P9-CBT-640

WRONG NUMBER

WRONG NUMBER

The Breakup of AT&T

ALAN STONE

BASIC BOOKS, INC., PUBLISHERS

NEW YORK

Library of Congress Cataloging-in-Publication Data

Stone, Alan, 1931–
  Wrong number.

Bibliographical notes: p. 339.
  Includes index.
    1. American Telephone and Telegraph Company—
Reorganization.   2. Telecommunication—United States—
Deregulation.   I. Title.
HE8846.A55S73   1989   384.6'3   88–47895
ISBN   0–465–09277–2

For Celeste

CONTENTS

Preface   ix

PART ONE
BELL CANTO

CHAPTER 1
HELLO, CENTRAL: THE TELEPHONE IN PERSPECTIVE   3

CHAPTER 2
THE BELLS ARE RINGING   34

CHAPTER 3
SILENCE THAT DREADFUL BELL: THE NEW DEAL AND THE
WESTERN ELECTRIC CASE   59

PART TWO
RINGING IN THE NEW

CHAPTER 4
THE VOICE OF CHANGE   83

CHAPTER 5
THE WARNING BELL   119

CHAPTER 6
RINGING IN THE NEW: THE RISE OF MCI   153

CHAPTER 7
THE BROKEN CONNECTION: COMPUTERS AND
INTERCONNECTION   195

PART THREE
CLOSING THE RING

CHAPTER 8
BUSY SIGNALS: MCI'S RENEWED ATTACK AND COMPUTER II   239

CHAPTER 9
"NO" FOR AN ANSWER: UNITED STATES V. AT&T   273

CHAPTER 10
WHAT'S MY LINE?   314

Notes   339

Index   371

PREFACE

It is commonplace that major political decisions occur in the judicial and administrative arenas as well as the presidential and legislative ones. Certainly, for example, civil rights policy owes far more to the courts than to the president and Congress. Courts and regulators have had far greater impact in recent years than the president and Congress not only in social policy, but in important economic areas as well. This book is concerned with the politics that led to the massive restructuring of the telecommunications industry and the public policies regulating it. These changes, culminating in the breakup of AT&T on January 1, 1984, are largely the work of the courts and the Federal Communications Commission (FCC).

While Congress played some role in these changes, its last major act occurred in 1934 with the enactment of the Communications Act and the creation of the FCC. Various presidents have prodded and urged, but they have never stood at the forefront in telecommunications policy. Politics at the judicial and administrative levels takes place in settings more formal than Congress or the presidency. The vocabulary and concepts employed in courts and administrative agencies are technical. They are not the discourse of electoral politics or legislative debates. Nevertheless, in all of these areas choices are made. Governing concepts such as "deregulation" and "privatization" are employed to justify policies and political values that are being implemented.

Politics, in a word, is the key to understanding the events that culminated in the AT&T breakup. But politics in the judicial and administrative arenas is less understood than politics in the legislative and presidential arenas. Crude notions that regulators are inevitably beholden to the large firms they regulate are still commonplace. But as this book will attempt to show, such notions are misleading. AT&T, for example, has both won and lost battles before the FCC, state regulatory bodies, and the courts. The politics of regulatory agencies and courts is far more complex than such crude ideas as the co-opting of regulatory agencies. Rather, the evidence in this book demonstrates that policy changes occurred because companies, trade associations, so-called public interest groups, and others succeeded in persuading courts and regulatory bodies that their new conceptions of the public interest should displace older ones in order to further statutory goals.

The process of change is a gradual one. Those seeking policy changes initially request experiments, modifications, and the like. This is in keeping with a basic ground rule of the Anglo-American legal system which applies to regulatory bodies just as it does to courts. Precedent is a weighty consideration, and sweeping reversals of past policies done all at once are rare. Rather, the erosion of the older conception of the public interest through particular exceptions and caveats gradually leads to a general change. For this reason, understanding the AT&T breakup requires reaching back into time. Indeed, the breakup and related changes in policy can only be understood through a historical perspective.

As I traced the changes in telecommunications policy, I was struck by how pervasively written documentation explains every action taken. Not only were courts and agencies persuaded, but they tried in their reports, memoranda, and policy statements to persuade as well. For this reason, virtually every action they took is best analyzed and understood by examining the documents that seek to justify it. Interviews and recollections, of course, play roles in much research. But the extraordinary documentation available in telecommunications policy rendered personal recollections almost superfluous. To this end I relied largely upon the enormous record of *United States* v. *AT&T*, other court cases, federal and state regulatory proceedings, and archival material.

Much of the material I consulted was located at specialized libraries and research facilities, including the Harvard Program on Information Resources Policy in Cambridge, Massachusetts, and the National Archives Record Center in Suitland, Maryland. I was generously assisted in obtaining and examining documents by Mildred Ettlinger and Robert G. Lewis at the AT&T Archives in New York; Maureen Ryan at the FCC; Peggy Chronister at the Museum of Independent Telephony in Abilene, Kansas; Michael Altschul at the Antitrust Division; and Fred Henck at *Telecommunications Reports* in Washington, D.C. In addition, many other people associated with the telephone industry supplied me with documents and other information. A discussion with John Callender, president of the Fort Bend Telephone Company in Rosenberg, Texas, was especially useful in providing the viewpoint of the independent telephone industry on the dramatic changes that have taken place.

Accumulating and examining research materials were only the first steps in such an undertaking. Putting the massive amount of material in a coherent order was itself a substantial task. I was fortunate in having a diligent and able group of research assistants who assisted me in this endeavor: Lisa Auerbach, Christine Lindsey, Bernadette McKinney, Ralph Stone, and Gary Tschoepe. Funds and leave time for this project were generously provided by the National Science Foundation, the Alfred P. Sloan Foundation, and the Division of Social Sciences at the University of Houston. Deans Tom Mayor and Harrell Rodgers were supportive in many ways.

I discussed my research with many persons in academia, government, and the business world. I am indebted to Richard Barke (Georgia Tech) for much insight provided during the early phases. Several people read the manuscript or portions of it and I benefited much from them. Darrell Dobbs (Marquette University), Benjamin Ginsberg (Cornell University), and Hudson Janisch (University of Toronto) scrupulously read drafts and contributed much to the final shape of the manuscript. Because of them it is a much better book than it would have been otherwise. Most important, I want to thank my wife, Celeste P. Stone, to whom this book is dedicated, for editing, rewriting, typing, and most important, challenging me to consider and reconsider virtually everything in this book. It could not have been written without her efforts. Martin Kessler, president and publisher of Basic Books, provided consistently sound—indeed, basic—advice and judgment. I would also like to thank Charles Cavaliere, project editor, Wendy Polhemus-Annibell, copyeditor, and Elizabeth Cunningham, indexer, for their exemplary efforts.

I began the research for this book generally supporting the FCC's deregulatory moves and the restructuring of the telecommunications industry. As I became immersed in the material, I gradually changed my mind, concluding that many of the changes wrought were not in the public interest. This book attempts to show why, in my view (and that of most of the public), the government dialed a wrong number.

No single volume can cover all of the complex incidents relating to the AT&T breakup and the numerous FCC and state proceedings. I have chosen those that are generally viewed as the most important, such as the incidents involving MCI. Without rendering a judgment on each and every event, I believe that those discussed allow the reader to understand the politics of the telecommunications industry and the policy changes wrought.

PART ONE

BELL CANTO

CHAPTER 1

HELLO, CENTRAL:
THE TELEPHONE IN PERSPECTIVE

On 1 January 1984, AT&T, the largest corporation of any kind ever created, was dismantled as a result of a 1974 decree involving the company and the Justice Department. The breakup was the most dramatic of several actions that transformed the American telecommunications industry and the policies that govern it. Already a heavily regulated industry, the major responsibility for its regulation shifted from the courts and legislative bodies to independent state and federal regulatory agencies. After World War II, more and more responsibility moved from the state commissions to the Federal Communications Commission (FCC). Yet, in spite of these changes, there remained a remarkable continuity in policies until the late 1960s. But the FCC began to change policies with the support of court decisions. The instability and turmoil that followed led to the pressures that eventually persuaded the Justice Department to file the 1974 suit.

The target of these actions was a fully integrated corporation. AT&T had dominated every major part of the telephone business—local transmission, long distance, and the manufacture of customer premises equipment (CPE) and switching and transmission equipment. But it did so not to extract monopoly profits but as a consequence of its service obligations, many of which had been imposed by legislators and regulators. AT&T's predivestiture structure had developed over a long period of time in response to the practical conditions of the telephone industry. In many cases, AT&T undertook these new responsibilities reluctantly.

More importantly, AT&T's eventual structure responded well to all reasonable criteria for good performance. Few would deny that at the time of divestiture the American telecommunications network developed under AT&T's leadership was the best in the world. More than 90 percent of American homes enjoyed 24-hour telephone service, dependable connections, and high signal-to-noise ratios. The rates charged for this service, charted against inflation rates or price increases in other industries, were relatively low and were supervised by federal and state regulators. AT&T's productivity and efficiency were high relative to other large firms and to the economy as a whole, and the company was technologically progressive. Indeed, Bell Labs was one of the most formidable research resources in the nation, contributing in whole or in part the transistor, talking motion pictures, television, stereophonic sound, the artificial larynx, and laser technology—only a handful of the 19,500 Bell Labs patents granted by 1982.

AT&T was not solely responsible for the remarkable achievements examined in this book, nor was it flawless. It emerged as the network's overall manager after considerable development and resistance. Those responsible for making the American telephone system the best in the world included many other telephone companies and government agencies, such as the FCC, state regulators, and the Rural Electrification Administration, but AT&T deserves most of the credit for its success.

In Part 1, we examine the evolution of the public policy regime led by AT&T as well as its underlying tensions. In Part 2, we learn how that regime was undermined and, in Part 3, how it was overthrown. The enormous changes that occurred within the public policy regime in telecommunications happened not because of major failings in technological or economic performance but because of politics. However, when we speak of politics in the regulatory arena, we are not referring to the type of politics that exists at other levels. One political notion that does not apply here is that great corporations necessarily have great political power. AT&T does not control the governmental institutions that regulate it; on the contrary, it has lost most of its major confrontations before the FCC and the courts since the mid-1960s. In fact, MCI's win-loss record is far better than AT&T's in the political arena. The politics of the regulatory process is far more complex than a simple translation of economic size into political power. Nevertheless, in keeping with a widely held American belief, AT&T's size and success became important ideological weapons against it. Those involved in the political attack against AT&T argued that monopolies are inefficient and they exaggerated the relevance of minor incidents to mask the company's overall excellent performance. For example, occasional service difficulties were used to portray the monopoly as inefficient and technologically backward, even though substantial evidence existed that proved the contrary.

The charges brought against AT&T are contained in three related sets of proceedings. Although the most well-known case is *United States v. AT&T*, we must also consider the many interconnection and computer communications proceedings and those brought about by MCI against AT&T and others to understand the vast changes that have taken place in the telephone industry. *United States v. AT&T* is responsible for the fact that we now pay separately for local and long-distance service. The interconnection and computer proceedings led to our right to lease or own the equipment of our choice, whereas the MCI proceedings led to long-distance competition. It is necessary to consider all of these components in order to understand fully the differences between the older public policy regime in telecommunications and the one that exists today.

The changes wrought by the settlement of the antitrust suit were the most drastic of all. An industrial structure that took almost a half-century to evolve was broken apart. In Chapter 2, we learn that the Bell system's structure and the government's system of regulation evolved for very sound reasons. Yet the Justice Department's challenge in the 1974 case was directed not only at AT&T but at the adequacy of the regulatory regime as well. The Justice Department sought to show by way of eighty-one historical episodes (many containing multiple parts) that AT&T abused its power and that public service regulation was incapable of controlling the company. AT&T parried by attempting to show that public service regulation serves the public interest and that the company's conduct was guided by reasonable business considerations that served the public well. The case was a dispute over the historical interpretation of such events as AT&T's TELPAK tariff, the alleged exclusion of competitors in video programming transmission between 1945 and 1954, and the Bell system's restrictions on interconnecting into its network.

United States v. *AT&T*, the computer/interconnection, and the MCI sets of proceedings *are* ultimately matters of historical interpretation. Accordingly, Parts 1 and 2 of this book examine many of the relevant events that precede the 1970s, even the invention of the telephone. These historical events are not simply preludes to *United States* v. *AT&T* and the other major proceedings covered in Part 3 of this book, they are also critical components of the proceedings that constitute the recent politics of telecommunications. Ultimately, these politics are closely mixed with the ideological and intellectual issues of how the American telecommunications network can best perform to serve both individual and public interests. The ability to persuade regulators and other decision makers of which public policy regime is most appropriate for telecommunications—full competition, contrived competition, or regulated public service—is a crucial component of the politics of telecommunications. Those seeking to break down the regulated network manager system in the 1970s were backed by a trend against elaborate regulation. AT&T's rivals and their big-business clients were able to move the FCC and state agencies away from older styles of regulation. They were equally successful in obtaining government protection against AT&T and the local independents. How this was accomplished is a major concern of this book.

THE ROAD TO DIVESTITURE

Although the Justice Department's antitrust suit was filed in 1974, the roots of that litigation can be traced to action undertaken much earlier. Indeed, to limit the scope of this book to events that began in 1974 or even to the FCC's liberalization actions that began in 1968 with the *Carterfone* decision, would be to undermine our understanding of the pre- and postdivestiture telecommunications industry. This does not mean that an understanding of the new telecommunications industry entails a history of every event that has occurred. But to understand the public policy grounds for the old system and the political reasons for its undoing, we must reach back to such critical events as the invention of the telephone in 1876 and the creation of the FCC in 1934.

The seeds of AT&T's dismemberment and the restrictions imposed on it can be traced to resentments and suspicions sown much earlier. The telephone was born in a bitter patent controversy. AT&T's opponents have claimed that the company's enormous size and dominance of the telephone industry can be traced to a patent fraud that gave it an undeserved head start. This argument is tied to the notion that big companies are inherently dishonest in economic competition, whereas their smaller competitors are almost always virtuous. As our historical examination will show, the Bell patent was a deserved one. Further, the company retained its monopoly position in spite of threats from competitors because experience convinced most actors (including those in the independent telephone industry) that a regime of regulated local monopolies under AT&T's leadership would best serve the public.

AT&T's rivals have not only used these resentments and envy as ideology, they have also used economic theory to justify their political goals. Several factors converged during the 1970s to promote a resurgence of faith in competitive markets, including the intellectual and moral bankruptcy of controlled economies—principally of the socialist variety—and the various performance failings of several heavily regulated industries, especially in transportation. Microeconomic theory, purporting to show the benefits of free competition in most situations, was given presidential approval beginning with the Ford administration's plea for deregulation of all regulated industries, even though regulation worked well in the telephone industry. AT&T's opponents successfully capitalized on economic theory just as they did on envy of the powerful. In both situations, the opponents engaged in one of the most important ploys of regulatory politics: to portray one's self-interest as *the public interest*. If successful, this tactic achieves two results. First, it enlarges a group's constituency to embrace others who will not experience pecuniary gain as a result of action but who are often active in a field. For example, naderites, free-market economists, and the FCC staff did not gain monetarily from the various decisions that benefited MCI, but their support was important to the ultimate success of AT&T's rivals. Second, to be politically successful with regulatory agencies depends to a considerable extent on the process of defining and redefining the "public interest." Because intellectual arguments are a critical component of regulatory politics, it is important to understand the arguments of older public policy regimes that once governed telecommunications as well as how "public interest" arguments benefiting AT&T gave way to newer ones benefiting MCI and other competitors.

From the early Western Union to the more recent MCI, AT&T has continuously faced rivals and critics eager to employ economic and ideological arguments to gain some benefit at the expense of the Bell system. Although the dramatic dismemberment of the corporation is a recent event, the restructuring of AT&T has been a concern of many for a long period of time. Attacks on the Bell system have come not only under the banner of free and open competition but under the flag of its opposite as well—central governmental planning and stringent public control. The early New Deal, for example, was a time when free and open competition was in considerable disrepute. When the FCC was created, the centerpiece of the Roosevelt administration's economic policy was the National Industrial Recovery Act, which was based on centralized compulsory economic planning. Ironically, this public philosophy, in many ways the diametrical opposite of free competition, allowed the proponents of deregulation to attack the structure of the Bell system. Indeed, the 1974 suit and the other important changes in telecommunications policy can be traced to the Communications Act of 1934 and the subsequent investigation of the Bell system, as they were premised on stringent government control of communication.

AT&T also developed a conception of the public interest referred to as the *regulated network manager system*. The system did not develop all at once or without serious internal division within the Bell system. Nevertheless, during much of its early period, AT&T was led by Theodore J. Vail, a remarkable manager who indelibly placed his stamp on the company he served. Vail's views and the performance of the telecommunications industry under his leadership contrast to what followed.

Like the public policy regime of contrived competition that now prevails, the regulated network manager system favored one private interest over all others. Under the current system such firms as MCI are favored, whereas in the older system AT&T and the independent telephone industry were favored. In both cases, the favored firms have wrapped themselves in the flag of the public interest for political reasons. While each side's demands are self-serving, the public, or segments of it, can nevertheless benefit more from one set of policies than another set. For example, residential subscribers can pay more under one set of policies.

As we will learn throughout this book, the overall results of public service regulation under the old regulated network manager system benefited especially the ordinary ratepayer but not necessarily the high-volume user. Goals such as universal service and high average quality of transmission were achieved. Indeed, the American telephone network was the envy of the world.

Why, then, was the system so fundamentally restructured? A *Wall Street Journal* editorial published the day after the 1974 Justice Department suit was filed comments, "Out of all this we arrive at one question: where is the problem that justifies risking possible damage to the efficiency of a vital part of the U.S. infrastructure? . . . If there is a problem that justifies all this we can't find it."[1] Ten years later, in the aftermath of the settlement of the biggest and most expensive antitrust suit in history, the American public overwhelmingly endorsed the judgment made by the *Wall Street Journal*.[2] Eleven months after the formal breakup, the American public, by a margin of 64 to 25 percent, believed that the AT&T divestiture was a blunder and that business users rather than residential subscribers would be its main beneficiaries. The public had a reasonable understanding of the changes that would be wrought and expected local service rates to increase rapidly, service quality to deteriorate, and consumer repair costs to escalate.

Most of the public did not support a restructuring of the telephone industry. Congress never decreed the drastic actions taken by the FCC and several courts. There was no national debate on so fundamental an act as restructuring a basic part of the American infrastructure and the way it might perform. Why, then, did the momentum for drastic changes begin to occur in the late 1960s and culminate in the extraordinary changes of the 1980s? Although an overall level of bad performance can be ruled out, as this book will show, AT&T's performance as it affected several important and powerful actors in the telecommunications industry was less than optimum. This does not mean that to these actors AT&T's performance was unsatisfactory, but rather that service, rates, or other factors conceivably could have been better. The question here is a profoundly philosophical one and exists in other contexts as well, such as tax rates or access to medical care— Should the wealthy subsidize the nonwealthy? As we shall see later in the book, the public service notion under which the Bell system operated provided a justification for cross-subsidy arrangements in telecommunications.

At times, AT&T allowed other telecommunications firms to offer supplementary services or products that it was unwilling or unable to provide itself. However, AT&T was usually unwilling to provide a new service because of the threat it might pose to rate averaging, universal service, cross-subsidy, network reliability, or some other goal for which AT&T was primarily responsible. But the relentless pressures of competitors, large-volume users, and others gradually transformed the telecommunications industry. Although MCI was one of the most important and well-known actors in this drama, the roles of Westinghouse, American Petroleum Institute, IBM and other members of the computer industry, the New York Stock Exchange, and a host of other giant firms and trade associations were also influential in forcing these changes to take place. Ironically, AT&T, the largest firm of all, was committed through goals such as universal service and rate averaging to the interests of the small subscriber, whereas those with whom AT&T came into conflict, such as MCI, were primarily concerned with the interests of large business subscribers. The main political achievement of AT&T's rivals was their collective ability to portray their own interests as the "public interest," and in the process to gain important allies at every decision-making level. Their ultimate triumph occurred with the 1984 divestiture and with the system of contrived competition, in which new rivals were granted advantages denied to AT&T in such markets as long distance.

THE POLITICS OF TELECOMMUNICATIONS

A common view of the regulatory agencies—the institutions responsible for making the most important decisions on telecommunications policy—are that they are usually beholden to the interests they regulate. If several such interests exist, this view holds that the largest of them prevails. Regulatory agencies are often viewed as overworked and incompetent at best, or dishonest and corrupt at worst. Yet a surprising lack of evidence supports this perception. Although there are instances of capture, corruption, and incompetence in regulatory agencies, theoretical and practical considerations militate against generalizing this view.

At the outset, any general conception of telecommunications policy must deal with an apparent inconsistency. As we shall see, AT&T won many FCC decisions in the period before 1968 in spite of the implacable hostility of many FCC commissioners and staff members. And although AT&T lost most major decisions before the FCC after 1968, it also won a few. Thus, the overall picture indicates a more complex decision-making pattern than a simplistic theory of regulatory decision making would suggest. Yet, there is an underlying consistency to these apparent FCC inconsistencies—it lies in the manner of decision making that takes place in regulatory agencies, which is fundamentally different from that which takes place in Congress, state legislatures, or other governmental bodies. Legislative bodies, through bargaining and logrolling techniques and their responsiveness to the pressures of public opinion and interest groups, are a model for most people's understanding of politics. Yet they are an inappropriate model for understanding the processes and policies of regulatory agencies and courts.

Thus, the dominant aspect guiding regulatory agency behavior is constraint. One is less likely to ignore the freedom and discretion of administrative agencies that enforce regulatory statutes, but it is far more common to ignore the formal rules and structures that restrict their actions. In many ways, regulatory agencies are bound by the same kinds of rules that control courts, such as precedent or appeal. Indeed, in some respects, the formal restraints are even tighter because of the labyrinth of administrative law and process that only indirectly applies to courts. This may be contrasted with the freedom enjoyed by Congress and state legislatures whose sole boundaries are within constitutions. In this sense, regulatory agencies are subject to a more stringent constitutional scheme of fundamental principles than are courts or legislatures. Like courts, though, regulatory agencies are bound by precedent and statutes governing jurisdiction, and they must justify the decisions they make. Their decisions must pass the scrutiny of informed judges, not the far less rigorous scrutiny of public opinion. The opinions of regulatory agencies must be based on facts that have been carefully screened through stringent rules of evidence. In contrast, legislators may use gossip or rumor as fact without having to answer to formal evaluation procedures. For these reasons, the demagogue is common in legislative affairs but rare in courts and administrative agencies.

However, the constitutional scheme of regulatory agencies is far more rigid than that of courts. A regulatory agency is bound by several factors: (1) the organic statute that sets up the agency and provides its basic rules; (2) other statutes that restrict and govern the agency's conduct; (3) executive branch supervision, often in the form of budgetary leverage; (4) congressional appropriations hearings and oversight; (5) an enormous body of administrative law governing procedures and how substantive decisions are made; and (6) a comprehensive appeals process undertaken both within the agency itself and in the court system. In short, regulatory decision makers must withstand scrutiny by courts, the executive, and the legislature.

Although all of this is well known, it is often forgotten by people who assume that regulatory agencies are inevitably captured or are dominated by the firms they regulate. But there is a more subtle difference between regulatory agencies and other governmental institutions that acts as a further constraint—the agencies must *continuously* supervise the industries they regulate. For example, legislators can with impunity pass a law affecting an industry, expect compliance, and then shift their attention to another issue. Yet if the law poses compliance difficulties or imposes costs not previously considered, the industry, and in some cases the regulatory agency, are blamed. Courts, too, delve into many matters, render individual decisions, and then turn their attention to other concerns. Only rarely do courts exercise long-term, continuous supervision over an institution—and even then, they supervise only an aspect of an institution rather than the institution as a whole. For instance, courts have exercised continuing supervision over school integration but not over school performance in general. In contrast, the constraints imposed on the politics of regulatory agencies are much more confining. If electricity or gas service is deficient, the companies providing these services and the agencies regulating them are both held responsible. Similarly, if rates are considered too high or safety lax, the agency and company are held equally accountable. Thus, regulatory agencies must take into account not only the short-term effects of their decisions but the long-term results as well. Indeed, regulatory agencies exist, in part, because of the perceived need for continual supervision.

The enormous supervisory apparatus in the legislative, judicial, and executive branches, and the likelihood that transgression or favoritism will be discovered, provide regulators with powerful incentives to obey the constraints that form their constitutions. The threat of transgression or favoritism being discovered is strengthened by the fact that in the most important regulatory proceedings there are several sides and few permanent alliances. For example, AT&T and Western Union were on opposite sides in a proceeding on the authorization to carry intercity television signals but were allies in the various MCI proceedings. AT&T, IBM, computer service bureaus, terminal equipment manufacturers, and others held different views on the complex issues within the FCC's computer inquiries. The politics of regulation are very much shaped by fleeting loyalties as well as the many ways an aggrieved party can register a complaint. Regulators are justified in feeling threatened, as there are many staff people eager to find ways in which the public interest is not being served and many legislators eager to build their own reputations at the expense of derelict regulators. There are also interest groups, the trade press, professional muckrakers, and the media to deal with. Thus, regulators are constrained to adhere scrupulously to the multitude of requirements imposed on them. Bribery, conspiratorial conduct, and undue influence are infrequent aberrations in regulatory behavior.

The constraints on regulators do not guarantee that their decisions will necessarily be correct, only that they will be reasoned and fair.

PUBLIC POLICY AND TELECOMMUNICATIONS

The First Phase

Since the period of its invention, the telephone has been government regulated. Although the telephone was born during a time dominated by laissez-faire doctrines—that is, the belief that governmental control of economic affairs should be limited as much as possible—the telegraph, railroads, and certain other industries considered "public services" continued to be highly government regulated.

Yet even before the telephone was born there existed for many centuries an elaborate theoretical structure that spelled out the obligations and privileges of public service companies. Although the particulars varied from industry to industry, there was a common core of policies affecting all public services, such as the obligation to serve the public without unjust discrimination. This public service idea was not the same as the more recent economic concept of natural monopoly; rather, it was a legal-ethical principle that included economic considerations. The public service principles were first applied to the telephone by courts and legislative bodies, but as the need for more supervision increased and the technical complexity of the industry grew, independent commissions began to regulate the industry.

The initial development of public policy toward the telephone industry under the public service principle occurred in the preindependent commission phase. Detailed amplification occurred in the state independent regulatory commission phase. Because of the experience of the industry and the number of issues it was asked to resolve, the PUCs (Public Utility Commissions) and the telephone industry had developed a system by the early 1920s called the *regulated network manager system.* Under this system, AT&T became the manager of a nationwide network consisting of its own subsidiaries and independent telephone companies. The regulated network manager system evolved gradually through trial and error. After the expiration of the basic Bell patents in 1893 and 1894, competition was first welcomed but then rejected in favor of local monopolies and a single long-distance carrier. The hostility that had existed between AT&T and the independents was transformed into cooperation as they integrated into a single network. Rate averaging and cross-subsidy principles were developed to attain the goal of universal service. Telephone companies were required—in some instances, against their wills—to provide end-to-end responsibility, including the maintenance and repair of telephones, transmission lines, and switching equipment.

When the FCC came into existence in 1934, it assumed jurisdiction over interstate communications from the Interstate Commerce Commission (ICC), which had supervised interstate telephone service since 1911. By the 1930s, most of the important principles and goals of the regulated network manager system had been established, and the FCC was expected to respect them. Even though many New Dealers carped at AT&T—it was, after all, a giant company in an era of virulent anti-big-business sentiment—it was assumed that the regulated network manager system would be left intact. Although there were specific complaints, most of them were without merit; even the big-business baiters conceded that the American telephone network was the best in the world. Rates and profits were reasonable, technological progress was remarkable, and virtually every other aspect of performance was considered superior. But when performance was deficient, the PUCs compelled the telephone companies to improve.

Under the concepts of jurisdiction that prevailed until the late 1930s, the FCC was not expected to play the major policy-making role in the telephone industry. Most traffic—then as now—was local and, thus, the PUCs were expected to play the major role in regulating the conduct of the industry. Although the PUCs' performance was remarkably good, events that began shortly after the enactment of the 1934 Communications Act conspired to reduce their influence over the telephone industry and to erode the regulated network manager system. But it was politics, not performance, that led to the downfall of the regulated network manager system and eventually to AT&T's breakup.

The Second Phase

Several factors contributed to the dramatic changes in telecommunications policy that began in the late 1960s. First, the conception of federal jurisdiction had been enlarged during the New Deal and thereafter. Consequently, even though most telephone calls remained local or intrastate, the FCC and the courts gained the power to assert jurisdiction under the commerce clause because of a local "effect" on interstate commerce, and PUCs were increasingly preempted. Second, some of the changes undertaken by the FCC were forced by activist courts that, as we shall see, misunderstood telecommunications policy and the rationales for FCC and PUC decisions. These court decisions began as early as 1956 and the FCC and PUCs were required to obey them.

The third major factor for change has its roots in AT&T's progressiveness and inventiveness. The closely regulated company was expected to devote its primary—if not its exclusive—attention to public service obligations. Through Bell Labs, AT&T invented or improved the radio, television, talking pictures, and stereophonic sound and sought to exploit many of these commercially in areas outside the narrow framework of telephony. This raised two basic questions. First, would AT&T be able to fulfill its public service responsibilities if it became involved in enterprises not regulated by public service principles? Second, would AT&T—and other regulated telephone companies—be in a position to compete unfairly in nonpublic service sectors against firms primarily in such sectors? From the 1920s to the present, the courts, the Justice Department, and the FCC have wrestled with these issues. Not surprisingly, firms and industries fearful of AT&T's resources and technological prowess have used the judicial, administrative, and legislative arenas in their attempts to curb AT&T's incursion into nontelephone-related enterprises. These rivals include General Electric in radio, the first to raise these issues against AT&T, as well as IBM in computers more recently.

Yet another major factor for change was the dual structure of policy command that developed in the telecommunications industry. Traditional public service regulation closely governs prices, entry into and exit from an industry, and the specific routes and markets that each firm may enter. In sharp conflict with these restrictions are the requirements of the Sherman Antitrust Law. Antitrust principles include independent, noncollusive pricing; the ability to enter and leave an industry without government approval; and the right to select product and geographical markets freely. Antitrust and public service are, in principle, inconsistent concepts. Nevertheless, complex sets of rules attempting to reconcile the irreconcilable have developed in various public service industries. The problem is complicated in telecommunications because of AT&T's involvement in industries that were not governed by public service principles, as well as by its decision to become its own principal supplier through Western Electric.

As is the case with most issues in telecommunications policy, politics are obscured behind such technical questions; in this case, AT&T's exemption from antitrust coverage. In 1949, the Justice Department brought a major antitrust suit against AT&T, principally aimed at the vertical relationship between Western Electric and the Bell-operating companies. The case was settled in 1956, but it did not resolve the problem of potential conflict between antitrust and public service regulation. Dissatisfaction with the settlement and numerous private antitrust suits raised the issue again. Eventually, the courts held that AT&T and other telephone carriers were subject to the antitrust laws. Thus, the regulators had to accord considerable weight to these laws.

In addition, many of the changes wrought in telecommunications policy since the late 1960s are the result of actions taken by the FCC—and, to a lesser extent, by state regulators. Why did the FCC change its outlook so dramatically, abandoning major policies that had been in effect since the 1920s? To answer this question, we must first understand the FCC's trend toward liberalization and its public interest standard that all regulatory agencies are required to uphold. The term *public interest* has no clear-cut definition and can be interpreted differently by different people. Each regulatory agency is entrusted with certain obligations that are outlined in its statutes, which define *public interest* for the agency but usually do not detail the policies required to achieve its obligations. The courts and the agencies themselves are required to consider these obligations as yardsticks so as to determine if certain agency actions are justified.

In the leading *New York Central Securities* (1932) decision, the Supreme Court concluded, "It is a mistaken assumption that the [public interest] criterion is a mere general reference to public welfare without any standard to guide determinations. The purpose of the Act, the requirements it imposes and the context of the provision in question show the contrary."[3] In that case, the court measured Interstate Commerce Commission actions against such statutory goals as efficiency, adequacy of service, and the best use of transportation facilities. The courts have reversed FCC decisions, like those of other agencies, when it was determined they were inconsistent with the agency's obligations. For example, in 1952, when the FCC authorized a competitive international radiotelegraph service between the United States and several other countries on the ground that Congress generally favored a policy of competition embodied in the Sherman Act, the Supreme Court required it to show that competition served "some beneficial purpose such as maintaining good service and improving it. . . . Merely to assume that competition is bound to be of advantage . . . is not enough."[4] From this, an important consideration in understanding the shift in telecommunications policy emerges. A regulatory agency's policies are always constrained by a set of performance obligations. Yet the agency may be confronted with newly discovered facts, emerging technologies, new demands, or novel service proposals that lead it to change its rules or even the structure of the industry from monopolistic to multifirm. However, the agency cannot simply expound a view such as "competition is good"; rather, it must *find* that given policies or industrial structures will probably result in the achievement of its obligations.

Section 1 of the 1934 Communications Act charges the FCC with promoting a "rapid, efficient, nationwide and worldwide wire and radio communication service with adequate facilities at reasonable charges." The charge is general, of course, but it implies that the agency must take into account far more than the well-being of a dominant carrier such as AT&T. The notion of adequate facilities, for example, implies that user demands, insofar as they are technologically and economically feasible, must be satisfied. When existing carriers are unable or unwilling to fulfill these obligations—such as during an era of rapid technological development—the regulator is constrained to allow others to do so. Thus, the FCC and state regulators must take into account the concerns of a variety of interests, including different user groups with discrete needs (for example, banks, retail chains, or data transmitters), suppliers of novel services or equipment, network broadcasters, business subscribers, residential subscribers, and the existing carriers, at least insofar as their financial health permits them to fulfill their public obligations. A kind of pluralism is built into the regulatory system, but it is not the type of pluralism that inexorably allows contending parties mutually to adjust or compromise their interests. On the contrary, the FCC may deny a proposed service if the projected market is small or if it interferes with the provision of a more important service because of spectrum allocation problems. Regulatory agencies are expected to assess the various alternatives that might fulfill their statutory obligations and to choose the one that will probably lead to the greatest net benefit. Theirs is a pluralism that recognizes that spectrum is a scarce resource, and they may sacrifice the interests of groups that conflict with important goals.

An agency builds a body of precedent in the same way that common law courts build systems of workable rules. Over time and through practical experience, various rules lead to the adoption of those considered the soundest. Rules that do not work effectively or that lead to unacceptable costs are modified or rejected. The important point is that in the common law system, judges have developed a body of law that allows those concerned to make reliable judgments on permissible and impermissible conduct. In the same way, state courts and PUCs were able to elaborate a practical set of rules based on public service principles for the telephone industry. For example, we will see that end-to-end responsibility by the telephone company precluded customer ownership of telephone instruments because the telephone companies could not guarantee the performance of customer-supplied equipment. Based on practical experiences, the PUCs uniformly supported such fundamental doctrines as local telephone monopolies, end-to-end responsibility, universal service, rate averaging, AT&T's role as network manager, and a host of other principles.

However, doctrines that work well under conditions of stability or gradual change are subject to severe strain when change—or the demand for it—accelerates. Time-tested precedents may be of limited value, or even counterproductive, in such circumstances, which is precisely what the FCC and PUCs found during the late 1960s. At this time, there was a surge of demand for change in many areas. New firms alleged that they had discovered novel telecommunications needs that the existing carriers, most importantly the Bell system companies, were not satisfying. Before World War II, the existing carriers were able to supply every significant customer need, but wartime advances in electronics, many of which were spawned by the Bell system, triggered novel opportunities that old and new firms were eager to exploit in the burgeoning telecommunications market. Coaxial cable, microwave relay, satellites, and other advances enlarged message transmission capacity and reduced long-distance costs. At the same time, the growth of the television and computer industries generated a demand for specialized telecommunications equipment such as modems. Thus, the FCC concluded that it could no longer fulfill its obligations under the old rules. But, as we will see, the new rules adopted by the FCC were not necessarily better than the old ones.

THE RESPONSES TO CHANGE

Almost immediately after World War II, the FCC and PUCs were asked to rule on issues that had profound implications for the regulated network manager system and AT&T's central role within it. The demands of television networks for rapid completion of their links and such novel technologies as mobile radio, recording devices, and answering machines first brought into question the rules that had gradually developed since the telephone's invention. In the immediate postwar era, the FCC and PUCs generally responded by permitting carefully prepared exceptions to the general rules. But if a proposed service or device threatened such goals as universal service or end-to-end responsibility, it was either not authorized or permitted on terms acceptable to the existing carriers. Although controversies arose, they were solved relatively easily in comparison to what was to occur later. In general, AT&T did not object to these new services and products because they did not threaten universal service, the high quality of the system, or other goals under the regulated network manager system.

In the late 1960s, however, pressures on the FCC and PUCs intensified. Large interests such as the American Petroleum Institute, IBM, the computer service bureau industry, department store chains, Westinghouse, and other firms and industries began to perceive communications as a central part of their operations. Accurate billing and credit information, an increased need for transmitting accurate technical data, customer ordering, and making hotel and airline reservations are only a few of the many activities in which efficient telecommunications could play an important role. Improved telecommunications came to be perceived as a way a firm could differentiate itself from competitors and induce higher employee output per unit time. As a result, firms became increasingly sensitive to the costs of such services and large communications users, as well as those who supplied them with services and hardware, began to ask two related questions: "Why should we help to subsidize residential subscribers and local service through high business and long-distance rates?" and "Why should we not obtain service and equipment tailored to our particular needs?"

At first, the firms that offered to supply these big-business customers (for example, MCI and Carter Electronics) proposed that they be permitted to supplement telephone service and hardware. They claimed not to be challenging the public service idea nor AT&T's role in the regulated network manager system, but were seeking only peripheral submarkets that AT&T would not satisfy. Ironically, these new entrants pointed to AT&T's efficiency and enormous success in serving most of the public to argue that the markets they sought were too small to harm AT&T's ability to engage in rate averaging. Whether the new firms actually intended to restrict themselves to submarkets not served by AT&T is not known. But AT&T opposed many of the new proposals, prophetically claiming that the markets were uneconomic and that the newcomers' supposed "innovations" were actually minor variations of services already offered by AT&T. Moreover, AT&T and the independent telephone companies—many of which received subsidies from AT&T for local carriage of long-distance calls—argued that the FCC should consider the principle of creamskimming and not treat each instance or kind of service as discrete. Under that concept, some competitors can choose only the lucrative markets—skimming the cream—while others are required to serve less profitable or profitable ones.

However, under considerable influence from staff members sympathetic to MCI and the other new entrants, the FCC accorded the newcomers every benefit of doubt. Pursuant to the mission of the Communications Act, the FCC was expected to assure adequate facilities for user needs. The newcomers claimed that AT&T was not satisfying whole classes of customers, especially those with data transmission and other specialized needs. Creamskimming was treated not as a general issue but on a case-by-case basis; the agency promised to examine the issue more closely if it got out of hand. The promises and projections of the new entrants regarding the new markets were accorded great weight, whereas the objections posed by AT&T and others were viewed mainly as self-serving.

Since the FCC believed its actions were not undermining fundamental principles, it required AT&T to treat the newcomers not as competitors but as independent telephone companies with such rights as interconnection. But competition from some of these firms began almost immediately, and AT&T was, in effect, required to treat competitors as customers, even though time-honored telecommunications policy rules dictated otherwise. The FCC's principal mistake here was to believe it had not encouraged competition to occur. Based on highly optimistic predictions of future telecommunications trends, the agency did not want to fail to plan for a time when the telephone would operate robots in distant factories and perform similar miracles. The FCC accepted, virtually on faith, the new firms' claims that they—and not AT&T—would lead us into this world of the future. The FCC also accepted that the new entrants would be too involved with novel and innovative services to compete with AT&T.

As the promises made by MCI and others failed to materialize, their financial situations suffered. Consequently, the newer firms began to offer products and services that closely resembled or duplicated those offered by AT&T and local independent telephone companies, causing numerous disputes over interconnection to be brought before the FCC and the courts. Technology also undermined the notion that the newcomers only offered something different than the traditional firms. For example, the enhanced capabilities of customer premises equipment, switching and central office gear, and transmission blurred lines between add-on and principal equipment and between computing and communicating. Also, the same housing could incorporate a wide variety of functions, and the same line links could accommodate voice, video, and data traffic.

By the fall of 1973, the FCC's actions had led to a hopeless muddle. Instead of resolving issues, the volume of litigation and the acrimony between the various interests attested to irresolution. Having launched its experiment, the FCC undertook step after step to assure the success of its new offspring as these firms encroached further into the traditional activities of AT&T and the independent telephone companies. The FCC did not consider the virtues and drawbacks of competition and of the old regulated network manager system. Rather, prodded by the increasingly important role of the courts, it backed into a system of contrived competition in which AT&T was forced to guarantee the survival of at least some of the new firms—most importantly MCI, which was certainly a legal innovator if not a technological one.

1974 AND BEYOND

From the late 1960s, when the new applications began to proliferate, until the fateful year of 1974, the FCC conducted numerous proceedings. It was clear that important changes were occurring in virtually every aspect of telecommunications and that the distinction between telecommunications and computing was blurred. Now was the time for the FCC to reconsider first principles. For example, should the public service conception—the foundation for telecommunications policy since the telephone's invention—be confirmed, modified, or, in some respects, abandoned? If a general change is required, what should be the new decision rule? Should the regulated network manager system be superseded? If changes in principles are required, what effect would these have on such goals as rate averaging, universal service, and Bell Labs' ability to engage in fundamental research?

But the FCC did not address these fundamental issues. Rather, it continued to rely on vague promises of innovative services, on the simplistic principle of choice for new services, and on the assurance that each new offering would not impair the goals of the regulated network manager system. In 1974, however, the FCC began to lose control over telecommunications policy as the federal courts increasingly became involved in fundamental issues.

In March of 1974, MCI filed an antitrust suit against AT&T, the first of many that would be brought by equipment vendors, private line and long-distance companies, and others against AT&T. In response to these suits, the courts rendered decisions that intruded on FCC and PUC policy in important ways. Knowing that the courts (especially the Court of Appeals, District of Columbia Circuit to which FCC decisions are appealed) had adopted a new activist stance, MCI made an important move in the regulatory arena when, in late 1974, it quietly filed the EXECUNET tariff for a service that would compete directly with AT&T's long-distance service. The FCC, especially those staff members who had previously advanced MCI's cause, felt betrayed. But MCI, with allies in many other quarters, was emboldened. In 1978, MCI was vindicated as Judge Skelly Wright, a quintessential activist judge, held that the FCC could not prohibit MCI or others from offering long-distance services in competition with AT&T. As we shall see, few court decisions better illustrate the nineteenth-century wisdom of moving policy-making in regulatory areas from courts to specialized administrative agencies.

Yet as devastating as these 1974 MCI moves were to FCC policy-making, the greatest shock was still to come. On 20 November 1974, the Justice Department filed a major antitrust suit against AT&T, requesting the virtual dissolution of the Bell system that had been so carefully constructed for almost a century. The ensuing years saw numerous court decisions involving private antitrust cases brought against AT&T and independent local telephone companies, as well as those involving regulatory matters. In addition, there was much congressional "noise" (if not laws) and, most importantly, the rulings in the government's big antitrust case. The FCC was constrained to follow a new standard of "competition," although the nature of this competition and its relationship to the principles that had so successfully guided the development of the telephone industry were not described. But worst of all was the effect of this uncertainty on AT&T's plans and the future of the network. In 1974, the company announced that it would fight the government's suit, but by early 1979, when Charles L. Brown succeeded John de Butts as AT&T's chief executive officer, the new political realities had impressed themselves on AT&T's leadership. The company would lose more through prolonged chaos and confusion than through an adverse settlement of the big case. After several unsuccessful attempts, the parties announced a settlement in January 1982, which, with certain important modifications, was accepted by Judge Harold F. Greene.

On 1 January 1984, the old Bell system was dismantled. Forgotten in the details of the divestiture, in the plans for the future of the telecommunications industry, and in the attention given to the diverse needs of business users were the best features of the old system and the Bell system's role in it. John de Butts summarized it in 1975 as follows:

> The Bell System's goal . . . is to ensure "the widest availability of high quality communications services at the lowest cost to the entire public." That is my definition of the basic social purpose for which this business exists. It is my definition of the public interest.[5]

THE PUBLIC SERVICE PRINCIPLE

The old AT&T was not, of course, flawless. Yet, guided by the public service principle, AT&T and the local independents had performed well. Since this book attempts to show how political alliances led to the downfall of the Bell system, we must first understand the fundamental principle to which de Butts referred. The changes wrought in telecommunications policy and the AT&T breakup fundamentally challenged the historic doctrine of public service that had governed telephone service through World War II and beyond. It is critical, therefore, to understand the old policy regime and its underlying public interest conception.

While the period beginning in the 1960s is often regarded as the era of the information revolution, the role of information (or what was termed *intelligence* in the nineteenth century) and the means by which it is conveyed were as critical to the changes that took place in the 1800s as they are to the changes that have occurred in the last quarter century. Less than 25 years after Morse's invention of a practical telegraph in 1837, there were 32,000 miles of pole line transmitting five million messages per year.[6] In 1861, coast-to-coast telegraph communication began, and in 1866, the Second Atlantic Cable opened, permitting rapid communication between the United States and Europe. Among the effects of the telegraph were the expansion and integration of markets, the reduction of information and transaction costs, and the facilitation of capital movements. The time required to enter into transactions dramatically diminished and, as a result, the number of transactions increased enormously. Moreover, the telegraph made possible the development of institutions that ushered in the modern complex business system: commodity exchanges, a national securities market, wire service, and rapid dissemination of general and business news and credit reporting, which itself encouraged transactions by lowering credit risks. The telegraph, in short, was not simply another new invention; rather, its impact was felt throughout the American political economy. In fact, the telegraph, together with the railroad, were critical components in the development of our national economic system.

Based on early common law principles, policymakers such as judges and legislators drew distinctions and developed or adapted principles applicable to economic activities considered public services, such as the telegraph, telephone, railroad, and electric lighting. Although the nineteenth century was characterized by laissez-faire attitudes in Britain and the United States, exceptions were made. Chief Justice William Howard Taft, speaking for a unanimous Supreme Court in 1923, commented, "Freedom is the general rule, and [governmental] restraint the exception."[7] The telephone and telegraph were among the industries included within the exceptions to the general rule of freedom; they were described as "affected with a public interest," "clothed with a public interest," "public service companies," and "public utilities." (To avoid ambiguity, we use the term *public service company* here.)

The concept of a public service company can be traced to English common law, and was incorporated into American law. In general, the concept is based on a noncontroversial observation: not all economic activities are of equal importance to a society. Crude notions such as describing certain items as "necessities" and others as "luxuries" approximate the same point (for example, the processing of drinkable water is far more important than the production of pet rocks). But this vague, noncontroversial observation does not reveal how to develop workable definitions or how to devise public policy principles applicable to important economic pursuits. From the fourteenth-century conception of a "common calling," common law judges attempted to develop precise definitions and policies, and eventually they fashioned the concept of a public service company and set out its obligations. When public utility commissions came into existence to regulate communications, transportation, electricity, gas, water, finance, and other sectors, their basic rules were premised on the public service ideas of the common law.

Although the public service conception is now largely consigned to the province of history, it is important to the story of the telephone in the United States. Under the public service conception and the policies based on it, the telephone industry grew, flourished, and served the public well. The cooperation that developed between the private and public sectors contributed to the exceptional achievements of the telephone, electric, and other industries subject to public service regulation. Those who look to deregulation and competition to solve economic and social problems ignore the achievements of the public service conception; instead, they focus on the few failures. Adam Smith, unlike those who claim to be his intellectual descendants, accepted that certain activities are of a different nature and that the state has an obligation to assure the provision of certain services. This does not imply state ownership, but rather private-public collaboration.

It is necessary to note that although the public service conception has economic characteristics, it is *not* an economic conception. That is, economics is a guide to the problem of efficiency—it does not describe justice—whereas justice is a primary concern of the public service idea. This distinction is an important one, as public officials and others concerned with the structure of telecommunications often employ only economic criteria when making policy recommendations. Under this view, if it can be shown that an industry is not a natural monopoly—that is, if production is accomplished most efficiently by a single firm—the industry should not be subject to economic regulation. In contrast, even if water distribution could be economically undertaken by one hundred firms and emerald processing by a single one, firms in the former industry would be classified as public service companies and firms in the latter category would not.

Although monopoly plays an important role in the policy-making of public service companies, it is not the defining characteristic. Early British public service occupations included chimney sweeps, cartmen, and auctioneers. References in important cases to monopoly, according to leading legal historian Breck McAllister, "seem to be for the purpose of emphasizing the size and importance of the business and not delimiting a necessary condition to regulation."[8] Indeed, in the important case of *Brass* v. *Stoesser* (1894), the Supreme Court concluded that the approximately six hundred competitive grain elevators along the line of the Great Northern Railroad in North Dakota were public service companies.[9] Most importantly, telephone systems were considered public service companies even when they were engaged in vigorous competition.

The rapid economic expansion that took place during the nineteenth century, including the development of new industries in communications and transportation, led the courts to clarify the public service conception and the obligations of public service companies. As laissez-faire attitudes spread throughout the American and British economies, it became increasingly important to specify why certain activities were exempt from the general rule. Three elements that define a public service industry emerged. First, the product or service must be requisite to the community's level of civilization or necessary to its economic life. Thus, even if a new technology is in its infancy, a vision of its potential may make it appropriate to the community's level of civilization. Obviously, what is requisite to a primitive society is different than what is requisite to modern industrial society. Second, the activity in question must have widespread external effects on a community. And third, the unrestrained mechanisms of the market will probably not provide significant segments of the community with the service or product in sufficient quality and quantity.

Consider the railroad as an example. The importance of the railroad has been described well by the distinguished nineteenth-century economic theorist Henry C. Adams:

> The industry of transportation is fundamental in the industrial organization of a community. He who controls the means of communications has it in his power to arbitrarily make or destroy the business of any place or any person.[10]

In the latter part of the nineteenth century, railroads supported the well-being of businesses and of entire communities. Individually, collectively, or collusively (a considerable amount of collusion did exist), railroads had the power to thwart the principle of free competition by arbitrarily favoring one firm or community over another. Railroad policies could determine the vitality or stagnation of whole communities and, indeed, of the nation. In brief, they had widespread external effects on the economy and society.

While the telephone did not achieve the *commercial* importance of the railroad until many years after its invention, the telegraph had already attained critical importance and the telephone's importance was grasped immediately. The 1910 congressional statement in support of including interstate telephone and telegraph service under Interstate Commerce Commission (ICC) rate regulation commented: "Now the telegraph line and the telephone line are becoming rapidly as much a part of the instruments of commerce and as much a necessity in commercial life as the railroads."[11] In short, future and immediate strategic centrality was important in determining public utility status. For this reason, the telephone was considered a public utility almost from its inception, even though its revenues were modest in comparison to the railroads'.

Similar ideas can be seen in other early cases involving businesses not usually considered public services. For example, ten tobacco warehouses in Louisville, Kentucky, were a necessary conduit between producers and dealers; no practical alternative existed to this method of transacting a principal business in that region. Accordingly, the Kentucky Supreme Court held in 1884 that tobacco warehouses were public service companies.[12] For similar reasons, irrigation companies in Colorado and Arizona were held by their state supreme courts to be public service companies in 1888 and 1906, respectively.[13] Without irrigation in the arid regions involved in these disputes, farmers could not grow their crops and, obviously, could not obtain water by means other than irrigation.

Consider another example: fire insurance. A 1909 New Jersey law fixing premium rates was challenged by 121 fire insurance carriers conducting business in the state. The New Jersey Court of Errors and Appeals, after observing that neither monopoly status nor state condemnation of land for eminent domain purposes determined public service company status, carefully traced the development of the fire insurance business in the latter part of the nineteenth century. Noting the rapid growth of the business, the court observed that other businesses could no longer obtain credit without obtaining fire insurance, which was universally employed as collateral security. Since credit is the lifeblood of industry and commerce from the smallest retail establishment to the largest industrial facility, fire insurance occupied precisely the same strategic position that the railroad had. In the court's words, fire insurance "ramifies in its effects from the greatest banking houses, through the homes of the unemployed, or the badly paid, to the smallest retail shops."[14]

As the preceding examples illustrate, monopoly, or competition in terms of the number of units in an industry, does not define public service, nor does the number of units determine the obligations of the firms within an industry. Rather, the policymaker determines whether unrestrained competition will provide the service to the community in the quality and quantity desired. For this reason, public service regulation has traditionally imposed time-of-day requirements, since there can be off-peak times when service necessarily runs at a loss. Consequently, no firm will perform the service during those hours. Further, locations with low population densities or that are relatively inaccessible are often underserved without public service regulation. As one can see, then, cross-subsidization and rate averaging are major instruments of public service regulation, regardless of the number of firms providing the service in a given market. The justification for monopoly, therefore, is different than the justification for public service.

THE TELEPHONE AS A PUBLIC SERVICE

Alexander Graham Bell claimed to have invented the telephone in 1876—a claim that was subjected to bitter dispute, as we will see in Chapter 2. In 1878, Bell predicted that "future wires will unite the head offices of the Telephone Company in different cities, and a man in one part of the country may communicate by word of mouth with another in a different place" and that the telephone would become a means of communication among businesses, hospitals, police, and fire stations as well as the general public.[15] Nevertheless, at the outset most observers were not convinced of the telephone's future and conceived of it as a means to transmit music, drama, and news. At this time, the central switchboard and other devices necessary to a modern telephone system were dimly conceived, if at all.

The rate of the telephone's adoption was rapid in its early phases

TABLE 1.1

Telephones in the United States, 1876–1885

(in thousands)

Year	Number	Year	Number
1876	3	1881	71
1877	9	1882	98
1878	26	1883	124
1879	31	1884	148
1880	48	1885	156

SOURCE: *Historical Statistics of the United States: Colonial Times to 1970*, 2 vols. (Washington, D.C.: Government Printing Office, 1975), 2:784.

even though density was extremely low by contemporary standards, as Table 1.1 indicates.By the early 1880s, even those most skeptical in the beginning were more receptive to the telephone's rapid spread and improvement. Of course, growth alone does not render a new technology a candidate for public service status. The telephone's similarity to the telegraph—notwithstanding important differences—and public policy toward the telegraph provided the model for government regulation of the newer industry. Legal treatises generally considered the two technologies together during the nineteenth and early twentieth centuries.

Consequently, the telephone industry was treated as a public service business from the time the telephone was recognized as important. The telephone's early uses were seen as virtually the same as the telegraph's, but the telephone has several major advantages. First, it can be used by the ordinary person, whereas the operation of the telegraph requires the experience of a person familiar with Morse Code. As a result, the potential for commercial use of the telephone was viewed as much greater than that of the telegraph. Second, the telephone permits discussion by reproducing speech; in contrast, the telegraph requires the transmission of a complete statement before a reply can be made. And because the telephone can transmit ordinary speech, it allows the listener to detect the nuances and emotional content of the information being conveyed by the speaker. Also, translation of ordinary language into code followed by retranslation into ordinary language is not required in telephone use, making it a more accurate device than the telegraph, which has faced litigation over the issue of negligent mistranslation. For the same reason, the telephone is a much faster device for conveying information than is the telegraph. Further, because of its many advantages, the telephone was soon regarded as a more cost-efficient and reliable device than the telegraph. Finally, although the initial uses of the telephone were largely business related, it became a social instrument as home use increased.

The advantages of the telephone increased even further as a result of important technological advances made in the telegraph. Because of the demands made on telegraph use, Western Union and other telegraph companies sought to increase the capacity of wires to carry messages. Initially, the duplex, which allows separate eastbound and westbound transmissions over the same wire, was employed in 1872. Soon after, Thomas A. Edison developed a quadruplex system in 1874, and private telegraph lines within cities were developed as early as 1849. Central-office switching, which allows telegraph subscribers to communicate with each other, was employed in New York and Philadelphia as early as the late 1860s and proved valuable to banks, stockbrokers, and others. Finally, telegraphically operated burglar and fire alarms, as well as district telegraphs—which allow the placement of simple signaling devices in homes connected to central offices—were in place at the time of the telephone's invention.[16] Although the progressiveness of telegraph technology may have discouraged the telephone's adoption initially, the telephone actually benefited from these innovations only a few years after its invention.

Thus by the 1880s, there was universal agreement that telephone firms were public service companies, a view that would continue without challenge after 1894, when competitors to the Bell system emerged following the expiration of the basic Bell patents. An 1885 Nebraska case, in which a telephone company refused to allow a lawyer to become a subscriber, illustrates the sentiment of the time. Forbidding the telephone company to make such an unjust discrimination, the Nebraska Supreme Court stated:

> While it is true . . . that it has been organized under the general corporation laws of the state, and in some matters has no higher or greater rights than an ordinary corporation; yet it is also true that it has assumed to act in a capacity which is to a great extent public, and has . . . undertaken to satisfy a public want or necessity.
> The demands of the commerce of the present day make the telephone a necessity. All people, upon complying with the reasonable

rules and demands of the owners of the commodity . . . should have
the benefits of the new commerce.

It has assumed the responsibilities of a common carrier of news.
It has and must be held to have taken its place by the side of the
telegraph as such common carrier.[17]

In addition to court decisions, states enacted statutes regulating telephone companies as public services or making telegraph laws applicable
to telephones. When challenged on the ground that such laws were
unconstitutional in that the telephone industry was not affected with a
public interest, courts almost uniformly upheld their constitutionality.
The Indiana Supreme Court in 1886, upholding a state law regulating
telephone charges, said the telephone

has become as much a matter of public convenience and of public
necessity as were the stage-coach and sailing vessel a hundred years
ago, or as the steam-boat, the railroad, and the telegraph have become in later years. . . . No other known device can supply the extraordinary facilities which it affords. It may therefore be regarded,
when relatively considered, as an indispensable instrument of
commerce.[18]

The principle that a telephone company is a public utility received the
approval of the Supreme Court in 1892, ending any future possibility
of challenging the regulation of such companies.[19]

Thus, the telephone fell into the category of devices that are heavily
regulated because they serve larger purposes for the public. In the 1886
Indiana case cited earlier, this meant that the patent rights granted by
the federal government could not override a state's right to prescribe
maximum charges for telephone use. In general terms, once the firms
in a certain industry are placed within the public service category, they
must abide by a set of general principles. The fundamentals of public
service include, first, an obligation to serve all who apply and agree to
abide by the reasonable regulations of the firm. From this requirement,
public service companies have been required to extend their facilities
so as to meet reasonable demand. Second, they are required to serve the
public adequately; under this obligation, they must be technologically
progressive. Third, they cannot unjustly discriminate among customers.
(Competitors, it should be reiterated, were not initially held to be customers.) Finally, public service companies must charge reasonable rates.

Volumes of decisions have been rendered amplifying and construing these general principles.

Hence, the telephone was born into a world of government regulation under the public service principle. Many of the legal obligations faced by the industry had been in place even before the invention of the telephone. Yet the telephone was also born in controversy, which it has experienced ever since. On the same day in 1876 that Bell filed his patent application, Elisha Gray, another notable inventor, filed a document with the Patent Office purporting to show that he had invented the telephone. Before long, many others claimed its invention. AT&T's predecessors withstood each of these claims, but the early experience of being under siege coupled with the telephone's intimate connection with government regulation had important affects on the company's culture through the 1984 breakup. Under the leadership of Theodore J. Vail, AT&T gradually developed an elaboration of the public service principle that would justify its dominance in the telephone industry. The regulated network manager system, conceived in large part by Vail, was, of course, self-serving for AT&T, but it was also much more. Vail was acutely aware that incanting words of obligation were insufficient to ward off the threat to AT&T. In a world of enemies, AT&T would continuously have to justify its public trust by action. Its performance would have to be exemplary. But even this would be insufficient to withstand the political onslaught.

CHAPTER 2

THE BELLS ARE RINGING

Why had AT&T become such a large, fully integrated company instead of one involved in only one or two phases of the telecommunications business? Integration played an important role in many of the episodes in *United States* v. *AT&T* as well as in the computer-interconnection and MCI cases. Indeed, much of the government's animus toward AT&T that began during the New Deal was based on the suspicion that through its integrated structure AT&T sought to extend monopoly control unreasonably from one part of the telecommunications industry to others. The government claimed that vertical integration allowed AT&T to favor its affiliates in procurement and to pad the rate base by inflating the cost of equipment. AT&T counterargued by claiming that its structure had developed gradually over time and for sound business-related reasons. Further, integration led to greater efficiency than would prevail in a more fragmented industry, which allowed AT&T to serve the public better. Notwithstanding considerable opposition, AT&T was able for a long while to persuade the major political actors—many of whom had a deep antipathy to giant corporations—that its integrated structure would best serve the public. Thus, the company's history was a critical issue in *United States* v. *AT&T* and the other major proceedings.

THE INVENTION OF THE TELEPHONE

Alexander Graham Bell was a teacher of the deaf and an experimenter who became interested in the development of a "speaking telephone." Bell was in competition with Elisha Gray, another brilliant inventor, who was also trying to develop the telephone. Both Bell and Gray received much financial backing and encouragement from scientists. Yet many others were engaged in the pursuit of developing a voice-grade telephone as well, and after Bell's victory, many of them claimed that their inventions preceded his.[1]

On 14 February 1876, Bell filed his basic patent application for a telephone transmitter employing a magnetized reed attached to a membrane diaphragm—an apparatus capable of transmitting sounds and changes of pitch but not speech. Nevertheless, the patent application, like others drafted by skilled patent lawyers, was sufficiently broad to cover other apparatus for transmitting speech. Only several hours later, Elisha Gray filed a caveat (a notice of pending patent application) for a method of transmitting and receiving speech, but there is serious doubt whether Gray's instruments were able to convey speech. It was not until 10 March 1876, that Bell was able to convey this famous message over a telephone to his assistant: "Mr. Watson, come here; I want you."

The events surrounding Bell's and Gray's same-day patent filings and the suspicion that Bell may have unlawfully amended his original application after seeing Gray's caveat, together with the claims of many others that they had invented the telephone, led to much litigation. Nevertheless, the 1876 basic process patent (and Bell's 1877 basic receiver patent) withstood approximately six hundred lawsuits and patent interference proceedings, including a suit brought by the United States for patent cancellation.[2] In 1887, a divided Supreme Court upheld Bell's claim against five challengers. Although doubts about the telephone's true inventor and the fairness of patent laws of the time will always remain, most evidence and authority support Bell's claim. However, AT&T's rivals continued to claim that the patents were unlawfully obtained and upheld by a conspiracy embracing a majority of the Supreme Court, patent examiners, and numerous circuit court judges. Thus, even at its birth, AT&T was accused of having hidden powers and of being uncontrollable by usual government processes.

THE FIRST ERA OF TELEPHONE COMPETITION

Prior to his patent filing and invention of the telephone, Bell and his partners—Boston businessmen Gardiner Hubbard and Thomas Sanders—formed the first predecessor enterprise to AT&T on 27 February 1875. Under the Bell Patent Association's agreement, Hubbard and Sanders supplied the capital and the three men shared equally in any patents Bell obtained. Hubbard offered to sell for $100,000 the 1876 patent to Western Union shortly after it was filed, but was turned down because Western Union's management believed the telephone was impractical. But by November 1877, Western Union recognized that it had blundered and organized a subsidiary called the American Speaking Telephone Company. Western Union, then far superior in resources in comparison to the Bell enterprise, acquired several telephone patents (including Gray's) and employed Thomas A. Edison, recognized as a brilliant inventor, to develop telephonic inventions. Thus, the first era of competition in the telephone industry had begun.

Western Union was not only able to undercut Bell rates but, moreover, much of its equipment and technology were superior to that of Bell's. The Bell enterprise could battle in two ways: they could (1) develop or purchase superior technology or (2) bring a patent infringement suit against Western Union. The suit was brought before the court in September 1878 and was settled in November 1879. Under the terms of the settlement, Western Union agreed to withdraw from the telephone business if in exchange it was paid a 20 percent royalty on all telephones used in the United States. Western Union also agreed to assign existing and future telephone patents to National Bell, the Bell interests' company. This agreement terminated with the expiration of the basic Bell patents. Hence, the first era of telephone competition ended only shortly after it began.

Why had it ended so abruptly? Western Union clearly was not hoodwinked, for four days after the November settlement, National Bell's shares were sold at $955.50—an increase of $505 above the September market price. Western Union's management was privy to the sentiment of the financial community. Bell had won a victory and Western Union knew it, but the evidence indicates that Western Union settled for several reasons. First, financier Jay Gould had organized a new telegraph rival in May 1879, with a capital of $10 million. Moreover, Gould threatened an alliance with the Bell interests and promised to bankroll the infringement suit. Rather than fight two fronts, according to this view, Western Union made peace on the telephone front to wage war more effectively on the telegraph front.

However, the "two-front factor" cannot alone explain Western Union's reasons for agreeing to the 1879 settlement. The telephone's commercial importance at the time was trivial in comparison to that of the telegraph's. Western Union's contest with the Bell interests was not a true battle, as the company could have fought further if it believed it could have won the patent in court. Rather, Western Union agreed to a settlement because its attorneys and other officials were convinced that the Bell interests would continue to fight and ultimately prevail. Because Western Union attorney George Gifford believed Alexander Graham Bell had invented the telephone and that Western Union was an infringer, he urged his client to settle.[3]

The patent wars and the competition from Western Union would impress the Bell interests in an important way. Patents would become a critical component of telecommunications, of which the basic transmitter and receiver were only the beginning. When the basic patents expired in 1893 and 1894, the Bell interests sought to be well ahead of their adversaries, which entailed obtaining more advanced patents through internal development or from independent inventors. The latter alternative was at first the most desirable, as inventors working in their own shops could make continuous and significant contributions to telephonic advance. But when telephonic research became sufficiently complex to require large capital investment, major group effort, and advanced mathematical skill, a major research laboratory was needed. In this sense, the patent battles and the competition from Western Union led to the creation of Bell Labs.

THE BUSINESS OF COMMUNICATIONS

Early telephone service and equipment were rudimentary by contemporary standards. Yet even in its earliest phases the Bell interests were compelled to devise policies based on the peculiar characteristics of telephone communication. The single most important characteristic is the *interactivity* of the network; that is, a weakness in any part of the system can reduce the ability of the other parts to operate to their full potential. For example, a bad transmitter will cause inferior sound to flow to the receiver. Early on, the Bell policymakers realized that weaknesses in any part of the system can retard the expansion of the network, lower its quality, or otherwise impede its more widespread acceptance and use, with a resulting negative impact on revenues. For this reason, the Bell policymakers sought to control the quality of each piece of equipment and service that comprised the network. This, in turn, raised the issue of whether such control should be exercised under a system of ownership or a system of licensing according to standards. Since licensing entails a considerably smaller capital outlay, it is not surprising that the Bell interests first chose this path in that the system's size would grow more rapidly if others provided the funds for local systems, equipment supply, and so forth.

Another peculiar characteristic of the telephone business is that the value of telephone service to any subscriber depends on the number of persons with whom he or she can communicate. This consideration compelled the Bell policymakers to focus their attention on switching, which remains a priority today. Without a central switch, forty-five lines are needed to connect ten nodes, whereas with one central switch only ten lines are required. Gradually, the idea of a network evolved, consisting of switching centers distant from each other but connected by trunk lines, and hierarchies of switches. As the network grew, the company was impelled to invest resources not only in engineering problems but in basic research as well. In many cases, the basic science and mathematics on which the engineering would be based was yet to be discovered.

When one combines the interactivity of the network with the ever-increasing complexity that results from expanding it, the theoretical justification for direct ownership of each part of an integrated network—local loops, long distance, CPE and switching, and transmission gear—becomes clear. Economic and technological considerations led to the integration of research, planning, engineering, design, manufacturing, and operating capabilities within one firm. Economist R. H. Coase has done the pioneering theoretical work in determining whether a firm is more likely to use the market or integration within the company to achieve a result.

> When we are considering how large a firm will be the principle of
> marginalism works smoothly. The question always is, will it pay to
> bring an extra exchange transaction under the organising authority.
> At the margin the costs of organising within the firm will be equal
> either to the costs of organising in another firm or to the costs in-
> volved in leaving the transaction to be "organised" by the price
> mechanism. Business men will be constantly experimenting, control-
> ling more or less. . . .[4]

The Bell system followed this dynamic—the more complex and changing a product or service is, the greater the costs incurred in instructing
others who are responsible for component parts; the less the tolerance
for deviation, the larger the costs will be for the failure to fulfill one's
part in an overall interactive system. When complementarity is critical,
and the components of an industry progress at uneven rates, the costs
of discoordination can be very high. If licensees or independent sellers
did not have an incentive to cooperate with the Bell interests in implementing or developing a new technology quickly or in meeting a Bell
target or rising standard of service, the effects would be felt throughout
the network—and they would be costly. The transaction costs in telephony are high, and negotiation, changes, and discussions of scientific
and technological matters are more common than in many other industries. Thus, transaction costs are reduced if a single firm has the authority to enforce its will on the various segments of an industry. Moreover,
in an integrated network, the opportunities for coordinating all components of the system permit cost savings, an argument that AT&T consistently made in the major litigation.

Of course, it does not follow that only a single firm monopolizing
all parts of the system is possible. However, the idea that a dominant,
vertically integrated firm capable of enforcing its will on reluctant independents—the network manager role that AT&T undertook—was
the direction in which telephone technology impelled the Bell interests, sometimes against their will.

THE FOUNDATIONS OF AT&T

The predivestiture structure of AT&T—a holding company that embraced operating companies and divisions in all phases of the telephone
business—was created in December 1899. Although much changed in

the interim, many contemporary AT&T policies (e.g., telephone leasing) were in force on New Year's Day, 1900. AT&T, which had existed as a long-distance company since 1885, took over the property of the American Bell Telephone Company, its parent, and until 1 January 1984, performed several functions in the Bell system.

First, AT&T operated the Bell system's long-distance service through the Long Lines Department. Second, it operated as a high command, making decisions for and coordinating the system as a whole. Third, it owned controlling shares in Western Electric, its supply and manufacturing company, and in local operating companies. Over the years, AT&T's shares in operating companies tended to increase. For example, AT&T had acquired 50.1 percent of Pacific Telephone & Telegraph's shares by 1905; by 1980, that figure had jumped to 90.18 percent. In two cases—Southern New England Telephone (SNET) and Cincinnati Bell—AT&T owned less than 30 percent of the companys' shares, and although the shares were not affected by the divestiture, they were sold.

Bell Telephone Laboratories (Bell Labs), the last important component of the basic predivestiture structure, was incorporated in 1924 and quickly became one of the preeminent research organizations in the world. Bell Labs was jointly owned by Western Electric and AT&T and was formed to better coordinate research and development, which had been previously undertaken by Western Electric Research Laboratories and various AT&T research and engineering departments. It is not uncommon for large corporations to have sizable research departments, but the research conducted is almost always of an applied nature. In contrast, Bell Labs made enormous contributions not only in applied research but in pure science and mathematics as well. In large part, the Bell system's early commitment to science and technology was encouraged by technical problems that could not be solved without advances in these fields.[5]

Although the complex structure of the Bell system evolved gradually from the invention of the telephone, it was not until 9 July 1877, that Bell, Hubbard, and Sanders superseded their 1875 partnership agreement and formed the Massachusetts Trust (a then-popular business form) entitled the "Bell Telephone Company, Gardiner G. Hubbard, trustee." By February 1878, it became necessary to finance expansion of the business. Accordingly, the next stage entailed the formation of the New England Telephone Company, capitalized at $200,000. This company, which was restricted to the New England states, appointed agents to develop exclusive territories and who were compensated by commissions on telephone and call bell rentals. The markets opened up by the development of switching and other new services, the fight with Western Union, and other factors continued to impose an enormous financial burden on the Bell interests that the New England Telephone Company only partly alleviated. Accordingly, Hubbard and Sanders incorporated the Bell Telephone Company (a corporation, not a Massachusetts trust) in July 1878, but as they sought and obtained new investors, they saw control begin to slip away. The new company, capitalized at $450,000, attracted as general manager Theodore J. Vail, a man who combined extraordinary managerial abilities and a keen political sense. Beginning as a mail clerk for the Union Pacific Railroad, Vail's ability and energy in transportation services lead to a meteoric rise. He established a system of fast mail delivery for the Postal Service. At the age of 30 in 1876, Vail was appointed general superintendent of the Railway Mail Service. Dissatisfied with Congress's economizing measures, he joined the Bell interests with an enthusiasm about the telephone's opportunities and the promise of a New York City franchise.[6]

Few large institutions have ever borne the imprint of one person as thoroughly as Vail's on AT&T and its predecessors. Vail settled the Western Union suit and assertively moved to enlarge the use of the telephone. Among his first moves were expansion of the central switchboard exchanges, telephone fire-alarm systems, and long-distance (or toll) lines that, though modest by contemporary standards, were pathbreaking at the time. However, these ambitious projects led to further financial strain and the creation of a new company in March 1879, the National Bell Telephone Co., capitalized at $850,000. At this point, the original partners were no longer able to control the fortunes of the telephone. After the Western Union settlement, under which the Bell telephone interests were required to purchase Western Union's and American Speaking Telephone's equipment, the need for additional capital led to still another transformation. The American Bell Telephone Company was incorporated on 17 April 1880, and capitalized at $7,350,000.

AT&T owes its creation to Vail's dream of long distance. Even though the technology was incapable of carrying conversations very far in the 1880s, Vail was committed to the promise of allowing every subscriber to converse with every other subscriber. Because American Bell met with little success in interesting its local licensees to jointly engage in long distance to and from their territories, it incorporated AT&T as a long-distance subsidiary in February 1885. Interestingly, the certificate of incorporation purported creating a network that would extend throughout the United States, Canada, and Mexico. By 1888, under Vail's leadership, the new company was confident that long-distance service would be successful.[7]

Ambitious plans entail substantial risks. Typical of large-scale projects undertaken for the first time, the costs of creating a long-distance network were greater than initially planned. In 1888, AT&T was compelled to float a $2 million debenture issue to finance long-distance expansion. This issue, together with later expansion undertaken through public stock and bond offerings—a common feature in AT&T history—have acted as long-term incentives for AT&T to be efficient in its operations. In its frequent resort to capital markets, especially in sales of debentures, notes, and bonds, AT&T has had to appeal not to potential customers of its telephones but to investors who are ordinarily indifferent to the product or service in which they are investing but who focus on risk, yield, and other financial variables. Any company seeking to sell debt instruments in financial markets is expected to know that it must deal with sophisticated investors who will compare the seller's performance (and probable performance) to those of other prospective sellers of financial securities, including those in highly competitive industries. If a company such as AT&T, then, wishes to sell its debt on favorable terms, its performance and probable performance must measure up to that of its rivals in competitive industries. This, of course, is doubly true if it plans to make repeat sales of such financial instruments, for it is unlikely that potential investors will be twice fooled. Thus, the expansion of a company such as AT&T through frequent resort to financial markets (instead of almost entirely through retained earnings) has an important consequence: the discipline imposed by the financial markets acts on the firm as a surrogate for competition. Of course, this does not necessarily guarantee that such a firm will be efficient any more than competition necessarily assures that a firm will be efficient. But in both cases a strong incentive to be efficient is provided. Thus, the commitment that AT&T made to long distance had important consequences for the firm's efficiency.

The Bell interests' spur toward increased capitalization met with resistance from the Massachusetts legislature, which led the leaders of

AT&T and American Bell to an important decision in 1899. In contrast to Massachusetts, New York, where AT&T was incorporated, was more liberal-minded on the issue of increasing corporate capitalization. Thus, in late December 1899, AT&T became the parent company and corporate headquarters were moved from Boston to New York.

By 1900, AT&T was on its way to forming a comprehensive vertical structure. Western Electric, already an electrical equipment manufacturer, had been acquired in a gradual process that began on 5 July 1881. The need to meet expanding demands for telephone equipment, coupled with dissatisfaction with prior arrangements because of delays, shortfalls, and imprecision, led to the decision to acquire a major manufacturing facility. Hence, the Western Electric acquisition is an example of the empirical findings of economic historians Harold Livesay and Patrick Porter: Firms engage in backward vertical mergers "by a desire to rationalize flows by . . . assuring needed raw materials rather than from a desire to add profits of the manufacturer to that of those downstream in the business."[8] Similar rational considerations governed the license relationship for local operating companies. After a number of experiments that proved unsatisfactory, American Bell in the early 1880s solved the problem of how best to exploit local markets—it would offer licensees permanent licenses in exchange for stock, thus becoming a partner in the local loop business. This allowed American Bell to conserve capital for long distance and other phases of the telephone business and at the same time to maintain considerable influence so to assure that licensees took a long-run view of the business. Thus, at this early stage American Bell assumed the role of network manager, of guaranteeing the overall performance of an interactive system. It could further assure that as new technological innovations came about the licensees would not resist employing them. In short, the AT&T-licensee structure came about not because of desire to exercise control but for sound economic and technological reasons.

Gradually, local licensees consolidated into larger territories for several reasons including economies in centralized management, lower transaction costs in larger exchanges, the high capital costs of some newer technologies, and increased coordination requirements. The final step was AT&T's increased equity holdings in the licensees—more than 90 percent by the mid-1930s—caused by the profitability of local loop operations and AT&T's dissatisfaction with minority ownership. AT&T officials found that some of the licensees were not cooperating in the development of long distance and were resisting closer uniformity in good telephone practice. Moreover, under the system of minority share ownership, some local managers were performing inadequately, impelling AT&T to incur higher supervision costs than would be the case with majority control. Consequently, AT&T purchased licensees' stocks whenever possible.[9]

The basic predivestiture structure of AT&T was thus complete. As noted earlier, the integration of each component into the Bell system occurred because of sound business reasons. As we will see, AT&T's dominant status as regulated network manager and the structure of local and long-distance monopolies also existed as a result of sound business reasons.

REGULATED MONOPOLY AND PUBLIC SERVICE

At 7 A.M. on 17 September 1945, the fuses in the offices of the Keystone Telephone Company were pulled, marking the close of the second era of competitive telephony. Forty years earlier, the Bell system faced competition in many local and long-distance markets. AT&T's ability to survive the competitive onslaught and attacks by prominent legislators and the Justice Department is another tribute to Theodore J. Vail's genius. For at a critical time in the company's history, he recognized the benefits of close public utility regulation through regulatory commissions, in exchange for which AT&T and its licensees obligated themselves to attain such goals as universal service and technological progressiveness. AT&T, in a word, had a private agenda wrapped in a conception of the public interest. But unlike later participants in the telecommunications industry, its private interest was in the interest of the general public.

The second competitive era began inauspiciously for AT&T. Antimonopoly sentiment was rampant in the 1890s, and telephone competition—then as in the 1970s—was expected to lower prices and spur progressiveness. Yet by 1920, the belief in competition as the best public policy in telephony had died and it was not revived in the anti-big-business attitudes of the 1930s. The overwhelming sentiment is summarized in a 1919 Missouri Public Service Commission report:

> Competition between public service corporations was in vogue for
> many years as the proper method of securing the best results for
> the public. . . . The consensus of modern opinion, however, is that
> competition has failed to bring the result desired. . . .[10]

Telephone competition fell into disfavor mainly because of AT&T's
political-economic strategy, which persuaded virtually every important
actor—even its rivals—that the public interest would be best served
under a regime in which public service commissions regulated telephone monopolies. After the basic patents expired, and after AT&T
sought unsuccessfully to buy sufficient patents to keep ahead of rivals,
competition began to develop gradually and by about 1900 more than
500 independent telephone companies were established annually for a
number of years. Moreover, AT&T was singularly unsuccessful in preventing municipalities from granting franchises to rivals.[11] At the same
time that competition provided a threat, so did nationalization. Manitoba in 1907 and England in 1911 had nationalized most of their
respective telephone service.

During this period, progressivism—a tenet of which was firm government control of large business enterprise—had come to the fore. One
of AT&T's critical moves after Vail's return to the company in 1907,
was to use the progressive sentiment to the Bell system's advantage. It
did so by first embracing the theory of natural monopoly, which had
become fashionable in academic circles at the turn of the century. Although today an industry is considered a natural monopoly if production is done most efficiently by a single firm as output increases, the
term had a somewhat different meaning during the Progressive Era.
Based on a wave of bankruptcies and deteriorated service that had occurred in the traditional public service industries when multiple franchises were granted, the earlier view holds that service to the public is
best undertaken by a single franchisee, or a natural monopoly. It is
important to note the distinction between the earlier and later conceptions of a natural monopoly; that is, *better* and more comprehensive
service based on empirical observation is different from a *theoretical*
conception that purports to predict what is *most* efficient. AT&T sought
to follow the older natural monopoly conception so to portray itself as
the bearer of the public interest.

When Vail accepted AT&T's presidency in 1907, he realized that one
of his most important tasks was the elaboration of the public interest

standard. Prior to his return, the AT&T leadership was split in its attitude toward the new commission form of continual supervision. Annual reports, therefore, avoided the important issue of the company's attitude toward the new mode of regulation. In the 1907 *Annual Report*, the first written since Vail's return, the company spelled out a refined theory of regulation that delineated the proper roles of private company and governmental supervisor:

> It is not believed that there is any objection to [public control] provided it is independent, intelligent, considerate, thorough and just, recognizing, as does the Interstate Commerce Commission . . . that capital is entitled to fair return and good management or enterprise to its reward.[12]

The 1910 *Annual Report* even more enthusiastically endorsed public regulation, adding that it should assure that the plant and service are of the highest possible standard and efficiency, and that service should be extended as far as possible—the universal service standard. In addition, the report pointed out that telephone companies are public service institutions and should be compelled by regulators to attain such standards, but that regulators should stop short of attempting to manage the business. Following is the report's critical argument in favor of monopoly.

> If there is to be State control and regulation, there should also be State protection—protection to a corporation striving to serve the whole community (some part of whose service must necessarily be unprofitable) from aggressive competition which covers only that part which is profitable. . . . That competition should be suppressed which arises out of the promotion of unnecessary duplication, which gives no additional facilities or service. . . . State control and regulation, to be effective at all, should be of such a character that the results from the operation of any one enterprise would not warrant the expenditure or investment necessary for mere duplication and straight competition. . . . Two local telephone exchanges in the same community are regarded as competing exchanges, and the public tolerates this dual service only in the fast disappearing idea that through competition in the telephone service, some benefit may be obtained. . . . Two exchange systems in the same place offering identically the same list of subscribers . . . are as useless as a duplicate system of highways or streets not connecting with each other.[13]

The 1910 *Annual Report* thus established the quid pro quo that would replace competition. AT&T and its affiliates were willing to submit to

commission regulation committed to guaranteeing efficient and progressive telephone service. Further, the commissions were expected to
prod the telephone system to attain high standards and to expand the
system. In exchange, AT&T committed itself as network manager of the
Bell-operating companies and noncompeting independents. However,
AT&T rejected interconnection with independent companies that competed with a Bell licensee or an affiliated independent on the ground
that such interconnection was redundant. It promised to improve
equipment and operating procedures and to continue expansion into
uneconomic, sparsely settled, and difficult-to-reach territories. Most
importantly, AT&T committed itself to attaining universal service, so
that virtually everyone who desired a telephone could have one and
could communicate with anyone else. Obviously, the public utility
commissions were expected to regulate telephone pricing so that
subsidy flows could allow these goals to be achieved.

It should be noted, too, that Vail used a shrewd political strategy in
dealing with the independents. AT&T did not advocate that it become
the sole provider of telephone service but rather the network manager
of a vast network that included Bell companies, Bell licensees, and noncompeting independents. Politically, this was important in that the independents often had strong ties to local elites. Merchants and other
businesses that increasingly relied on the telephone approved the regulatory commission idea because it promised stable and reasonable rates
as well as a high grade of service. They usually disapproved of competing service because nonconnecting systems prevented them from
communicating with some suppliers and customers.[14] Thus, the independents who favored competition and rejected the independent
regulatory commission idea were increasingly isolated both politically
and in terms of the goal of attaining a vast network in which any person
could converse with any other.

Notwithstanding some conduct that was sharply criticized, a major
antitrust investigation, and the threat of nationalization, AT&T had successfully wrapped itself in the mantle of the public interest by the
time of Vail's retirement in 1919. By the early 1920s, AT&T and the
independents were close allies. The independents have remained allies,
opposed to the more recent changes that the regulators and courts have
brought about.

THE PUBLIC-PRIVATE PARTNERSHIP

By late 1920, all but three of the forty-eight states had PUCs with the power to regulate telephone service. Since most telephone matters concerned local rates or service, the PUCs were the core of the regulation system. Their ability to regulate AT&T and the independents effectively was a central issue in *United States* v. *AT&T* and the other major proceedings.

Telephones first became subject to federal rate jurisdiction (by the ICC) under the 1910 Mann-Elkins Law. Under an agreement known as the Kingsbury Commitment, into which the Justice Department and AT&T entered in 1913, the company agreed not to acquire any competitors and to furnish interconnection to noncompeting independents into the Bell network. And in 1921, Congress enacted the Willis-Graham Act extending ICC jurisdiction over telephone mergers and acquisitions, thereby effectively abrogating the portion of the Kingsbury Commitment prohibiting AT&T acquisitions. By this time, controversy had subsided and every major actor had come to agree with Vail's 1908 formulation: "One policy, one System, Universal Service." In the thirteen years between Willis-Graham's enactment and the creation of the FCC in 1934, the ICC considered at least 274 merger and acquisition cases and certified 271. State PUCs capable of regulating telephone mergers generally approved them as well. The ICC's activities served to rationalize the industry, and a leading study of ICC telephone regulation concluded that acquisitions usually occurred "because the smaller system lacked capital, credit and revenues to extend or even maintain its plant or because the owners of the small enterprise desire to withdraw from the telephone business."[15]

Although the FCC supplanted the ICC in 1934 and gained greater powers, until after World War II the bulk of regulation occurred at the state PUC level. This framework lasted through the boom of the 1920s and the bust of the 1930s. It continued into the postwar era and, although the seeds of its destruction can be found much earlier, the late 1960s marked the beginning of its decline. Indeed, even though it has been modified and, as we will see, much policy is in conflict with it, the regulated network manager system has not been wholly abandoned even today. The system was never frontally attacked; rather, it has been eroded through "exceptions," "special cases," and "experiments," such that the new system of contrived competition has gradually replaced it. The regulated network manager system has never been directly attacked because such action would unleash an examination of its overall performance. Even a cursory look at the American telephone industry from 1920 to 1968 shows its remarkable progress under the regulated network manager system. Telephone company profits were reasonable and far from monopoly levels, in large part because they were rigorously controlled by public utility regulators. Of course, trends in communications are not unlike trends in other sectors—they are dependent in no small degree on general economic trends. Thus, a downturn during parts of the Great Depression as well as substantial growth during the boom that followed World War II were to be expected. Nevertheless, while the GNP increased approximately fivefold between 1920 and 1970 (from about $140 billion 1958 dollars to approximately $722 billion 1958 dollars), telephones increased almost ninefold (from 13,273 thousand to 120,218 thousand) during the same time period. Even more remarkable, while 35 percent of households had telephones in 1920, the comparable percentage in the larger 1970 population was 90.5 percent. And, of course, since interconnection of telephones was virtually completed by 1970, the value of the telephone to each subscriber was incomparably greater in 1970 than in 1920.

However, these considerations do not begin to exhaust the long-run achievements of the regulated network manager system. The telephone in America had achieved the status of a necessity for both business and residential users; the structures of commerce, entertainment (through radio and television), and social interaction became dependent on the telephone system. Americans needed to work fewer hours per year to obtain telephone service than residents of other developed nations. For example, a 1971 Department of Commerce study showed that the average American needed to work 26 hours per year to obtain basic telephone service, whereas the average French citizen required 179 hours. The number of Americans on waiting lists to obtain telephone service was lower than that in any country with a large telephone system. Moreover, the Department of Justice did not contest AT&T's exemplary record in national defense work or in operating during and immediately after natural disasters, nor did it deny the extraordinary research and development record of Bell Labs, the benefits of which have extended far beyond telecommunications.[16] As Donald Baker,

deputy assistant attorney general, Antitrust Division, stated shortly before the big case was instituted: "A.T.&T. has clearly outperformed the
foreign post offices and given us probably the finest message telephone
service in the world."[17]

Why, then, did the Department of Justice bring suit in the face of
the American telephone system's outstanding performance? In part, it
portrayed public regulation of the industry as ineffective. Competition,
according to the proponents of the vast changes in telecommunications
policy that had taken place, would better "regulate" the industry and
serve the public interest. Notwithstanding the Justice Department's
characterization, PUC regulation withstands scrutiny well. PUCs have
been under continual siege, charged with corruption, incompetence,
or disregard for the public. But considering the large number of cases
that they have handled, there have been very few cases of *proved* corruption or blatant disregard for the laws they are charged with enforcing.
PUC critics usually are satisfied with naked allegations of the agencies
being "captured" by regulated firms. And, of course, some dema-
gogues, claiming to represent the consumer's interest, oppose all rate
increases. Yet, as R. H. Coase has said, these claims are no more than
presumptions of what the consumer interest *should* be.[18]

Unlike the courts and antitrust authorities who assume that competition will lead to the best results and who can then turn their attention
to other matters, the PUCs are compelled to exercise continual—long-
term and short-term—authority over the industries they regulate. They
must consider both the consumers' interests and the producers' interests, for unless the producer can make a reasonable profit and attract
capital for expansion, the consumer cannot be effectively served. PUCs
cannot avoid blame for performance deficiencies; they cannot even
blame the regulated companies for deficiencies because their own lack
of foresight or inadequate supervision of the industry is viewed as the
primary source of failure. In short, PUCs should be obligation-oriented
and collaborative with regulated firms. Although collaboration is inconsistent with a strictly adversarial attitude, it is not inconsistent with
one in which the PUC does not act on or grant a company's request
unless the company's showing is clear and convincing.

What compels PUCs to behave in this fashion? As we learned in
Chapter 1, PUCs are constrained in many ways. Courts, the executive
branch, and legislatures exercise considerable supervision—and, more
importantly, power—over PUCs through hearings, legislation, appro-

priations, oversight, and enforcement. Information about alleged transgressions on the part of PUCs or the firms they regulate is readily available from a variety of sources, many of which have strong incentives to
exercise considerable scrutiny. There are many eyes on the results of
PUC regulation as well as on the ways in which the results are achieved.
All decisions, including regulatory ones, allocate resources so that
there are winners and losers. For example, if our utility rates increase
and our service does not improve, we know it; if we experience a
brownout, we know it. Sufficient criticism of this nature is used by
political actors willing to exploit it as an issue. In addition, others are
deeply involved in most regulatory decisions, either as close watchers
or as participants. Those economically concerned about PUC telephone
proceedings include (1) residential subscribers, (2) consumer organizations, (3) business users, (4) trade associations, (5) equipment suppliers
and potential suppliers, (6) competing carriers, (7) large telephone
companies, (8) independent telephone companies, (9) rural cooperative
telephone companies, (10) telephone company trade associations, (11)
companies involved in other markets or technologies on which decisions may impinge, and (12) government purchasers of telecommunications services, such as the Department of Defense. This, of course, does
not suggest that all of these economic interests are represented in every
proceeding. Rather, they do hire lawyers and lobbyists to scrutinize
what PUCs and the FCC are doing or plan to do, so that any economic
interest that may be affected by a proceeding usually has the opportunity to intervene. Further, a variety of governmental institutions claim
to represent not their own interests but the public interest, often with
varying and divergent views of what constitutes the public interest.
These "guardians" of the public interest include (1) other state PUCs,
(2) NARUC (the association of regulatory commissioners whose predecessor dates from 1889), (3) local governments, (4) other state and local
government agencies, (5) state attorney generals, (6) local prosecutors,
(7) the Department of Justice, (8) the Department of Commerce and
various divisions of it concerned with telecommunications, (9) the
Office of Management and Budget and parallel state agencies, (10) various watchdog agencies (such as the General Accounting Office and its
state parallels), (11) legislators who are attentive to public utility and
telecommunications issues, (12) legislative committees, (13) other
agencies (such as agriculture departments in rural telecommunications
matters and the Department of State in international matters), and, of

course, (14) the courts. Always present, too, is the threat of a special committee appointed to examine the performance of PUCs or regulatory agencies in general. Finally, there have been instances of agency staff, conceiving that a PUC has taken a wrong turn, leaking information to the media, legislators, and others.

There are also many private guardians of the public interest. Muckrakers such as Ralph Nader have existed even before public utility commissions. Although these would-be guardians of the public interest are often biased or simplistic or have failed to investigate a question reasonably well, they do serve a useful purpose. The threat of investigation provides regulators with an incentive to defend their actions and to show that the alternatives were less attractive. These "political entrepreneurs," as James Q. Wilson calls them, are adept at mobilizing latent public sentiment by revealing a scandal or capitalizing on a crisis.[19] In their endeavors, the private guardians of the public interest are often surreptitiously aided in obtaining information from PUC insiders. They are also adept at leaking what they have learned to media reporters.

In brief, legislative appropriations and oversight hearings, executive branch reviews, adverse publicity, the threat of forced resignations, and even criminal prosecution provide PUCs strong supplementary incentives to follow the paths dictated by statutory goals. PUCs do make mistakes and can differ among themselves, but, like courts, they establish principles that are developed over the years and that are based on experience, daily contact with concerned actors, and continuous supervision of regulated firms. Decisions are articulated in written opinions based on facts and reasoned to conclusions that regulators hope will withstand the scrutiny of courts, legislators, executive branch officials, and the attentive public. And, they have usually withstood this scrutiny.

By 1920 PUCs concluded, in the words of the California agency: "[a]fter a number of years of experience with two telephone systems in these communities, the subscribers almost unanimously demand a consolidation into one system. . . ."[20] Thus, the PUCs had accepted as the public interest the basic vision outlined by Vail. That is, in exchange for monopoly privileges, telephone companies are stewards charged with rendering cheap, efficient service of high and improving quality. Telephone companies must be held to the standard of end-to-end responsibility in which they are continuously charged with maintaining the quality, safety, and effectiveness of each component of the network. Since the telephone companies are charged with end-to-end responsibility, and the network's overall quality is adversely affected by the quality of the worst component of the system, PUCs required telephone companies to lease equipment. If subscribers supplied their own equipment, according to PUCs, quality could not be assured.[21] Finally, PUCs devised many quantitative standards governing such things as switchboard capacity, promptness in handling calls, and conversion time to higher grades of service.

Ultimately, the regulated network manager system must be judged by performance criteria. Did the system work? In later chapters we answer this question in detail, but in general we can say that the system worked well, and although there were some rough spots and downturns, it improved in the long run. Consider one example: Before World War II, the time required to establish a long-distance telephone call was approximately 3 minutes; in the 1960s, it was 1.5 minutes; and by 1973, it was further reduced to under 40 seconds. The same progress applies to other measures of telephone company performance as well, all of which occurred under conditions of reasonable, and often declining, rates. Labor costs are an important component of overall costs and, hence, rates. According to the Department of Labor, the Bell system's productivity gains between 1972 and 1977 exceeded those of all but one of the sixty-three industries that reported such data. Moreover, fifty-one of these industries had labor productivity growth less than one-half of the Bell system's. In the overall inflationary period from 1947 to 1977, the telephone industry's rate of price increase was about one-half that of all industries combined. Between 1960 and 1973, the consumer price index (CPI) increased 44.4 percentage points, but the residential telephone component increased only 14.6 percentage points. Further, during the highly inflationary period of 1973 to 1979, the CPI increased 84.3 percentage points and the telephone component only 16 percentage points. Between 1965 and 1977 more than 240 of the 264 items in the CPI showed rates of price increases greater than telephone rate increases.

Both the postwar and prewar record, we should recall, occurred as AT&T continuously engaged in extensive research and development to assure progressiveness and the attainment of universal service. And this occurred when rates were made in such a way that Bell profits were always reasonable. As the Department of Justice casually notes, it never charged that AT&T and its licensees made monopoly profits,[22] nor could it charge that the Bell system made unreasonable profits if measured against those in competitive industries.

THE BOUNDARY PROBLEM

The regulated network manager system gradually broke down not because of its overall performance record but because of political reasons, one of which I call the *boundary problem*. The system, and the public service principle that supported it, were conceived as carefully delineated exceptions to the competitive principles that should govern markets in a capitalist economy. Firms in such industries as water, electricity, or telephone never advanced an argument that, say, steel manufacturing or appliance retailing should be embraced within the ambit of public service activities.

A major difficulty arises when new technologies compete or converge with traditional telephone service. Under such circumstances, the political battle is fought over highly abstruse matters of definition and boundary. How radio should be regulated was a key issue during the 1920s in the confrontation between AT&T and the coalition led by General Electric. That is, should radio be regulated as if it were another form of telephony? The sequence of events that led to the deregulation of all terminal equipment, including ordinary telephones, stemmed from the difficult problem of resolving where computing ended and communicating began. Each company or trade association backed the side of the argument from which it would most benefit. Those who sought to exclude the new technology from public service regulation usually sought to prevent AT&T from entering the new industry and used government processes to achieve their goals.

However, AT&T's opponents did not launch a frontal attack on the regulated network manager system; in view of the company's overall success, they could not. But they transmogrified the system by carving out more and more exceptions. They secured allies, for example, by portraying AT&T as a greedy imperialist intent on extending its monopoly far beyond its proper boundaries. Since the newer rivals were frequently smaller than AT&T, it was possible to engage the sympathies of important actors who favored "the little guy." Of course, there were also allies who simply despised giant companies generally or AT&T specifically, as well as those in the policy arena who sought to limit regulated monopoly as much as possible or who sought to extend anti-trust principles. Ironically, then, AT&T's very success in developing new products and services significantly contributed to the undermining of the regulated network manager system. As AT&T developed or con-tributed to new products or services and considered exploiting them, its commercial rivals sought to exploit the resentments that already existed. Even as AT&T and the telephone independents were settling their controversies, a new one based on the boundary problem and AT&T's technological prowess was brewing. The radio controversy un-leashed considerable resentment against AT&T that would carry over into the anti-big business 1930s. The Bell system's successes in develop-ing other novel technologies, such as television and sound motion pic-tures, would contribute to a hostile FCC investigation in the 1930s and to the 1949 antitrust suit against the company and beyond.

At the close of World War I, few people envisioned that the most dramatic application of radio would not be in point-to-point communi-cation but in broadcasting. AT&T saw radio's potential in extending long-distance telephony and, accordingly, it invested its efforts in radio development and acquired patents of others. Its overall attitude before the radio boom was that radio telephony could never replace wire service but could be a valuable supplement to reaching relatively inaccessible locations.[23]

Unregulated firms such as General Electric, Westinghouse, and United Fruit became involved in radio research for their own reasons. General Electric and AT&T contested twenty radio-related patent in-terferences between 1912 and 1926, and the unregulated firms fre-quently blocked patents so that the others could not effectively use them without infringing on those held by another firm. Because these events occurred in the period around World War I, the United States government (principally through the Navy's Bureau of Steam Engineer-ing) sought to solve the patent tangle and, at the same time, to assure that control of the new technology and its development was in Ameri-can hands. The net result was the formation in 1919 of the Radio Cor-poration of America (RCA), closely linked with General Electric, and the creation in 1920 of a patent pool embracing General Electric,

AT&T, and others that allocated exclusive and nonexclusive fields in virtually every phase of communications, including broadcasting.[24] Even though the patent pool agreements were carefully crafted, bitter disputes, between AT&T on the one hand and a coalition led by General Electric on the other, soon erupted, largely because of ambiguities in the clauses concerning broadcasting. At the time the agreements were signed, none of the parties foresaw how rapidly the broadcasting boom would occur. Although they envisioned the radio as an adjunct to wire point-to-point communication and ship-to-shore service, they did not anticipate its importance as a medium of entertainment and information. The broadcasting boom began in 1920, a few months after the patent pool agreement was signed, when Westinghouse erected a powerful transmitter in Pittsburgh and developed a regular schedule for the station to broadcast nightly. AT&T and the other members of the patent pool then realized the lucrative opportunities in the new field of broadcasting. By 1925—only five years after Westinghouse's KDKA station was licensed—2,750,000 households in the United States had radios, yet this figure barely touched the vast market of families that would want radios.

The inevitable dispute was fought not only in the realm of interpreting the patent pool agreements but in the political area of defining the public interest in broadcasting as well. AT&T sought to embrace broadcasting on its side of the boundary, separating public service companies from those firms not so regulated, and it did so through a concept worth reconsidering in today's cable television market, a concept it called *toll broadcasting*. On 6 January 1922, AT&T issued a public announcement that stated it would operate a radio station:

> [AT&T] will provide no program of its own, but provide the channels through which anyone with whom it makes a contract can send out their own programs. Just as the company leases its long distance wire facilities for the use of newspapers, banks and other concerns so it will lease its radio telephone facilities and will not provide the matter which is sent out from this station.[25]

Thus, AT&T devised a plan in which there would be no relationship between program production and distribution to the public. Unlike the broadcasting system that prevails today, in which the networks and cable companies determine which programs will be distributed, the toll broadcasting idea envisioned the distributor as a conveyor of material over which it has no control. Just as the telephone company has no control over the conversations of its subscribers, radio-transmitting companies would sell blocks of time to programmers. Today, as television exhibits a bland sameness and cable companies can determine which programs to air and can exclude whole services, toll broadcasting has an appeal as an alternative that may have enlarged choice and diversity.

AT&T's attempt to employ public service principles in broadcasting soon collapsed. Although toll broadcasting does not necessarily imply monopoly in distributing programming, AT&T was attacked on the ground that it was seeking to extend its telephone monopoly. Further, the decision of the arbitrator appointed to decide the issue of whether AT&T could enter broadcasting under the patent pool agreement was adverse to the telephone company's position. The position of RCA and its allies—that AT&T should not be allowed to enter broadcasting— was reinforced by AT&T's assertion of its patent rights against radio stations infringing on broadcasting transmitter patents. Even though AT&T was legally entitled to protect its patents, the adverse publicity reinforced the fear that the company was attempting to enlarge its monopoly. Finally, legislative and executive attacks on the telephone "monopoly" intensified, and at the same time, some government officials expressed displeasure about certain news commentaries on an AT&T station. These factors eventually led to AT&T's withdrawal from broadcasting in 1926 and to its decision to sell its existing radio stations to RCA. The toll broadcasting experiment ended, demonstrating how difficult it would be to embrace novel technologies within the public service ambit. A long chain of events, beginning with the radio experience, would proclaim a peculiar irony and lead to AT&T's breakup. The creation of the FCC in 1934, and its notorious investigation of AT&T, would be the next links in the chain leading to the 1984 breakup.

THE CREATION OF THE FEDERAL COMMUNICATIONS COMMISSION (FCC)

Primarily, the FCC was created in 1934 to combine the radio regulatory functions of the Federal Radio Commission (FRC) and the telephone regulatory functions of the ICC into a unified agency.[26] AT&T opposed the creation of a unified agency when it was first proposed in 1929, but with the advent of the New Deal in 1933 and the climate of anti-big business feelings focused on public utility holding companies, AT&T expressed even more apprehension. Even though the major governmental reports advocating the creation of a unified agency emphasized that significant changes in existing law would not take place, AT&T had reason to be apprehensive. The House Report envisioned a future report by the new agency on such topics as whether AT&T should be compelled to engage in competitive bidding for equipment instead of relying on Western Electric.

The Communications Act of 1934 was, thus, intended to be noncontroversial—largely a matter of administrative consolidation. On the other hand, it was expected to be the prelude to much more drastic regulation and legislation that would follow an FCC investigation of telephone company practices. Certainly, the New Deal's first one hundred days justified AT&T's apprehension in which it was joined by the independent telephone industry. Among the statutes that then sailed through Congress were those that (1) divorced commercial banking from investment banking, (2) established federal control over new securities issues, and, most controversial, (3) created the National Recovery Administration, which was to establish federal supervision over virtually every facet of activity in almost every industry. From AT&T's perspective, then, the federal government had marched beyond the boundary between private management and regulation that Vail had elaborated. And the FCC was conceived of as a prelude to overly stringent regulation, even nationalization.

The forces favoring the FCC's creation were successful in part due to their ability to identify the public interest in administrative consolidation. After all, what could be more reasonable than a single agency to regulate all communication, as there was a single agency—the ICC—to regulate all transportation? With this central argument, the proponents of the new agency did not need to find examples of AT&T wrongdoing; vague accusations and calls for an investigation were employed as secondary arguments. The forceful statement of ICC Commissioner Joseph B. Eastman, a highly respected regulator, that the ICC was doing a satisfactory job of telephone regulation as well as declining interstate rates, were insufficient to overcome the call for a new agency. But as we will see, the FCC investigation of AT&T that ensued eventually led to the company's undoing.

CHAPTER 3

SILENCE THAT DREADFUL BELL:
THE NEW DEAL AND
THE WESTERN ELECTRIC CASE

THE NEW DEAL IN COMMUNICATIONS

The redefinition of the public interest in telecommunications that led
to the massive 1974 suit and the deregulation of telephone equipment
and long-distance service took place gradually. AT&T's regulated network manager system was questioned during the New Deal and was
followed by the Justice Department's immense 1949 *Western Electric* suit
brought with the full support of the Truman administration. The case
was settled in 1956, during the Eisenhower administration, over the
objection of many persons in Congress and the Justice Department and
others. This dissatisfaction, in turn, led AT&T's critics to scrutinize the
company's moves continuously, in the hope that they could redefine
the public interest as something that would not support AT&T's structure and practices.

The political climate of the New Deal, and the consequences of
AT&T's technological prowess in developing products that were not
narrowly in telephony, aided AT&T's enemies during the Roosevelt
administration. The 1930s were a time of deep antagonism between an
expanding federal bureaucracy and important business sectors, including parts of the communications industry. This, of course, does not
mean that most New Dealers sought to destroy the business system or

to replace it with public ownership, but that New Deal rhetoric was frequently critical of big business in general and of many large firms in particular. Although it is certainly arguable that the main thrust of the New Deal was to preserve the capitalist system, the rhetoric did reflect the view that big business, or some leading sectors of it, were largely responsible for the Great Depression. The failure of the New Deal to lift the nation out of the Great Depression only confirmed for some New Dealers that monopolistic behavior caused the failure of the Roosevelt program.[1]

The same ideological trends that occurred generally during the New Deal occurred in communications as well. These trends were typified in the work of President Roosevelt's Temporary National Economic Committee (TNEC), which, before beginning its investigation of the American economy, decried "the concentration of economic power and its injurious effects on the American system of free enterprise."[2] The issues for those holding such a conception were to discover exactly how big corporations were bad and to propose remedies. As we know from Chapter 2, the 1934 Communications Act was intended as a prelude to further legislation that would deal with structural and behavioral changes in AT&T. Particularly suspect was the relationship between the operating companies and Western Electric, their principal supplier. Indeed, the FCC launched a hostile investigation of AT&T shortly after its founding, but it took few formal actions against AT&T or its subsidiaries from 1934 to the onset of World War II.

Notwithstanding the bigness-is-badness public philosophy of the New Deal, even a cursory look at AT&T shows continued good performance in all pertinent areas despite the Great Depression. In long-distance rates—the area of greatest concern to the FCC—the company had announced its fourth general long-distance rate reduction on 1 January 1930. In 1936, it again reduced such rates throughout the country for calls longer than 234 miles and lowered overtime charges as well.[3] In the realm of service improvements, rapid progress was being made in replacing manually operated telephones with dial telephones. In 1929, only 26 percent of Bell instruments were dial-operated; by 1939, 56 percent were dial-operated. Technologically and scientifically, Bell Labs made great strides in the development of coaxial cables that could transmit much more information; when a general economic expansion took place, AT&T was ready for it. Equally important, the company further elaborated its public service responsibilities as it moved away from its radio involvement. In 1927, AT&T President Walter Gifford outlined this enhanced public service obligation:

> It would be contrary to sound policy for the management to earn speculative or large profits for distribution as . . . extra dividends. . . . Earnings must be sufficient to assure the best possible telephone service at all times and to assure the continued financial integrity of the business. . . . Earnings in excess of these requirements must either be spent for the enlargement and improvement of the service furnished or the rates charged for the service must be reduced. This is fundamental in the policy of management.[4]

Although Gifford's comments could be attributed to a keen sense of public relations, AT&T *did* behave in this way and it did impose on itself a high standard for future performance. As noted earlier, long-distance rates had been reduced both before and after the onset of the Great Depression. Local and intrastate long-distance rates are, of course, more difficult to generalize about because there are so many of them and their relative importance depends on different volumes of traffic. For example, a local rate reduction in New York City is far more meaningful than a similar reduction in a rural community. With this complicating condition in mind, it is notable that the FCC's final report on the telephone industry grudgingly conceded that in 1936, major reductions took place in New York, California, and other states.[5]

To the FCC staff conducting the AT&T investigation, the company's failure was not in performance but a question of its size. At the same time, the FCC did not want to redefine the public interest in favor of competition in the traditional public service markets of local loops or long distance. Rather, its principal focus was on equipment markets. Because of the facade of comprehensiveness and the pretense of impartiality, the report was an important Antitrust Division weapon in its attack on AT&T in the 1974 case.

THE FCC INVESTIGATION

The FCC investigation of the telephone industry called for by Congress in 1934 began quietly. AT&T voluntarily submitted to the FCC staff a formidable number of documents dealing with patents, research and development, manufacturing, long-lines operations, and other matters. The FCC staff assigned to the special telephone investigation began in 1935 to study a large number of telephone matters. As the investigation proceeded, the FCC's Telephone and Telegraph Division, charged with investigating specific complaints and proceedings against telephone companies for violations of the 1934 Act, received virtually no complaints and had docketed almost no formal matters against AT&T and its subsidiaries. Further, the FCC was clearly favorably disposed to the technological progress that AT&T was making in such areas as coaxial cable.[6]

The controversy between AT&T and the FCC's Special Telephone Investigation (STI) staff that would erupt in 1936 should *not* be viewed as evidence of overall FCC disapproval of AT&T. Rather, the bitterness erupted between the STI group, led by Commissioner Paul A. Walker, and AT&T. The company's principal procedural complaint during the investigative phase was that the STI staff refused to allow AT&T to bring its own witnesses or to cross-examine STI's witnesses. Although an investigation is unlike a trial, AT&T had not been accorded a fair opportunity to provide its own information in a reasonable manner. This suggests that the STI carefully selected evidence to bolster its foregone conclusions.

The STI hearings concluded on 30 June 1937. Superficially, the STI effort looked impressive—seventy-seven volumes of staff reports were introduced as exhibits and the testimony records consisted of approximately 8,500 pages. In addition, there were hundreds of supplemental exhibits and thousands of working papers and documents. However, beneath the scholarly facade was a deep antagonism toward AT&T. Without proof, the STI inferred that AT&T's long-distance rate reductions were caused by the STI investigation.[7] Most importantly, the STI staff reports tended to deprecate AT&T's conduct and to ignore the major facts about AT&T up to that time—its high and improving service quality, its low rates, and its technological progressiveness. While considerable space was devoted, for example, to banker control of the company in 1907, virtually no attention was directed to the then current conditions of widespread ownership of AT&T stock and the extraordinary lack of concentration in shareholding.

The STI investigation is important in that its influence and the hostility it generated toward AT&T persisted after the end of World War II. More than any other factor, it led to the 1949 suit against AT&T—the

Western Electric case—which was in large part based on the findings of the STI, especially those relating to the suspicion of excess profits resulting from the ties between Western Electric, on the one hand, and AT&T and the operating companies on the other. The evidence that Western Electric's profits were reasonable for an industrial corporation and that it operated efficiently were beside the point to the STI anti-AT&T zealots.[8]

The first STI report was submitted to Congress on 1 April 1938. Named as the *Walker Report* after FCC Commissioner Paul A. Walker, who directed the investigation, it was not adopted as an official FCC report. The 1938 FCC *Annual Report* states: "This proposed report previously had been submitted to the Commission with a view to subsequent determination at the earliest practicable date as to the form and content of the report which the Commission will later submit to the Congress."[9] In other words, the other commissioners would not endorse the *Walker Report*'s drastic conclusions, which charged that AT&T's rates were too high and that it had effectively evaded state regulation. Further, the report recommended that since Western Electric supplied a large proportion of the switching and transmission gear and CPE to AT&T and the operating companies, the prices of which are included in the rate base, Western Electric should be treated as a public utility subject to FCC control. In addition, the *Walker Report* endorsed the notion that AT&T and the operating companies should purchase equipment through competitive bidding.[10]

That AT&T would greet the *Walker Report* unfavorably was, of course, predictable. That the full commission would refuse to adopt it was far less predictable; indeed, it seriously undermined the report's credibility. Walker's hostility to AT&T and his differences with other commissioners was noted in the media almost from the outset of the investigation. In early 1936, for example, *Business Week* reported that

> Washington insiders say the investigation was virtually forced on FCC by Paul A. Walker . . . [who] used all his political pressure to obtain the congressional backing for his crusade, and the Capital wonders if he cherishes some private hate against the Bell System. It adds sadly that, anyhow, he is one of those pious parties who is apt to see a devil behind every rosebush.[11]

Notably, Walker did not raise the issues of breaking up AT&T or injecting competition in the local-loop or long-distance markets. Like every other major actor at the time, Walker viewed telephone service as a natural monopoly.

While other members of the FCC differed sharply with the *Walker Report*, their ability to prepare an alternative report was severely limited. The STI staff was under Walker's control, and the "facts" given in the exhibits were not substantiated; rather, data were often mixed with anti-AT&T interpretations. The FCC, under considerable pressure to complete a report, tempered the conclusions of the *Walker Report* but was compelled to rely on the findings of the STI staff. The staff's bias is illustrated in its report entitled *Politics of Control*,[12] which was largely prepared by economist N. R. Danielian, who subsequently published a book capitalizing on the Walker investigation and his important role in it. In his book, Danielian editorializes that AT&T had attempted "to substitute propaganda and 'public education' for sound indus rial statesmanship. . . . The picture of a corporation with its agents in every county of the country trying to 'educate' the public to its own point of view is not very reassuring for the preservation of democracy."[13] During an era in which the Roosevelt administration had adopted a strong anti-big business stance and the FCC specifically had spent large sums of taxpayers' money to attack AT&T, Danielian claimed that the real danger to democracy lay in AT&T defending itself against partisan attacks undertaken with the imprimatur of the United States government.

The Walker staff's attempt to overexaggerate a few minor incidents failed to show that AT&T strategically or systematically engaged in deception, undue influence, or duress. Although inference of undue influence was made through the fact that a Bell affiliate provided free telephone service to PUC commissioners, no such inference was made that the Walker investigators were unduly influenced by the free local telephone service and room space provided to them at AT&T's headquarters in New York. The Walker staff generalized about Bell system "subsidies" to publications from isolated incidents involving occasional purchases of large numbers of obscure low-circulation newspapers. And while the *Politics of Control* makes much of the Bell companies' tendency of trying to persuade PUCs that the Bell position is the correct one in various proceedings, no evidence was given of anything more ignoble than persuasion.[14] In its reply, AT&T did not question that some of the incidents used by the Walker group to draw sweeping inferences had taken place. The telephone company did, however, question the casualness with which wild generalizations were made and frequently the interpretation of events. For example, the *Walker Report* declared that "[t]here *are instances* . . . where banks have been penalized by the refusal of telephone company accounts when bank officials have opposed company efforts for rate increases" [emphasis added].[15] In fact, as AT&T showed in its brief, there was *one* such instance in the small town of Athens, Alabama, in 1927, from which the STI's sweeping generalization was drawn.[16] The task of rebutting and putting into context the numerous contentions made in the *Walker Report* and the accompanying exhibits was an impossible one.

As a result, the full FCC report, released in June 1939, was largely based on the Walker investigation's "facts," although the conclusions and recommendations had been toned down considerably. Obviously, the FCC could not have disowned the investigation without, in effect, admitting that it had wasted considerable time and money. Thus, the FCC praised the lengthy and costly investigation in its 1939 *Annual Report*. But less than one of the almost 250 pages in the report was devoted to the final report of the telephone investigation. After more than 4 years and $1.5 million—a considerable sum during the Great Depression—the FCC stated, "[t]he report suggests certain amendments to the Communications Act for the purpose of clarification, and also amendments to enlarge the Commission's authority over the telephone industry."[17] The 1940 *Annual Report* barely mentioned any need for new telephone legislation.

However, the FCC investigation would have an impact, although not until after World War II, during which any drastic action against large companies was out of the question. The final report accepted that both local and long-distance transmission were natural monopolies and public utilities. These services were "entitled in the interest of its patrons to reasonable protection from wasteful competition . . . but subject to public . . . regulation. . . ."[18] But state regulation, the final report asserted, was inadequate because states could not obtain facts about activities beyond their jurisdictions. Therefore, the FCC, without explicitly calling for preemption that might antagonize the states, vaguely called for enlarged federal administrative power over telephone companies. In fact, while the Supreme Court held that AT&T and Western Electric could not be *directly* subject to state PUC regulation (except in the states of incorporation), state PUCs in rate proceedings could obtain necessary and pertinent information from AT&T and Western Electric about equipment costs and allocations. This was accomplished in a rate proceeding because the burden of proof on the issues of charges made by AT&T and Western Electric, insofar as such charges formed part of the rate base, was on the local operating companies. Thus, contrary to the FCC's conclusion, state commissions could obtain the information they required. State commissions had been scrutinizing such costs charged to operating companies before the FCC had published its report, and they continued to do so.[19]

While the FCC and the state PUCs could, therefore, obtain information about Western Electric that would aid in rate determination, this did not make CPE or switching and transmission equipment manufacture a public utility or natural monopoly. In fact, the FCC, without recommending specific legislation, stated that competition in these fields of manufacture might reduce prices and create more efficient production.[20] The recommendation would be acted on not by the FCC but by the Justice Department after the war.

THE SIN OF SUCCESS

As pointed out in Chapter 2, AT&T's entry into businesses outside traditional telephony tended to backfire. The mere suspicion that AT&T was surreptitiously extending its monopoly or subsidizing prices in the new field from "monopoly profits" in telephony placed the company in an uncomfortable defensive posture. One way AT&T dealt with the problem of a new technology was to portray it as a public service and, therefore, as appropriate within its sphere. But radio showed the pitfalls in this strategy. Moreover, the traditional public service criteria could not be used to justify what amounted to little more than means of entertainment or adjuncts to such traditional media as newspapers and periodicals.

AT&T's successes in developing radio were followed by important breakthroughs in telephotography, television transmission, stereophonic sound, and talking motion pictures. The latter development led AT&T to a new approach to the problem of new technologies. In 1926, AT&T officials organized Electrical Research Products Inc. (ERPI) to exploit the patents and discoveries of its research having application outside AT&T's public service activities. But AT&T soon found itself in bitter disputes with competitors and customers or would-be customers (in this case, motion picture companies). Once again, AT&T was involved in patent litigation and was charged with attempting to extend its monopoly unlawfully. Even though ERPI was successful or settled cases amicably, the critics grew louder and were joined by Commissioner Walker and his staff.[21] Profits from ERPI were small in comparison to those from telephone operations and, in any case, were not worth the potential harm they could cause AT&T. During a time in which anti-big-business sentiment prevailed and Commissioner Walker's staff sought to attack the company, AT&T used sound political judgment in its decision to abandon the ERPI enterprise. The clamor for AT&T to get out of businesses unrelated to telephone transmission might extend to its ownership of Western Electric. Accordingly, in December 1937, AT&T sold most of the ERPI business to the Altec Service Corporation (organized by former ERPI employees) and became far more liberal in its licensing policies. Nevertheless, the underlying issue of which businesses a public service company could and could not enter continued to haunt AT&T. The issue would not be resolved until AT&T withdrew from all monopoly services under the agreements in *United States* v. *AT&T*, the computer and interconnection matters, and the MCI litigation.

PRELUDE TO THE *WESTERN ELECTRIC* CASE

World War II did not entirely suspend partisan politics—there was a presidential election in 1944—but most administrative actions and antitrust proceedings were postponed. While virtually every knowledgeable person expected a boom based on pent-up wartime savings and the unavailability of consumer goods, few expected the extraordinary economic growth that has characterized the post–World War II era. Rather, there was widespread fear of a depression that would follow the boom—unless policies could be designed to prevent the downturn. Although much important economic theorizing took place in the macroeconomic area, some policymakers looked to antitrust policy as the basic antidote to depression. Belief in this view was based on the sharp economic downturn of 1937. Antitrusters sought to place paramount blame for the recession on big business; essentially, they theorized that big business, exercising monopoly power, had instituted arbitrary price increases. When consumers were unable to purchase goods at these excessively high prices, big business did not lower prices; rather, they laid off workers, reduced output, and postponed investments.[22] Thus, to the antitrusters, the key to preventing another depression in the postwar era was vigorous antitrust action. Antitrusters were bolstered by the association of the Nazi German government with international cartels—the quintessential monopoly arrangement. One of the German monopolies, I. G. Farben, was almost as hated for its use of slave labor as was the German government, and some large American firms were defensive because of their roles in international cartels.

As the foregoing discussion suggests, to be against monopolies in the immediate post–World War II era was not only politically popular but economically popular as well, in that the theory addressed some of the major economic problems facing the nation at the time. President Harry Truman, an advocate of vigorous antitrust action, vetoed the Reed-Bulwinkle Act in 1948, which granted antitrust exemption to common carriers for jointly formulating rate and other agreements (Congress overrode the veto). Truman also vetoed a 1950 bill, this time successfully, that would have allowed certain basing point pricing practices to encourage more uniform prices. In both cases, Truman stated his strong support for the antitrust laws. However, antitrust is not primarily a matter of enacting statutes or of vetoing them. The Sherman Act is sufficiently broad to allow the Antitrust Division of the Justice Department to challenge a wide variety of practices. In short, antitrust is primarily a matter of executive branch enforcement. Therefore, it is in the activities of the Justice Department and the Federal Trade Commission that we must look to ascertain an administration's views on antitrust.

The Truman Antitrust Division was one of the most vigorous since the enactment of the Sherman Law in 1890. Aside from bringing the *Western Electric* case, consider its other activities in 1949 alone. The Truman administration pursued old and new cases vigorously, largely eschewing compromise in the form of negotiated settlements. A New Jersey court upheld the Antitrust Division's contention that General

Electric unlawfully monopolized basic tungsten filament incandescent lamp patents. A suit was filed to break up Great Atlantic and Pacific Tea Company, then the nation's largest food retailer. A major monopoly case was brought against the large tobacco companies, and another was brought to sever the stock and management relationships among DuPont, General Motors, and U.S. Rubber. American Can Company, the nation's largest manufacturer of tin cans, was charged with monopolizing. Other major pending cases, in some of which the government sought drastic restructuring remedies, involved Bausch & Lomb Optical Company, the four largest meat packers, major dairies, the three largest farm machinery manufacturers, seventeen investment banking firms, Eastman Kodak, Timken Roller Bearing Company, United Shoe Machinery Corporation, U.S. Alkali Export Association, and Yellow Cab Company. Meanwhile, the Federal Trade Commission was prosecuting some of the biggest cases it had ever undertaken—its targets included major steel manufacturers and cement producers. Thus, AT&T was in good company when the Antitrust Division brought its action, the major purpose of which was to divorce Western Electric from AT&T and to create three separate corporations from Western.

Although large size played a major role in the Truman administration's antitrust broadside and redefinition of the public interest, there had to be other factors *present* before action was taken. One of the most important factors involved the extension of market power from one market into others. The Supreme Court's favorable disposition in the 1948 Paramount decision to the divorces of motion picture production and distribution from exhibition constituted an open invitation to attack vertical integration when associated with substantial market power.[23] But from the perspective of antitrust law, the case that provided the closest parallels to the AT&T–Western Electric situation involved the Pullman Company. When a District Court decided the *United States* v. *Pullman Company* case in 1943 and it was upheld by the Supreme Court, the decision was viewed as a major breakthrough.[24] Pullman provided sleeping car service to the railroads since 1900, achieving dominance of such service through long-term contracts. It used the leverage of its service business to achieve an almost complete monopoly of sleeping car manufacture for a subsidiary that made the cars, effectively preventing others from any sales in the industry. The District Court held that it was not necessary for the government to show abusive conduct or intent; benevolent monopoly is monopoly nonetheless. The monopolistic effects of Pullman's arrangements with the railroads were sufficient to prove a violation of the Sherman Act, even though all of defendants' customers were satisfied and Pullman's business was run in an efficient, even exemplary, manner. As a result of the violation, the Court ordered the separation of the two components of Pullman's business. Thus, resemblance between the Pullman and Western Electric situations were readily apparent and might result in AT&T divesting Western Electric even if vertical integration was efficient and reasonable.

To some antitrusters, then, the dangers of vertical integration loomed larger than the reality of good performance. To them, the power derived from vertical integration or conglomeration allowed a dominant firm to strike its single product or single-stage competitors with impunity and without regard to issues of profitability. Money lost at the competitive level could be recouped at another level, with another product or at another time. The strength of a large and diversified firm is derived from the variety of tactics it can use and the vast resources it commands. Its aggregate assets are so great that it can take losses that would destroy smaller enterprises. Thus, the vertical integration of a firm dominant at one level erodes the benefits of competition at all levels, and only antitrust action can counter this tendency.

However, the antitrusters' theory did not acknowledge the benefits of vertical integration in reducing transaction costs between successive stages below what they would be in market transactions. Such considerations were irrelevant under the Pullman rationale. Ignored was the strong evidence that most vertical integration that took place between 1899 and 1948 "was apparently motivated by a desire to rationalize flows by assuring efficient facilities for sales and distribution or assuring needed raw materials rather than from any widespread tendency to add the profits of suppliers or distributors to the profits of manufacturing."[25]

THE *WESTERN ELECTRIC* CASE

Why did the Justice Department bring its 1949 antitrust suit against AT&T and the Bell system? Unlike the 1974 case, it was not triggered by the complaints of competitors. There were no complaints about

AT&T's performance. Moreover, AT&T's wartime record was exemplary in aiding the war effort and in developing military communications, and its immediate postwar performance was also outstanding. The number of Bell telephones more than doubled in the first 10 postwar years, from approximately 23.5 million in 1945 to 36.8 million in 1950 and 48 million in 1955. Nor did the suit stem from a failure of long-range planning; indeed, AT&T's planning was a model for other companies. As early as 1945, AT&T corporate planners were working on the plan that would link every subscriber to every other subscriber in the country through direct and unassisted dialing. The area-code system, born that same year, was designed to include independent telephone companies in keeping with AT&T's network manager obligation. Thus, AT&T was already planning a new postwar system that would handle more calls more quickly and more accurately.[26] Bell Labs was developing not only the transistor, which would supplant vacuum tubes, but also early computers, the ring translator (which converted the information necessary for correct billing), new mobile radio systems for use on highways and in urban conditions, and PBXs with vastly greater capacity than prewar varieties—only a handful of the vast number of AT&T's technological efforts and accomplishments.

The Justice Department's suit stemmed from ideas born during the Great Depression. In general, these ideas were based on notions of corporate size, economic power, and their link with the macroeconomic problem of depression. They were also related to a theory of vertical integration that emphasized its potential for abuse but ignored its benefits, and a sneaking suspicion—based on the Walker report— that the Western Electric–AT&T relationship was an insidious one. Added to this was the political view that "bigness is badness." Thus, the Western Electric suit came about not because of pressures or complaints from customers or competitors but because of the dispositions of autonomous officials who had a distinctive conception of the public interest.

Consider one of the earliest postwar demands for an AT&T breakup. In February 1946, Tennessee PUC Commissioner Leon Jourolomon, Jr., a longtime opponent of AT&T, used a labor dispute to renew his call for divorcing Western Electric from AT&T. Pointing to the Pullman decision, he called for the sale of Western Electric's facilities to independent manufacturers, and asked the Justice Department to dissolve "the telephone trust." Echoing the familiar refrain, Jourolomon

claimed that the sole purpose of AT&T's ownership of Western Electric
was to overstate the value of the telephone plant used by the operating
companies. According to this theory, by inflating the rate base, the
operating companies were able to increase rates above what they would
be if equipment was purchased in arms-length dealings with independent manufacturers.[27] The theory, which in its simplicity has an immediate appeal, played an important role in the 1949 case, in that the case
was brought largely because a few state and federal officials believed
in it.

The appealing belief in the venality and duplicity of the Bell system
would not, of course, be shaken by the analyses of investment counsel-
ors whose sole interest was to seek out the best investment opportunities for their clients. A 1947 *Business Week* summary of Wall Street's
perceptions of AT&T's financial future was far less optimistic than
would be expected from Jourolomon's theory. *Business Week* pointed
out that AT&T's payrolls during the early postwar years rose more rapidly than gross revenues, such that direct wage costs were a larger percentage of the company's total revenues than they were prior to the
war. By 1948, the Bell system's return on capital investments had decreased to 4.5 percent, the lowest figure in the company's history up
to that time, excluding the depression years of 1932 and 1933. Even
evidence of Western Electric's prices being substantially below those
of other manufacturers was not taken into consideration. In a January
1949, California PUC proceeding, Western Electric showed that its
prices were 45 percent below those of the independents' average
prices. However, the PUC disregarded this evidence on the grounds
that the purchases of Pacific Telephone & Telegraph were greater than
the combined output of independent manufacturers, and that it was
impossible to determine what the independents' prices would be if they
conducted more business.[28] A comparison of AT&T's earnings in the
postwar era to those of other large companies reveals that its returns
were behind those of the fifty largest manufacturers in the United
States. Further, its rates of return in the postwar era until 1957 lagged
much farther behind those of manufacturing firms than they did in
the 1925–1935 or 1936–1946 periods. Stock prices, too, during the
postwar era lagged well behind the Dow Jones Industrial Average.[29]
Thus, those intent on bringing the 1949 suit clung to their theory and
ignored evidence of this type.

The first mention in the media of a probable antitrust suit against

AT&T was in mid-December 1948, when *Business Week* reported that the Antitrust Division was preparing a "Pullman case" against AT&T to divorce Western Electric from the parent company.[30] The usually well-informed *Telecommunications Reports* stated that the Justice Department was making a preliminary study and had not then made a definite decision about the antitrust suit.[31] The Justice Department emphasized that only the Western Electric–AT&T relationship was under inquiry, and that it did not intend to separate the operating companies from AT&T. Only one month after antitrust attorneys declared that the investigation was preliminary and that the FBI had not begun a full-scale investigation of the AT&T matter, the Justice Department brought its antitrust suit against the company. An extensive FBI investigation had not been conducted prior to the suit because the case was based almost entirely on the Special Telephone Investigation unit's efforts. The complaint, consisting of seventy-three pages, described events in AT&T's history that went back to the turn of the century, and it proposed a divorce of Western Electric from AT&T and a division of Western's plants into three competing, independent equipment manufacturers. In a statement accompanying the complaint, Attorney General Tom Clark stated that the purpose of the suit was to

> restore competition in the manufacture and sale of telephone equipment. . . . This in turn will lower the cost of such equipment and create a situation under which state and federal regulatory commissions will be afforded an opportunity to reduce telephone rates to subscribers. Absence of competition in the manufacture and sale of telephone equipment has tended to defeat effective public regulation of rates charged subscribers for telephone service.[32]

Of course, Clark did not draft the complaint, but he had to approve it as he did the other big cases brought during his tenure as Attorney General. Antitrust was only one area within Clark's ambit, and it is safe to assume that matters such as espionage and internal subversion received more of his personal attention than did antitrust.

The complaint was largely prepared by Holmes Baldridge, the attorney who had previously worked with Commissioner Walker in the FCC's telephone investigation and who had been mainly responsible for the preparation and supervision of the *Walker Report*. After 1938, Baldridge worked for the Antitrust Division, heading its General Litigation Section, during which time he was a major participant in the Pullman case. His work on the *Western Electric* case began in February 1948, approximately eleven months before the filing. During this period, Baldridge claimed that he had not discussed the case with members of the Antitrust Division other than the Assistant Attorney General, who presided over a large number of antitrust cases that were brought or pending. An investigator on the case claimed that several Antitrust Division attorneys had reservations about bringing the case, but Baldridge's wish to do so prevailed. Although the general counsels of the Minnesota and Tennessee commissions suggested bringing the case, it is clear from Baldridge's own admission that no other PUC representatives nor private parties were intent on bringing the suit.[33] Thus, the impetus for the case came principally from Baldridge, who sought to carry out his earlier work with the STI. The following excerpt from a discussion between Representative Kenneth Keating and Baldridge summarizes the latter's critical role in bringing the suit. After agreeing that he disapproved of the FCC's final report on the STI because it moderated the conclusions and tone of the *Walker Report*, Baldridge was asked:

> MR. KEATING: And then having failed to get what you wanted in the Commission report, you left there and went to the Justice Department and you were the one who started this suit?
>
> MR. BALDRIDGE: That is correct.[34]

Although Baldridge's work on the case was formally reviewed, it is safe to assume that Attorney General Clark was easily persuaded by Baldridge because of the attorney's experience with the telephone industry. Further, Baldridge knew well how to argue that the *Western Electric* case was consistent with Clark's general views on antitrust matters.

Investor response to the suit was negative. The stock market reacted by lowering the price of AT&T stock 1.5 points on the day of the announcement. In a press statement on the complaint, AT&T noted that Western Electric had been an integral part of the Bell system for 65 years, that the close and continuous relationship between the component parts of the Bell system directed toward perfecting the telephone network had resulted in the world's best telephone system, and that disruption of the Bell system would have an adverse effect on national defense. The financial editor of the *New York Herald-Tribune* predicted that since AT&T was the favorite investment for widows and orphans, legislators would be besieged with protests over the action. Although most newspapers did not react editorially to the complaint, the West Virginia *Morgantown Post* angrily declared that "[i]f there's one well-run corporation in this country it's the . . . [AT&T]. But for some unknown reason the federal government has been out to 'get' AT&T for 10 years or more."[35]

AT&T had several weapons with which it could fight the antitrust case in addition to its legal one. It could attempt to mobilize public opinion and Congress against the suit, as well as employ its connections with the Department of Defense, which had increasingly called on the Bell system to undertake more technological development of new weapons. On the legal front, AT&T's efforts would be devoted not only to fighting the suit's allegations but also to reducing the drastic relief that the Justice Department called for to terms agreeable to AT&T if the charges in the Sherman Act were proved. It should be noted that the prayer for relief called for not only the divestiture of Western Electric but also for (1) AT&T to acquire all of its equipment by competitive bidding, (2) Western Electric to sell its 50 percent share in Bell Labs to AT&T, and (3) AT&T and Western Electric's successors to license all patents to all applicants on a nondiscriminatory and reasonable royalty basis[36] (even though AT&T had already voluntarily instituted an extremely liberal patent-licensing policy).

AT&T's 24 April 1949 answer to the complaint consisted of a general denial of the Justice Department's allegations, several technical legal arguments, and a recitation of the advantages of an integrated telephone system carefully regulated by government agencies. The heart of the defense to the government's call for drastic relief claimed that the costs of a vertically integrated system were lower than they would be with arms-length market transactions between independent manufacturers and the operating companies. "Since all the operating units of the System have common problems there are many things that can be done better and more economically in their behalf by a central organization. The American Company has undertaken to do these things either directly or through its subsidiaries."[37] These included (1) developing and recommending technical standards and operating methods, and (2) providing the research and development results of Bell Labs and the manufacturing and supply facilities of Western Electric. Some installations for operating companies were custom-made with considerable give and take among AT&T, Western Electric, and the operating companies. AT&T argued further that the public benefits from its efficiency gains and technological progressiveness, a result of the

> close collaboration between the American company, Western and Bell Laboratories at all stages of research, development, design and manufacture and a close working relationship between their personnel. . . . This unification of research and development, manufacturing and operation . . . is an important factor in promoting the efficiency, economy and dependability of the telephone service.[38]

AT&T claimed that its integration led to better service at lower cost than would be the case if the system was fragmented.

Hence, the differences between the Antitrust Division and AT&T were not only over factual and legal issues but also over how the American telephone system could operate most efficiently and progressively. In 1949, on the threshold of AT&T's greatest accomplishments in its history, the Antitrust Division argued vertical integration would retard technological development, raise the cost of telephone service, reduce efficiency, and, inferentially, retard the attainment of the universal service goal.[39]

THE CONSENT DECREE

On 24 January 1956, about 7 years after the antitrust suit was filed, AT&T and the Justice Department entered into a consent decree and final judgment in the *Western Electric* case. Although a long lapse of time between the filing of a complaint and its resolution is not unusual in complex antitrust cases, the *Western Electric* case was unusual in that so few formal proceedings had transpired in the interim. In contrast, during the 1974 *AT&T* case the pretrial proceedings were concluded, an enormous amount of trial testimony was taken, numerous formal documents were filed, and the trial judges rendered important decisions on both procedural and substantive matters. Few of these events occurred in the *Western Electric* case (the major exceptions being answers to interrogations and the filing of documents). And while one view holds that the Republican administration that came to power in 1953 capitulated to AT&T, it does not explain the lack of action between 1949 and 1953 when the administration that brought the case was in power. Moreover, a judicial trial, if in progress, is most often not controlled by political actors but by the court handling it.

The 1949 *Western Electric* case bears one interesting parallel with the settlement of the 1974 *AT&T* case. Major antitrust cases against IBM were disposed of at the same time. But whereas the later *IBM* case was dismissed largely because of the procedural tangles that had developed in the trial, the terms of the 1956 IBM settlement bear important similarities to the *Western Electric* settlement.[40] Rather than more drastic relief, which could have severely set back IBM, the company agreed to grant nonexclusive licenses on existing patents and on patents acquired or applied for within 5 years. In the *IBM* case, as in the *Western Electric* case, the Eisenhower Justice Department realized that the two companies involved were not just large companies but also natural resources, and that as such any drastic restructuring would weaken not only the companies but possibly the nation as well.

The prevailing conception of the public interest had changed dramatically in the 7 years since the *Western Electric* case was brought. When we combine this change with (1) the showing that AT&T made to Justice Department attorneys undermining the foundations of the case and (2) the support given to AT&T by the Department of Defense, we can readily understand the consent decree of January 1956. The most important aspects of the settlement concern what it did *not* do; that is, it did not require AT&T to divest Western Electric and it did not impair the relationship of Bell Labs and the other components of the Bell system. In short, the settlement left the structure of AT&T largely unchanged, except that Western Electric was required to sell the Westrex Corporation, a subsidiary that manufactured sound recording equipment for the movie industry. As a result, it became clear as early as 1950, when AT&T announced that Western Electric would no longer manufacture radio broadcasting transmitting equipment or television station apparatus, that the company would withdraw from businesses unrelated to telecommunications.[41] Although Western Electric's endeavors in these fields were promising in the 1950s, AT&T had learned through experience that any activity in nontelephonic fields would be troublesome and ultimately unsuccessful. Thus, AT&T agreed in the settlement that Western Electric would not manufacture products not required by the operating companies and AT&T, except for certain products like the artificial larynx and those manufactured for the United States government, most importantly the Department of Defense. Further, AT&T and its operating subsidiaries agreed not to engage in unregulated, nonpublic service activities with the exceptions of working for the federal government, doing experimental work, providing circuits, giving advice and assistance to other communications common carriers, and directory advertising. Essentially, AT&T and its component parts agreed to limit themselves to communications activities, defense-related work, and the network manager role.

This portion of the relief did not address the argument initially posed in the *Walker Report*: that it was not possible for state regulators to determine whether the prices Western Electric charged the operating companies were inflated, thereby increasing the rate base. Because the claim could not be substantiated, AT&T willingly agreed that Western Electric would be required to maintain cost-accounting methods "that afford a valid basis . . . for determining the cost to Western of equipment sold to AT&T and Bell operating companies. . . ."[42] As the Justice Department observed in its press release, state regulators would have more control over the prices the operating companies paid for equipment if they were part of the same family than if the operating companies purchased such equipment on the open market. In the latter situation, PUCs could not investigate the prices paid for equipment nor the profits of manufacturers because the independent manufacturers would be free of regulations. In contrast were the numerous post-1937 state PUC cases that required the submission of Western Electric cost information. Evidence showed the consistently lower prices that Western charged the Bell-operating companies compared to independent manufacturers' prices for numerous kinds of telecommunications apparatus. Further, AT&T had been working closely with state regulatory bodies through the National Association of Regulatory and Utility Commissioners (NARUC) to devise common Western Electric disclosure requirements as well as systems of allocating equipment costs between long-distance and local service.[43]

The final element in the 1956 settlement was the availability of AT&T-controlled patents to others. As noted earlier, the company's postwar patent policy was to license at reasonable terms. AT&T did not object in principle to the decree's patent-licensing provisions, even though the provisions were unprecedented in breadth and duration.

Under the terms of the decree, all past and future Bell-system patents were made subject to compulsory license to all applicants not controlled by foreign interests, without regard to their uses. Also, royalties in these cases were to be reasonable, and patents shared and cross-licensed with AT&T's former radio pool partners were to be licensed royalty-free. In both cases, advice and technical information were to be supplied with the patents.

Although there were other terms agreed to in the settlement of the complex antitrust suit, those mentioned in the preceding discussion are among the most important. The critics' main dissatisfaction with the agreement was that AT&T did not give up Western Electric, but to even consider that it would have voluntarily relinquished its manufacturing arm is unreasonable. In addition to guaranteeing a steady supply of the vast equipment required for both CPE and switching and transmission through ownership, AT&T believed the relationship would achieve other vertical economies not possible through arms-length dealings with independent manufacturers. These economies included complete control of specifications and of their coordination throughout the network, rapid flexibility in the adjustment of specifications and standards, closer coordination in planning the network and its interactivity, greater probability of meeting the end-to-end guarantee, and more rapid technological advances through a freer flow of information within the component parts of AT&T. Further, AT&T argued that close coordination of manufacturing, design, and operations engineers would allow modifications to occur before the large-scale introduction of new products, thereby reducing the likelihood of introducing defective or poorly performing products.[44]

AT&T was able to plead its case during a period of unparalleled prosperity and economic growth. Telephone service, too, was growing rapidly. AT&T had gained a valuable ally within the government—the Department of Defense—at the same time that the underpinnings for bringing the *Western Electric* case, rooted in the Great Depression, were crumbling. Few could argue in 1956 that the public interest would be served by the destruction of a company intimately linked with advancing prosperity. One of the few who did was Representative Emanuel Celler. While Celler correctly perceived that the Department of Defense forcefully objected to divestiture of Western Electric, he could not prove that its views influenced the decision to settle or the rejection of divestiture as a resolution. On the contrary, evidence suggests that

Attorney General Herbert Brownell resisted pressure from the Department of Defense to dismiss the case in 1954, and that only gradually did the Justice Department attorneys come to reject divestiture of Western Electric as a remedy. Progress in rate discussions between NARUC and AT&T, the opposition of the independent telephone industry to drastic remedies, the Bell system's overall excellent performance, and the general economic advance contributed to reshaping the view of the public interest and to shaping the final settlement.[45]

Nevertheless, in 1958, Celler began searching for evidence that would support a "sellout." The subsequent hearings would be useful as an attack on the Republican administration as well as a vindication of Celler's view that only a venal conspiracy consisting of AT&T, top administration officials, and the Department of Defense could have led to such a weak settlement. The Celler Committee's report does not reflect a careful evaluation of the testimony and documents collected in the hearings.[46] Only those who believe that it was wrong for AT&T to attempt to preserve itself can agree with the conclusion of the Antitrust Subcommittee's 1959 report that the *Western Electric* case should have been reopened.

The case would, of course, be reopened in the course of the *AT&T* case settlement. In fact, the settlement of the *AT&T* case would depend on the lifting of restrictions imposed on AT&T in the *Western Electric* case. As we will see in Chapter 4, the groundwork for reopening the case was already being quietly laid in regulatory proceedings. AT&T's opponents would have to await the ripening of opposition to Bell system policies by competitors and large customers before a credible challenge could be mounted—a process that unfolded slowly.

PART TWO

RINGING IN THE NEW

CHAPTER 4

THE VOICE OF CHANGE

The 1956 Western Electric consent decree appeared to settle some of AT&T's major problems that had lingered from the prewar era—although clearly not to everyone's satisfaction. AT&T had reason to hope that the complaints voiced by Representative Celler and others about the settlement would gradually subside. And, as we have seen, compulsory patent licensing, AT&T's withdrawal from noncommunications businesses, and the mandatory provision of adequate Western Electric accounting information to state PUCs and the FCC were influential in solving some of the complaints critics made against the settlement. Yet AT&T was satisfied with the settlement's terms because the company's structure (with few minor exceptions) remained largely intact. Since AT&T controlled the dominant portion of each market, it also controlled, subject to PUC regulation, the interfaces between the components. For example, if an independent local telephone company wanted to interface with AT&T's network, the latter determined the basic interconnection rules.

Yet while the *Western Electric* case garnered the headlines in telephone matters during the first postwar decade, other developments were quietly undermining AT&T's structure and its control over equipment and long-distance service. The more visible struggles that began in the late 1960s are best understood as outgrowths of the earlier challenges. The major change in the prevailing conception of the public interest in telecommunications is best understood as a series of small changes followed by the recognition in the 1970s that the old order had been undermined. Fundamentally, the problems and confrontations of the postwar era have their roots in technological changes that began to occur even before World War II but that were accelerated during the war. These changes generated entrepreneurial activity as old and new firms sought to seize opportunities to use telecommunications in novel ways. This, in turn, raised three new issues: (1) what interconnection rights into the Bell network should be granted to the entrepreneurs? (2) how should the newly available portions of the expanded radio spectrum be allocated (spectrum, like land, is a scarce resource)? and (3) how could regulators solve the problem of drawing the boundary between regulated public service activity and unregulated competitive activity? AT&T's reactions to these issues and the responses of federal and state regulators constituted a major controversy in the 1974 suit. During the first postwar decade, the regulatory agencies, most importantly the FCC, attempted to resolve the new problems within a traditional public service context. But even then, there were those who advocated a new framework that would grant a larger role to competition. The early postwar events concerning answering and recording devices in CPE and intercity television transmission in long-distance transmission constitute the first phase of the erosion of the public service conception. The second phase, culminating in a direct attack on interconnection restrictions, examined in Chapter 5, began in 1956.

The Justice Department essentially portrayed AT&T's interconnection policy as nothing more than monopolistic arrogance. With the approval of all state PUCs, the FCC, and the independent telephone companies, it prohibited (with few exceptions) customer-provided interconnection into the AT&T-dominated network manager system. AT&T provided CPE and switching and transmission gear, usually of its own manufacture, as well as long-distance transmission. Although its operating companies were joined by many independent local companies, the interfaces between local loops and the national network were controlled or supervised by AT&T. Such controls were exercised over all communications products, including voice, video, data, facsimile, and so forth. AT&T's interconnection policy was embodied in the company's related tariffs and had deep historic roots. For instance, one typical Bell tariff provision stated, "Equipment, apparatus and lines furnished by the Telephone Company shall be carefully used and no equipment, apparatus or lines not furnished by the Telephone Company shall be attached to or used in connection therewith. . . ." Another common tariff stated that "[n]o equipment, apparatus, circuit or device not furnished by the Telephone Company shall be attached to or connected with the facilities furnished by the Telephone Company, whether physically by induction or otherwise, except as provided in this tariff."[1] As these examples make clear, telephone company customers were precluded not only from attaching their own CPE to Bell lines but they also could not connect a long-distance circuit or transmitting device (such as those used in radio and television transmission) to the lines without Bell's authorization. The tariff, it should be noted, equally applied to instruments that were substituted for the Bell devices as well as those that were *added on* to the Bell equipment (such as answering machines).

As the FCC, courts, and state authorities began making major inroads on the restrictive tariffs during the postwar years, the Bell system usually resisted. Similarly, subject to limitations worked out in earlier eras, the Bell companies frequently sought to enlarge the amount of radio spectrum appropriated for telephonic purposes. The novel rate offerings devised by AT&T in the postwar era were coordinated with these activities. Much of the Justice Department's 1974 suit against AT&T was directed at these activities. Unraveling the development of these issues in the immediate postwar era is, in many ways, the key to understanding much that occurred later on.

THE INTERCONNECTION ISSUE:
THE ARGUMENTS OF AT&T'S CRITICS

At a superficial level, highly restrictive interconnection tariffs can be viewed as a method of extending monopoly from one of the four telephone segments to the others. According to this view, although interface compatibility among the several facets of telephony is a necessity, it is not technologically nor economically necessary that a single firm exercise market dominance of all facets. For example, it does not follow that even if there is a sound reason for monopoly in local-loop transmission (something that had been generally conceded), there should also be near monopoly in long-distance transmission, CPE, or

switching and transmission gear manufacture. Consider also that an automobile is a complex product that requires interface compatibility,
yet automobile manufacturers do not control the rubber tire industry.
Rather, tire manufacturers must carefully consider an automobile's
weight, acceleration capabilities, and other characteristics. Thus, with
this view, AT&T's critics concluded that its interconnection policy was
a way to enlarge market dominance from one sector to others. They
pointed to AT&T's market shares to illustrate their argument. However,
although it is possible to use a natural monopoly argument to justify
local monopolies in local-loop transmission, certainly the manufacture
of CPE and switching and transmission equipment were not natural
monopolies. Yet, in 1973 for example, AT&T's share of telephone set
manufacture was 75 percent and its share of central office transmission
equipment manufacture was 86 percent.[2] Moreover, one should appreciate that the market for both CPE and switching and transmission gear
has grown rapidly during most of the twentieth century, especially after
World War II.

Accordingly, economic theory suggests that new firms should have
taken advantage of the good growth and profitability opportunities in
the industry.[3] A strong inference exists that conditions of entry should
have been relatively easy. Many firms made equipment similar to (and
in many ways more complex than) handsets, PBXs (private branch exchanges), and other CPE, and other firms produced heavy electrical
equipment as complex as that used in switching and transmission. Euro-
pean and American suppliers to independent telephone companies produced equipment at both levels that was competitive with Bell's, and
since the available equipment in any industry can embody a wide variety
of design and quality characteristics, the potential for product differentiation was also high. In short, if other reasons did not exist to preclude entry, one would have predicted considerable competition at
both the CPE and network-switching and transmission-gear levels. That
such competition did not occur AT&T's critics attributed to a combination of willful Bell behavior and regulatory permissiveness.

Critics of the Bell system made much the same kind of argument
in the case of long-distance transmission as they did with respect to
equipment manufacture. The economic argument in favor of natural
monopoly in long-distance transmission was severely weakened as microwave relay supplanted wire as the principal means of carrying long-
distance messages after World War II. In the late 1960s, microwave

transmission costs approached a minimum at approximately 1,200 circuits, yet there were approximately 60,000 circuits connecting New
York and Philadelphia alone.[4] Nevertheless, not until considerable time
after the natural monopoly justification in long-distance transmission
disappeared did competition actually appear. According to this view,
in long-distance transmission as in equipment manufacture, AT&T's
market dominance persisted notwithstanding the absence of any economic justification. Again, the reasons lay in governmental policies and
in AT&T's willfulness, as economists Walter Adams and James W. Brock
have pointed out:

> Even if one were to concede Bell's prowess as the purveyor of local
> telephone service, its ability to determine who shall be allowed to
> compete in long distance transmission or who shall be able to com-
> pete in the sale of terminal equipment was not conducive to rules of
> the game which would award victory to the competitor endowed
> with "superior skill, foresight and industry." Bell's ability . . . to re-
> fuse interconnection with its local network . . . enabled it to attain
> and retain system dominance over the entire vertical chain of the
> communications industry quite irrespective of efficiency, progres-
> siveness or other competitive virtues.[5]

Clearly, the argument's straightforward and clear-cut analysis has an
immediate appeal, but further examination of the reasons behind
AT&T's interconnection policy undermines not only the argument itself but an important part of the Justice Department's case as well. That
is, by examining the history of interconnection policy—often at the
insistence of regulatory agencies and against the objections of telephone companies—the reasons for its widespread adoption become
apparent. Most important is that the marginal costs of organizing interconnection within a single firm are lower than if market transactions
among different firms prevail,[6] which is why telephone companies and
regulators preferred meticulous interconnection restrictions.

THE ORIGINS OF INTERCONNECTION POLICY

The telephone industry has always had inventors who develop what are
called foreign attachments, instruments that supplement or substitute
for the components supplied by the operating companies. Bell policy

generally had been antipathetic to these devices for a variety of reasons. In 1884, in letters directed to licensees about various attachments intended to amplify the sound of Bell instruments, Vail declared, "Their merits have been carefully considered and the various forms in use thoroughly tested . . . and we find that such attachments are injurious to the transmitters. We must therefore decline to allow their use in connection with our instruments."[7] AT&T had a clear interest in preventing the interconnection of any device into its system that might impair effectiveness, quality, or durability. The general rule was enforced even though some Bell licensees were reluctant to interfere with their subscribers' use of foreign attachments after they had been purchased.[8]

As telephone use grew in the early 1890s and the expiration of the Bell patents neared, the number of foreign attachments that could be made easily and attached to the basic instruments proliferated.[9] Some of these devices were found to impair the intelligibility of communication or the quality of the signal, such as an "ear pad for Telephone Receivers."[10] Still other devices during the late nineteenth and early twentieth centuries preyed on public fears, implying that the telephone mouthpiece was a health hazard! For example, a flyer for the Improved Antiseptic Nickel Mouthpiece Attachment claimed that "[t]he scrapings from many telephone mouthpieces were subjected to the microscope by Prof. Kauffman of the Board of Health and great numbers of bacteria germs were found . . . which shows that great danger actually exists in inhaling these germs in the mouth and nostrils."[11] Still another advertisement for a mouthpiece warned that telephones "may be infected with the most dreadful contagious diseases" because people touched the mouthpiece with sore lips.[12] Such flagrant claims, needless to say, angered Bell officials.[13] Other attachments sold to consumers did not work, and in almost all cases, there was some degree of transmission loss that resulted from interconnecting the device into the telephone network.[14]

Because of the interactive nature of the telephone network, telephone companies and regulators responsible for the overall quality of the network could not adopt a casual attitude toward such devices. Those adversely affected by foreign attachments that malfunctioned or reduced the quality of conversation included not only those using them but parties to conversations and subscribers using Bell equipment as well. Consider, for example, citizens band (CB) radios of the early

1970s, which interfered with nearby radio, television, and telephone reception. Another example is the problem faced by AT&T and other telephone companies because of the Hush-A-Phone. In 1922, AT&T's chief engineer tested this device and declared that it "introduces a very large transmission loss and materially distorts the clearness of the transmission. It is clumsy and hinders the placing of the receiver on the hook. The use of this device would be a positive detriment to good service."[15] The proliferation of foreign attachments and the difficulty of locating and testing them before their introduction into the network caused such engineering and technical problems as hazardous voltages, line imbalance, attenuation, other forms of quality deterioration, and substantial economic problems. Bell licensees and the telephone companies incurred high transaction and information costs resulting from (1) discovering such attachments, preferably before harm might occur; (2) testing the devices; (3) negotiating with their manufacturers and sellers; (4) proposing modifications and policing the manufacturers' adherence to the new standards; (5) retesting the devices; (6) installing them or supervising their installation; (7) instructing subscribers in the correct use and maintenance of devices so that the network would not be impaired; and (8) repairing them. Inevitably, too, a liberal interconnection policy would have imposed still other costs resulting from disputes. For example, if electric shock led to an injury, the subscriber, the telephone company, and the seller or manufacturer of the attachment would each abjure responsibility and blame the others for the mishap. In place of this invitation to high transaction costs, telephone companies and regulators chose a policy of low transaction costs.[16] Taking responsibility for the entire network—the end-to-end concept—made sound economic sense not only for the telephone company but for the subscribers as well, since it assured lower telephone company costs. For these same reasons, independent companies that were not integrated backward like AT&T usually imposed severe interconnection restrictions, although they were sometimes not as severe as the Bell tariffs.[17]

About 1896, contracts between Bell licensees and their subscribers began to include clauses prohibiting the attachment of customer-provided CPE to telephone lines. By 1899, strict interconnection tariffs were the general policy of telephone companies and were upheld by the state courts when challenged by subscribers. Further, as the concept of end-to-end responsibility became generally accepted, the restrictive tariff provisions were treated as an integral part of that responsibility, and the ICC, PUCs, and the FCC uniformly upheld these provisions as reasonable restrictions.[18] Indeed, they often compelled telephone companies to adopt the provisions. However, the tariffs did not bar all interconnection; rather, customer interconnection was prohibited unless a good reason to override the prohibition could be provided. Hence, information and transaction costs were largely shifted to the customer seeking the exception and were not imposed on other subscribers. Those granted exceptions tended to be reliable customers who could be trusted not to impair the network. For example, the United States Army had well-trained telephone personnel and for security reasons maintained control over CPE. Mining and railroad companies also were permitted to provide and maintain certain CPE because of the hazards telephone company employees would face in maintaining the equipment.[19]

PUCs AND INTERCONNECTION

When the PUC movement began, it was faced with the question of how to deal with CPE interconnection. Since most telephone calls were local or intrastate, PUCs were critical in establishing policy. It wasn't until the late 1930s that the Supreme Court widened the scope of the interstate commerce concept so that federal regulatory agencies could assert jurisdiction over activities previously considered intrastate.[20] And not until the postwar era did many federal regulatory agencies, including the FCC, take advantage of the opportunities that the Supreme Court opened. Thus, prior to the postwar period, we must look at the state level to understand interconnection policy. The remarkable consistency of the state agencies, often upholding interconnection restrictions against powerful interests, compels us to conclude that they had sound reasons for upholding the interconnection restrictions.

The starting point in understanding the PUCs' responses to the interconnection issues they examined is their overriding concern with service quality, which impelled them to do such things as order a reduction in the number of subscribers on a party line, require improved service in other ways, and require the upgrade or repair of equipment. The commissions uniformly responded to subscriber complaints about those telephone companies that required subscribers to furnish their own handsets by ordering these companies to own and maintain such equipment. They prohibited subscribers from owning and maintaining telephone equipment because it would impair a telephone company's ability "to render adequate and reasonable service." The telephone companies were charged with the sole responsibility for the maintenance of equipment "so intimately associated with the quality of service."[21] For these same reasons, the commissions ordered the discontinuance of rates, which provided subscribers with an incentive to install or repair CPE.[22]

In a 1915 state regulatory agency case involving five large downtown Chicago hotels, a telephone company objected to customer-supplied CPEs.[23] Each hotel had installed lobby telephone booths and conduits running to a switchboard owned by the telephone company but operated by hotel employees. Thus, a person wishing to make a telephone call gave the number to and paid the switchboard clerk, then returned to the booth to conduct the conversation as the clerk made the connection. The Illinois Public Utilities Commission sustained the telephone company's objections, holding that such divided responsibility for telephone service, in which one of the parties is unregulated, can lead to impaired service quality. In contrast, when telephone service is under the exclusive control of a firm regulated by the commission, the agency can fulfill its mandate to guarantee the character and quality of service.

It should be noted that in this and subsequent cases, the PUCs did not often find actual impairment of telephone service; rather, they were concerned with the principle the cases would establish and its effect on their ability to control the quality of service. As a 1920 New Jersey Board of Public Utility Commissioners decision observed:

> It is probably true that in some instances subscribers could obtain equipment of a type and quality which would operate satisfactorily in connection with the telephone company's system, but if an attempt were made to allow exceptions . . . it would be difficult, if not impossible, to draw a distinction between units of equipment owned by the subscribers which might be serviceable in connection with its system and those which could not satisfactorily be used.[24]

In 1934, the California Railroad Commission noted that low quality in senders' customer-supplied equipment necessarily had an adverse effect on the quality of transmission to other persons whose equipment was supplied by the telephone company. Thus, the California commission rejected the request of the City of Los Angeles to interconnect its internal communications system into the telephone company's system.[25] Other state commissions found that inexpert customer installation of equipment could subject subscribers to hazards, break connections, fail to ring numbers, and generally impair the delicate engineering system of the network. Further, the telephone company's costs of inspecting, testing, maintaining, and correcting customer-provided CPE would need to be passed on to subscribers.[26]

Until World War II, then, interconnection was governed by a uniform policy adopted for straightforward reasons. Over time, precedent reinforced the rule so that some PUC cases did little more than cite some of the earlier ones.[27] The regulatory matters invariably involved a plaintiff who sought to substitute equipment for that supplied by the telephone companies. That the telephone companies could not or were unwilling to supply customer needs was never an issue. Finally, the FCC did not involve itself in CPE matters because the cases did not involve disputes of widespread interstate applicability. In essence, the policy was efficient and promoted ease of administration.

When we place the interconnection problem in this context, we can better understand the reasons behind PUC decisions that would otherwise be unclear. Consider, for example, telephone directories. In the late 1920s, AT&T saw the value of controlling telephone directories and the classified advertising revenues that could be obtained from them.[28] As this use of residential and classified directories became a valuable adjunct to telephone service, PUCs began to assert jurisdiction over their form and content. For example, in a 1961 case, the California commission denied Pacific Telephone & Telegraph the right to divide a single directory into three; in contrast, New England Telephone & Telegraph was permitted to substitute four directories for one in a metropolitan area when one was too bulky.[29] In both cases, the PUCs' main concern was customer convenience. But as the use of classified directories grew, commissions began to appreciate that the substantial revenues derived from selling advertising in the yellow pages could be used to help maintain low rates for local residential service.[30] Keeping these considerations in mind, we can better understand the New York PSC ruling upholding the tariff restriction of a small independent telephone company, which forbade auxiliary covers or holders to be placed over its directory covers. The auxiliary cover in question was designed by a merchandising company so to sell advertisin g space. The PSC held that the auxiliary cover was a disservice to subscribers in that it obscured the emergency telephone numbers displayed on the telephone company's cover. Further, the PSC found that the auxiliary directory company had far less incentive than the telephone company to keep information on the cover up-to-date, and it could not compel the merchandising company to do so because it was not a public service company. Also, the auxiliary cover would reduce telephone company revenues, "thereby casting an additional burden upon the subscribers."[31]

The arguments in favor of unified telephone company control over all interconnection were, of course, premised on the telephone company's ability to fulfill its reasonable service demands. A telephone company could not refuse interconnection on the ground that it had insufficient capacity or that it felt expansion of its facilities unnecessary because novel uses of the network would fail commercially. In short, a telephone company had to meet demand, including novel uses of the telephone network. For example, in 1931, the PSC directed the New York Telephone Company to lease private lines to a company with the then novel idea of piping music over telephone lines to hotels, restaurants, and other customers. The PSC held that New York Telephone's assessment of Wired Music's commercial opportunities could not be used to deny the company the facilities it sought. A public service company is required to furnish reasonable service to all who apply for it.[32]

The breakdown of the general rule—that only public service companies or certain specific designees should have the right to interconnect into the telephone network—began during the post–World War II era. The great increase in demand on telephone companies was not only for traditional services but for novel ones as well. Nevertheless, the FCC and the PUCs attempted to operate, at first, within the context of the rules examined here, which worked well for quite some time.

AN OVERVIEW OF POSTWAR INTERCONNECTION

To a considerable extent, the growth in demand for telephone services during the postwar era was a result of an overall increase in business and prosperity. From 1946 to 1970, per capita GNP in constant dollars more than doubled, the number of telephones almost quadrupled, from approximately 31.6 million to 120.2 million, and the percentage of households with telephone service increased from 51.4 to 90.5 percent. Also, the Bell system was able to handle more than three and one-half times the number of daily local calls and even a greater multiple of daily toll calls in 1970 than in 1946.[33] Bell's postwar program to fulfill consumer demand began almost immediately after the cessation of hostilities. At the end of 1946, 80 percent of the prewar applications for service that were on hold because of the war had been filled; 70 percent of these had been filled as early as 1946, notwithstanding material and personnel shortages.[34]

This expansion had been accomplished, with its extraordinary capital requirements, during a period when AT&T was holding down prices more than most businesses in the economy. For example, between 1960 and 1973, the Consumer Price Index (CPI) increased 122 percent, whereas the rates for basic residential telephone service increased only 14 percent; similarly, from 1973 to 1978, the CPI increased 46.8 percent and residential telephone rates 14.1 percent. Between 1950 and 1978, aggregate long-distance rates increased only 8.6 percent, whereas the CPI increased 171 percent. Since Bell system compensation per employee increased 560 percent between 1950 and 1978, its exemplary rate record was achieved substantially through productivity gains.[35] AT&T was able to do so in large part because of rapid technological progress during and shortly after World War II that radically altered the telecommunications industry. At the CPE level, the development of telephone answering machines and recording devices, coupled with wartime advances in electronics, triggered the invention of new products that could be used in the telephone network. Further, while voice was by far the most important communication product of the network in the prewar era, the dramatic growth of the television and computer industries generated much demand for the carriage of video and other nonvoice data in the postwar era. In turn, these developments encouraged firms to design and market CPEs related to these products (for example, modems). The computer, too, led many businesses to realize the advantages of centralized data storage and transmission, which allowed them to keep close watch on their individual units and to react quickly and centrally to local developments.

The capacity to transmit information grew by vast leaps because of coaxial cable, microwave transmission, the transistor, electronic switching, and, later, satellites. AT&T contributed to or was responsible for many of these developments, as were other firms and the United States government. As early as 1935, when AT&T's coaxial cable development was in its experimental stage, Bell Labs' president, Frank Jewett, predicted that the new technology would greatly increase the number of simultaneous telephone conversations over a single circuit to 200 or more.[36] But the progress in transmission systems has been far more dramatic than Jewett anticipated. The LL coaxial cable, for example, could carry 600 two-way channels per pair of coaxial tubes in 1946, and in 1980, the L5E coaxial cable could carry 13,200 channels per pair of coaxial tubes. Microwave transmission underwent similar development; the capacity of a single microwave radio route increased from approximately 2,400 two-way channels in 1950 to more than 35,000 in 1980.[37] The increased capacity of distribution channels led to lower costs per channel mile at full load. For example, between 1950 and 1976, the cost per channel mile for microwave systems was reduced almost 80 percent. Similarly, from the 1950s until 1980, the cost per channel mile of coaxial systems was reduced nearly 80 percent.[38] Increased capacity, lower costs, increased demand stemming from such new technologies as television and computers, and the general economic boom together revolutionized telecommunications within a short period of time. No one firm—not even one as large as AT&T—could possibly seize all of the opportunities as rapidly as they could be realized. At the same time, prospective lucrative markets attracted entrepreneurs who sought to plug into the network through new CPE or who had modest private systems that could become far more valuable by interconnecting into the public-switched network.

The typical interconnection questions at this time were not whether local hotels might control telephone booths in their lobbies but, for example, the uses of devices like recording machines manufactured with a national market in mind. Thus, the implications of the postwar CPE industry placed the FCC rather than the state commissions at center stage, and because of the greatly increased importance of telecommunications to both providers and users, it raised incentives to intervene in regulatory proceedings. The FCC had, of course, the prewar precedent of state regulatory proceedings on which to rely, but it could not do so entirely because the implications of the 1934 Communications Act's mandate had become more complex. Whereas in the prewar era, regulators primarily defined the public interest in terms of service reliability, safety, quality, and efficiency, the communications explosion following the war led the FCC to weigh heavily the future needs of users. The major provisions of the 1934 Communications Act, like those in state statutes and the Mann-Elkins Act, were general and granted broad discretion to the FCC. Among its major provisions, Section 1 charged the FCC with promoting "a rapid, efficient, nationwide and worldwide wire and radio communication service with adeqrate facilities at reasonable charges." Section 201(b) required all common carrier "charges, practices, classifications and regulations . . . to be just and reasonable." Section 201(a) ordered common carriers "to furnish such communication service upon reasonable request therefor." While the language is general, it is not devoid of content. The concept of adequate facilities, for example, implies that user needs must be satisfied insofar as technologically and economically feasible. When existing carriers are unable or unwilling to satisfy such needs—such as during a time of rapid technological development—the regulator is constrained to allow other firms to meet the unfulfilled needs. Again, a carrier's obligation under Section 201(b) to make its practices "just and reasonable" implies that when a user or other intervener can show that a carrier's justifications for a tariff restriction are flawed or may lead to policies that will result in a less effective communications system, the tariff provision must be suspended. In order to prevail, the business groups seeking change in telecommunications policy had first to change the FCC's basic views of the public interest within this framework.

AT&T'S RESPONSE TO INTERCONNECTION

AT&T was not hostile to every attempt at interconnection. Its postwar interconnection policy must be placed within the contexts of politics and its postwar plans. It is clear that the company was in a difficult political position amidst anti-big business zealots. In 1972, for example, FCC Commissioner Nicholas Johnson proposed, at a "people's state of the union" meeting, that AT&T should be broken up or nationalized.[39]

AT&T's clashes with other firms were inevitable because of its postwar strategy to serve every market possible. In February 1945, AT&T foresaw a boom in frequency modulation (FM) and television broadcasting and claimed that it could meet the requirements of these new industries. H. S. Osborne, AT&T's chief engineer, claimed that it was technologically able to do so and that the company's existing long-distance program "provides a fund of experience which should be useful in the design, construction, maintenance and operation of networks for either FM or television transmission."[40] Large-scale manufacturing facilities were readied for this purpose. The cost of AT&T's ambitious program for FM and TV transmission as well as its other postwar plans were borne by raising vast sums of capital and by making efficiency gains, rather than relying on rate increases that the PUCs were reluctant to grant.[41] The competition for funds in financial markets, in turn, acted as a surrogate for competition to act efficiently. As noted earlier, large-scale investors (that is, purchasers of bonds and debentures) usually are not tied to investing in any particular industry or group; rather, their main concerns are yield, risk, and other financial variables. In this respect, AT&T had to compete against industrial corporations, government institutions, and so on, which provided it with strong incentives to become more efficient, and thus profitable, and to enlarge the use of telephone service (which included the universal service goal).

As a result of these pressures, the Bell system instituted a greatly enlarged sales effort. By the early 1950s, the AT&T sales effort included demonstrations to businesses of long-distance and teletypewriter service in accounting, engineering, purchasing, sales, and administration. Promotion of new long-distance uses was only a part of the new AT&T sales effort designed to tap the huge potential market in new telephone usage. The Bell system had designed more than 400 offerings, including mobile and aviation services, colored telephones, extension telephones, automatic answering and recording services, key systems, PBXs, telephones with illuminated dials, private line service, and so forth. By 1955, AT&T added to these anticipated markets special circuits for computer-processed data, closed-circuit television, and even factory automation.[42] The company's marketing efforts also extended to credit sales, being one of the first in the postwar period to anticipate the credit card explosion. In the early 1950s, AT&T was issuing credit cards, pointing out to business users that the cards were not only a convenience, especially to sales forces, but enabled businesses to monitor and record calls more efficiently. Even telephone booths were redesigned to stimulate increased use. However, not every new product and service was initially a success. In the 1945 to 1949 period, AT&T averaged only slightly more than a 5 percent return on capital. The company was able to cling to its traditional dividend only by paying out more than it earned. In the first half of the 1950s, the return on capital rose to 6.3 percent, and by 1958, to 7 percent. In addition to efficiency gains, the rising return on capital was also attributable to the successful sales of the new services, products, and attachments (which the company termed "vertical growth"). These contributed about 48 percent of the company's increased income in 1968 and were heading upward as a percentage of total growth.[43]

It is within the context of AT&T's sales strategy, and the enormous importance attached to nontraditional services—those besides local calls made by the traditional black telephone—that the company's interconnection policy must be considered. Clearly, interconnection was not a marginal component of the Bell system's postwar plans—it was a critical one. Its views, however, should be assessed as more than a means of profit maximization. One important consideration is a concept that some AT&T officials called "appliqueing"; that is, that the newest equipment must be designed so as to be compatible with all other new and old equipment in the network.[44] Failure to attain system-wide compatibility, according to the Bell system, could cause numerous problems, including hazardous voltages or currents, leakage of currents, crosstalk, noise, erroneous data transmission, excessive signal power or mixing, improper signaling, audible clicks, transmission interruptions, disconnections, inefficient use of central office and switching equipment, and other impairments to quality.[45] While potential harm to the network influenced AT&T's hostile attitude toward interconnection by others, critics counterargued by claiming that it is possible to impose strict standards on interconnections that prevent such problems from occurring. In fact, the critics' solution was the one eventually chosen. However, even if such compatibility is possible, this does not make it the most desirable solution. At the least, there remains the problem of divided responsibility, which was raised in some of the state proceedings referred to earlier. That is, if a problem exists in the net-work, it is easier and less costly for a regulatory agency to deal with the one telephone company responsible and to compel that company to solve the problem. In the case of divided responsibility, on the other hand, the regulatory agency is faced with the added expenditure of having to determine which company is responsible for the problem, as well as disputes among the companies unwilling to assume blame and the fact that it is far more difficult to hold responsible a large number of firms, some of which may be less reliable than others or located in distant areas such as Taiwan, Korea, or Thailand. Further, the added costs of divided responsibility are passed on to the telephone companies and subscribers. In general, the interconnecting firm is the principal beneficiary of relatively free interconnection.[46]

In addition, AT&T argued that relatively free interconnection would retard putting new technologies and devices on-line. Since the tele-phone network is interactive, it argued, the reciprocal effects of any new technology or device on all other parts of the network must be carefully considered before it can be put into operation. Since the pre-divestiture Bell system was a closely coordinated structure in which information was freely exchanged (including information on new tech-nologies and projects and trade secrets), the interactive problem could be considered on an ongoing basis. Indeed, the unified responsibility of network management imposed by regulators is an incentive to ex-change such information. In contrast, independent firms dealing at arms-length have a disincentive to share information. Thus, the likeli-hood of incompatibility and of potential problems in a complex interac-tive system is greater if responsibility is divided and there is relatively free interconnection. Further, even if an interconnecting device is orig-inally approved in a certification program, it may later prove incompati-ble with newer developments or it may lower overall network quality.[47]

Looking at interconnection in a dynamic rather than a static manner, AT&T also argued that when modifications are required due to incom-patibility among the components controlled by different firms, higher transaction costs result in the need to determine which firm will make the modification. And, the more costly the modification, the more re-luctant the firms are to undertake it. Although negotiation among the firms can lead to a solution, a command structure, such as that which prevailed at AT&T, is more efficient in arriving at a solution. For in-stance, with the introduction of electronic switching it was found that certain terminal equipment was incompatible, yet AT&T's command structure was able to impose a reasonable solution more quickly and cheaply than if other firms had been involved.[48]

Finally, AT&T argued that a registration program categorizing CPE as "harmless" or "harmful" would be misleading, in that harm cannot be measured by examining the characteristics of individual devices in isolation from the remainder of the network. The cumulative effect of permitting the proliferation of devices into the system, each of which may or may not be found to be individually harmless, could be injurious to the performance of the entire network. AT&T had built the highest quality telephone system in the world, and the introduction of large numbers of new devices, each harmless, might lower the quality of the network without any savings to most subscribers.[49]

Although AT&T's arguments were not immediately rejected by the FCC and state PUCs, the FCC gradually rejected them, sometimes prodded by the courts, and the state PUCs generally followed suit.

POSTWAR INTERCONNECTION—THE FIRST PHASE

As early as 1946, the first postwar challenge to AT&T's general noninterconnection policy was mounted by the U-Dryvit Auto Rental Company of Cambridge, Massachusetts. Although New England Telephone & Telegraph provided seven channels to the automobile rental company for use between its offices and radio-telephone facilities, the telephone company would not permit U-Dryvit to connect them into the public-switched network. New England Telephone & Telegraph felt that the interconnections in this case would cause direct competition between itself and the auto-renting company.[50] While U-Dryvit's activities were largely intrastate, its rejected claim that the telephone company's tariff violated the 1934 Communications Act was indicative of what was to follow.

The first important federal postwar interconnection case involved recording devices designed to attach to telephone handsets.[51] The instruments had been in use since 1916, but they were greatly improved during the war and demand increased; those using the device included attorneys, auditors, doctors, engineers, banks, insurance companies, hospitals, manufacturers, and transport companies. Although the Bell system had made two installations of the devices in 1936 for newspapers, neither it nor the independent telephone companies expressed any postwar interest in their manufacture. The telephone companies did not object to the devices but expressed concern over such issues as assuring the confidentiality of telephone conversations and preventing harm to the network through installation and maintenance safeguards. In 1945, at the insistence of the United States Navy and recording machine manufacturers, the FCC instituted a general inquiry into the matter. It focused not on whether recording devices should be an exception to general interconnection tariff restrictions but on the conditions that would have to be met for approval of the exception.[52] The participating manufacturers at the hearing carefully showed that their products would not impair the network and that they were willing to accept the telephone companies' conditions. They also showed that the products, which at that time could be activated only by manually picking up the phone, posed no safety or quality threat to telephone service and could fill many business uses. They further agreed that the telephone companies should be responsible for connecting and maintaining the devices. In view of the evidence on safety, reliability, and quality, neither AT&T nor other telephone companies opposed the use of the devices but treated them as interconnection exceptions. And although some firms sought to bar AT&T from manufacturing the recording machines or monopolizing the manufacture of devices connecting them with the network, the proceedings were relatively free of acrimony.[53] Thus, the FCC treated this matter as an exception to the general tariff prohibition, and in November 1947, it issued a final order authorizing the use of telephone recorders as of January 1948. The telephone company was ordered to provide, install, and maintain the equipment necessary to connect the recorders to telephone lines. Other requirements included (1) that the recorders be physically detachable from telephone lines or switchable to on/off positions at the will of the user, and (2) that they sound a tone warning when in operation.[54] Most important about this case, however, is the attention the FCC gave to market demand. The inference, even then, was that the FCC had to intervene if AT&T was otherwise unwilling to attend to market demand and sought to block others from doing so.

The next important interconnection case involving CPE was contro-

versial and led to a split FCC decision. In the 1954 *Jordaphone* case, the
FCC refused to authorize the interconnection of automatic telephone-
answering devices.[55] Instead, after concluding (against AT&T's objection) that it had jurisdiction over these devices and finding the AT&T
tariff prohibitions unreasonable as applied to them, the FCC deferred
the matter to the state and local commissions. This meant that each
state PUC would need to authorize and license particular answering
devices before they could lawfully be used in that state. The question
of why the FCC and AT&T treated answering machines differently than
recording machines can be answered by considering the technological
differences between the two devices. The former had to be activated
manually; the latter was automated and far more complex and unreli-
able at the time. The most popular answering machine in the early
1950s was the Telemagnet, a 27-pound instrument that automatically
lifted the receiver on the second ring of a telephone call, played (on a
phonograph record) an outgoing message of instructions to the caller,
and recorded (on a primitive tape recorder) the incoming message.[56]
As other telephone-answering devices were produced, the FCC, in June
1950, broadened the inquiry from one involving the Telemagnet and
another device to one including all answering devices.[57] By generalizing
the matter, the FCC would have to consider with caution the prospects
of both high-quality machines that would not impair the network and
low-quality machines that could. Tests conducted during the hearings
revealed a number of difficulties with some of the telephone-answering
devices. For example, there were problems like "false starts" from
electrical impulses other than telephone rings; handset lifting mechanisms that did not operate properly, resulting in an off-hook condition
that tied up the telephones and party lines to which they were attached;
transmission of a permanent signal to the telephone company's central
office; unintelligible recorded messages; and interference. Some machines could operate with only a few types of telephones, not including
some of the more recent types being installed by the Bell system. Several manufacturers implicitly conceded the serious problems of the
new answering machines, arguing that improved construction had
solved some of them.[58] Yet even those machines that worked with Bell
equipment often did not work well or at all with the telephones
supplied by the independent companies.[59]

The FCC Common Carrier Bureau began in this proceeding to play a
role it would increasingly occupy in the postwar era—a role character-

ized by hostility toward and skepticism of the Bell system's position. Far from being persuaded by AT&T, the FCC staff often overemphasized its independence. In the *Jordaphone* case, the FCC staff readily conceded that several of the automatic telephone-answering devices could have an adverse effect on telephone service and telephone company equipment. Nevertheless, it recommended that interconnection be permitted when the devices were connected to telephone lines by means of connectors or isolation units, which would assure protection to the services and to the facilities of the telephone companies. But the staff agreed that devices manipulating the handset, such as the Telemagnet, should not be permitted. The staff accused the Bell system of retarding the development and use of automatic answering devices, which had been in use in Switzerland. Finally, and most portentously, the staff disagreed with the Bell system's view that such attachments are an integral part of telephone service and that they must, therefore, be supplied by telephone companies or their designees.[60]

In view of the conflicts and competing considerations—especially those concerning the varying quality of the devices—hearing examiner Basil B. Cooper, presiding over the *Jordaphone* case, recommended that the FCC reject a general tariff modification that would allow interconnection of these devices. He noted that state and local authorities were in the best position to determine whether particular devices were likely to cause problems in conjunction with the telephones used locally. None of the devices, he observed, functioned with satisfactory technical efficiency in conjunction with all kinds of telephones. At the time, three states had already rejected complaints against the interconnection prohibition, while one, Wisconsin, required the AT&T affiliate to permit subscribers to use the Electronic Secretary.[61] Thus, when the FCC decided the matter in May 1954, it had at its disposal the experience of several state commission decisions as well as the examiner's views. In the important California case involving the Telemagnet, the PUC found that the device impaired telephone service and was susceptible to interference. Further, the California commission found that the Telemagnet was impracticable with most kinds of telephones.[62] In one of the most carefully prepared decisions, the Louisiana PSC found serious problems with the Telemagnet but felt that automatic answering machines eventually would be perfected and that a substantial market would develop. Nevertheless, the Louisiana PSC rejected the Telemagnet application, holding that the commission would best be able to

protect consumers if telephone companies, over which it asserted jurisdiction, selected, maintained, and operated such equipment.[63]

Confronted with a new, experimental technology and torn by conflicting approaches, the FCC upheld the interconnection tariff restriction, except where state and local authorities specifically authorized
the use of particular machines. The FCC found a substantial public
demand for automatic telephone-answering devices but, in a legalism
designed to accord with its holding, found that most of the demand
was to answer intrastate long-distance and local calls. Because of the
limited interstate impact and because states were already actively embarked on a program of approving and disapproving particular brands
and models, the FCC deferred the matter to the state agencies. At the
same time, it rejected AT&T's demand to bar devices not approved by
telephone companies even though FCC tests revealed that the automatic telephone-answering devices sponsored by the Bell companies
performed better than other machines.[64] It was clear, then, that AT&T
had won a skirmish but hardly the war. In fact, the *Jordaphone* case
demonstrated that the FCC would no longer treat the interconnection
prohibitions in the Bell tariffs as sacrosanct. Rather, the agency made it
clear that if probable public demand existed for a new communications
product or service that AT&T would or could not provide in sufficient
quantity or quality, independents would be allowed to enter the market. At the same time, however, the FCC deliberately hindered the
widespread application of a new technology in its unproved stages, for
it feared that a decision made prematurely and in the face of insufficient
technical information could move the new technology in an undesirable
direction. A sound concept of the public interest imposed such caution
on regulators—temporary inaction is most often less costly than a huge
outlay of resources on a new technology in its infancy. When a technological development is more advanced and future demand is less uncertain, regulators will attempt to facilitate the new technology or allow
the market to determine the outcome.

Although regulatory caution made it appear as if AT&T had won a
victory in the *Jordaphone* matter, it really had not. AT&T had carefully
to avoid being portrayed as an obstacle to technological progressiveness. In the aftermath of World War II, the public interest clearly lay
in satisfying consumer demand for new products and services, one of
the most important of which was television transmission.

THE POLITICS OF TELEVISION
TRANSMISSION TECHNOLOGY

One of the most serious charges that the Justice Department brought against AT&T in the 1974 suit was that it contrived to monopolize the intercity video market so that it alone would carry television network traffic. The charge involved much more than a historical debate, for, if true, one would have to conclude that AT&T deliberately delayed the expansion of nationwide television transmission. The inference that the Justice Department wanted to draw was that AT&T generally delayed the deployment of newer technologies if it was in the company's interest to do so and that it had the monopolistic power to make such decisions. Thus, monopoly retards innovation. The necessary inference of the Antitrust Division's position is that competition is the necessary spur to the deployment of new technologies.

To evaluate this argument, we must begin by examining the two principal technologies that could then carry intercity video—coaxial cable and microwave relay. For, as we shall see shortly, one aspect of the charge against AT&T is that, in part, it encouraged coaxial cable and discouraged microwave relay because the former was more susceptible to its control.

At the dawn of commercial exploitation of television that began after World War II, the dominant mode of distributing television programs was not known. What was known from the outset of experimental telecasting was that the twisted pair of wires used to carry telephonic transmission was inadequate to carry television signals over long distances. The range of frequencies to be carried in video transmission was simply too broad for both ordinary copper wires and cable.[65] The two principal contenders for the lucrative television transmission market were microwave relay and coaxial cable. While coaxial cable bore a clear resemblance to ordinary copper wire or cable, we cannot assume that AT&T necessarily favored coaxial cable to microwave relay. That AT&T had a strong historical commitment to coaxial cable is evident, as it was in large part developed by AT&T precisely to transmit television signals. During the 1930s, AT&T had been encouraged in this endeavor by RCA, which would become the largest customer of television program distribution.[66] Coaxial cable, consisting of a special cable in which one conductor is completely surrounded by a second one, greatly reduced attenuation and distortion and dramatically reduced power losses at high frequencies. Additionally, the increase in transmission paths compared to traditional two-way voice channels was dramatic. As early as 1935, Frank Jewett, president of Bell Labs, noted that coaxial cable would be capable of more than 240 simultaneous telephone conversations over a single circuit compared to the four conversations over the multiplex system then in general use in the Bell system. Thus, coaxial cable would permit AT&T to experience a great increase in telephone capacity and at the same time allow it to accommodate an anticipated television boom.[67]

However, at the end of World War II, microwave relay loomed as an alternative for both long-distance voice and television transmission, although it was not necessarily conceived of as a competitor to coaxial cable. While it was entirely possible that one of the two technologies might be the sole survivor for economic or technological reasons, AT&T then contemplated that each would serve its purpose in the television and telephone long-distance markets, and that distance, terrain, and other variables would determine which would be the most economic between any two points. In AT&T's view, both technologies had to be considered in transmission of voice and television, and as such they were within the jurisdiction of regulators and public service companies. Thus, to understand the regulatory decisions made concerning television transmission and interconnection with the telephone system, we must first be aware of the feeling at the time; in the words of O. B. Hanson, NBC's chief engineer in late 1944, "[i]t is likely that a national television network will be a combination of coaxial cable and radio relays."[68] Similarly, in a 1944 response to a question posed by NBC on postwar television plans, AT&T vice-president Keith McHugh commented: "We released to the newspapers a statement regarding our proposed plans for the trial between New York and Boston of a radio relay system for the transmission of both telephone messages and television programs." McHugh also mentioned that coaxial cable was being readied for television as well.[69] At this stage in its development, microwave relay was still experimental and only through trial links (such as that under development between New York and Boston in the mid-1940s) would it be possible to determine the system's dependability and economic and technological characteristics.[70] While experimentation with ultrashort waves had been conducted since the 1920s in hope of finding a use for the unused part of the radio spectrum, the first commercial ultrashort wave telephone system was launched by the Bell system in February 1941,[71] at which time coaxial cable was far more developed than microwave relay. The project was successful, but it was still a far cry from a large system using shorter waves than had ever been employed commercially. In microwave relay, the microwaves travel only slightly above the horizon and must be retransmitted at towers approximately 25 to 35 miles apart. They are subject to fading because of atmospheric conditions. A comprehensive microwave system requires the design of (1) repeater circuits; (2) antennae with high gain, good directional qualities, and a low capacity for distortion; (3) filters that can connect a number of different radio channels to a common antenna (thus reducing the quantity of antennae otherwise needed); and (4) repeater amplifiers to compensate for transmission loss in the previous path.[72] But the complete microwave system is more than a sum of its parts; indeed, the larger the system became, the greater were the questions of transmission quality, flexibility, dependability, and economy. Certainly, coaxial cable was a more proven and dependable technology in the mid-1940s, yet the promise of microwave, with its wide bands of available frequencies and low-power requirements, was enormous.[73]

Thus, because of the experimental nature of microwave technology, as noted earlier, the FCC would have to act cautiously. The costs of caution were preferred to the costs that the public may have incurred if the agency had approved widespread deployment of an underdeveloped technology.

THE FCC AND SPECTRUM ALLOCATION

With an understanding of the technological considerations in regards to television transmission just discussed, we can better evaluate how AT&T came to dominate intercity video traffic. We might ask, for instance, why it was AT&T and not Western Union, the broadcast networks, the independent transmission companies, or some combination that dominated intercity video traffic as a result of the critical regulatory decisions and nondecisions made in the 1940s and 1950s. As we know, the issue was an important concern to the Justice Department in the AT&T case. Without overtly charging that the FCC was corrupted by AT&T, the Justice Department concluded that "[t]hroughout this period, in an effort to monopolize the emerging and important intercity video transmission market, AT&T consistently sought preferred status for itself from the FCC . . . [and] denied interconnection both to private companies and other common carriers. . . ."[74] Donald C. Beelar, a communications attorney, has argued in an influential article that AT&T had engaged in a clever five-step move, employing interconnection refusal as a major weapon to remove in sequence its rivals. In this way, Beelar concluded, AT&T gained control of the intercity television microwave industry by 1950.[75]

However, the FCC's actions point to its desire to plan postwar spectrum allocation comprehensively, which formed its conception of the public interest in these matters. Unless we can assume that increased competition can solve every problem in telecommunications (contrary to the FCC's mandate), the problems posed by the new technologies developed before and during World War II impelled the FCC to design principles of priority for the new frequencies. As early as 1936, the FCC was confronted with the problem of large numbers of potential users of a scarce resource—radio spectrum. The guiding framework that the agency would use in the postwar proceedings was formed in the crucial 1939 *Mackay* decision, in which Mackay Radio & Telegraph, RCA Communications, IBM, and other applicants sought unused portions of the spectrum in frequencies above 30,000 KHz.[76] Because many of the characteristics of this range of frequency, including interference, were not known in a practical manner, and because the FCC was reluctant to grant spectrum without a comprehensive view of the uses to which it would be put, the agency instead employed a concept called *experimental license*. The concept, which would play an important yet misunderstood role in microwave transmission of television, allowed the FCC to grant temporary licenses that could be cancelled without notice or formal hearings. The purposes of experimental licenses were to gather information about performance in certain frequencies and to allow the temporary use of frequency until permanent arrangements could be made.

Equally important to the course of future proceedings were the general principles of priority that the *Mackay* case established. Foremost among them is that priority in frequency allocation would be given for uses that benefited the public at large (such as the telephone system) or that provided essential needs such as safety. On this basis, the FCC rejected IBM's request for more frequencies to operate a radio-actuated, high-speed typewriter, then useful only to large enterprises with many units (such as retail chains). Another important principle established in the case was that, because of spectrum scarcity, it would accord a low priority to radio spectrum uses for which a reasonable wire alternative existed. Thus, microwave relay of television was accorded a low priority for spectrum allocation because coaxial cable showed great promise. It should be noted that Commissioner Walker, certainly not an ally of AT&T, joined in this decision, which RCA contested.

The war, of course, suspended high-frequency allocation activity. But in the summer of 1944, the FCC instituted Docket no. 6651 and ordered hearings to determine "[t]he present and future needs of the various classes of non-governmental services for frequencies in the radio spectrum."[77] The review was prompted by advances in radio made during the war as well as increased demand for radio use that the post-war world would bring. Among the anticipated users of the frequencies were taxicabs, buses, railroads, vessels, airplanes, airports, medical services, police, foresters, firefighters, rural telephone users, citizen amateurs, FM radio and television broadcasters, meteorologists, facsimile and educational broadcasters, government, the petroleum industry, and a host of other industries that had discovered uses for radio frequencies.[78] Between 1940—the last full peacetime year—and 1945, much progress had been made in microwave transmission.[79] Even though AT&T and others had made substantial progress during the war in the development of microwave equipment and its capacity, the FCC could still reasonably anticipate that demand for use would substantially outstrip available frequency in the first postwar years. This expectation reinforced the FCC's resolve to operate according to the principles that it had established in the *Mackay* decision. Thus, in May 1945, after extensive hearings and numerous exhibits, the FCC refused to make permanent allocations for microwave relay, concluding that "[a]ll available information concerning relay systems was the result of experimental work in laboratories only. . . . There was no substantial practical experience under actual operating conditions."[80] Accordingly, the agency decided to issue experimental licenses only, which would have to be shared (over AT&T's objection) with other nongovernmental services. In short, the FCC was still guided by the principles of circumspection and frequency economizing that it had established in 1939. At this stage, AT&T was confronted not only with the possibility of other microwave carriers (which it did not then oppose) but also with the even more severe prospect of a constricted spectrum for radio relay purposes.

During the 1940s, nine companies received experimental radio-relay system licenses in the microwave and other bands. Among them were Philco, a radio manufacturer that also operated a Philadelphia television station (the company employed VHF frequencies and equipment—not microwave—to transmit video signals between Philadelphia and Washington), and Dumont, a now defunct television network that ran a small experimental video microwave link between Oxford and New Haven, Connecticut, which linked its New York television station to one in New Haven. As these examples show, experimental microwave was at this time in small-scale use and the companies involved with it were of insufficient size to construct a nationwide television transmission system, even with the aid of other firms.[81] During the same period, the FCC was overwhelmed by the number of other kinds of spectrum requests. For example, Raytheon Manufacturing Company had developed microwave cooking devices designed to operate in the 3,000 MHz region, and other interests, such as those representing medical diathermy and industrial electronic heating units, clamored for microwave space. Indicative of the potential for overcrowding, the police assailed such devices as diathermy because of the interference it created on police frequencies.[82] Again, the incentive for the FCC was to be cautious.

As we will see, the FCC was able to allocate frequencies and mediate competing demands for space through the concept of spectrum economy. And although spectrum economy clearly favored the telephone common carriers in television transmission, this was, in contrast with the Justice Department's view, merely an outcome rather than the purpose of the concept.

SPECTRUM ECONOMY AND TELEVISION TRANSMISSION

In August 1946, the FCC issued a frequency allocation report concerning the mobile radio service of buslines. Although AT&T and the independent telephone industry did not object to an exception covering buslines, they urged the commission to adopt a general public utility approach to newly used frequencies. They argued that the public utility approach, precluding private systems, would lead to the greatest economy in the use of frequencies available for mobile bus communication. Accepting the telephone industry's general argument, the FCC nevertheless held that the bus industry's communication needs should be handled by that industry and not by common carriers.[83] The agency's main reason for the exception was that the primary purpose of such communications was to assure passenger safety, and buslines know best how to construct and operate communications systems intended for this purpose. For the same reason, buslines would not be required to share their assigned frequencies with other users. Even though AT&T lost the skirmish, the FCC once again accepted the spectrum economy argument. Public utility control of frequencies would best economize frequency use and preclude the waste of this resource that would occur if the FCC permanently allocated the spectrum to large numbers of private users. Only such reasons as safety could carve out the exceptions to the general rule.

During the summer of 1946, as the FCC considered the *Bus Transportation Frequencies* case, AT&T attempted to improve the long-distance transmission characteristics of microwave relay. However, definitive answers to such technical questions as optimum repeater spacing, critical to the design of the new system, could not be obtained until the results were available from tests planned for the summer of 1947. In June 1947, anticipating rapid progress, AT&T announced proposed television rates that would apply to both coaxial cable and microwave relay. More importantly, AT&T's aggregation of the two new technologies promised a nationwide system that would include major cities in every region of the country.[84] Its plans were far more advanced than those of other microwave relay experimenters granted licenses to transmit television. Moreover, AT&T's proposed facilities would carry voice transmission as well, thus better satisfying spectrum economy considerations than television signals-only systems. However, the young television industry opposed the rates, which AT&T left open for negotiation by noting they were tentative. The three major networks present at an FCC engineering conference stated that they preferred common-carrier transmission of their television programs, which was similar to the transmission system used for radio programs. Only Dumont, then a small, newly formed network, preferred banding together with the other networks to transmit television programs by microwave relay. GE, on the other hand, planned a small private television network using microwave in New York but did not object to common-carrier operation, whereas Raytheon felt that the nation was not ready for a large-scale television microwave network and, accordingly, contemplated a relatively small-scale system among several large cities. Western Union, which also held an experimental license, announced that it had been unable to obtain microwave equipment and did not know when it could provide video relay service.[85] In short, then, only AT&T was ready, willing, and able to provide full nationwide television distribution with reasonable dispatch. Moreover, its distribution network would be available not only for network television but for other traffic as well, thus satisfying the spectrum economy idea.

By February 1948, the television networks' plans were greater than AT&T's combined coaxial-microwave relay system could handle. The Television Broadcasters Association (TBA) urged the FCC to provide frequency space for a private intercity television relay operation; it argued that "[e]xisting and proposed communications carriers were not presently in a position to meet the needs of the television broadcasters for network facilities."[86] The FCC restated that spectrum economy required intercity television to be handled by the communications common carriers, but at the same time it recognized that the television networks' requirements were then outpacing the intercity television transmission growth of the public service companies. Accordingly, the FCC allotted certain frequencies to the television broadcasters for mobile service (that is, for telecasting from a temporary place, such as a parade) and STL (the links from the television studio to the transmitter) and, secondarily, for intercity television relaying. The latter was explicitly a temporary measure, the costs of which the television broadcasters were ordered to amortize quickly.

At this time, the charge had been made that AT&T retarded nationwide television deployment because its rates were excessive. Yet, prior to February 1948, the FCC had not permitted AT&T to charge for experimental intercity television transmission, which allowed Dumont, Philco, and other firms to use AT&T transmission facilities without cost. In February 1948, the FCC ordered AT&T to file a tariff for video transmission that would become effective on May 1. The tariff led to controversies that the FCC handled under a new docket, no. 8963. Subsequently, the TBA proposed that the television broadcasting industry continue to receive free intercity service and it claimed that the rates proposed by AT&T and Western Union were unreasonably high. Rejecting the TBA proposal, the FCC ordered a full-scale hearing to examine rates and other important issues, and if television relay rates were found to be unreasonable, the television industry would be permitted to seek refunds under the Communications Act.[87] But AT&T was ready to defend itself against the TBA's claims with a detailed cost and investment study based on anticipated growth of television networking, its relative requirements for telephone services, and other variables.[88]

INTERCONNECTION RESTRICTIONS AND TELEVISION

Rates were not the only important issue in the AT&T tariff filing that led to extended controversy, for AT&T's intercity video tariff also contained an interconnection restriction similar to those contained in telephone tariffs, particularly private line tariffs. In essence, Tariff 216 permitted a telecaster to interconnect with AT&T local telephone facilities, but interconnection to non-Bell intercity channels was not permitted except when the Bell system was unable to provide facilities. Once the Bell system was able to provide intercity facilities, the telecaster was obligated to connect into it. The interconnection provisions were protested by Philco and Dumont, which were involved in both telecasting and transmission, the TBA, and Western Union.[89]

Were the interconnection provisions an indication of AT&T's desire for monopoly power in the lucrative intercity television market, or were the provisions reasonably justified by AT&T? To answer this question, we must first review the lengthy history of interconnection regulation. AT&T was the only intercity video distributor that intended to create in the future a nationwide system akin to the nationwide telephone system, whereas its rivals only intended to connect the most lucrative markets. Thus, AT&T conceived its rivals' behavior as creamskimming. Based on precedent, AT&T could reasonably expect the interconnection tariff provision to be upheld, as virtually all similar ones had been. As we have seen, telephone companies were often compelled to assume complete control over their entire systems, the reasons for which are succinctly summarized in a 1914 New York PSC case:

> Efficiency of service requires that the telephone company should have complete supervision and control (a) over the design of an installation, (b) over its maintenance, (c) over relocations and extensions, (d) over operation. . . . [W]hile in individual cases . . . abuse might not occur, the existence of the opportunity would certainly lead to the abuse if . . . established as a general practice.[90]

While the FCC was considering AT&T Tariff 216, the company refused to transmit an NBC video program between New York and Boston because it had been transmitted previously from Philadelphia to New York over Philco's facilities rather than AT&T's. Two weeks after the refusal, Philco launched a judicial attack on the interconnection provision, seeking a preliminary injunction compelling AT&T to transmit telecasts also transmitted by Philco. The court rejected Philco's request, deferring it to the FCC to decide the underlying interconnection issue.[91] Next, the television industry interests sought to have the FCC divorce the interconnection and rate issues. AT&T vigorously opposed what, on first impression, seemed to be only a simple procedure but what was actually a critical factor of time. Since the Federal District Court refused to enjoin the interconnection ban, it would remain in effect until the FCC acted. Obviously, this was to AT&T's advantage, especially since rate issues usually take longer to decide than do service issues.[92] But the FCC granted the motion for divorce—AT&T's first important loss in the television matter.

In 1949, the Justice Department brought its antitrust suit against AT&T and the television interests found new allies and new arguments. The principal new argument was that AT&T sought to control intercity television transmission so as to allow Western Electric to dominate equipment manufacture in the market. Based on the essential theory of the Justice Department's *Western Electric* case, the argument also brought FM broadcasters into the fray on the side of the television industry.[93] But while AT&T's enemies grew in number, so did its intercity video network and the volume of its business with the networks.[94] Thus, when the FCC's proposed interconnection report was released in early September 1949, essentially setting aside the interconnection provisions of AT&T's tariff, the Bell system had effectively won the battle on the economic front. Not surprisingly, the Bell system took vigorous exception to the FCC's proposed report, which ironically used AT&T's decisive success in creating a nationwide video transmission system as a reason to reject the "creamskimming" argument. Basically, the FCC held that "creamskimming" is inapplicable when there is so little cream to skim! Since the FCC ruled out two competitors in the same market, the little intercity video traffic left to independents could not adversely affect AT&T's intention to link all points, including those difficult and costly to serve.[95]

The FCC's final decision reflected the conclusions of its proposed report.[96] Reiterating the spectrum economy theory that led it to conclude that only communications common carriers (essentially, AT&T and Western Union) should permanently handle intercity video traffic, the FCC noted that the common carriers were not yet ready to handle all of the traffic that telecasters required. Although the Bell system was well on the way to completing such a network, the commission concluded that it alone would not be able to meet the full demand in the near future.[97] However, the FCC made it clear that it would consider any firm's application to be a common carrier, but not a competitive one. Further, the agency rejected the applicability of the creamskimming argument and found that, although the problems of interconnecting different systems existed, they were not insurmountable. Finally, the agency concluded that the interconnection restriction would impede the spread of television by denying intercity links and, accordingly, was unlawful because it conflicted with the public interest requirements of the Communications Act.

WESTERN UNION v. AT&T

While AT&T had lost the battle it had won the war, for the common carrier principle in video transmission was once again affirmed. The commission reiterated the concept of spectrum economy in stating:

> The limitations thus imposed on private intercity TV relaying result from the concrete fact that there is insufficient space in the radio spectrum to accommodate fully all the desirable radio services, and *that common carrier operation in general is more flexible and economical with*

respect to frequency utilization than would be private operations in this field
[emphasis added].[98]

Thus, the interconnection requirement with broadcasters would be
only temporary. Finally, the commission deferred the question of
whether AT&T would be required to connect with another common carrier—Western Union—which raised issues different than
those raised in connection with broadcaster interconnection. In the
Western Union case, interconnection raised the issue of *permanent*
interconnection.

By October 1950, the AT&T intercity television network had expanded as far west as Omaha, Nebraska, and as far south as Jacksonville,
Florida. On the west coast, San Francisco and Los Angeles were connected. Approximately one-half of the mileage at this point was coaxial
and the other half was microwave, with the latter in clear ascendancy.[99]
As AT&T locked horns with Western Union, no other firm had applied
for common carrier status. AT&T's principal argument in the 1950
hearings on whether it should be required to interconnect with Western Union was based on relative size. The company argued that it alone
was capable of meeting all demand for intercity video and that no other
company was constructing a multipoint, multipurpose nationwide system. Accordingly, AT&T stressed that interconnection would, in essence, provide a "private subsidy" by the telephone company to the
telegraph company by enlarging the latter at the former's expense.
Moreover, Western Union's service was technologically backward—it
could offer service in both directions only by changing the direction of
a channel, whereas AT&T could offer an additional channel so that both
directions could be utilized simultaneously.[100]

Meanwhile, other events were undermining Western Union's position. In mid-1950, the television networks were lukewarm to Western
Union's participation in video transmission.[101] Further, private microwave intercity video applications, including one filed by GE, were being
turned down because common carrier facilities (essentially, AT&T's)
were available.[102] Since private intercity video competition was denied
on spectrum economy and other grounds, there was little justification
for Western Union intercity video participation. Thus, the FCC's Common Carrier Bureau, often antagonistic to AT&T, held that an AT&T–
Western Union interconnection was neither necessary nor desirable because mandatory interconnection would disrupt Bell's overall planning.

While AT&T had assumed the responsibility of creating a nationwide video transmission network, Western Union reserved the right to pick and choose the facilities it would provide. Accordingly, if Western Union failed to provide a transmission system that it was considering providing, and Bell did not provide it, a full-scale intercity video network would be retarded and local stations in such areas would be adversely affected. Further, broadcasters had made clear that additional intercity video channels between New York and Philadelphia, one of Western Union's prime marketing targets, were not necessary. And Western Union admitted uncertainty as to its plans and failed to accept the full public service responsibility that AT&T had undertaken. These reasons persuaded the Common Carrier Bureau to reject mandatory common carrier interconnection. The same arguments also persuaded the FCC's hearing examiner, who held against Western Union in January 1951.[103]

The arguments that led to the initial decision were upheld on appeal to the full FCC. But while AT&T won at the commission level, it was by a surprisingly close 3–2 vote.[104] The majority held that the Communications Act clearly notes that interconnection cannot be required simply to serve the private interests of a carrier such as Western Union; rather, under the public service standard, a carrier must show that interconnection will best serve the public. Thus, the majority accepted the arguments of the Common Carrier Bureau and found that mandatory interconnection between AT&T and Western Union served no public purpose.[105] Finding that AT&T's channels were sufficient to satisfy present and future needs in the markets that Western Union sought to serve, the FCC rejected the telegraph company's request. Western Union did not, like AT&T, propose the creation of an intercity video network; rather, it admitted that it intended to choose markets selectively. Nonetheless, Western Union persuaded two members of the commission to dissent on the ground that the FCC's decision would give AT&T a monopoly position in intercity video. But the majority rebutted this argument, stating that while the FCC has an obligation to consider the national policy of competition embodied in the antitrust laws, much more is at stake in a public service field like telecommunications. The majority observed that its decision was not an endorsement of a Bell monopoly in intercity video, for it would approve other intercity video common carriers able to demonstrate a need for interconnection with the Bell system. Each case would be judged separately, based on the applicant's plans, readiness, and ability and the need for the service. In 1954, the FCC did approve the first such case.[106] The minority view, however, would come to represent majority opinion in future telecommunications policy. The view, which accords little significance to the public service idea, holds that unless an industry is a natural monopoly, competition produces better overall results.

AT&T's success on the economic front and its commitment to bringing television to the entire nation rather than only to the most lucrative markets, allowed it to represent its private interest as the public interest. As is shown in this chapter, contrary to the notion that AT&T's activities thwarted the deployment of new technologies, the policies approved by the FCC actually advanced progress in the television industry. Even so, the strong dissent in the *Western Union* case was to portend a shift in the FCC's conception of the public interest.

CHAPTER 5

THE WARNING BELL

THE CHANGING PUBLIC SERVICE STANDARD

In earlier chapters we have seen how the public service standard in telecommunications evolved within AT&T's regulated network manager system and how it came to be accepted by regulators as the best means to serve the public. Through the public service standard, AT&T's private interests coincided with the FCC's paramount obligation to assure "to all of the people of the United States a rapid, efficient, nationwide and worldwide wire and radio communication service with adequate facilities at reasonable charges."[1] In this chapter, we examine how the FCC handled the growing problem of reconciling the regulated network manager system with the increasing demands of new entrants and others calling for its erosion. These new competitors and the business interests they served attempted to show that their private interests reflected the public interest. At first, their emphasis was not competition but the availability of choice.

AT&T's resistance to the changes proposed by new competitors was an important Justice Department concern in *United States* v. *AT&T*. The Justice Department argued that AT&T's resistance constituted an unreasonable exercise of monopoly power. However, our close examination of this issue will reveal that AT&T was justified in its opposition to the proposed changes. From AT&T's perspective, these demands occurred at a time when a short-term service crisis played an important role in the FCC's behavior.

The FCC's changes in regulatory policy were shaped immeasurably by a subtle change in judicial behavior. Under traditional standards of administrative law, the reviewing courts could not substitute their own views of sound public policy for those of administrative agencies if the agency could support its policy preferences in evidence and law.[2] While the distinction between "appropriate review" and so-called "judicial activism" is often unclear, some cases are easily categorized as one or the other. As we shall see, the decision in the *Hush-A-Phone* case clearly overstepped the bounds of the traditional court-reviewing role and in important ways contributed to the FCC's changes in telecommunications regulatory policy described in this chapter.

It is clear that as early as the 1950s, some FCC personnel wished to introduce a general competition standard. In the 1952 *RCA* case, the Supreme Court reprimanded the FCC for *generally* preferring competition without showing its need in a particular situation.[3] Accordingly, AT&T's opponents pressed their private claims in a different way. In an age that celebrated the consumer, the opponents called for consumer sovereignty by demanding free choice and by criticizing AT&T's dominance of telephone service and equipment. Thus, competition entered the scene, the FCC appeared to be upholding its statutory obligations, and the private advantage of the new entrants and their allies appeared to be in the public interest. Moreover, if, in the FCC's judgment, AT&T and the independent telephone companies were unable or unwilling to provide certain telecommunications services and products for which a reasonable demand existed, the agency would have to remedy the situation. Otherwise, potential users and would-be suppliers could reasonably complain to the FCC and the courts that the agency was not assuring adequate facilities to all people of the United States. This, of course, does not mean that the FCC was obligated to allow an entrepreneur to supply any unmet demand that AT&T could or would not supply. Rather, the agency was obligated to examine the extent of the demand and to measure the costs and benefits of meeting (or not meeting) it in alternative ways. A variety of factors would have to be weighed, such as the commercial possibilities of new technologies, safety and quality of the network, and economic impact on common carriers. Within this context, and under the prodding of many interests intent on showing that AT&T would or could not meet their needs, the FCC's position gradually shifted direction, culminating in the 1968 landmark *Carterfone* decision.

THE *HUSH-A-PHONE* CASE

Like so many events that lead to the establishment of important principles, the *Hush-A-Phone* case has its origins in a relatively small and simple matter. As noted in Chapter 4, the Hush-A-Phone device was rejected as early as 1922 by AT&T's chief engineer, who found that its attachment to a telephone resulted in distorted sound and transmission loss and hindered placing the receiver on the hook. The device, consisting of a simple cuplike attachment that could be snapped onto the telephone handset, was intended to assure relative privacy. It was entirely acoustic and did not involve any electrical or inductive connection into the network. As such, the Hush-A-Phone—unlike most interconnection devices—did not raise the issues of physical harm, network safety, or technical compatibility.[4]

AT&T and its affiliates objected to the Hush-A-Phone principally because it reduced the intelligibility of communication. Because the quality of telephone conversations between users and other parties was lessened by the Hush-A-Phone attachment, the Bell system determined that the device degraded the network. As the FCC observed in its 1955 decision,

> The design of a plant to give a prescribed grade of service is based upon having telephone sets and instruments at the terminal of the connection which will perform as expected from the design. If the performance of a telephone set is lowered, the expected overall transmission performance will not be realized. This will affect not only the user of the set at the station at which it occurs but also users of the telephone system at other stations which are connected to the degraded station.[5]

In keeping with its role as regulated network manager and its tariff provisions generally prohibiting interconnection, the Bell system notified several Hush-A-Phone customers (most of them department stores) that the attachment was illegal and should be removed. As a result, the Hush-A-Phone company brought action against the Bell system in 1948, requesting the FCC to change the interconnection provisions of AT&T's tariffs so to permit the use of the device. In response, the Bell system claimed that the Hush-A-Phone was ineffective in that it impaired the intelligibility of telephone service and did not afford any significant increase in privacy. The Associated Telephone Company, then the nation's largest independent and a defendant in the *Hush-A-Phone* case, claimed that the device

> destroys the natural characteristics of the individual's voice and thus loses the advantage of ready recognition and identification; that in the case of many voices it tends to muffle and make indistinct the speech of another person using it; and that in the case of almost all voices it has a "blasting" effect.[6]

Telephone engineers, including some not employed by telephone companies, also complained that the Hush-A-Phone raised the transmitters of certain telephones above their cradles when the instruments were hung up, which tied up central office lines and delayed incoming calls. Associated also noted that the California PUC's policy was to deny interconnection rights if a device *might* impair the network because the administrative costs of policing such devices would be too high.[7]

In a major concession, Hush-A-Phone admitted that the device impaired the quality of telephone conversations, although not to the extent that AT&T charged.[8] W. H. Martin, vice-president of Bell Labs, testified and submitted evidence showing that the Hush-A-Phone resulted in a median transmission loss of thirteen decibels and a receiving loss of seven. In perspective, the total was greater "than the total of all the improvements" which had been incorporated in Bell handsets and station apparatus in the prior 20 years. Further, Martin argued, cupping one's hands over the receiver provided more privacy than did the Hush-A-Phone.[9] The FCC's Common Carrier Bureau agreed that the Hush-A-Phone and similar devices generally deteriorate telephone service, and therefore agreed that it was neither unjust nor unreasonable for telephone companies to prohibit the use of the device.[10] For these reasons, the FCC concluded that the use of the Hush-A-Phone impaired the quality of telephone transmission and that the privacy gains of the device were minimal under most conditions.[11] But under its statutory obligation, the commission also had to consider whether there was significant demand—actual or potential—for the device. For if it found that Bell had failed to fulfill demand, the FCC would have to consider ways in which it could encourage the dissemination of the device within the context of the general interconnection prohibition. The demand for the device was marginal, at best, even though it had been on the market for 27 years at the time the complaint was issued in 1948. Western Electric did not manufacture a similar device, and only 125,000 Hush-A-Phones had been sold since they were first introduced. More significantly, 80,000 of the total number sold had been made for the pedestal telephone, which was being phased out. Most of the devices were sold during the 1920s, after which sales dropped sharply; for example, in 1949, only 5,300 Hush-A-Phones were sold.[12] Finally, users of the device appeared not to be concerned about it, as none was willing to testify on the company's behalf.

In February 1951, in an *initial* decision, the FCC unanimously voted to dismiss Hush-A-Phone's complaint, but stated that each foreign attachment must be treated separately on a case-by-case basis.[13] It was not until December 1955 when an almost entirely different group of commissioners ruled 6–0 that the Hush-A-Phone impaired intelligibility, naturalness, and voice recognition. The FCC, relying on the long-employed state commissions' concept of network quality impairment, held that "[t]he use of the Hush-A-Phone affects the quality of telephone service not only . . . to users, but also to all other subscribers who are connected with the same telephone system and who may call or be called by Hush-A-Phone users."[14] Since the Hush-A-Phone directly impaired telephone service and was not an advance in telephone technology that could lead to significant public demand, the FCC had no difficulty in dismissing Hush-A-Phone's complaint.

The Hush-A-Phone *Appeal*

In 1956, Hush-A-Phone appealed the FCC's decision to the Court of Appeals, District of Columbia Circuit. Although the interconnection tariff provision had a rich history in the regulatory bodies and state courts, this was the first time it was considered by a federal court. Under usually accepted administrative law principles, courts almost always defer to regulatory agencies in matters of fact (such as whether a device impairs the quality of the telephone network); that is, in the interpretation of statutory terms that are technical rather than legal and their application to facts.[15] Nevertheless, in recent years many seasoned observers of administrative law have commented on a nascent judicial activism in which courts sometimes substitute their views on technical matters for those of regulators and even Congress.

The leading institution in the new judicial activism was the United States Court of Appeals, District of Columbia Circuit, which reviews a large number of administrative decisions. The court expanded its policy-making role by employing several concepts that are pertinent to comprehending its decision in the *Hush-A-Phone* case. The first is an expansion of the conception of rights beyond the traditional ones embraced within the Lockean and constitutional ideas of life, liberty, and property.[16] The second concept can be described as judicial self-righteousness. Implicit in many of the court's decisions is the notion that judges are more honest and intelligent than regulators:

> A court does not depart from its proper function when it undertakes a study of the record, hopefully perceptive, even as to the evidence on technical and specialized matters, for this enables the court to penetrate to the underlying decisions of the agency.[17]

While superficially reasonable and modest in tone—"hopefully perceptive"—the language here is fraught with danger. Instead of reviewing to make sure that an agency's views are consistent with a statute, the quoted language, in conjunction with the expanded notion of rights, has been used to substitute a court's judgment for that of experienced regulators.

The *Hush-A-Phone* case, decided in November 1956, is an early example of judicial activism.[18] Since there was no federal judicial precedent in the area of interconnection, the court was relatively free to vent its views on the subject without constraint. Accordingly, it ignored the network concept and every reason that the PUCs and FCC had provided to support interconnection restrictions. The court disregarded the facts that regulatory agencies have an interest in the quality of transmission and that statutes (including the 1934 Communications Act) direct them to consider quality and promote improvements in the network. In effect, the court held that if an interconnecting device does not physically impair any of the facilities of the telephone company, any commission restriction on interconnection is an "unwarranted interference with the telephone subscriber's *right* reasonably to use his telephone in ways which are privately beneficial without being publicly detrimental" [emphasis added].[19] One searches the Communications Act and the Constitution in vain for any 'right' that was accorded subscribers to attach things to the telephone system. Completely ignored in the court's proclamation were the numerous reasons that every PUC had advanced over the years in upholding interconnection restrictions.

Notwithstanding the surprising result in the *Hush-A-Phone* appeal, it is important to appreciate what the court's decision did not do. Although the court's comment, "privately beneficial without being publicly detrimental," would open the door to the introduction of more such devices, the court did not command the FCC to deregulate CPE interconnection or to promote competition, aₙd it certainly did not warrant any substitution for Bell-provided equipment. Accordingly, the FCC, upon remand, directed AT&T to amend its tariffs so as to distinguish between harmful and harmless interconnecting devices. Thus, the company could not prohibit devices that did not injure or impair the system or its operation.[20] The amended AT&T tariffs were filed in April 1957, in accordance with the decisions, but in an accompanying statement, AT&T made it clear that liberalized interconnection did not apply to electrical devices because these did create a safety hazard.[21]

Hush-A-Phone, which eventually redesigned its device to meet Bell's original objections, was satisfied with the court's ruling and asked that its FCC complaint be withdrawn after the new tariffs became effective.[22] But the *Hush-A-Phone* decision did not end controversy in the foreign attachment field nor did it clarify the court's ambiguous and difficult-to-apply language. The state PUCs treated the decision as only applying to acoustic CPE devices and maintained their traditional opposition to many electrical and induction CPEs. The FCC, too, was unwilling to permit uncontrolled dissemination of new foreign attachments.[23] But the *Hush-A-Phone* outcome was a clear defeat for AT&T and the long-standing interconnection restriction principle. It would encourage others, especially as more and more spectrum opened up, and new user needs would create a need for new CPE fashioned to meet those needs. For this and other reasons, the FCC's attitude in the continuing frequency allocation issues was critical. And these issues would continue to be important in the *United States* v. *AT&T* case. In brief, the Justice Department claimed that AT&T used flawed arguments before the FCC to thwart competition and to preserve its monopoly, a charge that deserves further examination.

SPECTRUM AS A SCARCE RESOURCE

Rapid technological developments during the 1950s shaped AT&T's strategy and the FCC's policy on spectrum allocation of microwave frequencies. AT&T had major plans for microwave use. As early as the

1956 Annual Meeting of the Industrial Communications Association, an important users group, Bell-system representatives spoke of "office automation"—the integration of computing and communications that would revolutionize record-keeping, ordering, and other business functions. Richard W. Miller, an AT&T merchandising official, promised the industrial users:

> We want to know a lot more than we do now about your present and future needs for other services, too—private line telephone and teletypewriter services and long distance telephone service, for example. We plan to make market analyses for these services as early as we can. . . . [Later in his talk, Miller noted the] likelihood of a coming need for a variety of service offerings available for data transmission. For example, it may be desirable to provide private line channels of various bandwidths ranging in grade all the way from telegraph to television. Channels of very wide band width would be required if, as seems probable, the time will come when companies will want to directly interconnect computers located in different cities.[24]

The stakes for AT&T in the microwave battle were high. As early as 1954, *Telecommunications Reports* related AT&T's strategy of providing increased services to customers:

> The approach is to make the service more valuable to the customer. This has very definite monetary as well as public service advantages— the customer getting the most from his telephone services, uses them more and more and keeps them longer, and is more receptive to a second suggestion when he is satisfied with the first.[25]

The strategy was successful in that nontraditional services composed almost 50 percent of the Bell system's income growth by the mid-1960s.[26] But many other firms also had major plans to use portions of the microwave spectrum. Thus, the inevitable struggle for frequency allocation could only be decided by the FCC. In the critical *Above 890Mc* proceeding, which sought to establish such allocation principles, the agency established a set of ground rules and allocations.

Technological breakthroughs in the 1950s made the institution of a decision rule on allocation more urgent. New AT&T technology gave the company a flexibility to provide new services in a manner hitherto undreamed of. In 1954 and 1955, AT&T scientists and engineers began the transition from controlling communications functions and switching through hardware (such as diodes and transistors) to software. The older control system required the design of new hardware and circuits on a continuing basis to meet new needs. Under the new system, however, "[d]etailed engineering of large numbers of logic circuits would be eliminated. To change a sequence of actions, add new functions, or modify old [ones] it would be necessary only to change the program in the permanent memory."[27] Stored program control thus promised to revolutionize telephone switching. It made available a variety of new services providing extraordinary flexibility within each service, including direct-distance dialing, centrex (in which central office switching is arranged to recognize and complete calls within a group of lines representing subscribers), and a host of data services. The same flexibility that added services in the public-switched network could also be employed in private network offerings and mobile radio service.[28] Thus, demand for new services would grow rapidly, and since spectrum for new services could be scarce, the stakes in the *Above 890Mc* proceeding were high.

As noted in Chapter 4, the battle for spectrum can be traced to the pre–World War II era. As early as 1946, the fight to employ microwave frequencies for novel purposes began. For example, when police radio interests complained about the interference caused by medical diathermy machines, the FCC made available the 2450Mc frequency range for diathermy and industrial heating equipment, thus assuaging the police force.[29] In 1947, Philco and the California Forestry Service cautioned the FCC not to grant too large a share of the microwave spectrum to AT&T.[30] The problem of microwave spectrum pollution had barely begun, yet the prevailing sentiment of those who sought to use the microwave spectrum was expressed well by a Television Broadcasters Association spokesperson: "We seem to have arrived at a point where . . . a policy of conservation as well as exploitation is prudent."[31] In particular, the petroleum industry—an important actor in both the *Above 890Mc* and *Carterfone* proceedings—typified the burgeoning interest of many industrial and commercial sectors in the enormous possibilities of telecommunications. In October 1947, the American Petroleum Institute (API) created its Central Committee on Radio Facilities, of which ocean-going vessel-to-shore communications, petroleum pipelines, and geophysical exploration were only the beginnings of its new-found interests in telecommunications.[32] The head of the API Committee projected that

Practically every division or branch of the petroleum industry can well be served by one or more adaptations of radio to effect economies in operation, increase safety or raise efficiency. Radio may, perhaps, provide new methods of processing oil to supplement or even replace the present catalytic refining processes.[33]

Other potential uses outlined by the API included activation of remote control systems to start and stop motors at isolated wells and policing of pipelines.[34]

Many other industries gradually discovered what the petroleum industry did early in the postwar era—telecommunications was a valuable resource. This realization raised for industry representatives a host of issues, including whether they should have the choice of a private system or telephone company-provided service, interconnection rights and, of course, frequency allocation. The cross-cutting conflicts meant that not only could industrial and commercial microwave users have interests in conflict with telephone companies but with each other as well. For example, the API and the theater television interests clashed in 1952 over the allocation of certain microwave frequencies.[35] The political battle over microwave frequencies came to resemble a barroom brawl, but with one difference: virtually every interest took a position in conflict with AT&T's. In 1953, the Radio-Electronics Television Manufacturers Association (RETMA), desiring a degree of predictability on how to plan the manufacture of sets in the future, requested that the FCC conduct an overall study and promulgate microwave rules in accordance with current and future requirements.[36] As the FCC prepared to act, a dozen user organizations, including railroads, motor carriers, and forest industries, banded together in 1954 as the Microwave Users Council. To them, the paramount problem was to prevent a recurrence of the intercity television situation in which the common carriers (principally, AT&T) were accorded control of the traffic.[37]

THE PROCEEDINGS IN THE *ABOVE 890Mc* CASE

As the FCC grappled with individual matters and fragmented issues, it became apparent that the agency needed to institute a general proceeding. It did so in November 1956, ordering hearings to begin in the spring in a docket formally entitled "Allocation of the Frequencies in the Bands Above 890Mc," or more commonly, "Above 890Mc." Oral hearings were held from May through October in 1957, during which time the FCC heard 160 persons and organizations and had accumulated more than 5,000 record pages. The proceeding was to be a major step in changing the prevailing conception of the public interest in telecommunications. Big-business interests would play principal roles in the transformation as well. While the FCC delineated nineteen separate issues, *Telecommunication Reports* observed: "The principal controversy shapes up as a battle between the common carrier communications industry and proponents of unlimited or liberalized use of private point-to-point microwave systems."[38] Already pending were the private microwave applications of Minute Maid Corporation and Central Freight Lines of Texas, which the common carriers bitterly protested.

Before the *Above 890Mc* proceedings began, the Antitrust Division of the Justice Department recommended in a letter to the FCC that the agency reject common-carrier operation of microwave systems. Competition in microwave, claimed the Justice Department, will lead to competition in microwave equipment manufacture, whereas common-carrier microwave operation will lead to monopoly in such manufacture. The Justice Department made the highly tenuous argument that the 1934 Communications Act favors competition except where exceptions are specifically carved out.[39] Section 314 of the Act, on which the Department relied for its view, explicitly applies to radio (not to telephony or common-carrier services generally) and forbids anyone in the traditional radio business from controlling any telephone or telegraph company when the effect may be to lessen competition substantially. Even though the argument, legally tenuous at the outset, was discredited by the Supreme Court in 1953,[40] the Antitrust Division would continue to use it throughout subsequent proceedings. In contrast, the industrial users did not press this argument in the hearings; rather, most adopted the view made by RETMA's representative that the microwave spectrum is "virtually unlimited." Consequently, they argued, there was sufficient spectrum space for both common and private carriers.[41] While some attempt was made to rebut this estimate on engineering grounds, the principal common carrier argument, effectively made by General Telephone's president, Donald C. Power, was based on the concept of creamskimming.

> If existing or prospective subscribers are permitted to substitute their own private systems for existing telephone company facilities or facilities which the telephone company can readily provide in a reasonable time, the economic well-being of the telephone company is adversely affected. The telephone company can look to only one source to replace the revenue siphoned off by privately owned, competing systems. Added revenues sufficient to make up for that lost by the establishing of private systems must be obtained by increasing the rates to the general public served by the company.[42]

For this reason, Power argued, it is irrelevant whether the microwave spectrum is virtually unlimited, as those interests favoring private microwave systems contended.

Thus, the issue of private microwave pitted large users, who would find a privately owned system economical, against the public service companies, who were united on this point. The common carriers used the argument that their rates in the lucrative private-line market cross-subsidized lower rates to smaller business users and residential subscribers. Exceptions to the general rule, they proposed, included (1) right-of-way companies such as railroads, power companies, and pipelines; (2) instances in which a communications system is responsible for safety or security such as the police; and (3) situations in which the common carriers were unable or unwilling to supply private line. The Bell system announced that it would introduce a private-line tariff to meet private system competition and to make common carrier private lines more attractive.[43]

As the *Above 890Mc* hearings proceeded during the summer of 1957, it became apparent through their continuous and active participation that users of telecommunications services had never before evinced such intense interest in an FCC proceeding. For example, the National Association of Manufacturers opposed the common carriers' position, complaining that "[t]he use of microwave point-to-point communications systems by the manufacturing industry has been effectively strangulated by the existing rules and policies of the Commission."[44] Also, the National Retail Dry Goods Association (NRDGA), representing the nation's large department stores, argued that the rapid suburbanization that had taken place after World War II changed retailing dramatically. Retailers had to follow population shifts, leading them to establish a larger number of units, and private microwave was necessary to coordinate main stores, branch outlets, and warehouses within and between regions. Further, the growth of retail credit sales, then in its infancy, required rapid private communication between credit authorization centers and selling outlets.[45] As more and more witnesses were heard, it became apparent that virtually every big-business interest in the country vehemently opposed public service company control of microwave. The big-business interests claimed to want only free choice, largely ignoring the creamskimming arguments made by the telephone companies. The apparently reasonable insistence on "free choice" was coupled with claims from important industries that the economy as a whole would suffer if the FCC did not decide in favor of the big-business position. Thus, the Automobile Manufacturers Association claimed an urgent need for microwave in production, accounting, and distributive functions: "The highly competitive nature of the automobile industry makes it mandatory that privately operated systems be considered in comparison with common carrier charges."[46]

While industry in general opposed common carrier control of microwave transmission, it was the petroleum industry's opposition that was voiced most strongly. William H. Morris, president of Sinclair Refining Co., emphasized the exceptional importance of telecommunications in the petroleum industry, claiming that his firm's experience was typical of the integrated oil companies and pointing out that 5 percent of Sinclair's costs were for telecommunications.[47] W. M. Rust, Jr., of Humble Oil, speaking on behalf of the American Petroleum Institute, predicted that microwave would become even more important in coming years with the growth of offshore drilling operations. Rust asserted that unless the petroleum industry could operate its own microwave systems, national defense and the well-being of the petroleum industry and its consumers would be impaired. The common carriers, he argued, should not have a stranglehold on the petroleum or any other industry.[48] Summarizing the petroleum industry's perspective, Shell vice-president E. J. Strawn proclaimed that "a dangerous philosophy has crept into the attitudes and policies of the communications common carriers. . . . A theory of control and domination of all communications, large or small, public or private, solely on the basis that they . . . somehow have been chosen to provide such service."[49] (The "dangerous philosophy" was, of course, the public service principle.)

Thus, for the first time in an FCC proceeding, virtually all big business—led by the petroleum industry—was arrayed against AT&T. Each firm or industry contended that it needed privately provided microwave to serve its unique requirements. And each disregarded AT&T's argument that the big industrial and commercial interests would be free to choose between private microwave or the public network for each section of the network. Obviously, according to AT&T's argument, each company would choose the least-costly alternative, based on route, time of day, volume of traffic, and other factors. Thus, while the telephone companies would continue to engage in cost averaging, in which the less costly routes would subsidize the more-costly ones, private microwave systems would be free to pick and choose only the least-costly routes. Not surprisingly, they would thus be able to undercut the common carriers in some routes. Accordingly, the public service companies would have to adjust rates upward for their other customers. Moreover, the common carriers argued that it was unfair competition to require one group to serve all comers and another to pick and choose freely.[50]

The Above 890Mc Decisions

The FCC found itself in a difficult position as it approached the 1959 decision in the *Above 890Mc* case. The 1956 antitrust settlement, the controversy generated by it, and the growing telecommunications demand of large users together influenced important government and big-business actors against AT&T, which was portrayed by its opponents as a monopolist. The FCC's decision to liberalize the use of private microwave was based on its evaluation of two central questions: (1) How adequate was the supply of microwave frequencies? and (2) Would the licensing of privately owned microwave systems economically injure the common carriers? It should be noted that in this important proceeding, many basic questions were not addressed (for example, whether the FCC should abandon the public service concept in the microwave spectrum).

If the FCC's decision to open up private microwave had been partly based on the Bell system's inadequacy in meeting some of the microwave demand placed on it, it would have been justified. For example, representatives of Freeport Sulphur and Minute Maid expressed dissatisfaction with the limited availability and poor quality of Southern Bell's microwave service.[51] Although the first *Above 890Mc* decision briefly mentioned the common carriers' inadequate microwave provisions, the consideration did not play a major role in the decision. If it had been an influential factor, however, it would have led to a decision rule akin to the intercity television rule, in which private companies would have been granted temporary licenses until the common carriers could meet private-line needs. But the FCC refused to limit itself in this way. Rather, it undertook a revolutionary step on rather narrow grounds.[52] First, it found that a frequency shortage did not exist at the time and that a shortage was not likely to develop in the future. Second, the FCC projected, on the basis of economic considerations, that there would be few private microwave users. Therefore, the intense demand of a few private-line users (demonstrated by their vigorous participation in the hearings) and a projected small overall private-line demand were the key reasons the FCC agreed to permit private microwave. Because the agency viewed private microwave as an exception to common-carrier control of intercity communications, the issue was treated much like a military or police service, for which there is little or no need to discuss boundary questions between public and nonpublic services. The FCC also expected common-carrier interconnection re-strictions to "operate as a limiting factor."[53] Later developments in interconnection, and even the implications of the Court of Appeals' *Hush-A-Phone* decision, made this argument tenuous.

In view of the FCC's favorable disposition on the right of private microwave system operation, the Commission next had to determine whether privately controlled, private-line microwave would creamskim from AT&T by causing it to raise rates for residential and business sub-scribers not able to afford private microwave. But again, the agency failed to consider general principles and instead focused on the specific evidence adduced at the hearing, concluding that the small amount of traffic covered in the proceeding would not significantly affect AT&T.[54] Also, consideration was not given to the many exceptions with which the agency was dealing or would deal in the future. As we shall see, in most of the proceedings the FCC tended to avoid creamskimming as a general issue by treating as discrete each application and each excep-tion to the general rule.

After having assumed that it would not confront other situations that would weaken public service company control of telecommunications, the FCC next examined the evidence concerning economic impact. The only specific projection present in the evidence was a flawed study offered by Motorola, which concluded that the Bell system would not be significantly affected by privately controlled microwave. The common carriers did not offer detailed impact projections, and even the FCC, engaged in a fundamental rule-making effort, did not prepare its own studies or request projections from the public service companies. Accordingly, the agency concluded that "[t]he record is *inconclusive* on the question as to the specific nature, extent, and magnitude of any detriment which the licensing of private point-to-point systems would have on the ability of common carriers to serve the general public" [emphasis added].[55] Then, in a procedure more appropriate to an adversary proceeding than a rule-making one such as *Above 890Mc*, the telephone and telegraph companies' failure to show *specific* adverse economic impact was interpreted by the FCC as meaning that the problem did not exist. Of course, the agency promised to reexamine the issue in the future if economic conditions changed.

Thus, AT&T and the other public service companies suffered a major defeat because the FCC ignored fundamental issues, made questionable arguments, and inferred conclusions from limited evidence. Clearly, the agency was impressed by the intensity expressed by large users of private microwave and felt obligated to accommodate their interests. Of course, the petroleum industry was pleased with the outcome.[56] And, not surprisingly, when the Commission reconsidered *Above 890Mc* in 1960, it upheld its original decision, largely on the grounds set forth originally.[57] Although the door for competition was not yet opened wide, it certainly opened considerably more as a result of the *Above 890Mc* case.

THE *TELPAK* CASE

The First TELPAK Offering

Less than four months after the FCC's 1960 reconsideration opinion of *Above 890Mc*, AT&T instituted its competitive response in the private-line market. A new private-line, bulk-rate communications offering known as TELPAK was filed on 16 January 1961. The offering consisted of four classifications—A, B, C, D, providing 12, 24, 60, and 240 voice-grade channels, respectively—and was AT&T's first response to the new competition between private line and common carrier approved by the

FCC.[58] To evaluate TELPAK, we must consider that it was AT&T's first response to the revival of competition in the postwar era. The earlier *Hush-A-Phone* case involved an add-on device rather than a product or service already provided by AT&T, and *Above 890Mc* failed to provide AT&T with reasonable guidance on what it could and could not do or on the limits of the new private-line competition. The FCC's response in TELPAK, however, shows that once it authorized a new service, it would attempt to protect the providers against AT&T. In short, the FCC was being drawn not into support of full and free competition but into a kind of contrived competition in which it protected competitors without any clear rules. For its part, the Justice Department not only condemned AT&T's monopoly but its competitive responses as well, pointing to TELPAK as particularly egregious conduct.

The novel situation created by *Above 890Mc* made AT&T unsure of precisely how to compete. Its attempt to formulate a response to private-line microwave began in 1960, when the Bell system formed a task force called the Broadband Rate Planning Group to determine how it would compete with private-line microwave and, generally, how it would respond to the first *Above 890Mc* decision. The task force's conclusions were expressed in a September 1960 document whose title, "Broadband Report," reflects one of its major concerns. That is, prior to *TELPAK*, AT&T had not provided a tariff offering under which a large customer could order a specific frequency bandwidth (or broadband channel), which could be set aside for all of the customer's voice, facsimile, data, telegraph, and other requirements.[59] The "Broadband Report" concluded that there was a large market for broadband services whose needs were not being met by AT&T and that multichannel use was growing rapidly. The report anticipated that the broadband growth rate would increase as data transmission—then in its infancy—and computer sales expanded. It also anticipated new telecommunications functions to become commercial, such as telewriting, telemetering, control of industrial operations, and voice response. The task force found that AT&T's current multiple-channel rates were not competitive with user-provided microwave costs and that customers would not seek its services in this area unless rates were made competitive. Accordingly, the report urged that the Bell system design a new tariff offering so that it would not lose substantial sales as a result of the *Above 890MC* liberalization.[60] But more controversially, the "Broadband Report" recommended a relatively hard-nosed interconnection policy, which was based on the problems of network reliability and safety that a more liberal policy would cause, as well as on other reasons developed in PUC hearings. Accordingly, the report rejected liberal interconnection.[61]

Internal AT&T approval of the "Broadband Report" 's basic ideas was only the first step in the production of the TELPAK tariff offering. Realizing that the offering would be carefully scrutinized by the FCC, potential users, and others, AT&T prepared an accompanying "Grey Book" that contained an explanation for the filing, detailed cost data, a description of the potential market, rate principles, and rate levels. Armed with the "Grey Book," AT&T officials met with FCC personnel in December 1960 to discuss TELPAK. The "Grey Book," developed with the public's and the FCC's responses in mind, asserted the common carriers' need to offer services at rates competitive with bulk communications privately provided microwave so as not to lose increasingly large amounts of business. However, the book stressed that the rates were compensatory and would not be set so as to impose a burden on residential or small business subscribers whose communications needs were too small to qualify for TELPAK.[62] Thus, AT&T clearly delineated its new tariff offering, the justifications for it, and its relationship to such established principles as universal service and cross-subsidization.

TELPAK A through D was publicly announced in late January 1961. The U.S. Independent Telephone Association (USITA), representing the independent telephone companies, had discussed the tariff with AT&T before the public announcement and had urged the independent telephone companies to join the Bell system in a joint provision of TELPAK. The National Association of Manufacturers' (NAM) radio committee, representing both large and small manufacturing firms, was more skeptical, but not hostile, about the offering. It felt that more study was needed because TELPAK seemed to discriminate against small users. By May 1961, the independent equipment manufacturers, fearing that sales to private microwave users would fall if *TELPAK* proved successful, called for an FCC investigation. Motorola, a leading microwave equipment manufacturer, argued that the *Hush-A-Phone* decision compelled the FCC to require AT&T to adopt a liberal interconnection policy, and that the TELPAK rates were not compensatory. Thus, conflict over TELPAK between AT&T and the independent microwave equipment industry had developed by early 1961.[63] That TELPAK would become an imbroglio was clear when Western Union also filed an objection, claiming that it was at a severe disadvantage because it could not offer voice service. Western Union also charged that instead of applying TELPAK rates to bulk communications needs over dedicated lines, AT&T was offering the rate to selected customers for ordinary private-line channels furnished over diverse facilities between various points. Western Union questioned the underlying cost data that AT&T supplied to justify the tariffs and requested that the FCC undertake a full-scale investigation. AT&T replied that it was

> not our purpose to stifle competition, but to more effectively meet the competition of private microwave systems which the Commission in the Above 890 Megacycle decision made generally available. In that decision, the Commission stated that users should have freedom of choice between common carrier and private microwave service.[64]

Before March 1961 had ended, the FCC told AT&T that TELPAK rates could only apply when a single communications path of specified width was subdivided into channels of lesser width for each customer.[65] AT&T at first resisted the FCC's requirement, declaring that the TEL-PAK tariff described services rendered to customers, not the particular routes or facilities employed to deliver those services. Although objections to the FCC's views were filed by the General Services Administration, the FCC upheld its original construction of *TELPAK*. This would not be the last time that AT&T would be caught in the vise of conflicting government demands. AT&T declared that the FCC's interpretation of *TELPAK* greatly restricted its flexibility. The company felt it was better able than the FCC to determine how to deliver the services offered under TELPAK most efficiently.[66]

Thus, the advent of competition had the effect of dragging the FCC more deeply into the area of company management decision making. The agency now extended its obligations to protecting competitors from the alleged predations of AT&T, which, in turn, exacerbated controversy among the contending interests. Under the new conception of the public interest, the FCC would now be the arbiter of competing interests, especially those seeking to make inroads into AT&T's domain. The Bell system was gradually being thrust into a position in which it was both public service company and competitor, and these contradictory roles would generate controversy that the FCC would be called on to resolve.

The Modified TELPAK Offering

When the FCC turned down AT&T's petition for reconsideration and AT&T filed a modified tariff in August 1961, the situation was still far from resolution. In the new TELPAK tariff, AT&T explicitly sought the right to furnish the service "by whatever facilities the company may find most appropriate."[67] The company explained that it had intended such flexibility from the onset. Needless to say, Western Union and Motorola again requested the FCC to suspend the modified TELPAK tariff. Over AT&T's objections, the FCC suspended the new tariff schedule for three months and ordered a full-scale investigation.[68] The tariff was suspended notwithstanding widespread user support for TELPAK and Motorola's concession (which it later contradicted) that the rates were compensatory to AT&T and no lower than necessary to meet the competition of private microwave systems. The General Services Administration (GSA), the federal government's principal purchasing branch, pointed out that

> in this proceeding not one customer has complained. Not one customer has alleged discrimination or preference; and a wide range of customers has been represented in the multitude of *TELPAK* pleadings . . . that have been filed with the Commission during the past six months.[69]

As the FCC's *TELPAK* hearings proceeded during 1962, there were only two conclusions to which all parties subscribed. First, it was agreed that the private-line market would become increasingly important in the future because of the development of business customers' bulk communications needs, especially in the data field. Second, there would be simultaneous cost reductions in the costs of supplying such needs because of anticipated improvements in communications technologies. Moreover, both trends were expected to accelerate. It is important to note also that in 1962, space communications was in its infancy but the new communications technologies that would develop because of the space program would stimulate additional demand and reduce costs.[70] Because of these factors, AT&T argued that the TELPAK tariff would actually aid subsidy flows toward residential subscribers. Without TELPAK, such revenues would be lost to AT&T; with it, profit and revenues from increased traffic would more than compensate for the lower unit rates.[71]

The FCC issued its tentative decision in March 1964 and its final decision in December of that same year. The Commission largely focused on Section 202 of the Communications Act, which prohibits unjust or unreasonable discrimination in charges or services for like communications services. Nondiscriminatory treatment is a central public service obligation, and the most basic issue raised when discrimination is charged is whether the rate differences can be cost-justified. When competitive considerations are introduced, as they were because of the *Above 890Mc* decisions, the situation becomes more complicated, for competitors are expected to meet the price offerings of their rivals— an intrinsic part of the competitive process. But the inexorable tendency of meeting the moves of one's rivals is to create discriminations within or between classes. In the *Above 890Mc* case, the FCC had failed to consider adequately the ramifications of encouraging competition, yet it had embarked on the road of preserving Bell's competitors by restraining AT&T. Not surprisingly, then, the TELPAK tariffs were rejected. In its tentative decision, the FCC concluded that no evidence was shown to justify *TELPAK* rates relative to other AT&T private-line tariffs. It conceded that

> AT&T's engineering witness made a convincing showing that to require TELPAK to be furnished on a discrete broadband spectrum assignment would disrupt orderly circuit assignments, result in delays serving a customer where special construction might be necessary, require more channel terminal equipment than would otherwise be necessary, bring about unnecessary congestion of terminal facilities, increase the amount of circuit mileage devoted to the service, and complicate the problem of providing satisfactory transmission.[72]

The FCC also acknowledged the widespread user satisfaction with TELPAK service. Nonetheless, taking the narrow stance that the tariff was like other AT&T private-line offerings, the FCC concluded that the discriminatory rates could not be justified. Further, TELPAK A and B— the lower-volume offerings—were held not to be justifiable on grounds of competitive necessity because "rates for the equivalent number of channels offered under ordinary private line tariffs are reasonably competitive with the costs of private microwave systems." While TELPAK C and D were held to be apparently justified "in terms of meeting competition from private microwave systems . . . [the FCC was] unable to determine on the record that the rates . . . are compensatory in relation to the costs of furnishing the services. . . ."[73] The FCC's primary emphasis had shifted subtly from issues of public service—such as the quality of service, progressiveness, rates, and availability—to questions of competition. That AT&T representatives were able to show that the TELPAK rate structure would not adversely affect residential subscribers was not to the FCC an important factor, nor was the overall satisfaction expressed by TELPAK users.[74] The FCC's new position, not yet fully developed nor explicitly articulated, focused almost exclusively on the two firms seeking to compete with AT&T and private microwave—Motorola and Western Union.

The FCC was, thus, embarked on a new path. Much of its subsequent activity through the AT&T breakup would consist of attempts to reconcile the public service conception with competition, which it accepted as a desirable goal. Not surprisingly, a majority of the Commission affirmed its tentative *TELPAK* decision in a memorandum opinion and order of 23 December 1964: the FCC was fully aware "that numerous users of service under the TELPAK tariff have intervened to support the propriety and lawfulness of such tariff. The thrust of their presentation has been that under TELPAK rates they have been able to use more and better quality communications services, thus improving their business methods."[75] Nevertheless, the Commission ordered AT&T to revise its tariffs so to eliminate discrimination between TELPAK A and B and single-channel, private-line rates. The FCC ordered the record reopened on TELPAK C and D to determine whether they were compensatory. At this time, the FCC did not realize how long the *TELPAK* controversy would persist until AT&T would ultimately withdraw the tariffs in 1981. The controversy would be one of the Antitrust Division's major charges against AT&T, as the company's competitive response to private-line competition would be viewed as an abuse of monopoly power.

PRELUDE TO *CARTERFONE*—THE OPPOSITION MOUNTS

The interval between the December 1964 *TELPAK* decision and the FCC's momentous 1968 *Carterfone* decision was a time of dramatic telecommunications development, heralding even greater changes in the

TABLE 5.1

AT&T's Telephone Rates, 1940–1967

Average Price of Service	1940	1953	1967
Local	100	138.7	149.5
Intrastate toll	100	122.5	116.6
Interstate toll	100	83.4	75.7
CPI	100	190.7	238.1

SOURCE: U.S. Department of Labor in Subcommittee on Antitrust and Monopoly, Committee on the Judiciary, *The Industrial Reorganization Act*, Part 6 (Washington, D.C.: Government Printing Office, 1974), p. 3976.

future. Aggregate data during this period document AT&T's continuing progress in all major facets of the telephone industry. The total number of telephones in the country increased from approximately 84.5 million in 1963 to 109.2 million in 1968, and the percentage of households with telephones increased from 81.4 to 88.5 percent during those same years.[76] AT&T's impressive record was associated with price increases (using the year 1940 as a base) that were far lower than the consumer price index (CPI). In the case of interstate long distance, rates had even declined, as Table 5.1 shows. These developments were accompanied by a steady upgrading of technology—indeed, an expanding commitment by Bell Labs. Nevertheless, many big-business communications users magnified their dissatisfactions as general ones. For example, *Business Week* headlined an important 1967 article "Behind the Communications *Mess*" (emphasis added).[77] The "mess" turned out not to be related to any allegations that the Bell system provided poor service to residential or most business subscribers—indeed, the low cost and high quality of such service was not mentioned in the article but simply assumed—but to the intensifying disputes between AT&T, on the one hand, and big-business users and their would-be communications suppliers on the other hand. As we have seen, this pressure was already manifest before 1965, but the trend accelerated thereafter, as *Business Week* observed:

> For the first time, many companies are taking an active interest in which way the regulatory winds are blowing. They want to participate in a huge growth industry. . . . [T]oday companies are finding that FCC regulations and telephone company policies affect a lot more

than their own telephone service. So they are either trooping to Washington or making sure that an industry association is pleading their case for them.[78]

The principal example of user dissatisfaction that *Business Week* provided was a chemical company that unsuccessfully sought to interconnect its computer system into the telephone network.

As computers and computer software applications became more common in American industry, tensions rose between the public service companies and the industrial and commercial enterprises seeking maximum flexibility and control together with their suppliers (for example, IBM). The first FCC computer inquiry that sought to define the boundary lines between computers and telephony was in progress, pitting AT&T against computer firms and big-business users. A new small company called Microwave Communications, Inc. (MCI) petitioned the FCC on 31 December 1963 in regards to its desire to be recognized as a broadband common carrier for business between Chicago and St. Louis. Obviously, many business firms operating in high-traffic, lucrative markets agreed with MCI's position. Yet another major challenge to AT&T's dominance in intercity communications loomed in the form of communications satellites.

AT&T was at this time under attack on many fronts, but all of its rivals shared the common goal of redefining the public interest to allow greater entry in telecommunications. Many episodes in *United States* v. *AT&T* involved AT&T's opposition to these new entrants before the FCC and PUCs, the forums in which these disputes are expected to be resolved.

SPACE COMMUNICATIONS

The unique history of the American space program is responsible for the distinctive economic structure of the communications satellites industry as well as for AT&T's strong, but not dominant, position within it. While the story of satellites began before the Soviet Union's launch of Sputnik I on 4 October 1957, certainly that event had great impact on the ultimate structure of the industry. The United States suffered a serious blow to its prestige in science and technology, which, in turn, led to a strong American commitment under government guidance to space technology. Thus, communications satellites became not just a business; they became intertwined with national prestige and a substantial commitment of government resources. At the very least, patents developed under the government's auspices as well as its exclusive control over satellite launching would inevitably lead to cries of blatant favoritism if only existing common carriers were allowed to deploy communications satellites. Nevertheless, the Eisenhower administration made it clear that it had "achieved communications facilities second to none among the nations of the world. Accordingly, the Government should encourage private enterprise in the establishment and operation of satellite relays for revenue producing purposes."[79] Yet the government's commitment to "private enterprise," a policy endorsed by the Kennedy administration over the objection of several big-business baiters in Congress, did not specify the future structure of the satellite communications industry. It did not address such issues as whether the industry would be dominated by AT&T; if a number of common carriers would jointly operate satellites; or the roles of the aerospace companies and television networks. Moreover, even if government operation of the industry was ruled out, the government could still play a major role by participating in joint ventures.

AT&T's plan for satellite communications was based in part on the argument that public service principles should prevail in telecommunications regardless of the transmission means—satellites, wire, or microwave. Because AT&T anticipated the charge that it sought to monopolize satellite communications, its plan specified that all U.S. international common carriers should have full access to the satellite system and to ownership participation. AT&T's vice-president James Dingman, appearing before a Senate subcommittee on monopoly in August 1961, stated that if firms other than common carriers were included in the ownership or operation of satellite communications, "regulatory complexities" would result.[80] The corporation that was finally formed represented a compromise among the various interests and was far from the type of structure that AT&T sought. The 1962 Communications Satellite Act established the Communications Satellite Corporation (COMSAT), which would operate satellites for international communication. Although communications common carriers could hold stock in the new corporation, their ownership and voting participation was sharply limited: only six of the fifteen directors could be chosen by the carriers and no single carrier could vote for more than three directors. In short, the statute established a structure in which COMSAT would be free of dominance by the existing international common carriers. And, since the suppliers of telecommunications equipment now included aerospace companies, a new carrier's entry into international satellite communications would, in turn, raise the hopes of those seeking to enter domestic satellite communications when technologically feasible.

The successful launch of Hughes Aircraft's *Early Bird* satellite in 1965 led the ABC television network to request the FCC to allow it a private satellite that would link its network. This precipitated the FCC to institute its domestic satellite inquiry to investigate general domestic satellite problems.[81] By 1966, the battle had grown as AT&T opposed privately operated satellites on technical grounds (for instance, interference with microwave facilities) and argued that prohibitive costs limited the system's usefulness. The networks, with the support of the Ford Foundation, argued that a satellite system could relay programs for considerably less cost than what was paid to the public service companies. Since the Ford Foundation expressed no interest in operating a domestic satellite system, AT&T was in the unenviable position of attacking the proposals of an organization that had no financial interest in the outcome.[82] By 1969, AT&T announced that it would end its opposition to the television networks' operation of private satellite systems[83]—but by then, the company was in full-scale retreat on many fronts.

THE SERVICE CRISIS

AT&T's vulnerability during the period between the 1961 *TELPAK* decisions and the 1968 *Carterfone* decision was partly due to the company's own failings. As noted earlier, AT&T had clearly outperformed industrial America in the postwar period through the 1960s. But, as the company readily admitted, its own high standards caused it to experience a service crisis in the late 1960s. It is important to remember that many other great companies in competitive industries have suffered quality declines or other crises, and while some have recovered, others have not. This dynamic is part of a process that the distinguished economist Joseph Schumpeter has called "creative destruction."[84] Thus, AT&T's failings cannot be attributed to its regulated status just as Chrysler's cannot be attributed to its unregulated status. Rather, what matters most, in *economic* terms, is how a company responds—and in this regard, AT&T rectified its problems excellently in the long run. However, in the *political* arena events are often measured in the short run. In this regard, AT&T was forced to defend its short-term performance as it accumulated major rivals in many fields.

Although it is difficult to determine exactly when the AT&T service crisis began, the New York Public Service Commission (PSC) dates it from mid-1967, based on a rapid increase in consumer complaints. Like so many events that are described as "crises," the symptoms existed long before they were fully recognized. But AT&T's 1969 and 1970 *Annual Reports* conceded that the "crisis" existed. The 1970 Report stated: "I assured share owners then [1969] that we were sparing no efforts . . . to make matters right."[85] The company concluded that the convergence of a number of adverse factors contributed to the crisis, including an unforecasted rapid surge of demand for business traffic, a poor switching system, faulty trunk maintenance and administration, inadequate training of maintenance personnel, and poor main distributing frames administration. (For example, since 1893, Bell maintenance employees had left unneeded jumper wires attached to main distributing frames [which connect each customer wire pair to the line terminal in a switching center] with no ill effect, but the growth in traffic caused the weight of the dead jumpers to impede the operation of the main distributing frames.[86]) However, AT&T not only admitted to and rectified the problems, but, as we learned in earlier chapters, it also had to deal with the regulatory commissions' demands for rapid improvement. The New York PSC, for instance, imposed standards of acceptable service on the New York Telephone Company and delineated reporting procedures so that it could monitor the company's progress.[87] In short, the regulated public service company conception worked well, and within a reasonable time period the problems were corrected and service quality attained levels higher than ever before. Only one example of the vast number of improved services initiated after the service crisis is when, in 1971 and 1972, the Bell system introduced a computer-based system (COMAS) that more effectively recorded and correlated ineffective call attempts.[88]

Unfortunately, however, the short-run service crisis occurred at a difficult time for AT&T. The company was under attack from a number of interests: the FCC was conducting a major rate investigation; the *TELPAK* proceedings were under way; data processing and satellite technology presented many new problems (as well as opportunities); and the country itself was sharply divided over American involvement in Vietnam. Some of the antiwar sentiment was directed at defense contractors, such as AT&T, and as a result onslaughts against big business again became popular. President Johnson appointed Nicholas Johnson to the FCC, whose opposition to AT&T culminated in a 1972 statement at the so-called "people's state of the union" that AT&T should be broken up or nationalized.[89] The momentous *Carterfone* decision must be considered within the context of these events.

THE *CARTERFONE* CASE

In April 1967, Benjamin A. Javits, president of United Shareowners of America, recommended that AT&T take over the operation of the U.S. Postal Service: "There is no reason why the postal service shouldn't make money and easily can under skilled and dedicated management such as is available in AT&T."[90] However, Javits's favorable disposition toward AT&T was not representative of the attitude of those active in telecommunications policy-making. At this time, AT&T was defending itself against complaints made by regulators, big-business firms, and big-business baiters, which would ultimately redefine the public interest to permit more liberal entry into every phase of telecommunications except local service. The principal focus of the attack would become the issue of interconnecting subscriber-furnished, customer premises equipment. As early as 1966, the House Small Business Subcommittee on Regulatory Agencies heard testimony from antique telephone dealers complaining of the interconnection restrictions, even though the Bell system and other telephone companies had gone far in accommodating customer demand for antique and decorator telephone housing.[91] However, the problem went far beyond antique and decorator telephones as numerous business interests sought interconnection rights. For example, the large National Retail Merchants Association stated that its inability to interconnect privately owned systems into the public-switched network was a major impediment to its full use of private microwave systems.[92] But AT&T and the other telephone companies felt justified in maintaining interconnection restrictions. Yet the difficulty of supervising CPE worsened because of the postwar proliferation of such devices. Moreover, the FCC's final word on the issue in the *Above 890Mc* (1959) decision approved tariff regulations that limited interconnection,[93] whereas *Hush-A-Phone* was treated as a narrow exception to the general rule.

During the period immediately preceding the FCC's 1968 *Carterfone* decision, state commissions largely upheld the interconnection restrictions. For example, in 1966, the Pennsylvania Commission upheld the interconnection tariff, pointing out the eventual problems of circuit drain and line interference that could otherwise debilitate the network. In the same year, the Wisconsin Commission upheld the interconnection prohibition against a taxicab company's use of an automatic dispatching device, while in 1965, the New Jersey Commission refused to require New Jersey Bell to provide equipment for the interconnection of private emergency alarm systems when the electrical connection might cause interference on the circuit.[94] Thus, prior to the *Carterfone* decision, AT&T and the other telephone companies were provided with a clear decision rule: the interconnection restriction in tariffs would be upheld against devices that might harm any component of the network, *except* if there was widespread public demand for a device and a simple telephone company adjustment could alleviate the safety or quality problem. In 1965, the Hawaii PUC approved such a modification to accommodate the burgeoning interest in antique telephones.[95] Finally, under the rule that the Minnesota Commission announced in a closely argued 1965 decision: "The Hush-A-Phone uses no interconnection at all and the Hush-A-Phone case . . . was not an interconnection case. Neither the FCC nor the court in that case dealt with the interconnection problem."[96]

The Carterfone, the device that changed telecommunications regulation, was invented by Thomas F. Carter in 1959. Carter, who had been involved in two-way radio, office intercoms, and other communications systems since 1946, discovered in the mid-1950s that his customers with two-way radio-equipped vehicles sought to connect with telephone users for various reasons. Reminiscing in 1985, Carter said, "The men in the field decided they wanted to talk directly to the supply house to eliminate third party errors. I started designing a little item that would allow these people to do that."[97] The Carterfone device, which was not offered by the Bell system, permitted direct voice communication between persons using the telephone network and those located at remote mobile radio terminals. When attached to a telephone, the Carterfone allowed communication to take place between the mobile radio user and those using the telephone network without the need for a base station operator to relay messages manually. The instrument worked by having the mobile station base operator place the telephone receiver on a cradle in the Carterfone to effect an inductive and acoustic connection between the telephone line and the mobile radio channel.[98] Not surprisingly, then, the Carterfone met with considerable demand. Carter Electronics's Texas location probably helped bring the device to the attention of oil companies. Although not the only customers of Carter's corporation, they were among the most important and provided strong support during the FCC hearings. Because offshore drilling became an important activity of the petroleum industry during the 1960s,[99] the American Petroleum Institute strongly endorsed the Carterfone's value in this area at the hearings. Yet offshore drilling was only one of many uses that petroleum companies found for the device. Other endorsements for the Carterfone and Carter's position came from utilities, the United States Air Force, the National Aeronautics and Space Agency, the Antitrust Division, the National Retail Merchants Association, and, within the FCC, the Common Carrier Bureau.[100] Thus, the Carterfone benefited from much support.

In a March 1965 letter to FCC Chairman E. William Henry, Carter requested legal clarification of how the interconnection restriction applied to the Carterfone instrument. Told that the restrictions prohibit interconnection "except as specifically provided in the tariffs" and of his right to lodge a formal complaint with the FCC, Carter instead filed a private antitrust suit against AT&T, Southwestern Bell, and General Telephone of the Southwest, charging violations of the Sherman Act. The District Court referred the case to the FCC on the ground that the agency had primary jurisdiction and that the court could not act prior to the FCC's action.[101] Thus, in the fall of 1966, the FCC began its action on the interconnection issues, and on 30 August 1967, the hearing examiner issued an initial decision, finding against AT&T, Southwestern Bell, and General Telephone of the Southwest in almost every particular. However, the FCC hearing examiner considered the view of the National Association of Regulatory and Utility Commissioners (NARUC) that a ruling adverse to the telephone companies would cause an enormous rise in administrative costs to the PUCs and disrupt the carefully constructed rate structures. Further, the Mississippi PSC contended that a liberal interconnection policy would lead to substantial telephone company revenue losses, and state regulators implored the FCC to determine possible adverse economic, safety, and quality impact on a case-by-case basis.[102] Thus, under the view of the state regulators, even if the interconnection restriction was improperly applied to the Carterfone, the long-standing structure of telephone regulation should not be destroyed by changing the prevailing decision rule; that is, the primary issue was not the Carterfone device but the potential breadth of the Carterfone principle. Despite these considerations, however, the hearing examiner found that (1) users (notably, oil companies) were satisfied with the Carterfone, (2) a substantial unfilled demand existed for the device, and (3) it did not impair the safety or quality of the network. However, in consideration of the NARUC's views, the examiner held:

> We here consider only a specific device and the evidence as to what, if any, effect it will have on the system. The issue is limited, and is to be determined on the narrow basis of evidence, not the broad basis of theory.[103]

The examiner also pointed out that the Carterfone put "nothing into the system except the sound of a human voice into the mouthpiece of a handset."[104] Accordingly, the hearing examiner ordered the telephone companies to revise their tariffs only to the extent that they would no longer prohibit the Carterfone device.

In contrast to the moderate decision rule proposed by the hearing examiner, the Commission went much further in its June 1968 decision. Upholding the examiner's factual findings on the Carterfone as the basis for a decision of considerable breadth, the FCC held that there was "no material distinction between a foreign attachment such as the Hush-A-Phone and an interconnection device such as the Carterfone so far as the present problem is concerned."[105] The new rule advanced by the agency held

> that a customer desiring to use an interconnecting device to improve the utility to him of both the telephone system and a private radio system should be able to do so, so long as the interconnection does not adversely affect the telephone company's operations or the telephone system's utility for others.[106]

In spite of numerous earlier decisions upholding—sometimes even requiring—interconnection restrictions, the FCC concluded in *Carterfone* that the AT&T tariff had been unlawful from its inception, in that the company, not the Commission, had filed the tariff. In view of the tariff's unlawfulness, the FCC claimed,

> there would be no point in merely declaring it invalid as applied to the Carterfone and permitting it to continue in operation as to other interconnection devices. This would ... put a clearly improper burden upon the manufacturers and users of other devices.[107]

In short, the FCC encouraged companies to interconnect into the telephone network. Further, the Commission essentially argued that AT&T and the other telephone companies were incapable of supplying the burgeoning needs of modern business communications: "No one entity need provide all interconnection equipment for our telephone system any more than a single source is needed to supply the parts for a space probe."[108] Although the FCC's statement was clearly true, it failed to consider carefully the probable impact of the new rule. As *Business Week* succinctly recognized in 1967, "[t]here are almost 100 million telephones in the U.S. and they comprise a vast market for gadgets."[109] Even though the economy was becoming increasingly dependent on sophisticated communications and AT&T was in the throes of a service crisis, these were not reasons to change established rules. Recall that interconnection of user-supplied CPE was already being permitted when need was shown, telephone companies were unable or unwilling to satisfy need in the quantity or quality desired, and reasonable standards for the product were shown. The FCC ordered the telephone companies to revise their tariffs without considering the enormous expense they would have to expend in discovering, testing, certifying, amending, inspecting, and repairing these devices and other interacting parts of the network. Nor did the FCC consider the possible impact of its decision on residential subscribers, rates, or the universal service goal, or the cumulative impact that *Carterfone* might have in conjunction with other actions such as those involving MCI, private microwave, or satellites. Again, the central issue here was not the Carterfone device, which should have been granted interconnection rights, but the breadth of the FCC's holding in the case.

Petitions for reconsideration of the *Carterfone* decision were filed by AT&T, GTE, USITA, NARUC, and ten state regulatory commissions. Opposition to the reconsideration was filed by the FCC's Common Carrier Bureau, the Antitrust Division, the National Retail Merchants Association, the American Petroleum Institute, and, of course, Carter Electronics. As expected, the FCC's opinion on reconsideration affirmed its prior decision, but the Commission took a major step in its commitment to a new conception of the public interest: it viewed the new liberal entry policy as a spur to the development and deployment of new technologies.[110] Thus, the FCC reiterated its original holding, emphasizing that a device must fill a significant market need and must not impair the telephone system to be approved.[111] It also rejected GTE's contention that the *Carterfone* decision opened the door to customer ownership of telephone handsets on the ground that this issue was not relevant to the case. In brief, on reconsideration the FCC refused to project where the *Carterfone* ruling would lead.

In late August 1968, AT&T announced its revised interconnection tariff regulations. The new liberal provisions permitted the direct electrical connection of customer-provided CPE or other terminal equipment (such as computers) or customer-provided microwave systems to be interfaced with the network subject to several restrictions.[112] The first important restriction specified that some devices (such as computers) would be connected into the telephone network through a telephone company-provided control device. The provision was, of course, an invitation to raise the issue of why only telephone companies would provide these devices. Nevertheless, even before the *Carterfone* decision, AT&T was considering its own liberalization program. For example, in late 1967, Board Chairman H. I. Romnes, speaking before the American Petroleum Institute (then in dispute with AT&T), conceded that "[k]nowledge and skill in communications technology, which used to be found in the communications companies . . . have now spread all over the place. . . . Let us do all we can to arrive at arrangements that will provide for new devices that meet new communication needs."[113]

Another major restriction, which also had potential for dispute, was AT&T's new tariff prohibiting the use of any customer-provided device that interfered with network signalling functions. In the only victory AT&T saw in the *Carterfone* case, a later FCC decision held that a customer may not provide any substitute telephone instruments, poles, loops, or switching equipment for that provided by the telephone company: "Our decision dealt with interconnections and not replacements of any part of the telephone system."[114] Commissioner Johnson, whose opposition to AT&T was detailed earlier, was dissatisfied with AT&T's one victory in the case, calling for a free market in telephone instruments.

Thus, even at this early stage, the battle over whether the *Carterfone* doctrine should be expanded further had begun. The distinction between add-on devices and basic equipment would become more difficult to maintain, especially with the development of sophisticated computer devices in the 1970s. At the same time, the microwave battle was gaining renewed intensity. In general, the decisions raised more disputes than they resolved, and as AT&T lost more and more battles, its rivals increasingly sought to limit the company as much as possible. The continuing disputes over how to define the public interest in telecommunications ultimately led to the question of restructuring AT&T. Two adversaries—MCI and the computer industry—were primarily responsible for furthering the movement toward the breakup and easier entry into the telephone equipment and long-distance markets.

CHAPTER 6

RINGING IN THE NEW:
THE RISE OF MCI

THE AGE OF ANXIETY

The presidency of Richard M. Nixon, from his inauguration in January 1969 until his resignation in August 1974, was a time of repeated crises. The atmosphere in telecommunications policy during this period paralleled that of the nation. *Carterfone* and the other important FCC decisions had not ushered in a period of certainty nor clear policy direction. Rather, as Table 6.1 indicates, they created a time characterized by unprecedented anxiety. The volume of litigation at both the agency (including state PUCs) and federal levels had increased dramatically. Microwave Communications, Inc. (MCI), more than any other firm, group, or institution, was responsible for this instability. Its political maneuverings advanced the disintegration of the old regulated network system, ended the long-distance monopoly, and triggered the Justice Department's 1974 antitrust suit against AT&T. Further, many of the episodes that the Antitrust Division used to interpret AT&T's conduct as monopolistic concerned its relations with MCI.

How MCI gradually changed public policy in telecommunications by portraying its self-interest as the public interest is a critical part of this story—and of the breakup of AT&T. As in the case of CPE, a demand for immediate full-scale competition in long distance would have been rebuffed by the FCC and PUCs. The political dynamic in the case of long distance was similar to and complementary to that in CPE. MCI

TABLE 6.1

Number of Active Antitrust Cases Pending Against AT&T
at Year End, 1960–1982

Year	Number of Cases	Year	Number of Cases	Year	Number of Cases
1960	1	1968	15	1976	47
1961	2	1969	13	1977	50
1962	3	1970	21	1978	54
1963	3	1971	26	1979	50
1964	5	1972	31	1980	51
1965	8	1973	29	1981	60
1966	9	1974	38	1982	59
1967	14	1975	47		

SOURCE: *Antitrust at a Glance* (AT&T Report) (December 15, 1982), in AT&T
Archives.

and others did not at first challenge AT&T's monopoly of long-distance
service; rather, they initially made the reasonable request to be allowed
to serve markets not being served by the Bell system. Although peripheral competition with AT&T might exist, the main thrust of the new
entrants would be to enter new markets. In the 1960s, the extraordinary potential of the computer, particularly in data transmission, provided the principal arguments for the new firms seeking entry. That is,
neither AT&T nor any other single firm could be reasonably expected
to serve fully the enormous markets that would be opened up by data
transmission. Consequently, the public interest demanded that new
specialized firms be permitted to enter carefully delineated segments
of the new markets.

Once MCI and other new firms successfully portrayed themselves as
representing the public interest, the FCC was virtually committed to
their survival. Because it usually takes time for firms in new services
and industries to become profitable, the FCC adopted a protective
stance toward the young firms. In fact, MCI used a political strategy to
exploit the FCC's commitment: be aggressive toward AT&T and the
independent telephone companies. Demand and litigate. In this way,
the FCC and the courts would be further encouraged to preserve MCI.
Forgotten in the particular battles between MCI and other new entrants, on the one hand, and AT&T, on the other, would be the original
reason for MCI's license—to develop new markets innovatively, espe-

cially in data communications—as neither MCI nor its allies would do so.

In contrast, AT&T continued its record of excellent performance. In 1965, an already high 85 percent of households had telephone service; by 1975, the figure had risen to 93 percent. During the same period, the total number of telephones in use (including company, service, and private) had risen from 82 to 130 million. The Bell system accounted for most of the totals as well as the increases,[1] and it achieved these results at high levels of productivity. Even so, the company's critics *theorized*, to the contrary, that the regulated network manager system was not efficient. Yet, according to a study conducted by the Department of Labor, in the period between 1972 and 1977, the Bell system's labor productivity growth exceeded that of all industries but one (hosiery). AT&T's price performance was also found to be exemplary— from 1947 to 1977, the telephone service industry's average price increases were about half that of all other industries combined. Whereas the CPI between 1960 and 1973 increased by 44.4 percent, the residential telephone component of the index increased by only 14.6 percent.[2] Further, from December 1964 to May 1974, the CPI rose 55.6 percent, food prices increased 72.1 percent, housing 56.5 percent, and medical care 67.3 percent, whereas rates for telephone service rose only 18.5 percent.[3] Thus, AT&T's overall economic performance was undoubtedly high. Its technological and scientific progress between 1969 and 1973 were equally impressive, laying the groundwork for future improvement. For example, in 1969, Bell Labs developed (1) the UNIX operating system for minicomputers; (2) the spin-flip RAMAN laser (the first tunable high-power laser in the infrared region); (3) superconducting alloys; and (4) a computer program that produced artificial speech from printed English words and sentences. In the realm of customer services during these years, AT&T had unveiled (1) a telephone that allowed customers to dial emergency numbers (such as 911) without initially depositing a coin; (2) major breakthroughs in dataphone service; (3) the touchtone dial; (4) the 698A Code Com set, which provided communication capability for the deaf and blind through combinations of flashing lamps, vibrating finger pads, and sending keys; (5) conference telephones; and (6) higher capacity PBXs. Comparable progress was made in central office equipment, especially in the realm of data switching. Notable, too, was the Automatic Intercept System (AIS), which told customers how to complete calls that reached nonworking numbers. During the same period, great improvements were even made in such traditional components as cable and connectors.[4] Moreover, AT&T's plans for the future were not limited to short-term goals. The 1971 Bell Labs *Annual Report* described research in areas that would not be fully developed for some time. For example, the report devoted considerable space to the development of fiber optics—a technology that would not come on-line until the late 1970s and early 1980s.[5] In addition, the report described scientific work in such diverse areas as superconductivity, lasers and holograms, glassy metals, radio astronomy, and econometrics.[6]

However, the short-run view was not forgotten. The combination of AT&T's resources and technological effort, coupled with regulatory demands, solved the company's embarrassing service crisis. In 1970, the FCC instituted monthly reporting on AT&T service quality in twenty major cities, and coverage was expanded in 1972 to each of the Bell system's seventy-five administrative areas. The Commission also instituted a comparable system for seven independent telephone companies. Establishing a number of service criteria "bench marks" that constituted good service, the agency defined a "weak spot" as the failure to meet a bench mark in a single area in a single month. On this basis, the number of "weak spots" decreased substantially, from 395 in 1970 to 66 in 1979, and as early as 1974, the number had diminished to 80.[7] In short, AT&T had gone far in correcting the problems of the service crisis within a reasonably short time period, which became clear to the FCC soon after it began its service measurement program. In summary, then, since AT&T made excellent progress in economic, technological, and service areas during the period between the *Carterfone* decision and the Antitrust Division's case, MCI's success can be attributed not to its economic or technological superiority but to political factors.

THE CENTRAL ISSUES

MCI was born at odds with AT&T, and rivalry soon gave way to enmity. As we shall see, MCI's entry into telecommunications challenged the public service principle that had developed and been applied to telephony during the nineteenth and twentieth centuries. According to *Fortune*'s succinct and sympathetic summary, MCI's users would be business firms that had a need for its services, not res.Jential nor most small business subscribers:

> John D. Goeken, . . . the founder and president of a little company called Microwave Communications Inc., . . . contended that he would provide service not offered by the common carriers. He promised wider choice of bandwidths, greater speed, greater flexibility, a guaranteed maximum error rate and prices as much as 94 percent cheaper than AT&T's. While the MCI system will carry voice transmissions, too, its greatest appeal is to those who want to send data or a combination of data and voice messages.[8]

Inevitably, MCI's selection of choice communications customers and the most lucrative routes without an obligation to furnish services to other customers served to raise the issue of creamskimming. According to AT&T's view, MCI could undercut its rates because MCI did not incur AT&T's universal service obligations. A statement prepared for AT&T by Alfred Kahn, William Baumol, and Otto Eckstein—three of the nation's most distinguished economists—argued that

> nationwide rate uniformity and the entry of substantial numbers of competitors are incompatible. . . . The greater the degree of competition, the less the likelihood of Bell's being able to continue uniformity, supplying their sparse routes at their present prices which are relatively low in relation to costs. It will be unable to make up its losses among the denser routes because competition will render that impossible.[9]

This view, above all others, determined AT&T's behavior toward MCI and other alleged "creamskimmers." Further, to AT&T it was the principle that was most significant and not the particular amount "skimmed." At stake was AT&T's commitment to the principle of nationwide rate averaging. In the aggregate, it is unarguably true that each individual instance of creamskimming may not have been by itself a concern, but collectively they could make substantial inroads on AT&T's revenues, raise rates, and retard or even reverse the universal service goal. Similarly, FCC decisions affect not only individual matters but establish principles that act as precedent. As we have seen, the FCC had already allowed major inroads into the regulated network manager system without making clear their boundaries or the new principles they established. For these reasons, AT&T consistently opposed MCI and the other companies whose activities would erode the regulated network manager system.

Obviously, AT&T's behavior reflected its perceived self-interest. But where did the public's interest lie in the MCI-AT&T controversy? Business firms that sought to escape from the system of rate averaging were in favor of the new entrants. But how would this affect residential subscribers? As we examine these issues, charges and countercharges, and the complex details of AT&T's battle with MCI, it is essential not to lose sight of the differing conceptions of the public interest.

THE RISE OF MCI

MCI, or more accurately one of the companies called MCI, began its regulatory life on the last day of 1963 when it filed a Section 214 application with the FCC for authorization to construct and operate a point-to-point microwave common-carrier system among Chicago, St. Louis, and intermediate points. Its proposed service would be both intrastate and interstate. Section 214 requires interstate carriers to obtain from the FCC a certificate that present or future public convenience and necessity will require the construction and operation of the line. Further, the FCC is required to notify the governor or designated state agency in which the construction will take place and to hear complaints about the application, which, in turn, entails a state hearing (usually conducted by the PUC). Section 214 was "designed to prevent *useless duplication* of facilities with consequent higher charges upon the users of the service" [emphasis added].[10]

Thus, to set the stage for one of the most protracted and complex series of events in the recent history of telecommunications policy, the burden of proving the necessity for a new or supplemental service was clearly on MCI. Although the statute presumed that monopoly service was desirable, it was rebuttable. Moreover, MCI had to satisfy not only the FCC but also the Illinois regulators in regard to the intrastate traffic it proposed to carry. A 1968 Illinois Supreme Court decision succinctly stated the state's long-standing rule on competition:

The method of regulating public utilities in Illinois is based upon the theory of regulated monopoly rather than competition. Before one utility is permitted to take the business of another already in the field, it must be shown that the existing one is rendering unsatisfactory service and is unable or unwilling to provide adequate facilities. . . . Where additional or extended service is required in the interest of the public and a utility in the field makes known its willingness and ability to furnish the required service, the commerce commission is not justified in granting a certificate of convenience and necessity to a competing utility until the utility in the field has had an opportunity to demonstrate its ability to give the required service.[11]

Accordingly, MCI argued that its new service was unique and not offered by the Bell system. Its principal selling point was flexibility. MCI's amended application stated that it proposed a microwave system that would provide users with "the bandwidth they wanted and [that they could] increase or decrease these bandwidths at any time to handle any changes in their communication load, or type of equipment."[12] The application also stated that MCI planned to permit (1) channel sharing, in which customers would use the same channel on an agreed-upon basis; and (2) channel splitting, in which customers would use a private line for different purposes at particular times of the day (for example, a channel for voice might be used during daytime hours and one for data during the evening). MCI claimed that for the first time small-demand users would have private-line service available through a common carrier and that the rates along the Chicago–St. Louis route would be substantially lower than those offered by Bell.[13]

In February 1964, AT&T and Illinois Bell petitioned the FCC to deny MCI's application. Later they were joined by GTE's Illinois subsidiary and Western Union. AT&T claimed that (1) it and the other common carriers had fulfilled every public need for which MCI had applied; (2) MCI's proposal was an attempt to attract only a more profitable segment of the total communications market—a creamskimming arrangement that would impose an economic burden on other Bell customers; (3) MCI had not shown a need for the proposed service; and (4) MCI had not sufficiently shown the investment that would be required, in that the costs of several necessary features of the system had not been documented. Finally, AT&T alleged that the MCI system was of questionable adequacy and reliability because each subscriber would be required to make its own interconnection with MCI and because there were no provisions for an alternate power supply or routing.[14] Further, Illinois Bell claimed that it "is and for several years past has been ready, willing and able to render any and all of the common carrier communication services proposed to be offered by the applicant."[15] Thus, in keeping with the long-standing principle described earlier, even if a need for MCI's proposed services could be shown, the existing common carriers should be granted priority to render the services. In addition, Illinois Bell disputed MCI's contention that the Illinois Commerce Commission had no jurisdiction over the matter. MCI, further, had not filed its Illinois intrastate rates with the Illinois Commerce Commission. Of these many arguments, the Bell system's most compelling was that of creamskimming. The Bell system's actual cost of voice-grade, private-line service on the Chicago–St. Louis route was below MCI's rates. Thus, only AT&T's rate averaging allowed MCI to creamskim [16]

Although it was in AT&T's interests to delay the proceedings as long as possible, most of the delay that followed until the FCC's August 1969 decision is attributable to MCI. On 10 May 1964, MCI filed amendments to the pending FCC application, modifying its list of shareholders and providing additional financial information. Next, the FCC informed MCI in August 1964 that the company had not obtained the necessary authorizations from the Illinois Commerce Commission, giving it 30 days to do so. At MCI's request, the time was extended to 6 November 1964. MCI argued before the Illinois Commerce Commission that it was not subject to state jurisdiction; Illinois Bell contested the argument. Then, because the Illinois Commission had not granted MCI authorization to operate by 27 November 1964, the FCC returned MCI's applications without prejudice to refile. Meanwhile, the Illinois Commission was holding hearings on MCI's applications. The events of 1964 came to a close with MCI's petition to the FCC for reconsideration of its order, again on the ground that the Illinois Commission had no jurisdiction over the matter.[17] But because the Illinois Commerce Commission had not yet concluded its deliberations, the FCC agreed to reinstate MCI's application with the proviso that it could not act on the intrastate aspects of MCI's proposed service until the Illinois Commission concluded its deliberations. Then, in June 1965, MCI again amended its original applications, limiting them to interstate telecommunications. The common carriers again filed petitions for denial on the substantive grounds discussed earlier as well as on jurisdictional issues. On 11 October 1965, the FCC requested that MCI file additional amendments to its applications, which it did in mid-December. Hence, from the original December 1963 filing until the beginning of 1966, MCI had formally amended its original filing three times.[18]

In some respects, the delay, largely due to MCI's filing deficiencies, played into AT&T's hands. Most obviously, AT&T was then in business; MCI was not. But in another more subtle respect the delay played into MCI's hands, for it was obvious to attorneys and others conversant with the government-business interface in telecommunications that changes in the direction of open entry were occurring. Therefore, the longer MCI would be able to hold on, the more likely it was that the company would be a beneficiary of sweeping changes. For example, in October 1965, at the request of the American Petroleum Institute's (API) Central Committee on Communication Facilities, the FCC announced that it would change its rules to allow a wide variety of joint or shared installations and operations of private-line arrangements previously barred by the agency. In early 1966, the long-time battle over liberalization of private microwave erupted, pitting a diverse group that included the API, truck and bus lines, and press services against AT&T.[19] Virtually every major FCC decision, as we have seen, had been decided against AT&T in the 1960s.

On 2 February 1966, the FCC designated MCI's applications for a hearing. But on 28 February 1966, MCI made yet a further legal move: it asked the FCC to delete from the forthcoming hearing issues relating to such matters as the need for and public benefit of its service, whether its service would be duplicative, and the financial aspects of its applications. MCI was well aware that AT&T and the other common carriers would fight these contentions. Then, making the legal situation even more complex, MCI filed a petition for reconsideration of the FCC's order designating its applications for a hearing on 10 March 1966. MCI now argued that its applications should be granted without a hearing! The Bell system, needless to say, joined issue on this petition as well. On May 10, an FCC Review Board denied MCI's motion to delete the issues noted earlier, and on May 18, MCI filed a petition for Commission review of the Review Board's decision. Then, on 31 May 1966, the FCC advanced the matter considerably, denying MCI's petition for reconsideration of the order designating the hearing as well as the petition to delete relevant issues from the hearing.[20] Even the FCC's Common Carrier Bureau, which in most instances was not an AT&T ally, opposed MCI's petition to delete relevant issues.[21]

Inevitably, then, the hearings took place before an examiner from February through April 1967. Important to events that would lead to a later controversy between MCI and AT&T, MCI's president John D. Goeken stated that he had told potential subscribers that MCI would attempt to interconnect with AT&T and the other carriers, but if the common carriers would not agree to interconnection, it would be the subscribers' responsibility to work out their own interconnection.[22] In brief, MCI essentially led the hearing examiner to conceive of its proposed service as entirely private line. While MCI would try to accommodate customers and go through Bell-system switches to enlarge its own network, this was not a central part of its offering. The Common Carrier Bureau, while conceding that serious questions had been raised about MCI's technical and other qualifications, urged the hearing examiner to give the company a chance to show whether it could succeed. The Bureau argued that

> there are communications requirements of the public that are not being met under present tariff offerings and that sub-markets exist today which are not being fully exploited by the existing carriers. Although MCI's tariff offering would be similar to certain present offerings in many respects, it would offer greater flexibility and control to the subscriber.[23]

The Bureau avoided the creamskimming issue by urging that the MCI application be treated as a single situation rather than an open invitation to others. Accordingly, it concluded that MCI's activities would not deprive the Bell system of significant revenues: "Widespread extension of MCI's operations might, of course, have such consequences. . . . Whether such competition will be destructive or antithetical to the public interest cannot be definitively assessed at this time. Experience with MCI's initial operations should provide meaningful data in this regard."[24] Although the Bureau described MCI's activities as "competition," it also adopted the inconsistent position that MCI was developing new markets not served by the existing carriers. It also did not explain why new entrants rather than existing carriers should provide novel services, especially when the structure of rate averaging was at stake. AT&T, for example, in its reply to the FCC's Common Carrier Bureau, noted that it and the other common carriers had followed the long-standing practice of offering the same private-line rates based on mileage for high- and low-traffic density and low- and high-cost routes.[25]

MCI ENTERS THE MARKET

Hearing Examiner Herbert Sharfman's October 1967 initial decision recommended the approval of MCI's applications for point-to-point service among Chicago, St. Louis, and nine intermediate points—the first of many MCI victories. Clearly sympathetic to MCI, Sharfman's decision was a plea to give the newcomer a chance.[26] The difficulties in setting up the MCI service would be substantial, in that subscribers or MCI would have to make arrangements to interconnect into the telephone network for complete end-to-end service. In short, MCI was then seen exclusively as a private-line service.

However, even within this framework MCI's offerings were not considered novel, as the hearing examiner reported:

> In recent years the Bell System Cos. have increased the variety and combination of services offered. Alternate use of private-line services has been provided, as well as switched private-line networks, arrangements whereby voice grade data channels can be subdivided by customers with their own equipment and other innovations designed to accommodate customer requirements. In the first 9 months of 1966, approximately 125 requests for variations in interstate private-line services were met. Many of these required tariff revisions, which were made.[27]

The examiner also found that all but one of the prospective MCI subscribers who testified at the hearings were using their own private-line or common carrier services and were satisfied with the provision of those services. Indeed, MCI's witnesses acknowledged that "MCI does not offer any services that the existing carriers do not."[28] But the examiner asserted that MCI could offer lower rates for two reasons. First, unlike AT&T, MCI would not engage in rate averaging, in which more costly-to-serve routes would receive subsidy flows from the less costly ones to serve higher-traffic density routes, such as Chicago–St. Louis. Second, MCI proposed lowering quality well below that of AT&T's; in the examiner's words: "The sites are small; the architecture of the huts is late Sears-Roebuck toolshed, and they are without the amenities to which Bell employees . . . are accustomed; and servicing and maintenance are almost improvisational. . . ."[29] Nevertheless, the system would work and no further exploration of the implications of a quality decline—whether it could become widespread, for example—was made. Quality decline, creamskimming, and other issues were scrupulously ignored.

In many ways, Hearing Examiner Sharfman's initial decision set the tone for many of the succeeding MCI matters. That MCI provided something called "competition" was the overriding consideration, but the nature of that competition and the costs associated with it were largely ignored. Yet from the outset of MCI's existence, these critical issues should have been raised. Competition is much more than two or more firms seeking the same customer. MCI has frequently boasted that its offerings involved new and innovative services,[30] but its claims meant only rate advantages gained from a combination of creamskimming and lower-quality furnishings of the traditional components used in microwave relaying. The competition that lies at the heart of a capitalist system's progressiveness is different than that MCI sought to provide. Economist Joseph Schumpeter was the first to spell out the most valuable contribution of competition: it is not incremental price competition "which counts but the competition from the new commodity, the new technology, the new source of supply, the new type of organization . . . that in the long run expands output and brings down prices. . . ."[31] Conversely, without the spur of competition, AT&T was one of the world's most innovative firms. In 1967 alone, for example, AT&T announced the development of LSA diodes, the use of aluminum conductor cable in place of copper, a new laser knife for use in surgery, and an improved electronically controlled page printer.[32] The point is not to denigrate MCI but simply to place in perspective the relatively modest contributions that the new firm made then and even later. The competition MCI brought into the marketplace was not of the kind Schumpeter described as the most valuable.

MCI's appeal to the Commission took place in 1968, shortly after the Commission had heard the *Carterfone* appeal. Although Commissioner Nicholas Johnson questioned the principle of rate averaging, MCI's attorney Michael Bader conceded its equity. Bader proposed that MCI sought to do something that the existing common carriers were not undertaking, but AT&T's general attorney George Ashley counterargued that MCI's only significant contribution would be to offer rates lower over a high-volume route with favorable terrain than AT&T's nationwide average rates for the same distance. Therefore, the hearing examiner's proposal that MCI should be given a chance to "prove itself" would only prove that it could creamskim over a highly favorable route.[33] In late 1968, rumors began circulating that the FCC was deeply split over the MCI application, which was believed to be the major cause of the agency's delay in rendering a decision.[34] During this period, William McGowan joined MCI, even though he had no previous experience in telecommunications. However, he was an expert in finance, an area in which MCI needed help. Like most experts in financial deals, McGowan had to work closely with lawyers, and it was from one of his lawyer contacts that McGowan met MCI's John Goeken. In August 1968, while the FCC was deciding the MCI case, McGowan and colleagues established a new company—Microwave Communications of America (Micom)—that would function to sponsor prospective MCI-operating companies in other markets. Further, McGowan, Goeken, and Micom would each receive 25 percent of the shares of each operating company and the remaining shares would be divided among private investors.[35]

While the FCC's decision was pending, it became clear that should MCI's application be approved it would also apply for others in lucrative markets who would then seek similar operating rights. For example, in December 1968, Interdata Communications, Inc. (which had ties with MCI) filed an application with the FCC for a microwave system among New York, Philadelphia, Washington, and intermediate points.[36] Knowing this would be the inevitable response, the FCC should have treated the MCI application as one that would open the door to competition in many selected lucrative markets. From AT&T's perspective, the prospect of many new private-line competitors together with new equipment competitors required it to undertake responsive action. The first response in AT&T's competitive strategy was the Series 11000 tariff offering, which was a result of AT&T cancelling its private line *TELPAK* A and B rates in January 1967. Recall that, in December 1964, the FCC had declared that *TELPAK* A and B, designed for small-volume bulk users, was not justified in terms of competitive necessity. The FCC ruled that AT&T's ordinary private-line rates were competitive with private microwave. Now that MCI proposed that the unique aspect of its offerings would be that small users could share private microwave, the situation had changed. As an outgrowth of this and prior proceedings and conferences, AT&T introduced Series 11000 in March 1969, to become effective in July but later postponed until November.[37] The tariff offering proposed use during an experimental 3-year period in densely populated portions of midwestern and eastern states. It consisted of discrete high-capacity channels that would be dedicated to the customer's exclusive use 24 hours a day. Series 11000 would also permit a customer to designate others as joint users, and each user would be billed separately based on use and allocation instructions. According to an internal document prepared in late 1968 by AT&T's marketing director for Private Lines Services Planning, the Series 11000 offering was experimental, would probably develop slowly, and "most likely . . . might develop primarily among small users to take advantage of the joint user provisions."[38] Although Series 11000 was discontinued in 1972 because it did not meet sales projections, its anticipated introduction while the Commission's MCI decision was pending made clear MCI's peculiar views on competition. MCI sought outright rejection or suspension of the tariff (even though it was priced well above cost) on the basis that telephone companies should not be allowed to depart from rate-averaging principles in individual competitive services. In spite of detailed Bell data that showed Series 11000 rates were priced about 20 percent above costs, MCI also charged that AT&T's offering was based on noncompensatory rates.[39] Thus, MCI's views on competition as well as a major component of its strategy were revealed in the Series 11000 episode; that is, competition meant that AT&T should not be permitted to provide offerings that conflicted with MCI's, even if AT&T's rates were fully compensatory. MCI claimed that it could provide its "unique" private-line service if AT&T did not offer competitive services. To achieve this result, MCI had to persuade the FCC that the Communications Act should be interpreted as adopting this version of competition. Under McGowan's leadership, MCI adopted a political-legal strategy; as an admirer of McGowan admitted, "McGowan spent the summer and fall of 1968 lobbying the government to grant MCI's license for Chicago to St. Louis. That consisted mainly of talking with people at the FCC and Congress."[40] This strategy would consist first of gaining legislative sympathy and publicity through congressional hearings aimed at AT&T. Since this was a time characterized by anti-big-business sentiment, it was not difficult for MCI to find influential legislators who were sympathetic to small companies seeking to compete against the world's largest firm. The other important MCI political strategy was to persist in litigation. As the Series 11000 matter indicated, MCI would intervene in all possible FCC proceedings against AT&T. And, as we will see later, it would use the courts directly and indirectly by prodding the Justice Department to bring its suit against AT&T. In short, the most basic MCI strategy was to keep AT&T on the defensive.

Never a technological leader like its rival AT&T, MCI would become the quintessential political entrepreneur, remarkably successful in the political-legal arena. Ignored in the battle were the interests of residential subscribers and of telephone companies far smaller than MCI. Ignored also were the comments of those like Walter Karnopp, manager and owner of the small Eastern Oregon Telephone Company, who charged that the MCI proposal was an "invitation to disaster." He claimed that the telephone industry could not lose "the high usage toll routes without destroying the entire average ratemaking structures that have enabled the industry to bring subsidized exchange service to many millions who would otherwise be unable to afford a telephone."[41] Thus, the delicate structure of public service was in jeopardy, yet the FCC would not listen.

THE FCC'S MCI DECISION

On 13 August 1969, in a 4–3 decision, the FCC granted MCI's Chicago–St. Louis application. The agency limited service to "transmissions between MCI's microwave sites making it incumbent upon each subscriber to supply his own communications link between MCI's sites and his place of business (loop service)."[42] The FCC claimed that MCI's principal market would consist of subscribers willing to sacrifice quality for cost saving: "while no new technology is involved in MCI's proposal, it does present a concept of common carrier microwave offerings which differs from those of the established carriers."[43] The Commission responded to the creamskimming argument largely by ignoring the precedential aspect of the case and the encouragement it would give others to provide "novel" services; rather, it claimed that:

> MCI is offering a service intended primarily for inter-plant and inter-office communications with unique and specialized characteristics. In these circumstances we cannot perceive how a grant of the autho-

rizations requested would pose any threat to the established carriers' price averaging policies.[44]

To have recognized the precedent it set, the FCC would have had to consider creamskimming as a principle as well as under what circumstances AT&T could compete with the new carriers. Indeed, it would have had to consider why a new carrier rather than an existing one—which could incorporate the new service into its rate-averaging principles—should provide the "novel" service.

An equally vexing problem that the FCC faced in its decision was the interconnection issue. As the preceding quotations make clear, the MCI service was expected to be outside the public-switched network. Nevertheless, few if any users of the service would attempt to make their own interconnection arrangements. Because the FCC suspected that the common carriers would be intransigent about providing interconnection, it retained its jurisdiction in the matter so to assure that MCI could conduct its activities, obtain customers, and remain confident of interconnection. Only if the carriers could prove interconnection infeasible would they be excused from providing interconnection into local-loop service. It should be noted that the FCC did not interpret interconnection as a substitute long-distance service; rather, if, for example, company A became an MCI customer, it would be able to establish communication between its branches in St. Louis and Chicago, but its St. Louis branch would not be able to communicate with company B in Chicago. Thus, the FCC majority concluded that:

> This is a very close case and one which presents exceptionally difficult questions. . . . We wish to make clear . . . that the findings and conclusions reached herein apply only to the frequencies specified, and for the areas described, in the applications now pending before us.[45]

Commissioner Nicholas Johnson interpreted the MCI decision in a more general way: "I am still looking, at this juncture, for ways to add a little salt and pepper of competition to the rather tasteless stew of regulatory protection that this Commission and Bell have cooked up."[46] The dissenting opinion of Chairman Rosel H. Hyde focused more on the principles involved than on the particular facts of the MCI Chicago–St. Louis application. In this connection, it is notable that almost immediately after the decision MCI announced its plans for a similar Chicago–New York microwave link.[47] Hyde pointed out that the public interest, not competition, was the FCC's standard, and that the Supreme Court explicitly directed the agency to avoid a standard of competition.[48] In this view, if a new innovation such as domestic satellites best serves the public interest through competition, it should be favored, but if competition is unnecessary, redundant, unproved, or inefficient, it should be avoided. Hyde also noted that MCI's proposal entailed a grossly inefficient use of the spectrum:

> The decision would authorize the use of a microwave frequency in one of the most critical bands for the benefit of at most 204 private line customers, according to the applicant's own marketing consultants. The same frequency could ordinarily be used to derive thousands of circuits, predominantly used for the benefit of the ordinary long distance message toll user.[49]

According to Hyde, the FCC majority was able to condone this violation of the spectrum economy principle because of its lower cost operation, but MCI was able to charge the lower rate because it engaged in creamskimming. If AT&T had not adopted the rate-averaging principle, its rates on the Chicago–St. Louis route would have been lower than MCI's. Hyde thus concluded that AT&T and the other extant carriers would be constrained to meet the competition of MCI and other successful applicants. The inexorable effect of the FCC's majority conclusion would be to destroy the *principle* of nationwide rate averaging. Commissioner Robert E. Lee's separate dissent pointed out that MCI's proposal clinched the creamskimming argument, in that the company did not propose to serve the sparsely settled areas between Chicago and St. Louis but the more lucrative points.[50]

In September 1969, the Bell system companies, Western Union, and GTE filed petitions for reconsideration. Their principal argument was again based on the rate-averaging principle, claiming that no carrier should be exempt from it. MCI rebutted, arguing that it should not be bound by the rate-averaging principle because it was not offering a public-switched telephone service.[51] However, the FCC turned down the petitions in January 1970, reiterating its prior findings and earlier arguments.[52] Of course, this did not end the AT&T-MCI controversy nor did it address the unanswered questions concerning competition, creamskimming, and the like. Rather, it opened the door to increased litigation as a result cf the agency's failure to provide clear decision rules. For MCI's limited view of competition applied not only to AT&T

but to other firms as well. For example, in December 1969, MCI counsel Michael Bader affirmed the company's opposition to applications
made by New York–Penn Microwave Corporation proposing a system
directly competitive with MCI–New York West's. In response, Bader
outlined plans for an interconnected 11,000-mile route system through
40 states operated by 16 regional affiliates.[53] Hence, even as the FCC
was evaluating the effects of the Chicago–St. Louis system, MCI had
even more ambitious plans for the future.

THE SPECIALIZED COMMON CARRIERS (SCC)
INVESTIGATION

An important Justice Department claim in the 1974 suit was that AT&T
used the regulatory process as a vehicle for self-serving dilatory tactics
intended to prevent MCI from operating. The Specialized Common
Carriers (SCC) proceeding was one of the critical ones that influenced
the Justice Department's charge.

Predictably, MCI's success before the FCC encouraged others to seek
entrance into different forms of long-distance transmission, particularly
in the most lucrative markets. By the mid-1970s, the applicants included, among others, (1) Data Transmission Company (DATRAN),
which sought authority to construct and operate a 35-city digital transmission network limited to data; (2) Southern Pacific Communications
Corporation, a subsidiary of Southern Pacific Company, which owned a
large private microwave system; (3) seventeen other companies affiliated with MCI; and (4) several miscellaneous common carriers (MCCs)
whose function was to provide limited video transmission service.[54] The
Bell system, Western Union, GTE companies, and Rochester Telephone
pointed out that the MCI Chicago–St. Louis route was no longer an
isolated experiment. In opposing these applications, the public service
companies focused on the impact of applications limited to high-
density routes on their rate structures. They argued that they were
better able to provide higher-capacity and lower-cost facilities, contended that the applicants would interfere with common carrier radio
transmission, and urged that the grants would lead to wasteful use of

scarce radio resources.[55] Most importantly, however, the existing carriers pointed to the underlying rationale of Section 214 of the Communications Act, which, as we saw earlier, sought to prevent useless duplication of facilities with consequent higher charges. At the very least, they argued, the FCC should have sought to determine whether the existing carriers or newcomers could more efficiently bring novel services to consumers. Again, under Section 201, the FCC could have ordered the existing carriers to provide necessary or desirable services, but if the existing carriers were unable or unwilling to do so, a licensing procedure for new carriers could have been instituted. Ironically, the new applicants offered little in the way of innovation in comparison with Bell.

During 1970, the year in which the FCC launched its Specialized Common Carriers (SCC) investigation, AT&T announced, for example, the creation of charge-coupled devices that could be used for logic and memory functions in computers; a semiconductor laser that could for the first time be operated continuously at room temperatures; and the F spec credit-card dialer that allowed businesses to obtain customers' credit data by inserting a perforated credit card into the telephone. AT&T continued its average record of one patent a day since 1925.[56] At the same time, the FCC's dealings with MCI were influencing the agency's changing conception of the public interest; MCI's minor advantages became to the FCC instances of "innovation" and its conception of competition—in which new entrants were protected from older ones—would soon become the FCC's as well. However, by June 1970, it was apparent that the FCC's MCI decision had caused havoc in the industry. Consider, for instance, the West Coast microwave situation alone. In addition to MCI Pacific Coast, five other firms had applied for microwave licenses, which, of course, MCI opposed. The established public service companies opposed all of the applications and were joined by the California Farm Bureau Federation, which feared that the FCC's actions would destroy the rate-averaging principle that benefited agricultural areas. Finally, a microwave relay company for television operators also opposed the applications.[57] Since the same sort of result could occur in other significant markets, it was clear that the FCC had to develop some general principles; that is, the agency could no longer claim that it was dealing only with a Chicago–St. Louis experiment.

Thus, on 17 July 1970, the FCC instituted Docket no. 18920—the Specialized Common Carrier (SCC) inquiry. The issues to be considered included (1) whether as a general policy SCCs should be permitted; (2) whether comparative hearings among the applicants are necessary; (3) technical problems; (4) service quality and reliability; and (5) the appropriate means of local distribution of the SCC service.[58] The Common Carrier Bureau argued that competition directed toward the development of new communications services, markets, and technologies was in order. It urged that the new firms would expand the size of the communications market, not draw customers from the established carriers. With this theoretical framework, the Bureau rejected the creamskimming argument, claiming that a tariff proceeding, rather than one concerned with the basic authorization of services, was the appropriate forum to argue creamskimming.[59] More importantly, however, was the Bureau's discussion of the competition that the SCC's were expected to provide. It is clear from the FCC and Bureau staff discussion that MCI and the other SCCs were not expected to provide full-scale competition in message toll service—a status some of them eventually attained.

MCI conceded that its market was not the public-switched network, claiming that there is "a distinct difference between a public telephone service which is a natural monopoly and a customized communications service offered on a private point-to-point basis."[60] This distinction was critical in the FCC's approval of MCI's offering. In other words, if MCI had then advanced that it wanted to construct and operate a rival long-distance network (which it conceded to be a natural monopoly), the proposal would have been flatly rejected by the FCC. Instead, it delineated a market that was private "point-to-point." MCI's conception of point-to-point communications was taken from the way in which railroads employed private communications along their lines. A railroad could only communicate with certain points along its designated path and only the railroad was involved in using those facilities, which were not in the public-switched network. And just as the private point-to-point service would be excluded from the public-switched network, so also would the public-switched network be excluded from the private point-to-point service.[61] However, there were exceptions in which a private point-to-point service could interconnect into the public-switched network. As the FCC undertook the SCC decision, the railroad private-line services provided the model for exceptions. Private lines, with AT&T's permission, could interconnect into the public-switched network for designated reasons, such as emergencies involving safety of life or property.[62] For example, a railroad employee might connect into the public-switched network to call a hospital, but he or she could not call a friend 250 miles away to engage in social conversation. The latter use would be alternative long distance, competitive with public service long distance, whereas the former would be a carefully pre-planned exception fashioned to the particular need of the company controlling the private line. As we examine MCI's broadening claims, it is important to bear these conceptions in mind.

The Bell system apparently suspected almost from the outset of the SCC hearings that MCI had plans that included much more than private-line operation. Commenting in 1970 on yet another MCI-proposed modification of the Chicago–St. Louis link, AT&T noted "the adverse impact which MCI's drastically altered proposed market may have on the interstate switched network through *diversions of toll business*" [emphasis added].[63] In the SCC hearings, other public service companies shared AT&T's views and reiterated many arguments made in prior hearings. Opposing them were the proposed SCCs, user groups, and equipment manufacturers who reiterated their charges that common carrier services were too costly and excluded potential private-line users, and that competition would lead to innovation, lower charges, and other benefits.[64]

In late May 1971, the FCC issued its "First Report and Order" in the SCC inquiry. The Commission, without dissent (but with one concurring opinion, principally on the ground that a 3-year moratorium on new applications should be instituted), opted for free entry in the services that the SCCs would provide. The lengthy decision accepted virtually all of the Bureau's analysis and added much of its own. Those who had expected a strict party vote (which had occurred in the MCI matter) were surprised at the unanimity in favor of competition. But the Nixon administration had made its predisposition toward open competition known in the prior year in its comments on domestic satellites.[65] In brief, the regulated network manager system was left with few defenders within the community of those who influenced communications policy. As is made evident in the decision, the FCC became favorably disposed to SCC licensing because it believed AT&T and the other common carriers would not be able to handle the enormously expanding market in data communications. In view of its conclusion, which stemmed primarily from the computer inquiry, the FCC had no difficulty in its decision to allow new carriers to operate in that market.

Because the voice market—Bell's dominant source of income—was also expected to grow at a rapid rate, the new entrants in the data-communications market would not engage in creamskimming. One cannot emphasize enough how important it was to the SCC decision that the SCCs were viewed as market expanders and not principally as competitors of AT&T's long-distance, local-loop, or other services. The SCCs would only compete at marginal points with AT&T. Indeed, the necessary tenor of the entire decision was that if the SCCs competed with AT&T in the Bell system's major markets, they would not be needed.[66]

Consider, for example, how the FCC justified competition in contrast to Section 214's injunction against wasteful competition and uneconomic duplication. Although the agency agreed that these factors must be considered, it contended that there was more to consider in regard to the public interest. Rejecting the common carriers' view that the FCC should not permit new entry except if the existing carriers were unable to provide proposed new services, the agency claimed that it could authorize new entrants even if it was unsure of the existing carriers' ability to provide new services. The FCC believed the Bell system would have its hands full keeping up with the "rapidly expanding growth in local and interstate use of the standard voice communications services of the Bell system—*services which the applicants do not seek to provide*" [emphasis added].[67] Further, the agency reiterated:

> While there may be some overlap between the services proposed by the applicants and the present offerings of the established carriers, we find sufficient warrant for the staff's conclusion that the applicants are seeking primarily to develop new services and markets, as well to tap latent, but undeveloped, submarkets for existing services so that the effect of new entry may well be to expand the size of the total communications markets.[68]

For the same reason, the FCC swept aside the charge of creamskimming without examining the evidence. It argued that the SCCs would not make significant inroads on the Bell system because they would largely be serving new and expanding data markets.

From the FCC's comments we can construct its conception of an SCC (which MCI has not resembled). The two principal applicants that the FCC had in mind were DATRAN and MCI. DATRAN proposed a switched, all-digital private network devoted exclusively to data transmission, and it sought to provide local distribution as well as the inter-city facilities. As such, DATRAN would operate outside the public-switched network and be entirely digital (unlike AT&T). MCI proposed only point-to-point private-line services that included data and voice. In both cases, the applicants indicated that they would be serving markets different than those served by AT&T. According to MCI, it would "be serving different markets from those now served by existing carriers, primarily new submarkets of the dramatically expanding data communications market."[69] Thus, it follows that an SCC would be unwarranted in providing a service already provided in a significant way by the existing carriers. The SCCs could not simply invent a new name to provide a service that AT&T already covered. The existing carriers were ordered to permit interconnection to allow the SCCs to provide end-to-end service for their private-line or private network customers. Or, the SCCs could construct their own local distribution systems. However, it was clear from the FCC's brief discussion of interconnection that it intended to assure that the existing carriers would not prevent the operation of the SCC's private system by arbitrary or unreasonable interconnection restrictions. The decision clearly would not justify an SCC's claim to interconnect into AT&T's public switched network that had been constructed and improved for almost a century, and use it to compete head on with AT&T. This was obviously AT&T's assessment of the matter. If AT&T then felt that it faced a head-on confrontation with MCI, it almost certainly would have appealed to a court. And although AT&T issued an optimistic statement after the SCC decision, the decision would not solve the MCI-AT&T controversy.

THE MCI-AT&T DISPUTE INTENSIFIES

To evaluate the events that led to MCI's 1974 private antitrust suit against AT&T as well as the Antitrust Division's coordinated action, we must first understand what the SCC decision meant to a reasonable observer of telecommunications policy at the time. We must ask such questions as, was AT&T engaging in predatory tactics to drive MCI and the other SCCs out of business? Or was MCI, with the connivance of the

FCC (especially that of its Common Carrier Bureau), gradually enlarging beyond reasonable limits the scope of the SCC decision, because MCI and the other SCCs could not effectively compete under the original guidelines?

The issues concerning permissible services, rates, and interconnection rights aggravated an already heated situation. And, as we have seen, the FCC's conception of competition in the SCC decision was narrow. The SCCs were not expected to compete directly against AT&T in the principal markets in which AT&T was engaged; rather, they were expected to enlarge the market by developing submarkets that AT&T had either not or insufficiently exploited. The SCC decision further emphasized that these markets were principally in the data field. And MCI, although it amended its applications on several occasions, did not change its fundamental conception first outlined in 1967: that it did "not propose a message toll or exchange telephone service. . . . Rather, it will offer a service to business and other concerns . . . for inter-plant and interoffice communications."[70] Thus, at the time of the decision, a reasonable observer could assume several rules: that (1) the SCCs could not compete with AT&T in a public-switched network; (2) the SCCs could not compete against AT&T in private line or other services in which AT&T had an established position at the time of the SCC decision; (3) the SCCs could compete in private point-to-point or private network service (such as DATRAN's proposal) if AT&T either did not occupy the submarket or did so only marginally; and (4) AT&T could compete with the SCCs (which, in turn, could compete with each other) within the new submarkets. Based on this reasonable understanding of the SCC decision, AT&T was not displeased and saw no need to appeal, stressing that it might depart from rate averaging and instead price directly competitive services. Western Union, too, welcomed the new pricing flexibility. The FCC had trumpeted the importance of the decision as well as how critical the undertaking would be to the expanding data field—indeed, to the very well-being of the United States.

If the SCC movement showed signs of foundering on the basis of the submarkets they had carved out, their natural inclination, of course, would be to expand into AT&T's older, more traditional markets. Accordingly, it was predictable that the FCC (and, especially, the Common Carrier Bureau) would enlarge the decision well beyond its clear bounds rather than allow the SCCs to fail. The permissible service, rates, and interconnection issues stemmed from a combination of MCI aggressiveness and FCC submissiveness. Contrary to an important Justice Department argument in the 1974 case, the events that we examine in this chapter are not attributable to AT&T's bad faith or dilatory tactics.

Although the interconnection and rate issues were important, they were relatively straightforward, whereas the interrelated issue of permissible special services under the SCC decision was far more complex. The stakes in special services were extraordinary and the politics were highly charged. Thus, WATS (Wide Area Telephone Service), one of the older sets of AT&T special services, was born in 1961 over the objections of Western Union, GTE, and many independent telephone companies. Even though WATS was mired in controversy for many years, its revenues made the battles worthwhile. AT&T's overall WATS annual revenues grew from $18 million in 1961 to $925 million in 1974 and to more than $1 billion in 1976.[71] Thus, WATS's great value demonstrates the stakes in the services at issue between MCI and AT&T—foreign exchange and common control switching arrangements. Foreign exchange (FX) allows a customer to make or receive local telephone calls through a distant switching center. FX effectively provides a long extension cord in the form of a dedicated line between the customer's location and a telephone company switching center at the distant location. As such, FX was especially popular among airlines and hotels because they can centralize their reservation systems. A person seeking to make a reservation calls a local rather than a long-distance number, which is routed to the foreign exchange. The FX customer received two bills—one for the private line that connects the customer to the foreign exchange and another for the telephone service that the customer used through the foreign exchange.[72] Although it had certain private-line features, FX service was also integrally tied to the public-switched network. Conceivably, FX may be used as an internal private system, but its principal and customary use was to link calls originating in the public-switched network to a dedicated line. Thus, under any reasonable construction, FX was neither a private line nor a private network service under the SCC decision.

The other service at issue between MCI and AT&T—common control switching arrangement (CCSA)—granted a customer with large communications needs (primarily voice grade) among many points access to the telephone company's central office switch, which routed calls to the customer's dedicated lines. CCSA, which originated in 1963, was an established AT&T service by the time of the SCC decision and, therefore, could not then be considered a unique or innovative service that AT&T was failing to provide. The public switch was used for many economic and technological reasons stemming from the fact that large users' PBXs and other equipment could not handle the volume of message traffic desired. Accordingly, additional hardware programming in a sophisticated switch, such as the Number 5 Crossbar, allowed a portion of the switch to be dedicated to a single customer. For instance, the large-user customer (such as the United States government) would dial an access code (usually 8) followed by a telephone number; the common control equipment in the Number 5 Crossbar switch would then translate this information into a route and destination, advance the call to an alternate route, forward the call to other switches, and so forth. A notable feature offered with CCSA was automatic off-net dialing, which enabled the customer to place a call to a telephone not on the CCSA network.[73] Government systems established under CCSA during the early 1960s included the Federal Telephone System (FTS) for civilian use and the Switched Circuit Automatic Network (SCAN) for use by the U.S. Army. By 1971, more than twenty-five CCSA networks had been established for commercial customers. Thus, at the time of the SCC decision, CCSA was an AT&T commercially viable service offering. Further, it was much more than the novel private-line service contemplated by the SCC decision.

With the preceding discussion in mind, we can now begin to evaluate how this phase of the MCI-AT&T controversy over the interconnection, rate, and permissible services issues evolved. AT&T's responses were, as we shall see, reasonable and timely *if* MCI's proposed service offering was within the contours of the SCC decision, as it was then reasonably understood. MCI first approached AT&T to discuss interconnection in September 1970. AT&T's initial response was that "there does not appear to be any reason why arrangements could not be worked out between MCI and the Bell System companies concerning interconnection."[74] The first meeting between the companies took place in October, and by early January 1971, AT&T had prepared guidelines for interconnection. But negotiations were held in abeyance until MCI received FCC approval of its construction modifications in January 1971. In March, AT&T submitted its revised guidelines to MCI, describing them as the basis for negotiations for a contract, and noted that rates were being developed. However, AT&T made clear that the underlying theory of charges was that in the long run they should be based on the actual cost of providing facilities to each SCC in the city in which the facilities would be provided. In the short term, until actual costs could be ascertained, an SCC would pay the intrastate private-line rates applicable to each city.[75] The June 1971 SCC order obligated both sides to reconsider their negotiations in light of the decision's language. The decision required rates to be nondiscriminatory and reasonable. Accordingly, AT&T would be required to devise compensatory rates based on each grade and quality of service involved in each area covered. The interconnection issue was also to be solved through negotiations. The SCC decision stated that the SCCs could construct their own local facilities to provide end-to-end service or, in accordance with paragraph 67 of the Notice of Inquiry, they could obtain interconnection or a dedicated leased channel. The principal method then in use was to route the private line into a Bell system or independent switching center that handled regular calls but to bypass the switch. Thus, the private-line connection would be a permanent one whereas calls going through the public-switched network were temporary connections.[76] Of course, since AT&T and the independent telephone companies were most fundamentally responsible for the public-switched networks and the technical problems that could arise, the Notice of Inquiry and the SCC decision were sufficiently broad to allow the public service companies flexibility in this respect. For this reason, AT&T filed post-*Carterfone* tariff revisions that would allow private-line interconnection at the customer's premises. However, these were subject to restrictions designed to protect the quality of the network and to prevent using a private line for switched, public network service.

AT&T's bargaining stance was based on these views of the obligations imposed by the SCC decision. But while MCI obviously sought to begin operations, it employed negotiations with a view of establishing a record of AT&T recalcitrance that it could use before the courts, Congress, and the FCC. Notably, former FCC Commissioner Kenneth Cox, who had sided with MCI in its authorization proceeding before the FCC, joined the company on 30 September 1970 (only one day after leaving the FCC). MCI already had excellent legal representation before Cox joined the company,[77] but Cox would be expected to employ his political expertise. The company's political strategy was to put AT&T on the defensive and to expand MCI offerings into services already provided by AT&T. As noted at a 13 July 1971, AT&T-MCI meeting, MCI, in addition to an interconnection contract, "wanted to have the freedom to offer its customers every service available from either long lines or Western Union."[78] Clearly, this posture went far beyond the limits of the SCC decision. And if MCI failed in this strategy, it intended to take the issue to the FCC for resolution, knowing full well the agency's commitment to making the SCC experiment successful. In view of this, AT&T sought to reduce the negotiating tensions between itself and MCI rather than face FCC pressure. Thus, Illinois Bell agreed to provide more costly dial access to the network instead of manual interconnection, even though the Bell system could have resisted doing so in light of the SCC decision's ambiguity on the point.[79]

The principal problem—the rates that MCI should be required to pay until more permanent arrangements could be made—should also be put in this context. MCI demanded that it should pay the same rates as Western Union for interconnection to the Bell system companies. AT&T, however, held that Western Union rates were inappropriate and, pending the development of an SCC rate structure, that the SCC should pay the higher intrastate private-line tariff. MCI's position was based on the idea of equal treatment, which it interpreted as meaning that it was entitled to the lowest interconnection rate. Although, superficially, MCI's argument was appealing, it ignored several important factors. First, AT&T held that Western Union rates were inappropriate because they were based on the mix of facilities that Western Union was provided for a nationwide system. In contrast, MCI was then requesting facilities for only a Chicago–St. Louis route, which would make AT&T's costs more closely resemble those in the intrastate private-line market than in the nationwide common-carrier market. Second, Western Union's contract with AT&T was for nonengineered facilities that did not guarantee voice-grade quality, whereas MCI proposed to offer standard voice-grade services. Third, Western Union rates were at this time of high inflation out of date and subject to renegotiation, as they were executed in 1970 and based on data collected in 1966. Thus, AT&T believed that Western Union rates would not be compensatory when MCI would begin operation in 1972. Moreover, as MCI's McGowan later admitted, Western Union was not a competitor of MCI in 1972.[80]

Notwithstanding these differences, MCI and AT&T reached an agreement in late September 1971, which was approved by the Illinois Commerce Commission. However, AT&T made most of the concessions, including its position on the dial access issue. In spite of considerable internal opposition, AT&T also yielded on the floating rate issue under which MCI's rates would be modified to reflect revisions in the intrastate tariff rates, even though Bell claimed that many such rates were below cost. MCI president John Goeken thanked AT&T's negotiators "for the effort that was put into this agreement. It is appreciated very much."[81] MCI and Bell filed the appropriate revised tariffs on 30 December 1971, and MCI began its operations in January 1972.

However, the rate issues were far from settled. The next rate controversy, in which the Justice Department would charge AT&T with an obstructionist posture, would center on the concept of capital contribution.

THE CAPITAL CONTRIBUTION CONCEPT

The Chicago–St. Louis link was only the first step in MCI's overall plan to establish a nationwide network. That fact, together with the certain entry of other SCCs into the field and Western Union's plans to expand service offerings, led AT&T in 1972 to plan the development of a uniform contract for such carriers. MCI and other SCCs entered into negotiations with AT&T, again claiming that they should be charged the rates charged Western Union. AT&T again took the position that Western Union rates were too low, arguing that if Western Union and the SCCs were to be treated equally, the former's rates would have to be raised, not the latter's lowered. AT&T's first general proposal, made in September 1972, was known as the *capital contribution concept*. Under it, the SCCs would make a capital contribution to acquire local facilities dedicated to them rather than lease such facilities. Bell also proposed to Western Union that its contracts should be modified and that Western Union should agree to the capital contribution concept.[82]

The proposed revision of Western Union's rates and the issue of rate concepts had been under discussion at AT&T for some time. For example, a 4 June 1971, high-level internal memorandum noted that Western Union rates had been based on a study completed in 1966. An AT&T interim cost study (which was later verified) of interexchange facilities leased to Western Union, completed on 28 August 1972 and listing estimated costs, concluded that the overall level of charges to Western Union should be nearly doubled to be compensatory. Based on these results and the projections of Western Union's prospective transition to a different mix of service offerings, AT&T proposed new higher rates to Western Union and the SCCs in January 1973. The new rates were based on the cost studies conducted in 1972, which showed that both Western Union's rates and MCI's Chicago–St. Louis facilities rates were noncompensatory. In turn, the SCCs and Western Union questioned the underlying bases of the studies.[83]

Principal blame for the dispute must lie with the FCC, which failed to explore satisfactorily the interconnection issue and the nature of competition it was creating. The FCC required AT&T, accustomed to serving customers and connecting carriers (such as independent telephone companies) with which it did not compete, to aid its competitors. Needless to say, in judgmental matters such as the cost-accounting bases of rates, AT&T would favor its own interests just as MCI, Western Union, and the SCCs would favor their respective interests. But the FCC's conception of competition went beyond even this serious problem, as the capital contribution concept demonstrates. A possible analogy might be, for example, if General Motors was asked to build the plant of a new automobile company, supply labor and expertise to its competitor, and accomplish within a short time period what it took General Motors decades to do. As a 1972 Bell high-level internal memorandum observed, it was

> unreasonable for new common carriers to go into business as a risk venture and make no capital contribution for a substantial part of their proposed business, expecting to lease circuits from Bell, thus taking advantage of Bell's capital raising commitments. If Bell were to lease circuits to the new carriers it would in effect be bankrolling its competition.[84]

Within this context, it is apparent why the disputes between AT&T and the SCCs were not resolved but instead became exacerbated in 1972 and 1973. In October 1972, DATRAN, requesting Bell to lease numerous facilities (apparently abandoning their plan to build their entire network as described in the FCC's SCC decision), was told that AT&T had no intention of being "their banker" and did not "propose to raise capital dollars for them."[85] DATRAN rejected the capital contribution concept in January 1973. What company, after all, would not prefer to shift part of its risk to a competitor? AT&T had not yet worked out the particulars of the capital contribution concept and saw that the SCCs would oppose it. Accordingly, in early January 1973, AT&T offered a lease approach, eventually dropping the capital contribution concept.[86] In part, AT&T's retreat from the plan—founded on the reasonable notion that a competitor should not be required to construct its rival's plant—was defensive, as the company knew it would inevitably be blamed for any difficulties in the negotiations.

MCI was, of course, aware of its advantages. International Telephone & Telegraph Company (ITT) had acted as an unwitting collaborator of MCI when it sued GTE on antitrust grounds that MCI might be able to employ against AT&T. In 1972, the Federal District Court in Hawaii rejected GTE's argument that the FCC had exclusive jurisdiction of the issues presented.[87] The antitrust law could be used in disputes between telephone companies. Thus, when MCI eventually presented its draft agreement to AT&T on 26 January 1973, it reiterated the equal treatment claim. Further, the delay caused by the controversy was politically advantageous to MCI. Not surprisingly, then, MCI's Michael Bader conceded in a 9 January 1973 meeting that, "We have to move—AT&T has always rightfully complain [sic] we delay in coming to them with needs."[88] Yet Cox, MCI's principal FCC contact, complained to FCC Chairman Dean Burch that "[i]f AT&T continues to be unresponsive and obstructive in regard to these matters, this could pose critical problems for us."[89]

On 26 February 1973, AT&T forwarded model contracts to MCI and the other SCCs. At the same time, AT&T was negotiating with Western Union to increase the local facilities rate (which AT&T held to be noncompensatory). Interim contracts providing interconnection were signed by MCI and the Bell-operating companies in May 1973. In addition, other SCCs entered into the model contract in April and May 1973. However, MCI persisted in its demand that its rates and Western Union's should be treated equally, and MCI exerted pressure on Western Union not to agree to AT&T's proposed higher rates. Laurence E. Harris, MCI's principal negotiator, noted in a memorandum of his meeting with Western Union: "I don't think there is any doubt whatsoever that Del [Harmon, vice-president of Western Union] understood what I was talking about and the ramifications of any change that Western Union might agree to in Contract No. 1."[90]

Western Union and AT&T did not reach agreement, MCI refused to make concessions, and agreements executed in the interim were not finalized. The rate problems remained unsolved, but in some ways they paled in comparison to the FX and CCSA issues. Once again, however, the FCC eventually gave in to MCI's aggressive demands.

FX AND CCSA

The controversy over FX and CCSA raised the level of antagonism between MCI and AT&T to unprecedented heights. MCI's victory in eventually enlarging its offerings to include FX and CCSA—preludes to the ultimate triumph of becoming a full-scale, long-distance competitor of AT&T—is evidence of the company's political activity in keeping AT&T on the defensive and in portraying it as a greedy monopolist. FX and CCSA are services that required the use of the Bell-switched network— clearly outside the ambit of the SCC rationale. What allowed MCI to claim the right to offer these services were AT&T's post-*Carterfone* tariff revisions.

Carterfone required AT&T to permit add-on devices, and the interconnection usually took place at the customer's premises. Private-line interconnection at the customer's premises was also included in the post-*Carterfone* tariffs. Thus, private-line operators had the option of linking their point-to-point service in addition to that of constructing their own facilities or using the telephone company's switching office. To Bell, the danger in private-line interconnection lurked in the potential ability of a customer to use local-loop service to tap into the public-switched network. Thus, the Bell system's carefully crafted post-*Carterfone* interconnection tariff amendments were designed to comply with the *Carterfone* rule as well as to prevent customers from abusing private-line services in this way. Although the FCC did not specifically limit the new SCC services to a set list, they were clearly intended to be private line and innovative—not then offered by AT&T. Yet, FX and CCSA were neither. While MCI insisted that FX and CCSA were private-line services, Laurence Harris, MCI vice-president and principal negotiator with the Bell system, did concede that if the Bell position was correct, there would be no obligation under the SCC decision to interconnect for FX and CCSA.[91]

While the SCC decision was handed down in June 1971, AT&T informed MCI much earlier in the same year that interconnection would be effected under the same terms and conditions as private microwave. Further, Bell told MCI and the FCC's Common Carrier Bureau that it would not interconnect with MCI so that the latter could use the public-switched network for FX and CCSA services. AT&T, in addition, filed tariff revisions with the FCC and the Illinois and Missouri state commissions that precluded direct access into the public-switched network. In accordance with this understanding, the Justice Department conceded that such language had been routinely used to preclude FX- and CCSA-type services.[92] Yet AT&T's policies regarding FX and CCSA were formulated in the context of the general tariff changes called for in the *Carterfone* decision. Anticipating that the FCC might mandate interconnection changes, AT&T formed the Tariff Review Committee (TRC) in 1967. Although the 1968 *Carterfone* decision, which dealt with terminal devices, did not discuss FX or CCSA, it did require the Bell system to revise the interconnection provisions of its tariffs. AT&T thus drafted its new tariff revisions and, on 22 October 1968, it filed important revisions together with an explanation of the new private-line interconnection arrangement: "Connection is made on a voice grade basis at a customer's service point. . . ."[93] The phrase "service point" (later defined as "customer premises") was sufficiently clear to be limited to "the point *on the customer's premises* where such channels or facilities are terminated in switching equipment used for communications with stations or customer provided terminal equipment *located on the premises*" [emphasis added].[94] That is, connections at premises other than that of the customer's were not contemplated by the tariff revision. The AT&T-imposed restrictions on interconnection were a result of the TRC's deliberations. Among the considerations that contributed to the TRC's hostility toward looser interconnection restrictions, quality, maintenance, and piece-out were the most influential. Bell argued that divided maintenance responsibility can lead to service deterioration and, hence, cost increase. While the argument was at one time used against interconnection generally, that issue had been settled by *Carterfone*. AT&T's post-*Carterfone* position on quality and maintenance was still premised on the same service concerns: (1) that it should control interconnection at the points it selected through AT&T-provided connecting arrangements and network control-signaling units; (2) that unrestricted customer choice of interconnection arrangements would undermine these objectives in that the need to test all proposed interconnection arrangements would impose high information costs on Bell and its subscribers; and (3) if such interconnection became as widely used as the FCC forecasted, its cost could exert significant pressure on AT&T's principle of rate averaging.[95]

Thus, when we combine the maintenance and quality argument with the conception of piece-out, we see that the arguments reinforce each other. *Piece-out* was defined as a situation in which a customer or other carrier seeks to provide a "piece" of an overall service over the high-density, low-cost portion of the route, leaving Bell to provide the low-density, high-cost portion.[96] For example, suppose that the SCC planned service from point A to point C through point B. If Bell's rates were lower than the SCC's rates in the low-density A to B portion of the route—a result of Bell's rate averaging—and if Bell's rates were higher than the SCC's in the high-density B to C portion of the route for the same reason, the SCC would choose the lowest cost alternative for each portion. Thus, piece-out allowed an SCC to creamskim and to undermine the structure of rate averaging. As the disputes between MCI and AT&T heated and became increasingly technical, it is important to note that creamskimming was in many ways related to these issues, including FX and CCSA.

The earliest FCC clarification of the FX issue was adopted on 24 December 1968. The date is important, for on 18 October 1968, MCI filed a petition to reject AT&T's post-*Carterfone* revisions to tariff FCC no. 263 on the principal ground that it was overly restrictive. The FCC rejected MCI's argument, holding that AT&T could bar the use of customer-provided, network control-signaling units. The agency held that the new tariff revisions complied with the *Carterfone* mandate:

> Our decision in *Carterfone* does not hold that a customer may substitute his own equipment or facilities . . . for that furnished by the telephone company in providing message toll telephone service. . . . Our decision dealt with interconnections and not replacements of any part of the telephone system.[97]

Among the categories covered by the tariff revisions and the FCC's rules was private-line service, which the agency defined as "a separate service *that does not use the switched telephone network*" [emphasis added].[98] Because MCI-provided FX or CCSA would use the switched network and would directly compete with AT&T in the provision of such services, we cannot conclude that MCI was entitled to provide these services at the time it demanded them.

The AT&T tariff revisions became effective in 1969. Among the tariff revisions' provisions were those that restricted customer premises interconnection to the originating and terminating points of telephone calls. The FCC approved the new tariffs over the vigorous objections of several business interests and the Justice Department.[99] Thus matters stood until the FCC's 1971 SCC decision which, as we have seen, did not contemplate that SCCs would offer services already available through Bell or services that were not private line. Nevertheless, the defeats that Bell had sustained encouraged MCI to continue to demand. MCI would use a strong offensive stance at the levels of the FCC, the courts, and Congress to better its chances of winning. MCI did not suddenly find justification for its "right" to engage in an FX service as a result of the SCC decision; rather, it had demanded such connections as early as 1970. Moreover, internal MCI memoranda conceded that it was unlikely that Bell would voluntarily provide FX connections—a judgment made even clearer in Bell system tariffs.[100] Thus, following the 1971 SCC decision, MCI again demanded FX-type interconnection and AT&T restated its position: "MCI had not been authorized to provide services directly connecting to the public switched network, . . . Bell was not obligated under the Commission's orders or policies to piece out or otherwise participate with MCI in the provision of end-to-end services. . . ."[101] Further, neither MCI nor any other SCC had requested the FCC to authorize such a joint-through service in their SCC pleadings, and Section 201 of the Communications Act clearly outlined the procedure for a "new" service with which MCI had not complied in connection with FX and CCSA. The steps included reasonable request, hearings, and a finding that the proposal was "necessary or desirable in the public interest." In this connection, we should recall that the FCC's fundamental focus in the SCC proceeding was on the burgeoning data market and that its underlying assumption—indeed, the underpinning of its commitment to the SCCs—was that private data transmission would be the SCC's prime market. While MCI did not propose a pure data service, it did lead the FCC to consider as its principal proposed market a special kind of service that Bell did not offer. Accordingly, if it sought to offer more, a separate Section 201 proceeding would have been appropriate. MCI, in fact, proposed "to furnish essentially the same type of service as that of private microwave systems, with the basic difference that MCI would render the service on a common carrier basis." Again, MCI "will serve the submarkets of business and government users that require only intracompany-interoffice, inter-plant communications capability . . . without the need for an elaborate nationwide switching network."[102] Finally (although there are numerous similar quotes), two MCI officials stated in 1971 in the SCC oral argument:

> What we are not going to do is furnish a telephone exchange service. . . . What we offer instead is the flexibility and benefits of private microwave. . . . That is our intention, a private line service is equivalent to private microwave.[103]

Although FX and CCSA remained unresolved issues, the evidence indicates that AT&T cooperated with MCI in providing interconnections during 1971. MCI vice-president T. L. Leming conceded in a memorandum:

> My general conclusion from the meeting was that AT&T is now taking the position that we are just another connecting telephone company in much the same manner that other independent phone companies operate with them. . . . Their only dogmatic position seemed to be that our circuit lease arrangements with them must, of necessity, go to the customer's premises as opposed to tying directly to the central office.[104]

In this respect, it is significant that MCI did not formally complain to the FCC in 1971 and 1972 that AT&T was misconstruing the SCC decision, even though the Commission stated that it would promptly resolve any disputes arising under its decision. The issue was financially important to MCI in that several of its major customers (such as Westinghouse) sought FX or CCSA services from it during those years.[105] While there may be other explanations consistent with MCI's failure in 1971 and 1972 to take formal action before the FCC in the face of AT&T's clear refusal to provide FX and CCSA connections, one is most patent—MCI would have lost a contest before the agency so soon after the 1971 SCC decision. The FCC and the Justice Department then stated that MCI's facilities would not be connected with AT&T's public-switched network. Thus, the new company instead sought to circumvent the tariff restrictions. As MCI vice-president Leming wrote to president Goeken on 23 September 1971:

I did not note in this draft agreement any reference to foreign exchange service. It seems possible that we may be able to circumvent any restrictions they might envisage under the requirement that the services will be provided only to our customers' premises.[106]

That MCI was intent on following a legal-political strategy in which strained interpretations would be tested was demonstrated further in a 1972 ploy. Using its customers to apply for interconnection at MCI offices, MCI sought to defeat AT&T's piece-out restrictions. That is, the MCI customer would lease space in MCI's offices and then demand interconnection at its "business premises"—MCI's offices—instead of at its regular business offices. In this way, the customer could piece-out by using MCI for the portion of a circuit in which it was the least expensive and AT&T for the portion in which it was the least costly. Obviously, a carrier like MCI without full-scale public service responsibilities would be pleased with this arrangement, whereas AT&T, whose rates were based on cost averaging, would reject the arrangement. As the controversy over such connections dragged on into 1973, the MCI strategy of building a case against AT&T proceeded deftly. MCI's customers were brought into the fray against AT&T, the company claimed that it was being harassed by AT&T, it requested an FCC investigation of these situations, and it protested that it "should make no difference whatsoever to Bell where the service is terminated as long as it is not used for an illegal purpose."[107] Surely MCI knew that it made a difference.

On 18 April 1972, Cone Mills Corporation, an important MCI customer, wrote a letter to Illinois Bell (sending a copy to MCI) demanding FX service. In essence, Cone Mills demanded a local telephone at its "offices" on the 97th floor of the John Hancock Building in Chicago, which happened also to be MCI's Chicago office. Further, Cone Mills' contact person was an MCI employee and the telephone number it provided Illinois Bell was assigned to MCI. The purpose of the order was to enable MCI to connect an MCI interexchange channel to the Cone Mills local telephone line—that is, to provide an FX-type service. Illinois Bell refused the request on the ground that MCI was not entitled to FX service.[108]

The stakes were high because FX and CCSA were larger than the conventional private-line market, and during this period MCI was under considerable financial pressure. Judge Harold F. Greene, in exasperation during the course of MCI's McGowan's testimony, sharply criticized the company's evasiveness in revealing evidence about its financial condition and other issues. Nevertheless, certain facts and admissions point to the conclusion that MCI desperately sought to enlarge its market in 1972 and 1973 because its original private-line projections were inflated and its financial position was distressing. MCI needed FX and CCSA badly. The facts indicate that in June 1972, MCI contemplated a 165-city network at a cost of $80 million, yet a September 1972 internal memorandum estimated that a sharply curtailed 34- to 41-city network would cost $100 million.[109]

On 11 April 1973, MCI's strategy of using government to meet its objectives was employed when Cone Mills complained to the FCC about Illinois Bell's refusal (the complaint was prepared with MCI's "assistance").[110] During the same period, MCI began its series of complaints to the FCC and the Common Carrier Bureau about AT&T's alleged high handedness. Portraying itself as a victim of AT&T, MCI was able to gain the support of those regulators who had put so much effort into the SCC decision and the new policies favoring competition in novel services and equipment—MCI's failure would undermine their hard work. In a variation of the then popular theme "what is good for General Motors is good for the country," MCI attempted to show that what was good for MCI was also good for the FCC and its new policies.[111]

THE *BELL OF PENNSYLVANIA* CASE

The event that triggered the first court contest between MCI and AT&T began on 23 October 1973, when MCI learned that Bell of Pennsylvania would not provide a loop to serve MCI customer Keystone Tubular in Butler, Pennsylvania. Bell of Pennsylvania denied the request on the ground that AT&T's obligation was to provide local interconnection only and that Butler was outside the Pittsburgh local distribution area— a concept AT&T employed to delineate its interconnection obligations to Western Union, MCI, and the other SCCs. Butler was approximately 36 miles from the MCI terminal and was located within an area served by an independent telephone company. The incident was only one of many in which MCI made demands for connections far outside the local distribution areas, including demands for areas considerably longer than one microwave hop as well as areas outside the state in which the principal city (such as Chicago) was located. Perhaps most importantly, while one could have questioned AT&T's definition of a local distribution area, MCI did not offer an alternative one but instead chose to demand and to involve the FCC and others.[112] Ambiguity was a way to challenge AT&T's FX and CCSA policy. Late 1973 was clearly an opportune time for MCI to strike hard, as AT&T was on the defensive on many fronts. It was besieged with equipment connection requests stemming from *Carterfone*, the FCC's restrictions on AT&T in satellite services, and a senatorial investigation led by Senator Philip A. Hart on alleged abuses of monopoly and oligopoly power in several industries, including telecommunications. In Hart's hostile investigation, former FCC Commissioner Kenneth Cox, then a top MCI official, was an important witness.[113]

MCI brought suit against AT&T in the fall of 1973, challenging Bell of Pennsylvania's Keystone Tubular action in particular and AT&T's interconnection policies under the SCC decision in general. During the same period, the FCC instituted Docket no. 19866 to clarify the complaints concerning local distribution areas and other matters arising under the SCC decision. Meanwhile, AT&T had announced its proposed HI/LO tariff offering, which departed from the concept of rate averaging so to compete with MCI and other SCCs in their markets and services.[114] MCI's own study, conducted by the highly reputable Arthur D. Little Company, concluded that private microwave was able to undercut Bell only because AT&T scrupulously followed the principle of rate averaging. MCI's concept of competition sought to preclude AT&T's ability to respond as it used the government to defeat AT&T at most every turn. In this respect, it had a valuable ally in the chief of the Common Carrier Bureau, a principal architect of the FCC's limited competition policy.[115]

Notably, as late as December 1973, the FCC acknowledged that its SCC policy was not meeting its hoped-for expectations. In a decision handed down in the same month, the FCC did not directly argue with AT&T's contention that the SCCs "offer nothing new, but rather will provide principally voice grade private line channels."[116] It also did not quarrel at that late date with the view that the SCC rule required SCC services to be novel and innovative. Rather, it claimed that experience was yet too limited for the agency to accede in AT&T's judgment. Further, the FCC argued that the dispute over the concept of local distribution facilities was delaying the deployment of the new SCC facilities.

On the last day of December 1973, the Pennsylvania Federal District Court upheld MCI's position on the local distribution area issue. Moreover, the court required AT&T to provide FX and CCSA connections, to enlarge the local service areas, and to provide "such other interconnection facilities as are necessary to enable plaintiffs to furnish the interstate services they are authorized by the FCC to perform."[117] MCI won in large part because it relied on a 19 October 1973 letter from Common Carrier Chief Strassburg, which stated that MCI was entitled to everything it sought from the court. The fact that the letter was advisory, from an FCC staff person, and that the FCC was in the process of deciding the very issues under consideration did not give pause to District Judge Newcomer. The judge did not come to terms with the rationale behind the basic SCC decision or of the December 1973 reconsideration, did not understand the concept of a private line or how it differed from FX and CCSA, and did not employ rate averaging and other considerations in his decision. Instead, Judge Newcomer relied on such limited views as that because Bell included FX and CCSA in its private-line sales literature, they must be private-line offerings.

However, in April 1974, the Third Circuit Court of Appeals vacated the District Court injunction. In keeping with established principles of administrative law, the Court of Appeals unanimously held that the District Court should have deferred to the appropriate administrative agency in the complex technical issues of FX, CCSA, and local distribution facilities. Moreover, the FCC was then considering the issues that Judge Newcomer had failed to consider. In keeping with its views on the proper role of the courts in such matters, the Court of Appeals stated: "An examination of these two Commission pronouncements reveals that the existence and scope of any such obligation on the part of AT&T is so unclear that deferral to the expertise of the FCC is both desirable and appropriate."[118] Noting that none of the SCC decisions had mentioned FX, CCSA, or local distribution areas specifically or by implication, the Court of Appeals decided that it would be presumptuous for it to decide the issues in MCI's favor, in that such a decision would inappropriately substitute the court for the FCC as the body responsible for decisions on such matters as the role of competition in telecommunications.

AT&T's victory was short lived. It did not anticipate the tenacity of MCI to become a viable economic entity nor the Common Carrier Bureau's desire to further its policy of attempting to assure the viability of the SCCs. Commissioner Charlotte T. Reid sharply criticized Common Carrier Bureau Chief Bernard Strassburg for exceeding his authority:

> I believe that the Bureau Chief went beyond his delegated authority. I believe this to be even more apparent when one considers the fact that there was a reasonable basis for confusion as to what interconnection had been ordered. Therefore, the Bureau Chief to conclude that such was not the case, without inquiry to the Commission, is simply more than I can accept.[119]

Nevertheless, it is apparent from the 1974 *Bell System Tariff Offerings* decision that Mr. Strassburg's persistence would prevail. His views certainly did not envision that MCI would become a full-scale competitor of AT&T in the long-distance market, but the conception of private-line competition had expanded since the MCI and first SCC decisions.

In a classic understatement, the FCC conceded that its "prior orders may not have been perfectly clear."[120] The Commission granted FX and CCSA service to the SCCs because they could only compete effectively against Bell with such services: "If MCI and other specialized carriers are excluded from this market, they will be at a definite disadvantage in obtaining and holding subscribers to any of their private line services."[121] Reaffirming its belief in the SCCs' ability to serve the public interest, the Commission declared that FX and CCSA were private-line services on the same ground that Judge Newcomer chose— because they were so described in AT&T's written materials. Neglected was the previously held idea that SCCs were to provide innovative and unique services, principally in the data field, as FX and CCSA clearly would not fit into the older concept. The FCC thus became committed to the survival of the SCCs and its concept of competition had changed—the SCCs would be allowed to expand their service offerings so to survive. For the same reason, AT&T was severely restrained in how it could compete. Thus, AT&T's executive policy committee authorized the filing of the HI/LO tariff in January 1973, in order to compete with the SCCs. In January 1976, after numerous proceedings and delays largely caused by AT&T's competitors, the Commission ruled the tariff unlawful on the ground that it was noncompensatory. But, obviously, AT&T's novel departure from the rate-averaging principle, in effect since 1893, raised many new and complex issues including discrimination between customers who had competitive offerings and those who did not. The FCC ruled the tariff unlawful on the basis that it intended to conduct further inquiry into its lawfulness, and invited AT&T to develop new data consistent with FCC guidelines. In 1977, the FCC conceded that the type of uniform system of accounts under the guidelines that it required AT&T to keep for rate purposes was inadequate. But even before that time, AT&T had supplanted the HI/LO tariff with another one.[122] Interminable delay is one way of preventing a competitive response.

In view of the restraints placed on AT&T, it is not surprising that MCI was not content with FX and CCSA. The shifting conception of the public interest to which MCI's victories attested was critical in encouraging the Justice Department and in supplying the material for its case. And, as we will learn in Part 3, MCI's victories eventually led to a contrived form of long-distance competition that also characterized the new telecommunications policy. The FCC had deeply eroded the older regulated network manager system. Events not only in private-line offerings but in other realms, most importantly the computer-communications interface (discussed in Chapter 7), were in the process of eroding the old system even further.

CHAPTER 7

THE BROKEN CONNECTION:
COMPUTERS AND
INTERCONNECTION

The postdivestiture telephone industry is marked not only by the breakup of AT&T and the availability of alternative long-distance service but by a deregulated equipment market as well. As a result, we can own or lease telephones, purchase them from a variety of sources, and pay high fees for service visits (in place of the old system that mandated telephone company end-to-end responsibility). The chain of events that led to the deregulation of the equipment markets can be traced to two principal sources: the computer industry and firms that sought to enter the telecommunications industry as a result of the *Carterfone* decision. As in the case of the long-distance market, the demands for a deregulated equipment market were, at first, relatively modest but gradually escalated. Companies in the computer and interconnect industries as well as their customers gradually persuaded the FCC that policies benefiting them were in the public interest. Again paralleling the long-distance situation, the Justice Department treated many of AT&T's responses in equipment interconnection matters as instances of monopolistic behavior.

If the distinction between computing—that is, the processing of information—and communicating could have been maintained, the policy issues we examine in this chapter may have been avoided. But technology tended to link the two areas, raising the issue of which policy principles should govern in the large border area. AT&T, which already had many adversaries, now came in conflict with IBM and other computer companies and a multisided battle ensued. The problem was complicated by the fact that computer hardware devices with communicating abilities were only one type of interconnecting CPE. Consequently, the many interconnection issues raised in *Hush-A-Phone* and *Carterfone* were fused with the computer boundary issues. Since the interconnection issue was tied to one concerning a crucial technology, the FCC had to treat it with heightened sensitivity. The agency had a public interest mandate to facilitate the progress of the computer and its applications. Thus, AT&T had to fight on yet another front against not only more traditional interconnecting companies but also computer companies. AT&T's traditional CPE rivals now had powerful allies and their claim of standing for the public interest became more substantiated. These forces sought to capitalize on the sentiment expressed by economist Almarin Phillips:

> There is an aversion to large businesses whether they are efficient or not. Part of AT&T's problem is that they are big and they do things efficiently and well. . . . Every time AT&T does something well, there are new antitrust regulations and suits. To the extent AT&T does well, it faces this dilemma.[1]

The argument used by the anti-AT&T forces was that the Bell system was staid whereas the young companies were innovative. Yet in 1973 alone, "staid" AT&T developed the following among its usual cascade of inventions and innovations: (1) artificial speech produced from printed English words and sentences through a computer program; (2) data sets capable of rapid transmission rates; (3) a new automatic call distributor capable of rapidly transferring incoming directory assistance calls; (4) an improved wire with greater temperature resistance and a tougher insulation known as irradiated polyvinyl chloride (IPVC) wire; and (5) LSV (line status verifier), a system that permitted repair service personnel to verify the condition of a subscriber's line immediately upon receiving a trouble call.[2]

While AT&T was still clearly doing much to benefit the industry and its customers, it clearly was not winning the battles in the political and legal arenas. John de Butts, the company's new chairman who assumed office on 1 April 1972, decided that one of his paramount tasks would be to reverse the political-legal trend. De Butts, an AT&T careerist, began working for the company in 1936, gradually rising through both AT&T and several operating companies to vice-chairman in 1967. As such, he was involved in AT&T's regulatory activities for a long period of time at both the local and state levels. Moreover, de Butts was at the company's highest levels during the critical period beginning shortly before the FCC handed down the *Carterfone* and *MCI* decisions. In January 1973, de Butts presided over a conference of Bell system presidents. His personal notes from the meeting indicated that AT&T would fight against further advances in interconnection liberalization

> because of impact on [the] average consumer and cost of service. . . . [We] [m]ust recognize manufacturers will fight hard before the FCC, Congress agrees and everybody else. We must do likewise, plus state regulators and also customers and shareholders. If we really believe in our position, we can win this one, but it [is not] going to be easy.[3]

Two points are notable in de Butts's summary: (1) a firm belief in the correctness of Bell's position and (2) the need to devise a political strategy based on the support of Bell's natural allies—shareholders, customers, and state regulators.

De Butts launched AT&T's counterattack before the 1973 annual convention of the National Association of Regulatory and Utility Commissioners (NARUC), one of AT&T's principal allies. While it is apparent why AT&T's almost three million common shareholders of record would constitute the bases of company support, it is not obvious why the trade association of state PUC officials would be allies. First, NARUC was concerned about the revenue loss to local telephone companies that could result from CPE liberalization. Second, they were concerned about complex revenue allocation issues known as separations and settlements, which first arose in 1930 when the Supreme Court required regulators to allocate costs between interstate and intrastate services.[4] As the post–World War II era proceeded, NARUC became intent on assuring that long-distance revenues were used to subsidize local service. The FCC admitted this subsidy arrangement. As scholars Peter Temin and Geoffrey Peters have summarized, a "series of further revisions continued the process of shifting exchange plant into the interstate arena, demonstrating the lasting imprint of the agreement between Congress, state and federal regulators, and AT&T reached in the early 1950s."[5] In this way, an increasingly larger share of the rate base was shifted to interstate long distance under the separations procedures. That is, when new long-distance competitors sought to make inroads on AT&T's market and thereby undermine the subsidy flows to local service implicit in the separations process, it is obvious why the state regulators would ally themselves with AT&T. (It should also be noted that an important theory of the Justice Department's 1974 suit was that subsidy flows were from monopolistic local services to competitive long-distance ones. As Temin and Peters show [and as the enormous increases in local rates after divestiture confirm], the Justice Department's position was untenable.[6])

Thus, de Butts had clearly chosen to address an important ally at the NARUC convention. He began by noting that although the regulated network manager system had served the nation well in economic and technological ways, there was an unprecedented challenge to it. He identified a diverse group of challengers: (1) manufacturers and importers of communications hardware; (2) carriers who sought to serve or were serving selected parts of the market; (3) their customers, mostly large businesses who saw an advantage in the new pricing arrangements "but who have no obligation—and therefore no disposition—to reckon the cost of those new arrangements to the public at large"; and (4) members of the regulatory community who were either resentful of AT&T's size or who treated competition as a shibboleth.[7] At issue, de Butts claimed, were the public service idea, the regulated network, end-to-end responsibility, and the other cardinal principles that had developed in the telephone industry. But these issues, de Butts argued, were not being squarely faced. Rather, the FCC and others were resolving issues one by one, without looking at the underlying principles or comparing competition to the regulated network manager system. De Butts proclaimed:

> The time has come to alert the public to what the public is largely unaware—and that is that regulatory decisions have already been taken in its name that, whatever advantages they may afford for some people, they cannot help in the long run hurt most people.[8]

Further, the public had been led to believe that a system of contrived competition, in which the Bell system was precluded from effectively competing with new carriers, was superior to the excellent record attained under the regulated network manager system. The public was not being told, de Butts claimed, of the costs in service and repair that would ensue with the onset of divided responsibility over the network when the Bell system would no longer be responsible for the state and quality of each part of the network. Nor was the public told by the advocates of the new contrived competition what the impact on rates and universal service would be as further experimentation ensued. Moreover, de Butts went on, the new carriers' claims of offering novel services were untrue. Noting that MCI captured over 80 percent of the point-to-point private-line market between Chicago and St. Louis, de Butts asked, "Why, then, did our customers switch? Not because MCI offers services that are in any significant way new or different from those the existing carriers offer."[9] They switched because MCI's rates were lower, but the rates were lower because MCI was not obligated to serve all subscribers in sparsely settled localities and difficult-to-serve areas. That is, MCI could creamskim. When Bell sought to compete through a two-level rate structure, the FCC was delaying the institution of the HI/LO rates even though they were compensatory. De Butts claimed that this typified the FCC's new approach, which was neither regulated monopoly nor traditional competition. Rather, the new system of contrived or regulated competition was little more than an arbitrarily imposed and artificially maintained division of the marketplace. Under the FCC's scheme of contrived competition, not all the parties enjoy the same freedoms, bear the same responsibilities, or endure the same constraints.

De Butts hoped that his speech before the NARUC would unify the state regulators and the independent telephone industry behind AT&T's positions on equipment and long distance. As it was, AT&T was combatting a coalition of big-business users, SCCs and other transmission firms, manufacturers and distributors of interconnection equipment, and the new services and industries growing up around the computer—a formidable list of opponents, who would participate in the proceedings concerning interconnection and the computer-communications interface. However, as we will see, AT&T's positions in these proceedings were somewhat different from the NARUC's and some independent telephone companies'—most importantly Rochester Telephone. Thus, instead of helping AT&T's positions, they would undermine them, further isolating AT&T and making its position appear not to be in the public interest.

THE BEGINNINGS OF AT&T'S COMPUTER INVOLVEMENT

The first modern computer was used in Cambridge, England, in 1949.[10] From its early deployment through to the present day, the manufacture, sale, and lease of the computer in the United States have been undertaken by private firms whose operations have been unencumbered by the continual supervision of regulatory agencies. As long as the boundaries between computing and communication remain clear and distinct, each activity can be governed by its own set of rules, but problems arise when the boundaries become blurred. Under such circumstances, either new working definitions separating the two activities must be devised or the distinctions must be abandoned and the firms should be allowed to compete (or not to compete) on the same basis.

Just as AT&T dominated communications, IBM dominated the computer industry. IBM entered the computer business in the industry's infancy, obtaining a significant market share early, but it did not outsell Sperry-Rand's Univac until 1956. By 1964, however, Sperry-Rand, Honeywell, and RCA began to erode IBM's mainframe market share. In that same year, IBM revolutionized the computer industry when it introduced System 360, which not only superseded its prior product line but made obsolete all other competitors' products as well. The 360 line had two distinctive features that stimulated a more widespread use of computers: (1) it allowed a single computer to perform both office management and engineering functions, and (2) it allowed users to move upward to a larger computer without the costly burden of developing new programs. IBM's bold innovation was so successful that it held more than 65 percent of the world's general purpose mainframe market from 1968 through the 1970s.[11]

Notwithstanding IBM's preeminence in computers, it would be a mistake to view the problem of delineating the respective terrains of computing and communications as a clash between IBM and AT&T. Clearly, there were differences in position between the two firms, but IBM was precluded under the 1956 consent decree (into which it entered) from engaging in the service bureau business, except through a completely separate subsidiary. And it is precisely in the service bureau part of the business that the initial difficulties arose. Service bureau activities are those in which customer data are manipulated or changed. While IBM was able, in small ways, to circumvent this restriction, its major business was computer mainframes and other hardware.[12] Nevertheless, it strongly supported the views of its many service bureau customers.

AT&T was early involved in computer development but in a different way than IBM. For the same reason that it was involved in talking pictures and a host of other inventions and innovations, Bell Labs was one of the first institutions involved in the development of both analog and digital computers. Bell Labs generally investigated the principles and processes of communications. But when one considers the enormous value that computers could be in such functions as billing or switching, it is apparent why Bell Labs became deeply involved in the field. As early as 1940, AT&T transmitted digitally encoded information, foreshadowing the use of telephone and radio circuits for computer data transmission that would develop 20 years later.[13] During the aftermath of World War II, the Bell system had enough to do in traditional telephony without entering the computer business, which was becoming a highly competitive field. In any event, the 1956 Western Electric Consent Decree appeared to preclude (1) AT&T to enter any industry except the regulated telephone industry or (2) Western Electric to manufacture anything other than equipment for telephone operations. Nevertheless, AT&T moved forward in the development of computers, peripherals, and software for its internal use. Computing capacity in the Bell system during the early 1960s grew exponentially with a doubling time of less than 2 years. By 1969, AT&T had developed the UNIX operating system, a major advance that allowed, among other advantages, programs to operate together smoothly.[14] By the mid-1960s, AT&T was in an anomalous position—although a leading firm in virtually all phases of computer development, it was precluded from entering the business because computing was not a regulated public service. As writer Gerald Brock has observed:

> If regulatory control could be extended to data processing services, AT&T would have an opportunity to control that market through its control of the communications lines. . . . If the regulatory line could be drawn narrowly around traditional communications, AT&T could be prohibited from entering the combined services by the Consent Decree.[15]

Of course, the places of many activities on either side of the border were clear, but a case was sure to arise that would lead to a border dispute. When researchers at MIT's Lincoln Laboratories developed a system in the 1950s for transmitting digital signals between air defense sites over analog telephone lines, the battle was inevitable.[16]

AT&T and others engaged in programs to develop and improve modems that would be able to transmit and receive data over telephone lines through paths originally or principally devised for voice transmission. As early as November 1956, AT&T decided to begin the development of a commercial data service. An experimental program called DATAPHONE began in February 1958, demonstrating the feasibility of sending data at various speeds over telephone lines. In this period, IBM, too, undertook important developments in the field of data communications. As the 1950s came to a close, data transmission over private lines and through the switched network constituted a rapidly expanding market.[17] For this reason, the public service companies became attentive to all matters that might establish a general principle. In particular, they remembered *Hush-A-Phone*.

TELEQUOTE AND COMPUTER I

The incident that triggered the FCC's major computer inquiries, which wrought such extraordinary changes in American telecommunications, was a relatively minor affair. The Bunker-Ramo Corporation, an early service bureau, had developed an information service for stockbrokers called Telequote III. Pursuant to this system, undertaken through arrangements with the New York and other exchanges, Bunker-Ramo gathered, updated, and stored in regionally located computers information important to stockbrokers. For example, a broker dialing a Bunker-Ramo computer could instantly obtain information about the last price sold, last price offered, and so on for any stock traded on the exchanges. The common carriers had no objection to Telequote III; indeed, one may surmise that they viewed it as the progenitor of many other lucrative dial-in services to computers.[18]

Telequote IV, which Bunker-Ramo sought to introduce in 1965, however, presented a problem to the carriers because it added a message-switching capacity that allowed any of the offices of the sub-scribing brokerage firms to communicate information to each other. Telequote IV, of course, took advantage of the fact that the same computer could not only store and transmit information but could switch it as well. Obviously, the speed with which information can be obtained and transmitted is critical to the brokerage business.

> Telequote IV would permit a buy or sell order from a branch office of a broker to be sent to and stored in a regional computer until polled by a central computer, checked for parity and forwarded to the broker's office or to the broker's representative on the floor of the exchange. Execution orders would be routed back to the branch office from which they originated in similar fashion. In addition to this message-switching service, Telequote IV was to afford information storage and processing services with respect to margin accounts and financial research. The computers were to be programmed so as not to allow any information except that specifically provided for in the Telequote III or IV proposals to be sent over the private lines.[19]

Before we consider the underlying reasons that Western Union, Bunker-Ramo's principal carrier, refused to provide Bunker-Ramo with private-line service for Telequote IV, we should first note that the refusal put Western Union and the other common carriers supporting the action on the defensive. Western Union, by refusing to supply private lines for Telequote IV, appeared to be blocking progress. Computers in 1965, as now, were considered important objects because of their extraordinary capacity to solve innumerable problems and make our lives better. Moreover, Western Union had taken on not only the computer service bureau industry but, more importantly, the entire financial industry (including brokers and banks), which even then could foresee major uses for message switching. The distinction between message switching and circuit switching should be noted. The latter involves a carrier providing a customer with exclusive use of an open channel for direct and immediate electrical connection between two or more points. The traditional telephone system typifies circuit switching, whereas the telegraph industry uses message switching, which is indirect in the sense of a temporary delay or storage of information prior to forwarding the message to its destination. While the FCC conceived of circuit switching by a computer as communications, message switching by a computer was the focus of controversy because it inexorably involved some processing by a computer.

Western Union and its ally AT&T must have been aware of the risks they faced, the potential affront to major communications users, and the fact that Bunker-Ramo would not abandon such a potentially lucrative service without a fight before the FCC and, perhaps, the courts as well. It is therefore necessary to consider carefully the arguments of the public service companies. Western Union advanced two basic arguments to justify its refusal: (1) Bunker-Ramo was not entitled to switched service under the carriers' tariffs; and (2) if Bunker-Ramo engaged in Telequote IV, it would be subject to FCC regulation under the Communications Act. Under the then-prevailing conception of private lines, they could not be connected to the general exchange system nor could switching be permitted between the stations. In 1942, the New York Public Service Commission stated: "Communication may be had between several stations and a central point but the different stations are not connected one with the other."[20] Thus, the switching of information through Bunker-Ramo's computers would be considered a common carrier activity, in violation of existing tariffs, and subject to FCC regulation. Further, the switching would be used by Bunker-Ramo to obtain compensation from customers—precisely the activity carved out for communications public service companies. Bunker-Ramo would, according to Western Union, become a retailer of common carrier services with Western Union forced to become, against its will, a wholesaler. To follow the logic of Western Union's argument, there would be no obstacles preventing any large enterprise from leasing what purported to be a private line from the telephone company for computer services, and then adding switching capacity so that all customers in the network could communicate with each other. This issue had become a practical one when computer technology permitted: (1) the installation of remote terminals that would transmit and receive data from computers and (2) time sharing. Prior to the advent of time sharing in late 1961, a computer user had to deliver his or her problem to a computer's managers and then wait hours or days for an answer that would take the machine only a few seconds to generate. Until time sharing, the computer worked on one problem at a time. In 1959, British physicist Christopher Strachey proposed methods that would allow a computer to work on several problems simultaneously. Following through Strachey's suggestions, MIT's computation center developed a time-sharing system in 1961, which contained many direct connections to the computer. Moreover, the MIT system was connected into the Bell and Western Union systems so that access to the MIT computer could be had from terminals anywhere in the United States and abroad.[21]

The time-sharing concept virtually begs for connection not only between users and the computer but also between the users themselves. Users can carry on communication among themselves through the machine, cooperatively examining a set of problems and sharing information. Although there were early difficulties in large-scale time sharing, by the mid-1960s it was clear that it was growing, in part because Bell Labs endorsed the concept in 1964 by ordering General Electric computers that featured time sharing.[22] The boom in time sharing lowered computing costs and drew more companies into computer use, which, in turn, stimulated the rapid development of service bureaus, some of which developed specialized software for a variety of business and scientific uses.[23]

The Telequote controversy was settled through negotiation in February 1966. Bunker-Ramo devised a modified Telequote IV service that it transmitted over the telephone. But Bunker-Ramo's complaint to the FCC and the more general questions that it raised about the appropriate terrains of computing and telecommunications, unregulated and regulated activities, cried out for comprehensive treatment. The FCC hoped that by addressing the issues raised by the computer-communications interface early in the development of the field, it could resolve many of them before they became full-blown controversies. Little did the agency realize, when it adopted a notice of inquiry into the interdependence of computers and communications in November 1966, that major questions would still be unresolved in the late 1980s.

COMPUTER I

The Notice of Inquiry

Like so many issues that the FCC considered in the late 1960s, the Common Carrier Bureau and its chief, Bernard Strassburg, played major roles in shaping the ways in which the issues would be presented. As we have seen in earlier chapters, the Bureau generally favored new entrants into the various telecommunications markets. Clearly, the issues raised by the Telequote controversy lent themselves to the Bureau's general approach. In October 1965, Strassburg revealed publicly for the first time that the FCC would engage in a general inquiry on the subject. Speaking at an institute on management information and data transfer systems, he reviewed the applicable precedents and discussed the implications of time sharing, one of which was that falling computing costs would make communications costs the major component of the combined computing-communicating package. Strassburg spoke of the switching capabilities of computers and of the competition that would result from the convergence of the two technologies between communications and computer companies, including in the area of message switching.[24]

Even though the Telequote controversy was settled in February 1966, the staff investigation into the general boundary question continued. During that period, interests that might be affected by an FCC proceeding began making their views known. In a letter to the FCC that outlined its position on the boundary question, IBM proposed a decision rule that would have sharply reined in the area of regulated public service activity. The IBM-proposed rule was based on what the ICC has termed the "primary business test," which in transportation was relatively easy to apply.

> It has long been established that the words "for compensation" . . .
> refer to that transportation supplied with a purpose to profit from
> the service performed as distinguished from transportation supplied
> merely as an incident to some other primary business, even though
> in the latter case a charge is collected which may or may not be
> identifiable as compensation for transportation.[25]

Although the FCC never adopted the primary business test that IBM proposed, it implicitly employed the distinction in a number of matters.[26]

The 1937 case that IBM employed as principal precedent was one in which an airline communication company was held not to be primarily involved in communication because its primary function was to advance airline safety.[27] IBM thus proposed the following test to determine whether communications is central or peripheral to computing: when the computer performs message switching without transformation of the content of the data, it should be considered communications; when information is fed into the computer and it engages in an operation on the material and the transformed information is sent to someone else, it should be considered data processing. Communications, although significant, was considered incidental: "There has been transmittal to and from the computer of different messages—separate communications functions—and the performance by the computer of a non-communications data processing function."[28] IBM then called for the development of effective procedures to distinguish the two kinds of operations. The other alternative—a wholly unacceptable one—would be to regulate data processing, an industry that had performed well under conditions of free competition. But while the distinction that IBM drew could be applied in theory, it was not known if it could work in practice. Further complicating the issue was a March 1966 Western Union statement. Western Union, unlike AT&T, was under no explicit bar from using its equipment for non-common carrier business. With the declining importance of its traditional telegram business, it was searching for new opportunities and had developed Candygram, long-distance shopping and flowers by wire services, which were exempt from FCC regulation. Since the charges for these services were strictly segregated and Western's common carrier facilities were available at the same rates to competitors, the FCC approved the arrangements.[29] Western Union argued, however, that it would be at a serious disadvantage in computer communications relative to computer service bureaus, which did not have common carrier obligations and were not required to file tariffs. Claiming the IBM distinction meaningless, Western Union asked for either a uniform system of regulation or free competition: "Unregulated companies are in the field and are furnishing message switching service; it seems quite immaterial whether the message switching is the principal, or of secondary, interest of the customer."[30] A formal notice of inquiry was issued on 9 November 1966. It observed the increasing importance of computers generally and computer communications specifically, and it emphasized the convergence and interdependence of computers and communications. Further, several trends were discerned in the inquiry. First, many computers could be programmed for message and circuit switching in addition to data-processing functions. Second, the communications common carriers were increasingly employing computers that could be used for data processing in addition to their normal communications functions. Third, many new kinds of CPE (such as the Touch-Tone telephone) had great potential as computer input devices: "The same buttons can be pressed to enter information into the computer or to query the computer and get back a voice answer."[31]

In the notice, the Commission was clearly concerned about the possibility of thwarting progress. Noting the increasing importance of time sharing, the agency observed that the computer's flexibility permitted the sharing of information through switching, a valuable opportunity. But this capacity allowed the data-processing industry to engage in an activity that previously had been limited to common carriers. Accordingly, the FCC asked whether some form of regulation or a free competitive market would best serve the goals of the Communications Act; that is, if rates, accounting practices, interconnection rules, and other principles should be modified as well. Because the agency contemplated that the inquiry would be substantial with numerous participating interests, it took the unusual procedural step of calling for parties to suggest new issues or modifications of the issues proposed in the Notice of Inquiry. While many participants proposed new suggestions, the agency largely held to its original items of inquiry. MCI again stated that one of its major concerns was computer communications.[32] Still other companies noted that attachments used with telephones were an important part of the converging market.[33] Thus, in 1967, before the *Carterfone* decision dealing with interconnection and the SCC decision dealing with novel services, not only would computers and communications converge but the computer issues would overlap those raised in other major proceedings. A computer terminal, after all, is in some respects just another kind of CPE.

The Inquiry

The participants in the *Computer I* inquiry did not have long to wait before gleaning a sense of how the FCC would treat the issues it had raised. In December 1967, the agency was asked to rule on Western Union's Securities Industries Communications Service (SICOM) offering. The FCC, as noted earlier, used the primary business test to rule that in such Western Union services as the candygram or flower delivery, communications were subsidiary to merchandising and, therefore, exempt from FCC regulation.[34] SICOM, however, was a nonvoice computer information service designed for brokers that included message switching. Acting on the request of Bunker-Ramo and others to suspend the tariff, the FCC trod warily, pointing out that it did not want to prejudge the computer inquiry. Nevertheless, it was compelled to decide whether SICOM included any significant noncommunications services. Finding that each of the SICOM functions had a counterpart in other common carrier communications services, the FCC gingerly concluded that it would not preclude the entry of either common or non-common carriers into the computer communications field, but that it reserved the right to change its decision in the full computer inquiry.[35]

Early in 1968, Common Carrier Bureau Chief Strassburg provided a more revealing glimpse of probable Commission (or, at least, Common Carrier Bureau) sentiment in an important address before the Conference on Electronic Data Processing of the National Retail Merchants Association. Without specifying the proposed policies, Strassburg promised that the FCC would avoid the "extremes" of regulating all computer services that are dependent on communications and of allowing monopolistic behavior in the computer or communications industry. In short, Strassburg implied that some form of competition would prevail in computer-communications.[36] As the 5 March 1968 deadline drew near, the FCC was barraged with comments in the computer inquiry. Most business opinion proposed, like the National Association of Manufacturers (NAM) statement, that the FCC should not regulate data processing and that competition would do the best job in spurring the spread of innovative computer services and driving down costs.[37] Further, business interests as well as the various components of the computer industry vociferously called for a radical revision of the interconnection tariffs and sharp restrictions on the right of the public service companies to provide data-processing services. While some computer firms called for outright prohibition, others called for the common carriers to establish separate subsidiaries that would deal at arms-length with their regulated parents. In brief, the voluminous filings showed that the public service companies were pitted against nearly every user industry and every segment of the computer industry.[38]

The June 1968 *Carterfone* decision went far in deciding the interconnection question, in that the FCC declared AT&T's restrictive tariff unlawful not only with respect to the specific device involved in the case but to all CPE. In a December 1968 clarification, the FCC included computers and private microwave systems within the ambit of the *Carterfone* rule; that is, that a customer may add on equipment to the telephone terminal if it does not adversely affect the telephone system's operations or its utility to others.[39] However, anticipating differing viewpoints on most other issues, the FCC commissioned the Stanford Research Institute (SRI) to analyze the Computer I responses. The SRI reports, released in May 1969, rather than giving clear policy recommendations, proposed that the FCC undertake more research so to improve its ability to predict the outcomes of policy decisions. This, in turn, led the FCC to request the Computer I participants to comment on the SRI study by late June 1969,[40] which, of course, afforded the participants the opportunity to restate their original views.[41] Notwithstanding the tentative nature of the SRI reports, the FCC used them to release its first *Computer I* report in May 1969—approximately two and one-half years after launching the inquiry. The agency pointed out the tentative nature of its conclusions because it had not comprehensively studied the SRI reports and other material. It made clear, however, its preference for competition in the manufacture and sale of special communications equipment and systems for use in connection with the switched network.[42] Additionally, the FCC raised new issues to replace the interconnection ones that *Carterfone* had solved, the most important of which was rate structures. For example, because large volumes of data could be transmitted over the switched network in bursts, computer service bureaus challenged the 3-minute minimum rate as uneconomical. Again, the agency raised the issue of constructing a digital network to supplement the analog one. The FCC concluded that because these and other issues required further study, the inquiry would continue.

The Tentative Decision

Obviously, a record as lengthy as *Computer I* required considerable study before the FCC could devise a set of decision rules. The long-awaited tentative decision was released on 3 April 1970, but it should be noted that the decision was labeled "tentative." The tentative decision began by noting the issues—interconnection, rates and service, quality and quantity—that were being solved in other proceedings. Future developments in these areas would also be monitored through informal procedures.[43]

Essentially, the *Computer I* inquiry would answer two principal questions: (1) the nature and extent of regulatory jurisdiction over data-processing services and (2) the circumstances in which common carriers should be permitted to engage in data processing. It answered that regulation should be limited to three situations: (1) where there is a natural monopoly, (2) "where economies of scale are of such magnitude as to dictate the need for a regulated monopoly," and (3) "where such other factors are present to require governmental intervention to protect the public interest because a potential for unfair practice exists."[44] Under other circumstances, the FCC said, free and open competition should prevail. Aside from the extraordinary ambiguity of the third circumstance, the most interesting aspect about the Commission's new conceptual framework is what it did not include—the public service principle, which was disregarded as if it was irrelevant to telecommunications regulation. Within this framework, computer services were held to operate well under a regime of free and open competition, for even small firms were able to sell services effectively because of product differentiation. Not only would the FCC not impose regulation on most computer services, but the existing common carriers (with the exception of AT&T because of the 1956 consent decree) would be free to enter data-processing services for three reasons. First, they would add competition and, possibly, innovation. Second, they might exploit economies resulting from integrated operation. Third, computer services might afford an opportunity for Western Union to diversify in the face of its declining message telegraph business. However, to prevent the ills that could result from admixing regulated and unregulated businesses (including subsidizing unregulated business with the profits of regulated business, or disregarding the primary responsibility of the regulated activity), the FCC required strict separation of the two sets of activities and nondiscriminatory treatment between the separate subsidiary and other customers.

The Bell system was, as we have seen, foreclosed from participating in such noncommon carrier services. Notably, the FCC did not suggest that the prohibition was unfortunate, even though AT&T's extraordinary record of technological prowess portended a great contribution to computer services. The FCC at that point basically feared AT&T's remarkable technological record and generally restricted its entry into new fields. We should examine the agency's attitude in its reluctance to allow AT&T's entry into new fields by its actions in domestic satellites—clearly a communications common carrier field. In 1970, the agency strongly indicated that it might restrict AT&T's role in that industry, but deferred action until a full evidentiary hearing.[45] In June 1972, the FCC issued its second report, in which it adopted a policy of open entry into the private-line domestic satellite communications

business for all technically and financially qualified applicants—except
AT&T! The latter was barred for 3 years from providing private-line
satellite service to nonfederal governmental customers.[46] Within this
broader context, it is clear that the FCC willingly barred AT&T from
computer services not only because of the decree but also because of
its overall policy of favoring smaller competitors, especially in newer
technologically based fields. This factor, of course, makes the issue of
what constitutes a computer service far more consequential than a matter of definitional craftsmanship, for if an activity was on the communications side of the boundary AT&T might be allowed to engage in it,
but if the activity was on the computer side it could not. The agency
invented the phrase "hybrid service" to determine the close cases,
those that combined data processing and message switching to form a
single integrated service. In such hybrid services, where message
switching was offered as an integral part of a package that was "primarily" data processing, it would be treated as data processing. But where
"the data processing feature or function is an integral part of and incidental to message switching the entire service" would be treated as
a communications service subject to regulation. The Bell system was
specifically warned to stay on the correct side of the line.[47] The pre-
sumption in a close case would be against allowing the Bell system to
engage in a service. But could this decision rule be applied in practice?

The Final Decision

One issue that did not arise in the *Computer I* tentative decision was
the wisdom behind the decision to bar AT&T from computer services.
The innovations that were restricted to the Bell system because of the
1956 consent decree could be of exceptional value to the outside
world. The principal investigator for the SRI study lauded AT&T's
achievements in the field: "With respect to the provision of new data
services the indication is that the telephone industry is responding as
effectively as can be expected considering its size and complexity."[48]
The Bell system's computer capabilities were growing rapidly, especially after the development of the UNIX system in 1969. Yet in its
final decision, although endorsing the wonders that the computer
would make possible, the FCC did not consider the Bell system's role
in the process. How would the Bell system's discoveries be dissemi-
nated? Or should the agency be content with using its discoveries and

advances for internal purposes only? Questions like these were not addressed.

Not surprisingly, the computer industry was generally satisfied with the tentative decision and hoped that the final decision would largely resemble it. For this reason, the mainframe computer manufacturing industry's principal trade association endorsed the FCC's tentative decision, although it urged more stringent restrictions on common carrier entry into hybrid services.[49] Similar general endorsements, coupled with a call for yet further restrictions on the public service companies, were made by the Electronic Industries Association (representing the manufacturers of many interconnection devices), computer time-sharing services organizations, the American Petroleum Institute, and the National Association of Manufacturers, representing business users. Western Union complained that the FCC's strict separation requirement would hinder the common carriers' ability to compete since they could not take advantage of important economies of coordination and scale that data-processing firms could obtain. Moreover, the common carriers would be deprived of the flexibility of shifting computer use that the service bureaus had. While AT&T assured the FCC that it did not intend to (and could not) offer data processing to the public, MCI charged that AT&T was trying to divert private-line data users to the switched network.[50]

It was not until March 1971 that the FCC issued its final decision in *Computer I*. The vote was a surprisingly close 4–3. The final rules went even further in agreeing to the requests of the nonpublic service companies than had the tentative decision. While generally endorsing the earlier framework, the FCC majority ruled that communications common carriers would be barred from buying data-processing services from their own affiliates. Further, the affiliates were prohibited from using their parents' names or receiving promotional or other assistance from them. Essentially, this drastic rule was adopted on the ground that it would be virtually impossible to investigate every dealing between a carrier and its data-processing affiliate to determine whether the transaction was conducted at arms-length.[51] Thus, the FCC, instead of solving the boundary problem, exacerbated it. The agency's rules guaranteed that the communications common carriers would appeal, and it assured continuation of the computer-communications controversy by announcing that it would determine whether a hybrid service was predominantly communications or computing on a case-by-case basis. The three dissenters observed that the majority's sense of competition was peculiar in that it imposed such severe restraints on the common carriers. The SRI study had considered, but rejected, just such a restriction: "Such carriers will be barred from obtaining data processing services from their affiliates even where an affiliate . . . offers service to its customers at the lowest prevailing prices."[52] Finally, the dissent pointed out that there was no evidence of a regulated company abusing its position to warrant this drastic action. The dissenters thus argued that in the name of competition the FCC was curtailing competition.

The public service companies were dissatisfied with the final decision, as were the service bureau companies and their allies whose view of competition excluded participation by the common carriers, even through a separated subsidiary that was not permitted to do business with the carrier. Bunker-Ramo argued that the FCC lacked adequate personnel to supervise the carriers and to assure that cross-subsidization flows from regulated to unregulated services did not occur. The FCC, rejecting changes to the rule, turned down the computer firms' requests on reconsideration of this point, adding that if the safeguards instituted did not allow the agency to meet its objectives, further action would be taken.[53] The public service companies (excluding AT&T), realizing that the FCC only rarely reverses its earlier decisions on reconsideration, appealed the final decision to various courts during the spring of 1971. Instituted by GTE, United Telephone, Continental Telephone, ITT, and Western Union, the cases were consolidated before the Second Circuit Court of Appeals in New York.[54] It is likely that AT&T did not appeal because of the 1956 consent decree, because it had other battles to fight, and because the Nixon administration in 1970 issued a major policy statement favoring competition in every communications market not considered a "natural monopoly."[55]

The Appeal

While the interests adversely affected by the *Computer I* final decision were contesting its rulings in the courts, legal scholars concerned with the computer-communications interface were also dissatisfied with the end result. One perceptive law-note writer concluded that:

> Despite the considerable time and effort expended . . . the regulations left many issues undecided or unclear. First and foremost is the question of the point at which unregulated hybrid data processing becomes regulated data communications. The "primary thrust" test

indicated by the Tentative Decision substitutes the visceral reactions of the Common Carrier Bureau and the commissioners for a reliable definition. . . .

A second question involves defining those "hybrid services" that are within the scope of the regulations. The regulations speak of a "single integrated service," yet neither the regulations themselves, the Tentative Decision nor the Final Decision explains this term.[56]

When the Court of Appeals' February 1973 decision in *Computer I* held that the FCC lacked the authority to regulate data processing, certain evidence suggests that the agency may have had doubts about its ruling. The court unanimously held that the FCC's rules, which restricted dealings between common carriers and their data-processing affiliates, were invalid. The court also rejected the provision that would have prevented the carriers and their affiliates from sharing the same corporate name. Upheld, however, were the rules requiring strict separation between the two kinds of entities.[57] The primary distinction made by the Court of Appeals was that the FCC may make necessary and proper rules to discharge its obligations in the telecommunications field, but that it could not concern itself with the structure or desirable behavior of the data-processing sectors. That is, the FCC may regulate the behavior of communications firms in other sectors insofar as their actions affect behavior within the telephone industry, but it may not regulate behavior in the telephone industry to shape behavior or structures outside telecommunications. On this basis, the court rejected GTE's complaint against the FCC rule banning a carrier's sale of excess computer capacity: "Its prohibition . . . is aimed at the protection of efficient telephone service to the public by eliminating the *possibility* of a diversion of facilities to other purposes" [emphasis added].[58] Thus, the FCC was granted the right to deal with matters pertinent to the telephone industry; even the possibility of impaired telephone performance would justify FCC action. This broad discretion afforded the FCC was consistent with established administrative law principles. The Commission amended its rules in March 1973 to reflect the Court of Appeals' decision.[59]

Even though it took nearly 7 years for the *Computer I* inquiry to be resolved, its decision rules still did not clearly delineate communications from computing. Most importantly, computers were considered only one kind of interconnection device into the telephone network, and the rules applying to them had to parallel those for other interconnection devices (subject, of course, to reasons for different treatment). The basic interconnection rules, beginning with the 1968 *Carterfone* decision, were in the process of dramatic change.

POST-*CARTERFONE* INTERCONNECTION—
THE CERTIFICATION ISSUE

Another important component of the Justice Department's 1974 suit was based on its assumption that AT&T used a variety of obstacles to prevent telecommunications equipment firms from competing effectively. On this basis, the Justice Department charged AT&T with unlawfully attempting to maintain its equipment monopoly.

In late 1968, AT&T announced its post-*Carterfone* tariff revisions, which permitted the interface of a customer-provided CPE or other terminal device (such as a computer) but which was subject to several important restrictions. First, the devices could be connected into the network only through telephone company-provided control devices. Second, the tariff revisions precluded the attachment of any customer-provided network-signaling control unit. Third, telephone company customers could only connect into the basic equipment supplied by telephone companies and could not substitute for such equipment. Fourth, customer-provided equipment could not be attached if it adversely affected a telephone company's operations or the system's utility for others. The immediate post-*Carterfone* decisions upheld these general principles of the tariff revisions.[60]

The Commission was at first content with establishing broad principles and with allowing the participants to work out the particulars. But it was the particulars that ultimately led to conflict. Additionally, there were serious jurisdictional issues between federal and state regulators. For example, suppose that a state PUC forbade the interconnection of particular devices for intrastate calls. Through NARUC, the state regulators had already made clear their hostility toward a liberal interconnection policy in the FCC proceedings, claiming that the public service principle and the goals of the regulated network manager system were paramount. The New Jersey Commission succinctly stated this view: "The reality of telephone service is more important to the public interest than the integration into the telephone system of collateral equipment . . . which may jeopardize that service and discourage its improvement."[61] Although the state commissions unanimously accepted Bell's post-*Carterfone* tariffs, it was not clear how they would construe controversies arising under them.

The FCC's first important step in anticipating the post-*Carterfone* controversies was to commission in June 1969 the National Academy of Sciences (NAS), through its Computer Science and Engineering Board, to study the technical factors of customer-provided interconnection. The NAS report, issued in June 1970, concluded that uncontrolled interconnection could cause harm to telephone company personnel, network performance, and telephone equipment. It determined that harm may arise as a result of hazardous voltages, excessive signal-power levels, line imbalances, or improper network-control signaling. Finding that the electrical criteria in AT&T's tariffs relating to signal amplitude, waveform, and spectrum were technically based and valid, the NAS concluded that two approaches were acceptable to provide the required degree of network protection: (1) common carriers could own, install, and maintain connecting arrangements and assure adherence to the tariff-specified signal criteria; and (2) a program certifying appropriate standards for equipment and for safety and network protection could be instituted.[62] The NAS warned that

> No certification program . . . will work unless proper standards have been established. In the case of telephone interconnection, standards must be developed to cover certification for installation and maintenance of equipment and facilities, as well as for equipment manufacture, since all of these combine to determine the net effectiveness of the program.[63]

Further, the NAS recommended periodic inspections of equipment and installation by qualified personnel, and cautioned that any significant division of responsibility for supervision and maintenance of the telephone system would jeopardize the performance of the network as a whole.[64] For these reasons, the NAS urged that the certification program be undertaken gradually, so to develop a meaningful base of knowledge and experience. Further, the first implementation should be in an area with a high probability of success but with sufficient complexity to test the program adequately. AT&T generally lauded the

NAS report for its awareness of the dangers to the network and stated that it would be pleased to work with users and manufacturers in the development of standards and procedures.[65]

While it was clear that the FCC would opt for the NAS-recommended certification program, it was faced with a major problem: Who would pay for the costs of administering the program and of supervising compliance? Because the early users of interconnection devices most likely would be business subscribers and other high-volume users, the question was raised of whether residential and business subscribers not interested in interconnection devices should pay a portion of the expense, which would undoubtedly increase as manufacturers and vendors of such devices proliferated. Under the Bell system's immediate post-*Carterfone* tariffs, customers seeking to use interconnecting devices were compelled to pay the costs of protecting the network through the protective connecting arrangement. While such costs would tend to discourage customer acquisition of interconnection equipment, the certification program raised the possibility that such costs would be borne by nonusers.[66] That is, residential subscribers would cross-subsidize high-volume business users, including those with large data-transmission needs. The FCC was called on to consider these economic matters as well as the technical ones raised in the NAS report. It thus hired Dittberner Associates, a communications consulting firm, to undertake further analyses and to evaluate the NAS study. While the NAS study was viewed as impartial by most interests in the interconnection controversy, NARUC accused the Dittberner firm of "a continuing heavy involvement in serving the interests of equipment manufacturers, interconnect companies and potential clients."[67] Other federal government telecommunications officials accused the consulting firm of preparing a shallow report, replete with easily obtained "filler."[68] In any event, the Dittberner report, released in August 1970, was at odds with the NAS study. It concluded that customers should be permitted to interconnect directly into the public network without the necessity of common carrier interface arrangements as long as the equipment used met FCC-certified standards. Criticizing the NAS conclusion, the Dittberner study rejected the technically sound program of standardization and certification because of such nontechnical factors as workforce power and funding availability.[69]

Although some type of certification program was inevitable, the differences between the NAS and Dittberner views raised other important issues. The Bell system sought to minimize the burdensome costs associated with testing, certifying, inspecting, installing, and monitoring interconnection equipment, which would be incurred when troublesome operation might be attributable to telephone equipment, service, or customer-supplied interconnection devices. Further, disputes over these matters would lead to additional costs in discovering and assessing fault, negotiating, settling disputes, and, perhaps, litigating. In short, the system of divided responsibility threatened to raise information and transaction costs above what they were under the pre-*Carterfone* tariffs. Thus, Bell's solution of a protective device was designed to achieve a reasonable compromise that would incorporate many of the benefits of unitary responsibility and at the same time avoid endangering the network:

> The Bell System hoped that the potential for conflict . . . could be avoided or at least minimized by the establishment of a single universal requirement for the interconnection of customer-provided equipment to the network—a protective connecting arrangement—thereby eliminating the need for the telephone companies to evaluate and pass judgment upon each item of equipment supplied by their competitors.[70]

Moreover, the Bell system argued that the problem was aggravated by the telephone network's flexibility and progressiveness, in that without interface protection any change in the network would entail incurring substantial costs in determining the compatibility of each kind of interconnection device. For the same reason, it argued that the Dittberner-type certification program would act as a disincentive for Bell network improvement.

Yet while AT&T's position on certification was based on concerns involving network quality and improvement, the NARUC focused on economic considerations. The NARUC's views are best understood in terms of three types of interconnection devices: (1) complex multiline station equipment, such as PBXs used by institutional subscribers; (2) data-transmission terminal equipment; and (3) ancillary equipment, such as answering devices or automatic dialers. Since neither the second nor third type of device was a significant source of telephone company revenue used to cross-subsidize residential telephone service, the NARUC was willing to endorse a certification program with equipment standards. On the other hand, the first type of interconnection device raised important economic issues for the NARUC. PBXs and key telephone systems (in which a number of telephone lines are connected to each telephone set in a system and a line is selected by pushing a button corresponding to one line) were traditional telephone company offerings and had been priced by the local exchange carriers at prices substantially above attributable costs. Consequently, revenues from PBXs and key telephone systems (KTSs) subsidized local rates, thereby making telephone service more widely affordable. To the extent that such revenues were diverted from local exchange service,

> the effect would be to eliminate the subsidy of local exchange service, and it would be the non-interconnected subscriber—in other words, the vast majority of the telephone using public, including the poor, those living on fixed incomes, and other ordinary individuals of modest means—who would be required to pay a higher rate for their service.[71]

The economic situation was further aggravated, in that technological improvements lowered the rates for long distance but such gains were not made in local-loop service. Accordingly, the NARUC claimed that a liberal interconnection policy would largely benefit a small number of business and other affluent users but not the majority of telephone users. Further, NARUC comparative studies of lines with and without customer-provided interconnection equipment showed much higher trouble rates when customers provided CPE. While this did not necessarily prove that customer-provided CPE was at fault, it did prove an increase in the expenses to telephone companies, which, the NARUC argued, ultimately would be borne by the ordinary ratepayer.[72]

AT&T'S STRATEGY

Faced with conflicting views on certification, the FCC chose to appoint yet more committees to provide additional information that would justify its eventual decision. While most interests approved of the NAS program of certification, Carterfone Communications claimed it was "misdirected, biased and erroneous," calling for the FCC to repudiate the distinguished panel.[73] Also, in February 1971, Arcata Communications filed an antitrust suit against AT&T and Southern Bell, charging, among other things, that the network protectiv e interface device was part of a monopolistic conspiracy to retain a monopoly in CPE.[74]

In 1971 and 1972, the FCC announced the establishment of advisory committees that would attempt to develop technical standards for protecting the network from harms that could result from customer-provided CPE. The committees included representatives from NARUC, the FCC, the common carriers, independent CPE manufacturers, suppliers and distributors, and others. Under the auspices of the committees, progress was made toward establishing standards agreeable to the various interests. AT&T, in June 1971, even revised its tariff to provide the interface protection device for voice-grade, private-line service at no additional charge.[75] Although the Bell system was not pleased by these developments, its dismal win-loss record before the FCC and the courts during this period made it clear that resistance would have been an ineffective strategy. Instead, an internal AT&T memorandum prepared for the company's Executive Policy Committee indicated the company's strategy:

> On May 17, 1971, the Executive Policy Committee reaffirmed that the Bell System must be responsible for overall communications service even though some of the equipment is customer owned. Since the *Hush-A-Phone* and *Carterfone* decisions removed our right to enforce performance standards of our own choosing, our problem still is how to exercise that responsibility within the imposed constraints.[76]

Thus, AT&T saw the need to cooperate with the other interests, including its competitors. Even so, its principal concern was to fulfill its obligations for network safety and quality under the regulated network manager system.

AT&T officials viewed the early 1970s as a critical period in this development because of the increasing use of computer communications. Another internal AT&T memorandum prepared for a 4 October 1971 Executive Policy Committee meeting indicated this concern:

> The fact that protective devices have not been required on private lines does not mean that they are not needed. When private lines were few, we could afford to ignore some irregularities; they could be given individual attention, and the probability of interference with

other services was small. However the continued growth of private lines business has changed that as has the proliferation of terminal devices. We cannot monitor and check all private lines. Moreover some forms of data transmission provide an incentive to exceed the power criteria—higher bit rates and lower error rates. . . . As time goes on, this situation will become even more serious as more diverse terminal equipment is connected to private lines. . . . Consequently, it seems wise to install minimum protection now before the task is overwhelming.[77]

This makes clear the company's position in the various informal and formal FCC proceedings that would critically shape interconnection policy. Fearful of the harms that could befall the network, AT&T would not favor a liberal certification policy. Whether such harms actually occurred is irrelevant, for as network manager the company had to prepare for a scenario in which such harms reasonably could occur. Moreover, because of the anticipated proliferation of computer communications, AT&T could reasonably assume that the problems resulting from customer-provided interconnection would worsen. A relatively liberal interconnection policy would also encourage customers to install less expensive, uncertified CPE, which were more likely to cause harm or quality deterioration to the network. As early as the fall of 1972, an FCC advisory committee warned that its work would be meaningless if nothing was done about the widespread sale of uncertified devices.[78] Western Electric's competitors were as concerned about the problem as the Bell system's manufacturing arm.[79] Since the FCC was not organized to send investigators into private homes and offices to determine whether illicit interconnection devices were in use, it would be AT&T's primary responsibility to investigate these problems—at great expense. Finally, in keeping with its status in the telephone industry, AT&T was sensitive to its role as a major ally of the independent local-loop companies. In a typical small community containing one or two companies that dominate the economic life of the town, a large customer "going interconnect" would impose substantial costs on the remaining customers. This led the NARUC and state officials to propose, on economic grounds, limiting the number of interconnection devices permitted.[80] Profit pressures on the independent telephone industry would, in turn, lead state regulators to demand increased separation and settlements contributions from AT&T to the independent companies.

AT&T, then, actively participated in the efforts of the FCC advisory committees to the extent that the latter expressed satisfaction at the progress being made.[81] Nevertheless, AT&T officials continued to speak out generally on the wisdom of interconnection. More practically, as president John de Butts stated at a 1973 AT&T Annual Meeting, the company would oppose any certification program that did not resolve quality of service, safety, and economic impact issues. During that meeting, the first at which the heads of all Bell local operating companies were introduced, AT&T emphasized service improvements at local levels.[82] As this indicates, the impact of interconnection and the probable responses of state regulators could importantly shape the policy ultimately adopted on certification.

LOCAL REGULATION AND INTERCONNECTION

On 14 June 1972, after appointing its advisory committees, the FCC, largely at the NARUC's insistence, instituted a federal-state investigation of interconnection in conjunction with state regulators under Section 410 of the Communications Act. The provision allowed the FCC to convene a Joint Board, consisting of state and federal regulators, to report to the agency on matters of joint interest. The Joint Board was asked to report on whether customers should be allowed to furnish their own network control signalling units (NCSUs) and connecting arrangements (CAs), and, if so, what rules the FCC should institute.[83]

Business interests, deeply concerned about the possibility of different states establishing varying standards and procedures, also viewed the Joint Board as an opportunity to obtain uniformity. For example, Xerox Corporation, a major participant in the production of telecopier transceivers, computer printing systems, and other interface equipment, actively sought the establishment of a Joint Board or other federal-state body to establish coupler standards and options. Xerox anticipated three options: (1) telephone company provision of coupling devices, (2) customer provision of them, and (3) equipment containing integral protective characteristics.[84] As Xerox had learned in the important 1972 New York PSC *Rochester Telephone Company* decision, some telephone companies had broken ranks, some state regulators were no longer foes of liberal interconnection, and manufacturers had diverse views. Thus, a Joint Board could bolster support for future FCC action liberalizing interconnection. After reviewing prior proceedings and proclaiming the correctness of *Carterfone* and the other cases to which it gave rise, the Commission asserted that it did not want prior questions reopened. Rather, the questions to be resolved by the Joint Board were "whether, and to what extent, there is public need for us *to go beyond* what we ordered in *Carterfone* and permit customers to provide, in whole, or in part, the aforementioned NCSU's and CA's in interstate MTS and WATS and, if so, what terms and conditions should apply." [emphasis added].[85] In summary, then, the FCC wanted to both assure conformance with its positions at the state levels and to assure that the general principle of liberal interconnection was not reopened in the many state investigations then being conducted.[86]

One of the most important events that influenced the FCC's decision to create a Joint Board was the then-pending New York State matter in the *Rochester Telephone* case. The New York PSC's August 1975 favorable comments to the FCC in regard to the operation of the Rochester Telephone interconnection program lent support to the plan for further interconnection liberalization. Even though the statistical significance and interpretation of the PSC's evidence were doubtful, the New York agency concluded that the Rochester Telephone program had not degraded the quality of service.[87] Rochester Telephone Corporation (RTC) filed interconnection tariff revisions with the New York PSC in early February 1971. In contrast to the Bell interface device described by the PSC as expensive and complex, the RTC plan called for the attachment of a simple device and a system of company-prescribed standards to which the customer agreed to subscribe. RTC would enforce the standards by certification of customer-owned equipment and periodic inspection. The tariff also included restraints, some of which were more confining than Bell's, on the intermixture of company- and privately owned equipment on the same access line.[88] Thus, the RTC plan differed from that of Bell and most of the independent local-loop companies not only in the simplicity of the coupling used but in other respects as well. The Bell devices isolated completely the DC current in customer equipment from the network. The Bell indirect linkage was accomplished through transformers that had the capacity to bar hazardous voltages. Because of this isolation feature, Bell (and most of the independents) had much lower costs in evaluating customer-supplied CPE, their installation, interfacing, inspection, repair, and so forth. Moreover, since the telephone companies still had control of the network, they maintained responsibility for it as in pre-*Carterfone* days. Accordingly, while the RTC plan assured that disputes over improper performance would occur among the telephone company, customer, and supplier of the customer's device, the Bell plan still largely maintained the principle of uniform responsibility. Perhaps, most importantly, the RTC device, unlike Bell's, did not guard against longitudinal impedance imbalance (which causes noise and interference or improper network control signaling).[89] On this basis, the Bell system and other independent telephone companies opposed the RTC plan. But more interestingly, Xerox, which was both an equipment supplier and a major customer of RTC, also opposed the plan. Xerox preferred the Bell plan because it did not want RTC or other telephone companies determining whether Xerox products could be used, especially since RTC would be a competitor in the provision of CPE. Under the Bell interface plan, telephone company approval and inspection would be unnecessary, or at least minimal. The Bell plan had the additional merit of nationwide uniformity. Even the PSC's staff rate analyst recommended that RTC customers should have the option of choosing either plan.[90]

The hearing examiner approved the RTC plan on 24 February 1972, following closely the recommendations of the New York PSC staff brief.[91] Three months later the PSC reiterated its faith in the virtues of certification and inspection programs of the RTC type.[92] Not surprisingly, the New York PSC voted 3–1 to approve the RTC program in August 1972, rejecting, however, some parts of the proposal, such as that barring a mix of customer- and company-supplied CPE. However, the PSC did not disapprove of or reject New York Telephone's post-*Carterfone* tariffs that it had approved in 1969.[93] The agency emphasized that the RTC plan afforded an opportunity for testing an alternative to the Bell plan; therefore, the PSC did not even suggest that the RTC plan should be extended throughout the state. Approval was based largely on the spirit of taking a chance and on the PSC's "expectations . . . that freer competition will afford subscribers a wider choice of equipment . . . will stimulate innovation . . . and will promote reductions in cost, especially for those subscribers who require equipment less elaborate than that provided by the telephone company."[94] The lone dissenter, veteran Commissioner Edward Larkin, decried what he termed "a regulatory adventure." He concluded that evidence supporting the ordinary RTC subscriber's benefit from the program was not presented, and that end-to-end service and the other goals of the regulated network manager system were not considered: "The majority bases its conclusions on assumptions, speculations and even hoped-for contingencies that might or might not be realized."[95] Larkin argued that the program would benefit some manufacturers of CPE devices but not RTC's subscribers. Yet, neither Larkin nor the majority considered the significant differences between a program that would cover Rochester and one that would cover the nation. Certification, inspection, and so on are manageable costs in a single medium-sized metropolitan area such as Rochester, but when applied to the nation as a whole they present problems of a different magnitude. Thus, even if the RTC plan showed good results in Rochester, this did not necessarily mean it would work nationwide.

Of course, other states, free to develop other rules, developed a variety of standards from the Bell system's to rules that looked askance at any restriction on interconnection competition.[96] Nevertheless, the *Rochester Telephone* decision occurred shortly after the FCC's notice of inquiry creating a joint board. The size of the record, the length of the decision, and the importance of the state in which it occurred helped to predispose the Joint Board toward more liberal interconnection policies. But this would not occur without a fight, for during 1972, differences among the FCC's advisory committees on certification, network harm, and other issues emerged.[97] Complaints from equipment manufacturers about AT&T mounted and were generally supported by the Common Carrier Bureau. Manufacturers of various devices sought FCC action to compel AT&T and other telephone companies to abandon "any requirement for a telephone company supplied coupler."[98] And, in 1972, private antitrust suits against the Bell system and based on the interconnection issues burgeoned.[99] As we will see, the claims in these private suits would become important components of the Justice Department's 1974 suit.

THE JOINT BOARD REPORTS

During 1973, the advisory committees continued to be mired in controversy as the FCC sought yet more comments on the interconnection issues it had raised. Most importantly, AT&T, which had been asked on several occasions to provide statistical data on the incidence of harm, finally released its report in April 1973. AT&T concluded that customer-provided equipment "is causing a much higher trouble rate than is experienced when all telephone company provided equipment is utilized."[100] In a 23-page memorandum, AT&T claimed that it gathered 10,224 trouble reports over a 2-month period involving the use of customer-provided equipment, 4,973 of which were caused by customer-furnished CPE. Moreover, subscribers who owned their CPE relied on the telephone company to determine whether trouble existed in their equipment, thus diverting AT&T's maintenance resources from telephone company problems.

However, AT&T's report claimed too much and it backfired on the company. Alvin von Auw, AT&T's vice-president and assistant to the chairman, conceded: "More serious than the failure of the harms argument to persuade the Bell System's regulators was its failure to persuade many of its own managers."[101] Many in the company even advocated abandoning the argument for which supporting evidence was not adequately gathered. Moreover, it was argued that even if trouble rates were higher when customer-provided CPE was interconnected than when the telephone company supplied the CPE, a well-designed certification program could satisfactorily solve the problems. AT&T's response to this argument was, according to president John de Butts, that the higher "trouble rate . . . was certainly an indication of harms, the potential for harms, and it was certainly obvious to me that if we were going to have our proliferation of the connection of customer-provided equipment, this was going to be a problem."[102] While reports of trouble are not necessarily equivalent to the existence of trouble, AT&T, the regulated network manager, is primarily responsible for (1) investigating a trouble report; (2) ascertaining probable cause and responsibility; (3) informing and, perhaps, negotiating with the equipment supplier, customer, and others about the cause of a problem; (4) periodically examining customer equipment in the light of new AT&T equipment, loop and long-distance changes; (5) policing to make sure that improper equipment is not attached to the line; and (6) a host of other activities that could have been circumvented with AT&T's program of a protective device. Thus, AT&T's most fundamental argument was that certification would impose substantial transaction and information costs avoided under the older system of undivided responsibility.[103] But this view was ignored in favor of the view that held if customer-provided CPE did not "harm" the network, certification was the best alternative. The burden of proving harm was placed on AT&T and, as we have seen, the Bell system's tactical blunders in some ways contributed to its defeat on the certification issue. While the RTC program supported the FCC's adoption of a certification program, it still faced the formidable problem of recalcitrant state commissions that adopted interconnection rules at variance with the FCC's. The FCC solved this problem by instituting a proceeding in September 1973 on whether FCC interconnection preempted state action. In early 1974, the FCC decided that it had "primacy over the interconnection of customer provided equipment to the nationwide telephone network,"[104] and a divided Court of Appeals upheld the Commission in 1976.[105]

Thus, the FCC had swept away one of the principal impediments to the imposition of a registration program, yet much depended on the action of the Joint Board. Numerous firms and trade associations submitted statements to the Joint Board and nearly all participants, excluding most public service companies, favored a certification program. The Justice Department, claiming that interconnection had created real benefits without any demonstrable harm, called for further liberalization—one of its last public statements before filing *United States* v. *AT&T*.[106] Congress, too, manifested its increasing interest in telecommunications as New York Representative Bertram Podell introduced one of the first mandatory interconnection bills in the House.[107]

By April 1975, when the Joint Board issued its First Report, the situation had changed dramatically. The Justice Department, MCI, and a host of other companies had instituted major antitrust suits against AT&T. The FCC had formally separated the economic aspects of customer interconnection from the technical issues in April 1974.[108] The Joint Board had accepted the NARUC's three-part division of terminal equipment and recommended the establishment of a registration program at the FCC for data terminal and ancillary equipment. The program recommended would apply to all customer-provided CPE other than PBXs, KTSs, main and extension telephones, and coin boxes. Nevertheless, the Joint Board stated that the RTC program, which included these kinds of interconnection devices, "has been satisfactorily received by both the telephone company and its customers. . . . We believe that the adoption of such a program may offer a practical solution to the technical problems raised concerning the interconnection of PBXs and key telecommunications."[109] In an appendix to its report, the Joint Board included an extensive set of standards and procedures for the registration program. The Bell system, in short, suffered another defeat.

In May, the FCC requested comments on the Joint Board's report as well as a California PUC registration program that the Board suggested should be examined.[110] The Bell system, which had submitted to the FCC a revised trouble-reporting system that still showed higher trouble rates for lines equipped with customer-supplied CPE, filed its comments in July 1975, essentially concluding that neither the Joint Board's registration proposals nor the California PUC's certification program provided adequate assurance of protection from harms. In addition, the Bell system criticized many of the particular standards and procedures of the programs. At the same time, it was fighting an antitrust suit brought by nine CPE manufacturers and coordinated by the North American Telephone Association (NATA), their trade association.[111] Thus, the Bell system was besieged on virtually all fronts—the courts, Congress, regulators, liberals, libertarians, equipment manufacturers, the petroleum industry, and others were politically arrayed against AT&T in CPE-related activities at every branch and level of government.

Before continuing our examination of AT&T's interconnection defeats, we should again pause to look at the company's service record during this period. If we were to look solely at the volume of activity and the intensity of criticism directed against AT&T at this time, we would conclude that the company's performance must have been poor. However, although there were grounds for criticism, especially in the realm of marketing, AT&T's record was still remarkably good. For example, the percentage of homes with telephones had steadily increased. And even though the CPI had increased 67 percent from 1960 to 1974, local telephone rates rose only 29 percent and long-distance rates remained virtually unchanged during the same period. Further, long-distance messages handled by the Bell system increased 69 percent from 1969 to 1974, and the number of Bell-system telephones in use rose from under 97 million in 1970 to over 114 million in 1974. In the later year, Bell companies met 96 percent of their appointments to install telephones on time, and 96.9 percent of long-distance calls went through to their destinations without interruptions or other difficulties.[112] Hence, AT&T's quality or quantity of service was not an issue. Rather, the FCC had embarked on an experiment in interconnection just as it had in specialized common carriage, and it was dedicated to its success.

THE REGISTRATION PROGRAM

Between April 1975, when the Joint Board issued its report, and November, when the FCC issued its First Report and Order, the agency clearly indicated the direction it would follow in interconnection. It would gradually break down the distinctions among types of interconnection equipment, leaving no exclusive preserve to the public service companies. Full-scale competition in all CPE would not take place all at once but gradually. Thus, in June 1975, the Commission issued an order in which it rejected the distinction that it had earlier made between a substitution for telephone company equipment and an add-on to such equipment. Partly based on AT&T's 1969 tariff, which did not make the distinction, the FCC concluded that the distinction made no sense in terms of implementing the basic *Carterfone* policy. In view of the increasing complexity and integration of equipment within one shell, the distinction between substitution and add-on would have become unworkable.[113]

In November 1975, the FCC issued its First Report and Order. Complaining that the common carriers had failed to devise an acceptable interconnection program in the 7 years that had elapsed since the *Carterfone* decision, the Commission adopted a registration program for carrier- and customer-provided terminal equipment other than PBXs, KTSs, main stations, party-line equipment, and coin telephones.[114] The agency indicated, however, that it saw no reason to exclude such devices even though the Joint Board had done so, in that the technical concerns raised by the Joint Board about these classes of equipment had "been mooted."[115] But since all of the parties did not have an opportunity to comment on these devices, the FCC deferred decision on the excluded equipment. It did include extension telephones within the registration program as "ancillary devices." The FCC adopted a simple decision rule in the First Report and Order. If equipment was not shown to cause harm to the network, tariff provisions could not limit the customer's right to make reasonable use of the services and facilities furnished by the common carriers. Any device registered could be used by a subscriber, and registration was to be based on "representations and test data [that] . . . are found to comply with specific interface criteria and other requirements. . . ."[116] The effects of the RTC program, the Joint Board Report, and other bodies played a large role in the adoption of the registration program. And, in view of the decision rule adopted, AT&T's arguments in favor of a telephone company-provided interface program that included lower costs and higher quality were considered irrelevant.

Various parties filed petitions for reconsideration of the First Report and Order and the Commission's New Part 68 of its rules and regulations, which were based on it. AT&T at this time changed its legal tactics considerably. Affirming that the First Report and Order would probably be upheld on appeal, AT&T made proposals for changes to some of the technical standards in the New Part 68.[117] While the FCC modified some of the particulars in Part 68, its Memorandum Opinion and Order of 13 February 1976 largely left the framework of the registration program intact.[118] Then, in March, in another memorandum opinion and order, the FCC modified several of the technical standards in response to AT&T's recommendations that were designed to make the standards more responsive to actual operating conditions.[119]

The focus next shifted to the hitherto excluded categories of equipment. In March 1976, the Joint Board issued its Second Report and Order in which it recommended against the inclusion of PBXs, KTSs, and main telephone systems in the registration program. This recommendation, consistent with the NARUC position, was based entirely on economic grounds. The Joint Board did not address the technical questions but urged that the issue should be deferred until the Commission examined the economic issues concerning interconnection: "This recommendation was based solely on the Joint Board's general fears concerning possible revenue losses the telephone companies might suffer as a result of competition in the terminal market."[120] However, the FCC rejected the Joint Board's view and extended the registration program to include PBXs, KTSs, and main telephone systems. Finding that the same technical principles applied to the other CPE categories could also be applied to the previously excluded equipment, the FCC reaffirmed the decision rule of the First Report and Order. Anticipating what it would do in the economic interconnection proceeding, the Commission majority noted that "[i]t is sufficient to note the absence to date of any showing before the FCC that any actual economic harm has been experienced much less that this has adversely affected any carrier's ability to serve the public."[121] The FCC claimed that it was not fostering further competition for its own sake but to allow subscribers greater freedom of choice, which was keeping with the agency's mandate since *Hush-A-Phone*. The Commission did not question the costs associated with the benefit; only Commissioner Benjamin Hooks asked the Commission to assess the social and economic implications of the decision.

Except for the separate competitive impact inquiry, it was now concerned with follow-up issues, such as clarifying the language of rules, grandfathering equipment that was being used before the registration rules went into effect, and technical engineering problems such as wiring or signal power limitations for data equipment.[122] Now the FCC was resolving such matters: "First we will permit an existing equipment cord, which is already 25 feet long (or less) to be extended once by a connectorized extension cord which is itself 25 feet long or less."[123]

The last major attempt by the common carriers to maintain control of a customer's array of CPE was made through the primary instrument concept. First proposed by the chairman of United Telecommunications in March 1977, it would have required all basic one-line telephone service to include one telephone instrument owned and maintained by the telephone company. The proposal, which did not apply to private lines or data services, was endorsed by almost every telephone operating company and their trade associations. The rationale of the concept was that it would affirm operating companies' responsibility for complete end-to-end service and at the same time preserve subscribers' choice of any other CPE. At the request of members of the House Subcommittee on Communications, the FCC instituted a Notice of Inquiry in February 1978.[124] The division among responding interests was based on the same grounds as in the interconnection issues. Large users, such as Computer and Business Equipment Manufacturers Association, were opposed to the primary instrument concept and argued that the concept was in direct conflict with the *Carterfone* and *Hush-A-Phone* views. MCI, of course, opposed it, and Rochester Telephone broke ranks with the public service companies by not taking a position. The Justice Department described the concept as one that would stimulate antitrust suits. Perhaps the most interesting comments were filed by the Michigan State AFL-CIO, which pointed out that many firms had begun importing CPE as a result of the *Carterfone* decision with a consequent loss of American jobs. But such considerations were irrelevant to the FCC, which concluded in August 1978 that the primary instrument concept was fundamentally inconsistent with its new interconnection principles.[125]

THE ECONOMIC INQUIRY

Just as AT&T had lost every battle on the technical front, so it lost the battles in the economics of interconnection inquiry. The FCC's First Report, released in September 1976 and consisting of approximately two hundred pages, simply stated that the agency saw no economic need or justification to reexamine or revise its conclusions on competition in either private line or CPE. The FCC concluded that "[c]ompetition has had little, if any, adverse impact on telephone industry revenues or local telephone rates *to date*" [emphasis added].[126] Further, the FCC concluded that competition would probably not have a significant impact on future revenues and rates, claiming that the cost-accounting studies independently prepared for AT&T and the United States Independent Telephone Association (USITA) indicating such adverse impact were flawed. The commission found that the studies did not identify or justify the allocation method used to separate the numerous components of telephone service. It questioned such other factors as present value and annuity computational methods, which led to predictions of high growth rates in interconnection penetration. The agency found no "convincing evidence" that telephone company CPE and private-line services were contributing to the cost of local telephone service.

Rather, the FCC concluded that, in the face of competition, AT&T should increase the rates for private-line services and terminal equipment. The agency did not find that AT&T or USITA were wrong. In an implicit shift in the burden of proof, the FCC stated that "direct revenues for terminal equipment *may not* be covering the full cost thereof, and that any finding of contribution *may result* solely from the improper attribution of toll settlement revenues to terminal equipment . . ." [emphasis added].[127]

Much of the FCC's decision was based on discussions and comparisons of the intricate cost-accounting methods and procedures utilized by the various interested parties. While generally complementing itself on its actions in the SCC and CPE interconnection areas and again lauding the probable effects on innovation that competition would bring, the FCC failed to consider some of the most important economic issues that AT&T and USITA raised. Arthur D. Little, a major consulting firm, prepared for AT&T a detailed study on the complexities of innovation, which concluded that neither theory nor evidence supported the idea that an increase in the total innovative output would occur if more firms were permitted to provide services or equipment.[128] But the FCC largely disregarded this study in favor of its view of the overriding value of competition. Further, the FCC also did not consider important arguments made by Systems Applications, Inc. (SAI) in its study for USITA. SAI argued that the inroads that would be made on the offerings of AT&T and the independent local companies would be great and constitute a "real and continuing threat" to the telephone companies.[129] It also noted, as we saw in connection with MCI, that the new entrants were not content with their original offerings, and that they tended instead to expand their offerings and to erode traditional telephone company services without incurring full public service obligations. In addition, newer technologies, such as rooftop satellite networks, would develop and be dominated by specialized firms without the more general obligations of the common carriers. SAI predicted that in time these new technologies would erode traditional markets, allowing large firms to bypass the common carriers.

The sole dissenter, Commissioner Hooks, had, since his term began in the FCC, focused on the impact that decisions would have on lower-income subscribers. In a memorable statement, Hooks argued that to believe telephone companies had priced their CPE far below cost is to believe that the companies were being run by Santa Claus or Daffy

Duck. Sharply criticizing the cost studies undertaken for the majority, Hooks feared that the revenue loss to the telephone companies would be greater than that contemplated by the majority.[130] But by then the FCC, abetted by the courts, Congress, and the administration, was caught in a movement that would redefine the public interest in ways that were expected to help AT&T's rivals. The telecommunications industry was in the process of being radically transformed.

PART THREE

Closing the Ring

CHAPTER 8

BUSY SIGNALS: MCI'S RENEWED ATTACK AND *COMPUTER II*

During the last days of the Johnson administration, the Antitrust Division brought a major antitrust suit that sought to break up IBM into smaller component companies. Thirteen years and 104,000 trial transcript pages later, the Reagan administration agreed to a complete dismissal of the case in 1982, concluding that it was "without merit."[1] Yet, at the same time in 1982, the Justice Department entered into an agreement that would radically restructure AT&T. Although we focus on *United States* v. *AT&T* in Chapter 9, in this chapter we examine the parallel changes wrought in the long-distance and equipment markets as a result of the *Computer II* proceedings and the MCI court actions against AT&T and other public service companies. The efforts described in Chapters 4 through 7 to overthrow the old public policy regime were extended in the events described here. Together with the 1974 case covered in Chapters 9 and 10, they would decisively transform the telecommunications industry and the older conception of the public interest. As dramatic as the technological changes in the computer industry were in the period from 1969 to 1982, the public policy changes were small in comparison to those in telecommunications. The computer industry (including IBM) was partly responsible for these changes in telecommunications policy.

In this transformation, AT&T's rivals were able to capitalize on a sweeping change in the concept of the public interest, which allowed them to portray their proposed reforms as part of a wider movement toward deregulation, economic liberalization, and antipathy toward monopolies. When the *AT&T* case was brought in 1974, Senator Philip A. Hart, the Democratic Chairman of the Senate Antitrust and Monopoly Subcommittee, had conducted hearings on the Industrial Reorganization Act that would have set up a special court and commission to dismantle the "monopolies." The term *monopoly* was not used in its dictionary sense or in the way it is used in microeconomics; rather, if four firms accounted for at least 50 percent of the sales in an industry, that would constitute a monopoly.[2] Senator Hart singled out the computer and telecommunications industries for special attention in 1974.

In 1973, the Federal Trade Commission attacked the four largest breakfast cereal manufacturers in one case and the eight largest integrated oil companies in another on the basis of a theory called "shared monopoly."[3] Under this concept, large firms not acting in concert were considered in violation of law. Thus, there was not much hope for AT&T at a time when such views were rampant among federal economic regulators. In the face of foreign competition, the zeal to break up large companies simply because they were large had been replaced with the sentiment that deregulation would importantly contribute to the solution of America's foreign economic and macroeconomic problems. This view, too, supported the interests of those who sought to continue their experiments in telecommunications. The prevailing sentiment on the expected impact of deregulation in finance, transportation, and communications was made clear in President Jimmy Carter's statement in signing the Staggers Rail Act of 1980 into law. The president expected that the statute would be "a major boost for the revitalization of the American economy, a revitalization that I intend will restore America's competitive edge and make possible full employment, and, at the same time, stable prices."[4] Traditional regulatory principles were clearly on the defensive. Although regulation would continue to exist, the agencies would have to show what areas within their domains should continue to be regulated and why. To defend their domains against the deregulation onslaught, they would have to develop coherent theories showing why competitive behavior should not prevail in certain activities.

More than thirteen years after the *Carterfone* and *MCI* decisions, the FCC still had not devised such coherent views, which was complicated by the fact that AT&T was increasingly being regulated by court decisions as well as by the FCC and PUCs. Judicial activism, as we shall see, played a major role in telecommunications policy. A memorandum prepared by FCC Commissioner Joseph R. Fogarty for the other commissioners and top staff after the *United States* v. *AT&T* settlement was announced demonstrates the tension present at the time:

> At the outset, I want to emphasize that while AT&T and DOJ may have reached a reasonable and proper private accord under the antitrust laws, such accord, with or without judicial approval, cannot oust, supplant or modify this commission's mandate, authority, and jurisdiction under the Communications Act of 1934. Indeed, in cases of irreconcilable conflict it is the antitrust law which must yield to the commission's broader regulatory jurisdiction.[5]

Nevertheless, it was too late for the FCC to begin worrying about such problems as inconsistency, ambiguity, and concurrent jurisdiction. Of course, the agency was not responsible for much that happened since 1968 in telecommunications policy, including the Antitrust Division's massive antitrust suit against AT&T or the private antitrust suits brought by MCI and others. But in other ways, the FCC bore responsibility for the turmoil that had beset telecommunications policy. The number of antitrust suits, the emergence of congressional interest in the subject, and the vastly increased numbers of times that the Commission itself was called on to decide controversies attest to its lack of clarity in the new directions it had taken. The FCC, after all, created MCI and the other SCCs. Its concepts of competition were unclear and provided advantages for AT&T's adversaries.

MCI'S 1974 OFFENSIVE

On 24 August 1974, MCI's vice-president, Bert C. Roberts, Jr., sent a confidential memorandum to William McGowan outlining the company's need to act on a new service called EXECUNET. The company's original plan—to rely on private-line offerings largely in the data field—had not met preplanned expectations. Consequently, the company devised EXECUNET which, as we shall see, was tantamount to

WATS and MTS (ordinary long-distance service). As we know, MCI won the right to FX and CCSA connections in April 1974 after the FCC decided that MCI needed these service offerings to compete effectively against AT&T.[6] But the FX and CCSA victories were treated as preludes to offering full-scale long distance, as MCI would only marginally seek to offer private-line service.

MCI's 1974 activities must be evaluated in light of its financial situation. Roberts commented in his August 24 memorandum to McGowan that many at MCI doubted that EXECUNET was a private-line offering (although he did not), and that "[e]ach day that goes by will tend to put MCI into a negative cash flow position on the start up of the project. . . ."[7] Generally, MCI was in a cash-negative situation in the fall of 1973 and sought to use government policies to reverse the problem. It opposed new Bell tariff offerings while at the same time expanding its own offerings. MCI admitted that it could not compete with Bell's TELPAK offerings in the private-line market.[8] Even earlier, MCI had drastically miscalculated the cost of constructing a private network. In June 1972, it estimated that $80 million would build a 165-city network, but Stanley Scheinman, MCI's chief financial officer, prepared an analysis in September 1972 that concluded $100 million would be required to build only a 41-city network. Scheinman further calculated that at the end of 1973, MCI would be in a deficit cash position of $15 to $20 million.[9] Further, a 1974 internal audit report prepared at the behest of MCI management concluded that the company was itself largely responsible for its difficulties. The report stated that the major cause of circuit installation delay was "poor coordination between and amongst salesmen, customers, one or both terminating branches in telco personnel. In many instances, this poor coordination has materialized as a general lack of direction and aggressiveness on the part of MCI to solve problems, or to obtain and communicate vital information in a timely manner."[10] While an MCI internal memorandum described the audit report as "extremely useful," even William McGowan, testifying publicly years later, conceded that the company was facing "internal difficulties."[11] Judge Harold Greene, after hearing exhaustive testimony on MCI's finances, concluded in *United States* v. *AT&T* that the severe scaling down of MCI's private-line plans "was attributed by MCI to causes other than the Bell System. And subject to the government coming up with something else, I may take it for present purposes that is established."[12] The cutback of plans, together with internal inefficiencies, were among the major causes of the company's financial difficulties.

With an understanding of MCI's financial background, it is clear why it sought to expand its offerings beyond private line. But to do so successfully, it would have to put AT&T even further on the defensive through a private antitrust suit. As early as 9 January 1973, MCI's top command decided to prepare a private antitrust suit against AT&T and the operating companies. At the same time, MCI officials agreed to prod the Antitrust Division into a major action against AT&T as well as to spur sympathetic FCC staff into action against AT&T in the administrative arena. McGowan mentioned the possibility of a private antitrust suit in a March 2 meeting with John de Butts. Then, on September 28, 1973 (and at other times), MCI officials met with Antitrust Division officials, including chief Donald Baker, in an attempt to convince the Justice Department to bring a major action against AT&T.[13] Obviously, a multipronged attack would be more effective, of which the private antitrust suit would be the first step.

THE *MCI* v. *AT&T* CASE

MCI expertly prepared the groundwork for its antitrust suit against AT&T, which it filed on 6 March 1974 in the U.S. District Court in Chicago. Instead of portraying AT&T's moves in the FCC, state PUCs, and courts as reasonable disputes, MCI characterized AT&T and its operating companies as a conspiracy intent on preserving monopoly against newcomers, notably MCI. As we have seen, the controversies surrounding FX and the other subjects of contention between the two companies were at least open to dispute. Nevertheless, MCI filed statements like the following, which it made in late 1973 before the New York PSC on Bell intrastate tariffs: "MCI believes that it and similar filings by other Bell System companies are intended to delay and obstruct the introduction of competition to Bell by specialized common carriers."[14] That the Bell system was required to file intrastate interconnection tariffs, as it had always done, would not fit into MCI's plans; thus, MCI portrayed itself as the innocent victim of AT&T. In November 1973, McGowan furthered the groundwork of the case by urging MCI customers and shareholders to complain to Congress and the FCC about AT&T's actions. "At the same time, we are also considering legal action under other federal laws [that is, the Sherman Act's Sections 1 and 2] to redress MCI for harm done by AT&T and the Bell System companies."[15]

MCI's antitrust suit, described by *Telecommunications Reports* as "long heralded,"[16] contained four separate counts: monopolization, attempt to monopolize, conspiracy to monopolize under Section 2 of the Sherman Act, and conspiracy in restraint of trade under Section 1 of the Sherman Act. MCI alleged that AT&T had committed twenty-two different types of misconduct that could be grouped into several categories held by the courts as antitrust violations—predatory pricing, monopolistic refusal to deal through denial of interconnections, bad faith negotiations, and unlawful tying. MCI requested a jury trial and stated that the full amount of damages sustained would be determined after discovery and proof during the trial. Under Section 4 of the Clayton Act, a successful plaintiff in an antitrust action is entitled to threefold the damages sustained and the cost of suit, including reasonable attorneys' fees. McGowan claimed that MCI refused to cite in its complaint an exact amount of the damages "because they're continuing to accrue each day."[17] Most of MCI's twenty-two discrete charges against AT&T were based on pricing and interconnection controversies, which we examine later in Chapter 11. However, at the time the suit was filed, most of these controversies were still being disputed. For example, it was not until 23 April 1974 that the FCC compelled AT&T to grant FX and CCSA connections, admitting that its "prior orders may not have been perfectly clear."[18] Nevertheless, the MCI complaint accused the Bell system of overtly and intentionally undertaking a series of unlawful actions, even though these actions had not been declared unlawful at the time and were subject to reasonable differences of opinion. This point is especially important because much of MCI's case was based on AT&T's actions before the courts, the FCC, and state regulatory agencies. Such actions are ordinarily protected as a matter of fundamental civil liberties in that they involve the First Amendment right to petition for a redress of grievances. Accordingly, the Supreme Court has held in what has become known as the Noerr-Pennington Doctrine that such activity cannot be the basis of antitrust liability unless it is done purely as a sham.[19] As the events described in Chapter 6 show, this clearly was not the case here.

In April 1974, AT&T answered MCI's complaint. In addition to denying the charges, AT&T filed an antitrust counterclaim against MCI that in some ways mirrored the MCI complaint. AT&T charged that MCI unlawfully sought to monopolize the relevant market, abused the FCC's regulatory processes, and unlawfully acquired competing SCCs.[20] Whether the counterclaim made by the world's largest corporation against a company whose 1973 revenues were only $200,000 was a smart move is questionable. In any event, the trial court did not permit the counterclaims to reach the jury, and AT&T did not challenge the propriety of that action on appeal to the Seventh Circuit Court of Appeals.

The *MCI* v. *AT&T* case was assigned to Judge John Grady. The first step involved pretrial procedures, which invariably took a long time in a case of such magnitude. As the pretrial proceedings drew to a close, AT&T filed a motion to dismiss the complaint on 7 April 1978, on the principal ground that the matters in the case were subject to exclusive FCC jurisdiction. AT&T argued that the public service standard with its necessary government control was inherently inconsistent with the antitrust law's reliance on free and open competition. Further, AT&T argued that because the FCC had approved each of its allegedly anticompetitive activities, it should obtain antitrust immunity for them. Of course, MCI opposed the motion to dismiss, but the issue would continue to be raised in virtually all subsequent telecommunications antitrust suits, including *United States* v. *AT&T*.

THE ANTITRUST IMMUNITY ISSUE

On 6 October 1978, the District Court denied AT&T's motion to dismiss the MCI complaint. In general, when a court decides a motion such as this, it is obliged to assume that the facts alleged in the complaint are true and that they would be proved in a trial. Under these assumptions, the court is asked to determine whether the complaint still fails to support a cause of action. Courts are, as might be expected, loath to grant a motion to dismiss if there is a reasonable possibility that the plaintiff can establish its case after a full-blown trial. Indeed, a judge is usually far less secure in his or her knowledge of the subject matter at the pretrial stage, especially in complex cases. Within this context, then, Judge Grady's decision was not surprising and should not be construed as a prejudgment of the case.

Grady began by drawing a distinction between exclusive and primary jurisdiction.[21] Under exclusive jurisdiction the regulatory statute is so opposed to the antitrust laws that the antitrust court is ousted of jurisdiction, whereas primary jurisdiction occurs when the defendant's conduct is arguably immune from antitrust liability because of the antitrust laws. The court refers the conduct in question to the administrative agency for a preliminary determination on the factual issues. The Supreme Court has instructed the lower courts to look with disfavor on exclusive jurisdiction: "Repeal of the antitrust laws by implication is not favored. Only where there is a 'plain repugnancy between the antitrust and regulatory provisions' will repeal be implied."[22] Thus, Judge Grady undertook a sketchy examination of the 1934 Communications Act's legislative history and did not find the plain repugnancy the Supreme Court required. In a cursory 2-page review of the Communications Act—undertaken without consideration of the Act's context or of its background in the public service principle and the telephone monopoly ideas of the 1920s—the court did not find anything specifically exempting telephone companies from the antitrust laws. Most other decisions, including that of Judge Greene's in *United States* v. *AT&T*, reached the same result by employing a similar approach.[23] This approach, together with the uncertainty created by FCC policies, were the principal causes of the proliferation of antitrust cases brought against AT&T and the other public service companies. And with each court decision, judicial intervention into the area of communications policy increased. For this reason, after the *United States* v. *AT&T* settlement, most people did not know whether the FCC or Judge Greene was primarily responsible for telecommunications policy. An exploration of the jurisdiction issue, therefore, is critical.

As we have seen in earlier chapters, the 1920s witnessed the near universal acceptance of the conception that the best structure for the provision of local-loop and long-distance service was a single firm in each market. Because earlier experiments in competition had failed, many states' utility laws contained monopoly provisions. One's ideological position on other telephone matters played no role in this issue; indeed, as Commissioner Walker and his Special Telephone Investigation staff showed, one could view AT&T as the devil but accept the provision of both local-loop and long-distance services as best done by monopolies. Since regulated monopolies were inherently inconsistent with the antitrust requirements of free competition (including free entry and complete pricing discretion within large limits), it became apparent that the comprehensive system of FCC regulation under the public service principles was inherently inconsistent with the antitrust laws. Thus, the legislative sponsors of the Communications Act of 1934 did not explicitly state that the antitrust laws should not apply to the common carriers over which the FCC would assume jurisdiction because it was simply too obvious to mention. Numerous statements in the Communications Act materials make this clear. For example, the Senate Interstate Commerce Committee's report states that "[u]nder existing provisions of the Interstate Commerce Act, the regulation of the telephone *monopoly* has been practically nil. The vast monopoly which so immediately serves the needs of the people in their daily and social life must be effectively regulated" [emphasis added].[24] Undoubtedly, a fully regulated system of monopolies was the accepted conception of those who drafted and supported the 1934 Act, regardless of which side of the political aisle they sat on. And there is simply no room for the antitrust laws in such circumstances. Nor was this conclusion changed when the FCC instituted a hybrid system, referred to here as contrived competition. Regardless of how one might criticize the FCC on the direction it took, it still attempted to create a comprehensive system of regulation different from the competition contemplated by the antitrust laws.

Notwithstanding the decisions that found a way to reconcile economic regulation and the antitrust laws, the logic of the situation, detailed in a brilliant *Yale Law Journal* note, points in precisely the same direction as the legislative history of the Communications Act.[25] The defining characteristic that removes regulated conduct from the antitrust ambit is pervasiveness. Pervasiveness is found when (1) the conduct challenged as well as the rates, entry, and investment are continually subject to agency supervision; (2) competition enters into the agency's considerations; (3) agency expertise is particularly useful in deciding issues in the antitrust suit; and (4) the antitrust suit involves important regulatory policy questions.[26] Applying these criteria to the

FCC, then, the agency continuously supervised rates, entry, investment, and every other facet of a public service company's behavior. Second, the FCC consistently considered competition in its deliberations; indeed, the courts have sometimes accused it of giving too much weight to competition.[27] As the Supreme Court held, the FCC must show that competition serves "some beneficial purpose such as maintaining good service and improving it. . . . Merely to assume that competition is bound to be of advantage . . . is not enough."[28] Third, rates, entry, investment, and other aspects of regulation are dependent on assessing cost criteria, engineering capabilities, and the like: "The FCC's familiarity with the technology and its experience in rate making render it better equipped than a court" to make determinations. Similarly, "The reasonableness of AT&T's refusals to interconnect with competing carriers depends in large part on technical engineering questions, which the courts are also ill-equipped to decide."[29] Finally, there is no question that the antitrust suits against AT&T involved basic questions of regulatory policy in the communications industry.

In brief, historical considerations as well as the logic of these criteria lead us to conclude that AT&T's motion to dismiss MCI's antitrust suit should have been granted. The same considerations should have led to the dismissal of the government's suit and the other private antitrust suits against AT&T. But, as we know, this did not happen and these cases went to trial. The policy morass, which still continues, serves to remind us that when different policy-making institutions make policy in the same subject area, the inevitable result is confusion. And the courts increasingly intervened in matters that regulators considered their province.

THE MCI TRIAL

The trial in *MCI* v. *AT&T* began on 5 February 1980. At the end of MCI's case, AT&T moved for a directed verdict on each charge in the complaint. The trial court granted AT&T's motion with respect to seven of the twenty-two charges but denied the others. The dismissed charges included (1) inducing Western Union to file a tariff that mirrored MCI's

Chicago–St. Louis charges; (2) increasing AT&T's capacity to conduct data communications business for the principal purpose of destroying competition; (3) disparaging MCI; and (4) bringing sham proceedings before administrative and judicial bodies. MCI did not appeal these issues. Those remaining pertained to the TELPAK and HI/LO tariffs, interconnection, and damages.

A major controversy developed when Judge Grady limited AT&T's defense to 26 days. He did so because MCI required only 15 trial days to present its case and AT&T was expected to be able to complete its case within approximately the same time period. However, in view of the complexity of the case, AT&T claimed that:

> The trial court effectively denied AT&T an opportunity to present its defense in the manner that it wished and effectively compelled a presentation that may have been unintelligible to the jury. . . . AT&T had intended to present a step-by-step explanation of the events . . . by witnesses who would have explained, in terms as simple and understandable as possible, the difficult economic concepts, technical principles and idiosyncratic terminology of the telecommunications industry with which the charges in this case were inextricably intertwined.[30]

Given the wide discretion trial judges are accorded in the administration of cases, as well as the opportunities AT&T had to present evidence in surrebuttal, the Court of Appeals found that the trial court did not abuse its discretion in this respect. But while the trial court may not have committed a due process violation, the Court of Appeals essentially confirmed AT&T's major argument. The typical jury usually sympathizes with the individual or small company confronting a large corporation. For this reason, vagueness plays into the hands of a person or firm accusing a large firm of predatory behavior. The problem of defending against such a charge is even more difficult when the subject matter is highly technical and complex, such as telecommunications. Although we may concede that AT&T requested too much time to present its defense, because ambiguity and a simplistic view of the facts played into MCI's hands, AT&T required considerably more time to rebut the charges than MCI required to make them. The time limitations on AT&T allowed the jury to think in a simplistic "little guy versus big guy" framework rather than the more complex one that might have led it to consider the charges differently.

Following more than 50 days of courtroom sessions, the trial ended.

During this period, MCI routinely opposed virtually everything that AT&T proposed before the FCC, including its application for authority to construct and operate a fiber optic cable system in the northeast corridor.[31] After a bitter controversy over the content of the judge's instructions to the jury that we shall examine shortly, the jury began its deliberations of 11,514 pages of testimony and about 1,000 documents on 11 June 1980. The verdict form required the jury to make a separate finding of liability as to each of the fifteen charges, but permitted the jury to award damages in a single lump sum, without apportioning MCI's claimed losses among AT&T's various lawful and unlawful acts. MCI's losses were almost entirely based on a lost profits study that was admitted into evidence over AT&T's strenuous objection. Judge Grady stated that "[t]hough the defendant raises substantial questions . . . without it, the plaintiff will not have a case."[32]

Two days after it began its deliberations, the jury rendered its special verdict in the amount of $600 million, which was trebled in accordance with Section 4 of the Clayton Act to $1.8 billion—the largest antitrust damage award in history. Not only was MCI pleased with the verdict, but so were other treble damage claimants and, more importantly, the Justice Department, whose suit to break up AT&T was in progress. William McGowan was not exaggerating when he gloated, "Fully half of the Justice Department case against AT&T is our case. We've provided the government with a blueprint on how to conduct the trial."[33] MCI's stock, which traded as low as $1.75 in 1977, was trading in the $25–$26 range in 1981. Thus, a $10,000 investment at two and one-half in October 1976 would be worth $100,000 five years later—a remarkable achievement for any company, but especially so for a telephone company.[34] The period between the verdict and the Court of Appeals decision was, however, to be MCI's high point.

MCI v. AT&T: APPEAL AND AFTERMATH

MCI had grand plans to finance expansion from the proceeds of its antitrust award. Considering that MCI's earnings in the fiscal year prior to the verdict were approximately $13.3 million, a $1.8 billion award was quite substantial. Even Judge Grady was reported as saying that the total judgment "seems unseemly, maybe even obscene." Half the jurors did not know the damage award would be trebled. One juror said she knew about treble damages from having typed a report for a college student the year before.[35] Unfortunately for MCI, the Seventh Circuit Court of Appeals overturned the verdict.

The first oral argument before the Court of Appeals took place in April 1981. At the same time, a second MCI antitrust case against AT&T was in progress, filed in the Federal District Court in Washington, D.C., to cover post-1975 conduct.[36] A second oral argument before a reconstituted Court of Appeals took place on 19 April 1982. At this time it became apparent that the issue of the cost basis to determine whether AT&T had engaged in predatory pricing was a concern of the panel, especially of Judge Richard D. Cudahy, who at one time had served as chairman of the Wisconsin PSC.[37]

At last, on 12 January 1983, the Seventh Circuit Court rendered its 258-page typed opinion and 40-page appendix, commensurate with the sizes of the record and the jury award. While both sides could not have been wholly satisfied or dissatisfied, AT&T clearly had the right to feel more satisfied than MCI with the result. From AT&T's perspective, the most important result was that the damage award was rejected and a new trial was ordered on the issue of damages. The heart of the court's discussion concerned the issue of defining cost. The importance of this discussion was MCI's charge that AT&T had engaged in predatory pricing in its private-line tariffs. Critical in this determination was whether AT&T's prices were below cost. Because AT&T and MCI chose different ways to measure cost, the Court of Appeals devoted enormous effort to determining whether MCI's fully distributed cost (FDC) or AT&T's long-run incremental cost (LRIC) should be the basis of evaluation.[38] The majority agreed with AT&T that LRIC—total company cost minus what the total cost to the company would have been if it had not produced the single product, divided by the single product—was the appropriate standard and that no court had ever in a predatory pricing case used FDC—average additional cost per unit of adding a new product to a preexisting line, which includes a portion of the firm's unallowable overhead assigned to the new product.[39]

The Court of Appeals criticized the trial judge for not providing guidance to the jury on the appropriate standard to use and for allowing the jury to choose a standard at will. The Court of Appeals concluded that AT&T's HI/LO tariff was not below cost under any standard. It further observed that the only evidence MCI presented on the issue was the testimony and accompanying exhibits of Dr. William Melody (who was also the Justice Department's key economist witness in *United States* v. *AT&T*). The Court concluded that Melody's evidence was unconvincing and devoid of the rigor required to support a predatory pricing claim. The same lack of rigor and persuasiveness compelled the Court of Appeals to reject MCI's damage study that formed the basis of the jury award.

Neither the TELPAK nor the HI/LO tariffs were predatory. Yet both the MCI study and the trial judge's directions failed to separate carefully AT&T's lawful and unlawful activities and to show the damages caused by the unlawful activities, which largely involved the interconnection charges. AT&T lost on the interconnection issues because the court, describing the FCC's SCC decision as opaque, permitted the jury to interpret whether AT&T should have known that the decision permitted FX and CCSA connections. As we saw in our discussion of the original SCC decision, there was nothing opaque about it; the FCC simply changed its mind later on. But, in a bizarre ruling, the Court of Appeals upheld the right of a panel of ordinary jurors to construe a complex sequence of technical FCC decisions, most importantly, the key SCC decision, as if they were matters of fact and not highly specialized FCC law. Moreover, the jury was asked to consider how AT&T's specialist attorneys would have construed the SCC decision. Now not only would trained jurists become involved in regulatory decisions but untrained jurors as well. Nevertheless, AT&T felt itself vindicated since the tariff issues were thrown out as being without merit.

The second trial began in early 1985, with Judge Grady again presiding. Meanwhile, as a 1984 *New York Times* article stated, "MCI [lost] some sparkle."[40] The company's shares, which traded as high as $28 in 1983, had fallen to approximately $10 in early 1984. Nevertheless, it was still succeeding as a litigant, although on a scale considerably more modest than the verdict in its first treble damage case against AT&T. MCI's settlement of some of its claims in the second antitrust case brought against AT&T and independent telephone companies replenished MCI's coffers. But it still awaited the verdict in the first case, requesting $5.8 billion in damages the second time around. AT&T conceded that damages in the range of $7.5 to $36.4 million would be appropriate for the interconnection charges on which it had been found in violation of the Sherman Act. The verdict finally handed down was in the sum of $37.8 million, which was tripled to $113.3 million. Virtually every analyst called the verdict a victory for AT&T.[41]

Finally, in November 1985, AT&T, the new regional Bell-operating companies, and MCI announced the settlements of all of the outstanding suits.[42] But MCI's first antitrust suit had triggered a host of others and had deeply involved the federal courts in telecommunications policy. The turmoil in telecommunications policy was furthered by another example of MCI aggressiveness—EXECUNET.

EXECUNET

While MCI's hopes in its treble damage actions against AT&T and its operating companies were far from realized, its attempts to expand beyond traditional private-line offerings were more successful. The gains made through the FX and CCSA authorizations paled in comparison to that made through EXECUNET. In this service, an EXECUNET customer gained access to an MCI intercity line by calling a particular MCI local telephone number in the originating city from any push-button telephone. When the connection was made and the customer was identified through an identification number, he or she obtained access to MCI intercity circuits. The customer then dialed any telephone in any city where MCI offered EXECUNET service. The call was transmitted over MCI's intercity circuits, which were interconnected through the local telephone company's switching facilities to the local exchange facilities in the distant city. The call then reached the telephone called. A push-button telephone was ordinarily used in the originating city because MCI's switching equipment responded to the signal tones generated by this equipment. However, a customer could use a dial telephone and generate the appropriate tones through a readily available "Touch Tone" pad.

With EXECUNET, MCI abandoned any reasonable pretense to offering only private-line service. It was a service that more closely approximated ordinary long-distance (MTS) or WATS service. Neither MTS nor EXECUNET dedicated particular intercity circuits to specific customers; rather, both used whatever intercity circuits were available as well as local telephone company switching facilities and circuits. Second, like MTS, any telephone, not only one within a private subscriber's ambit, could access EXECUNET. Third, any telephone in a large number of distant cities could be reached. Fourth, the EXECUNET customer used common local exchange plants at both ends and, finally, the EXECUNET customer, like ordinary long-distance customers, was billed for each call, based on time and distance, with no charge added at the distant city.[43]

Of considerable dispute were the circumstances surrounding the filing of the tariff, employed to justify EXECUNET service as well as the question of when the MCI top leadership conceived of it (if not necessarily by the same name). They raise issues of considerable importance in FCC policy-making. The FCC's 1971 SCC decision was based on the hope that SCC competition would offer new and innovative services. Since then, MCI, the principal SCC, survived not by offering new and innovative services but by encroaching on traditional long-distance services. Instead of reexamining the underlying wisdom of the SCC policy, the FCC simply accepted the outcome. The issue then became whether the enlargement of MCI's services injured the Bell system. If little adverse impact was found, the FCC assumed its policies were sound. But the expansion of MCI offerings and the FCC's "clarifications" of the SCC decision, undertaken to assure MCI's survival (and thus vindicate the agency's original judgment), only served to muddle further an already unclear situation. The FCC's lack of clarity contributed to what would occur in EXECUNET. Not surprisingly, then, MCI's September 1974 tariff filing, which was the basis of EXECUNET, gave no indication that it planned to offer the switched long-distance service. According to MCI's Bert C. Roberts, Jr., he devised the EXECUNET service in 1974. Nevertheless, AT&T introduced material into the record that suggested (but did not necessarily prove) that MCI planned to introduce such a service as early as June 1973.[44] In AT&T's view, the FX and CCSA controversy was merely an MCI subterfuge designed to determine just how far it could go in using the FCC's lack of a clear decision rule to expand service offerings. The dates are important here. The FCC's "clarification" on FX and CCSA, which, in fact, made things more ambiguous, was issued in April. MCI's EXECUNET tariff filings were issued a short time later, in September.

MCI's letter of transmittal accompanying its tariff revisions did not mention EXECUNET but stated: "This tariff revision proposes to broaden the private use service that MCI now offers. . . ."[45] By October, it was clear that MCI had something new in mind since it ordered a large number of new lines in conjunction with the new tariff. An early November AT&T inquiry to MCI suggested that MCI might be planning to violate AT&T's tariff restrictions. MCI's reply was not responsive to AT&T's inquiry,[46] and discussions with the MCI staff failed to clarify the matter. In January 1975, however, MCI began offering the EXECUNET service. AT&T contacted the FCC in May 1975 (with a copy to MCI), claiming that EXECUNET was long-distance message telephone service and that MCI was not authorized to offer such a service. AT&T's position was that EXECUNET threatened the entire structure of telephone service. AT&T's MTS service was offered at nationwide averaged rates and, therefore, was susceptible to carriers aiming primarily at low-cost, high-density routes that yield high profits. But EXECUNET also threatened the subsidy contribution that long distance makes to local service through the separations process. The EXECUNET service would remove substantial revenues from the separations process, which would result in increased local rates.[47] After MCI responded to AT&T's letter, the FCC, on 2 July 1975, released an order rejecting the EXECUNET service on the ground that it was switched public message service and MCI was authorized only to offer private-line service. Latent in the FCC's response was the anger of FCC staff and commissioners that MCI had betrayed them.[48]

After MCI appealed the FCC order to the Court of Appeals, the matter was held in abeyance until MCI and other interested parties could file briefs and comments. On 13 July 1976, the FCC released its decision, reaffirming that EXECUNET was an unlawful tariff and reminding MCI of the original rationale for its specialized service: "MCI asserted that there was a distinct difference between a public telephone service which is a natural monopoly and a customized communications service offered on a private line basis."[49] The FCC also reminded MCI that every filing the company had made before the agency and the courts was premised on this distinction as well as on MCI's denial of aspiring to become a public-switched network service. Further, the FCC argued, MCI did not show the need for another public-switched network service.

JUDGE WRIGHT'S REVOLUTION

MCI appealed the FCC decision to the Court of Appeals for the District of Columbia Circuit. To understand the strange Court of Appeals decision, we must appreciate that one group of judges in the Circuit greatly expanded the reach of its review of substantive administrative policy-making. Under traditional administrative law principles, if "there is warrant in the record for the judgment of the expert body it must stand. . . . The judicial function is exhausted when there is found to be a rational basis for the conclusions approved by the administrative body."[50] The scope of review applies to both new regulatory principles and traditional regulatory action. While other courts also have d'sregarded the rule in administrative law, none was as notorious as the Court of Appeals for the District of Columbia. Under the leadership of Judge Skelly Wright, the court extended judicial activism to such lengths that the highly respected Judge Bazelon criticized some of his fellow judges, deploring the dangers inherent in technically illiterate judges sifting through the details of mathematical and scientific evidence.[51] According to trial lawyer William Allen, the judges in the D.C. Circuit who engaged in judicial activism believed that they were better able to protect the public interest than the agencies whose decisions they examined.[52] The Supreme Court as well as distinguished commentators have rebuked the D.C. Court of Appeals for extending its role improperly by acting much like a third branch of the legislature. The Supreme Court caustically noted that the D.C. Circuit was not composed of experts in any substantive fields assigned to administrative agencies nor in the innumerable fields assigned to the federal agencies that deal with matters ranging from automobile safety to railroad rates. As such, the D.C. Circuit, according to the Supreme Court, did not have the right to impose its policy choices in place of an agency's.[53]

The Supreme Court's reprimand of the D.C. Court of Appeals decision did not occur until 1984. The *EXECUNET* decision was handed down in 1978 and, like the 1954 *Hush-A-Phone* decision, it had a devastating and unsettling effect on the telephone industry. The focus of the Court of Appeals decision was on Section 214 of the Communications Act, entitled "Extensions of Lines," the only section that dealt with entry into the telephone business. The court ignored the history behind the Communications Act, which indicated that its authors expected telephone services to be delivered by monopolies. Also ignored was the meaning of the phrase "common carrier" in Title II of the statute; that is, the comprehensive public interest obligations that such companies are required to perform under strict supervision of state and federal regulators. In numerous proceedings since the telephone's invention, the FCC had examined the structure of the communications industry and accepted the regulated network manager system on the basis of the technical and economic reasons delineated in PUC and court decisions. Moreover, the FCC had also considered the possibility and effects of competition in many important matters, such as the SCC decision. Within this context, Section 214 of the Communications Act held that the FCC had the power to issue or refuse an application for a new line on the basis of the public convenience or necessity standard. Further, if the FCC granted the certificate, it could impose "such terms and conditions as in its judgment the public convenience and necessity may require." Thus, to the average observer, the SCC decision imposed limiting terms and conditions on MCI's certificate, yet Court of Appeals Judge Skelly Wright interpreted the decision in a different way. According to Wright, the FCC should have considered whether the EXECUNET service should be permitted regardless of the limits imposed by the SCC decision. That the FCC had considered the overall provision of MTS and WATS on a continuing basis was to Wright irrelevant.[54] In a distortion of Sections 203–205, which apply to rates and practices, Wright held, in a legislative judgment, that "carriers should in general be free to initiate or implement new rates or *services* over existing communications lines" until the FCC decides otherwise [emphasis added].[55] Of course, services such as those proposed by MCI neither existed nor were contemplated in 1934 when Sections 203–205 were written, and thus they were not then considered. Under the Act, services were covered in Section 214's provisions concerning the terms of the FCC's certificate. Having made this imaginative leap in construing the rate provisions of the Communications Act, the court concluded without evidence that MCI intended to compete only "on the fringes of the message telephone market."[56] But, as we know, MCI did not intend to limit itself in this way.

Thus, the D.C. Circuit did not solve the controversy but instead exacerbated it. In 1978, the FCC reviewed the matter in the light of the D.C. Circuit's views and again concluded that AT&T did not have to interconnect with EXECUNET and a similar SPRINT service.[57] Once again, the Court of Appeals reversed the FCC decision, holding that AT&T must provide local interconnections for EXECUNET and similar services.[58] The Supreme Court denied certiorari, and the regulated network manager system suffered yet another defeat.

As a result, several events were inevitable. First, MCI and others would become AT&T's long-distance competitors in MTS and WATS service. Second, tariff conflicts would erupt and the FCC would become increasingly busy as carriers protested the tariffs of others. Third, because AT&T's services were nationwide and those of the other carriers' network were relatively small, the latter would seek to interconnect into AT&T's lines at many points so to enlarge their markets. Although AT&T was now required to interconnect, the rates and rate structures for interconnection had not yet been determined, an issue that would evolve into numerous controversies.

Thus, Judge Wright's participation would not establish firm decision rules but would instead create indecision and controversy within the telephone industry. Further, the FCC would continue to favor the newer entrants at the expense of AT&T, to which the FCC gave a new appellation—the dominant carrier.[59]

ENFIA

The ENFIA tariff illustrates the unsettling effect of the *EXECUNET* decision. Ultimately, the ENFIA controversy stemmed from the strange transformation that mandatory interconnection had taken. Under the public service doctrine in common law, mandatory interconnection with competitors was not required. Then, under the regulated network manager system, mandatory interconnection with connecting, but not competing, carriers developed so to enlarge the network and its utility to each subscriber. Contemporary interconnection was required to assure that AT&T's ineffectual competitors would be able to compete with the "dominant carrier."

In May 1978, AT&T filed BSOC Tariff No. 8 (Exchange Network

Facilities for Interstate Access), or ENFIA, which specified the charges that long-distance carriers would pay for local exchange service connections. In September 1978, the assistant secretary of commerce for Communications and Information urged the FCC to seek a negotiated settlement to the disputes arising under ENFIA. An interim agreement was reached in December 1978, and in April 1979, the FCC released a memorandum opinion and order accepting it, concluding that ENFIA was patterned after the method AT&T used to compensate local telephone companies for exchange facilities used for MTS and WATS service.[60] However, the decision did not end the dispute over ENFIA. The original ENFIA agreement covered only MTS and WATS services. Negotiations between AT&T and other carriers on FX and CCSA ENFIA rates, as well as those for other so-called enhanced arrangements, broke down in February 1980, when MCI vice-president Roberts claimed there was no reason to continue discussions on AT&T's proposals.[61] Disputes over the ENFIA rates and the existing agreements, primarily over the meaning and consequences of such terms as "gross operating revenues," continued through 1980. In July, the FCC rendered another decision on ENFIA tariff revisions.[62]

In 1981, after AT&T filed new exchange access tariffs for resellers, the various parties entered yet a third round of negotiations,[63] much of which was devoted to the exchange of interrogations.[64] During this period, MCI announced its first direct EXECUNET agreement with the 2,100-station Northwest Iowa Telephone Company, which would allow MCI customers accessing Northwest Iowa's facilities to dial the same number of digits as Bell system customers.[65] This factor, together with the changes wrought by the 1982 *United States* v. *AT&T* agreement and the *Computer II* decisions, would have an enormous impact on rates and rate structures. But the *ENFIA* disputes continued from 1982 through 1984. In late 1983, the Commission commented on the endless controversies in *ENFIA*. Describing the apparently simple term "billed minutes," the agency said it had "found the meaning of that term . . . to be the subject of seemingly endless dispute under the ENFIA tariffs."[66]

However, what was clear about the ENFIA tariffs was that MCI paid a much lower rate to local telephone companies than did AT&T.[67] The FCC, prodded by the D.C. Circuit, devised policies that favored one class of competitors without considering the social gains from this new competition. According to economist Almarin Phillips:

All things considered . . . there is enough . . . to suggest caution in permitting blanket entry into telecommunications services. Some special burden should attach to show social gains from entrance, and that burden must be more than to show that in a particular line the entrants' operations would be profitable and viable. The regulated firm is multiproduct, regulated, and does contribute to . . . goals [other than economic efficiency] because of regulation. Adverse social effects in other dimensions may easily offset the gains in the service areas for which entry is sought.[68]

COMPUTER II—THE TENTATIVE DECISION

The *EXECUNET* decision destroyed AT&T's monopoly of public-switched long distance, but the *Computer II* proceedings completely reformed the old system in the CPE area. However, *Computer II* also provided the wedge for AT&T to redefine in part the public interest by being allowed to enter noncommunications businesses and to employ its technological prowess within them.

Computer II was instituted in large part because the *Computer I* distinctions did not provide adequate guidance to computer communications firms and because great progress was being made in the field. While in 1969, less than 10 percent of the investment in computers in use could employ data communications, the percentage reached 45 in 1976. Moreover, it became difficult if not impossible to determine whether computing or communications was the dominant activity. Thus, one of the central distinctions made in *Computer I* broke down.[69] Further, post-*Computer I* computing equipment was capable of performing data-processing and communications functions simultaneously:

> Computer networks no longer followed the neat pattern of first processing information, and subsequently sending it over communications lines. Remote computer users could now receive raw or partially processed data at their locations and complete the processing themselves. In addition "smart terminals" which were capable of performing some data processing functions were being developed.[70]

Computer II also occurred as a result of a changing conception of the office during the 1970s. The office of the future would be equipped with such things as CPE, which could exercise control functions for activities outside the office, and devices that allowed more kinds of information to be economically transmitted over existing telecommunications distribution facilities (such as wires, microwave, and satellite) and new kinds of facilities (such as optical fibers). Thus, control of robots in distant factories, electronic funds transfers, transmission and analysis of medical readings, and a vast potential for work at one's home computer terminal and the appropriate CPE were components of the office of the future. The widespread transmission not only of data but of higher quality video information and facsimile, holographs, electronic mail, and even complex engineering blueprints are other examples. Although not all of these advances would occur rapidly, the major firms had to ready themselves for them.[71]

In view of this, the stakes in the computer-communications interface were high. In 1974, the combined dollar volume of the data-processing and telephone industries was $60 billion, with both industries growing 12 to 14 percent a year in revenues.[72] As the FCC, courts, and the Justice Department threatened to curb AT&T's opportunities elsewhere, the computer-communications market promised to be an attractive alternative. Although the 1956 *Western Electric* consent decree was a major impediment, AT&T could circumvent its impact by defining an activity as communications rather than computing. In addition, there was the threat latent in IBM's entry into satellite communications, for other large companies were permitted to enter traditional and new areas of communications but AT&T was not allowed to enter their businesses. Thus, through a new computer inquiry like *Computer II*, AT&T could reopen issues and possibly redefine its boundaries.

Among the many factors contributing to the onset of what the FCC knew would be a massive inquiry in *Computer II* was AT&T's Dataspeed 40/4 filing in November 1975. The Dataspeed 40/4 terminal was a smart remote access device that could not only transmit messages but also store, query, and examine data. Errors that were detected could be corrected locally without the need to interact with a mainframe computer. IBM, the Computer Industries Association (CIA), and the Computer and Business Equipment Manufacturers Association (CBEMA) petitioned to have the Dataspeed 40/4 tariff revisions rejected on the ground that the service constituted data processing rather than communications, which was not permitted under the *Computer I* rules. The Common Carrier Bureau agreed that Dataspeed should be

rejected because it was a data-processing service.[73] Arguing before the
FCC, AT&T pointed out that the Common Carrier Bureau's views would
effectively remove the company "as a provider of data terminal services, whenever customers wish to update their service in order to communicate more efficiently with a computer without the need for an
intervening operator."[74] That is, the Common Carrier Bureau required
AT&T to be technologically backward and, therefore, uncompetitive.
The FCC rejected the Common Carrier Bureau's recommendation,
holding that Dataspeed 40/4 was primarily a communications service.
The agency also recognized that the existing rules were becoming increasingly inadequate since the capacity of terminal devices to engage
in data processing had increased markedly since the *Computer I* rules
were established. In 1976, during the pendency of the Dataspeed 40/4
proceeding, the FCC launched its second computer inquiry. At this
time, mini- and microcomputers as well as other devices that could
compute at a user's premises and be readily interconnected into telephone lines had clearly rendered the old definitions and conceptions
obsolete. Further complicating the issues was the ability of the common
carriers to use some of their facilities to allow terminals to converse
with each other. In addition, the common carriers had become capable
of offering performance features that would otherwise be located in
a smart terminal, including automatic call forwarding, restricted and
abbreviated dialing, and special announcements. Accordingly, the FCC
proposed in its Notice of Inquiry a new set of definitions, which it
hoped would make distinctions superior to those made in *Computer I*.[75]
A supplemental notice questioned the possibility of common carriers
having a data-processing subsidiary separate from the regulated
entity.[76]

Although there were sharply differing views, the initial response to
the FCC's new set of definitions was primarily negative. In particular,
the Justice Department drew connections between *Computer II* and its
1974 *AT&T* antitrust case:

> Unless a more airtight case for rescinding the restrictions on diversi-
> fication contained in the 1956 decree can be developed than has
> been to date, the likelihood that those restrictions will be lifted by
> the court is not great. An equity court is not likely to focus entirely
> upon theories of economic efficiency and overlook recent conduct
> by AT&T respecting communications industry competition.[77]

AT&T was not ready in 1977 to enter data processing, at least not publicly. In June 1977, AT&T vice-president James R. Billingsley told the FCC that the Bell system did

> not want to become data processing entrepreneurs. . . . What we do want is to be allowed to continue to provide our customer flexible and comprehensive telecommunications services, and to be able to use our facilities and systems to do those things which our customers want and which we can do as an inherent part of our system's capability.[78]

AT&T hoped that the rules established under *Computer II* would allow it to offer a wide range of services that included data-processing capabilities as communications services. AT&T argued in its lengthy filing that the 1956 consent decree recognized the dynamic and expansive nature of "communications," including the equipment that would be designed to meet new needs. Accordingly, AT&T claimed that if the FCC properly resolved the issues in *Computer II*, modification of the 1956 decree would not be necessary.

Among the many varying comments filed in 1977 in response to *Computer II*, some of which called for retaining the old *Computer I* conception of a hybrid service, one of the most important was IBM's. Because IBM feared most FCC regulation, it recommended that only "communications common carrier services which perform the pure transmission function—the transportation of information from place to place" should be regulated.[79] That is, carriers and all others who engage in different services should be unregulated. IBM did not even suggest that the carriers should be required to place their unregulated activities in separate subsidiaries so long as they used accounting systems that properly allocated between regulated and unregulated activities and did not subsidize unregulated activities. It also recommended that AT&T should be free to provide unregulated services through either a modification of the 1956 consent decree or legislation. When AT&T filed its reply comments in October 1977, it focused principally on IBM's comments, probably because of the latter's apparent conciliatory and reasonable tone. AT&T argued that IBM's perspective was inherently unfair to AT&T because of the extraordinary difficulty it would have in attaining a modification of the consent decree. Thus, an expanded definition of "data processing" and the narrow restriction of communications services that IBM proposed would severely hamper

AT&T's ability to offer such communications services as Dataspeed 40/4. Turning to the issue of a separate subsidiary, AT&T concluded that such a requirement would give unregulated data-processing firms a substantial competitive advantage. Maximum separation would be anticompetitive because regulated firms "would be required to 'compete' subject to burdensome administrative and operational restrictions. Such restrictions would include the uneconomical establishment of duplicative engineering, installation, maintenance and repair personnel."[80] AT&T urged that the Communications Act was broad enough to include as "communications" those services that "include incidental data processing which enhances or supports the communication common carrier service."[81]

The FCC issued its tentative decision in *Computer II* in May 1979. Reversing the rules of *Computer I*, the new set of definitions recognized that technological advances had made the problem of defining the boundary between communications and data processing unworkable. The new framework focused "on the nature of various categories of services and the structure under which they are provided."[82] The FCC's tentative decision employed three basic categories: voice, basic nonvoice, and enhanced nonvoice services. *Voice service* was defined simply as the electronic transmission of the human voice, such that one person is able to converse with another. An *enhanced nonvoice service* was defined as "any non-voice service which is more than the 'basic' service, where computer processing applications are used to act on the form, content, code, protocol, etc. of the inputted information." Finally, *basic nonvoice service* was defined as

> the transmission of subscriber inputted information or data where the carrier: (a) electronically converts originating messages to signals which are compatible with a transmission medium, (b) routes those signals through the network to an appropriate destination, (c) maintains signal integrity in the presence of noise and other impairments to transmission, (d) corrects transmission errors and (e) converts the electrical signals to usable form at the destination.[83]

The central distinction that the definition sought to convey was that the original information was not transformed in content. However, the definitions applied to basic and enhanced nonvoice services were sufficiently complex as to invite controversy and difficulty in application. Essentially, the new definitions would allow the public service companies to offer enhanced nonvoice services only through a separate subsidiary, which would lease telecommunications lines on the same terms and conditions available to information-processing firms without a common carrier subsidiary. The new conception of transmission was based on the 1976 *Resale and Shared Use* decisions,[84] adopted over the objection of AT&T and most other common carriers. Under the FCC-established concept of a resale carrier, such carriers were permitted to lease facilities from underlying carriers such as AT&T. The resale carrier added enhanced nonvoice services to leased lines for resale to retail customers. Thus, the resale and shared use conception presumably allowed the FCC to assure that common carriers did not abuse their regulated positions by discriminating in favor of their own subsidiaries.

While AT&T was not pleased with the FCC's new definitions or with the strict separate subsidiary requirement, it was pleased with the FCC's discussion of the 1956 consent decree. Using Section V(g) of the decree, which permitted AT&T to provide services and products incidental to communications services, the FCC decided that many enhanced nonvoice services may fall within the incidental category. Noting AT&T's technological prowess, the FCC observed that the public interest would not be served if AT&T had to restrict internally developed computer hardware and software to the Bell system only. Accordingly, the Commission tentatively decided to permit AT&T to market such incidental products and services through a strictly separated subsidiary in situations "where market forces promise to be adequate and where full regulation is therefore not required but the offering . . . would be in the public interest."[85]

Thus, for the first time AT&T could enter the door of the unregulated computer business. As vice-president William G. Sharwell noted, the company's reaction was positive but guarded: "We are inclined to regard this action favorably, but we can't tell exactly what it will mean until we study the full written proposal."[86] The FCC conceded that its new general definitions were subject to reevaluation if necessary, that the new AT&T rules in particular would require case-by-case analysis, and that many issues remained unresolved. For these reasons, the FCC's decision was deliberately considered a tentative one and called for further comments from interested parties.

COMPUTER II—THE FINAL DECISION

The FCC received a flood of comments on the tentative decision in *Computer II*, most of which were critical. AT&T's vice-president Billingsley generally endorsed the FCC's resale approach but urged that the development of a resale organization within AT&T's existing corporate structure would accomplish the FCC's objectives. AT&T still felt, however, that there was sufficient ambiguity within the FCC's interpretation of the 1956 consent decree to require "legislative action that would deregulate certain categories of services coupled with consent decree relief which would permit us to participate in a broader and more diversified marketplace."[87] It appeared that in 1979, AT&T anticipated the possibility of having to give up something in the antitrust suit, and saw *Computer II* as an opportunity to compensate by entering new businesses.

IBM, on the other hand, did not endorse the FCC's tentative decision but charged that the new proposed rules would not solve the problems: the FCC "would perpetuate unnecessary regulation and would continue the attempt to draw regulatory lines where no distinctions exist in technology or in the marketplace."[88] IBM reiterated its view that if AT&T cannot provide computer services, it should seek changes before the court or in Congress. It proposed that FCC regulation should be limited to areas that exhibited significant natural monopoly characteristics. The computer industry trade associations generally joined in IBM's view that the tentative decision would expand rather than contract the ambit of regulation. Yet other participants felt that the FCC's interpretation of the 1956 consent decree was far too expansive.

The Justice Department's comments would, of course, be important for several reasons, including whether it concurred in the FCC's construction of the 1956 consent decree and how the connections between *Computer II* and the pending antitrust suit against AT&T were drawn. Indeed, some of the attorneys involved in the antitrust suit also represented the Justice Department in *Computer II*. The Justice Department declared that the new FCC definitions did not improve the distinctions made in *Computer I*. Further, it sharply criticized the FCC's interpretation of the 1956 consent decree, declaring that the agency had no legal authority to definitively construe the consent decree. The Justice

Department "specifically rejected the Commission's novel interpretation that the 'incidental to' savings provision buried in the 1956 decree permitted AT&T to diversify into the unregulated data processing business. . . . This interpretation of the 1956 *Western Electric* decree is simply wrong."[89] The Justice Department pointedly declined to state that it would join the FCC in seeking a modification of the 1956 decree.

The links between *Computer II* and the pending antitrust suit were now clear. IBM, Xerox, and a host of other large and small firms were drawn into the conflict. Not only were there conflicts among the firms but among the government agencies as well, such that AT&T was uncertain of what constituted the law even if it complied with the rules embodied in the forthcoming final *Computer II* decision. Indeed, shortly after the FCC's final decision was adopted on 7 April 1980, AT&T chairman Charles L. Brown declared that "legislation is the only thing that can clear up such ambiguities."[90] But in view of Congress's lack of action in telecommunications except in compiling lengthy hearing records, AT&T was hoping for too much.

Released on 2 May 1980, the FCC's final decision hardly sounded final. At virtually every turn the divided agency promised to review and reconsider its conclusions and rules. Six separate statements accompanied the 122-page decision,[91] and the changes and supplements to the tentative decision were substantial. Instead of three categories of service, only two remained, basic transmission service and enhanced services. *Basic transmission service* was "limited to the common carrier offering of transmission capacity for the movement of information." *Enhanced services* were defined as offerings over a telecommunications network that add computer-processing applications and "act on the content, code, protocol and other aspects of the subscriber's information."[92] Conceding that its prior definitions were faulty, the FCC was now satisfied that it had constructed workable categories that coincided with those used in the marketplace. It believed that an underlying carrier would now have clear guidelines on which services it could provide directly and which required a separate subsidiary. But the service distinctions, while having the merit of simplicity, would not definitively determine on which side of the boundary all of the new service offerings would be, especially those involving information storage.[93] Further, the FCC reiterated its basic views on the meaning and application of the 1956 consent decree. Sharply rejecting the Justice Department's views, the FCC reaffirmed its tentative decision views, especially its primary right to determine the construction of the 1956 decree and the meaning of such operative words as "communications." Even though AT&T would face uncertainty as a result of what the Commission termed the Justice Department's "strained construction" of the 1956 decree, it told AT&T that it would support the company in any contest on the decree.[94] Of course, from AT&T's perspective, being in the middle of a contest between two government agencies was not an enviable position.

Although AT&T achieved a limited victory on the 1956 consent decree issue, it lost on nearly every other one in which the *Computer II* final decision varied from the tentative one. Common carriers were required to submit tariffs for basic services that would account for all of the costs relating to those services. The disclosure requirement was intended to make it difficult to include enhanced service costs in the basic service rates. Data-processing companies, to whom the basic services were sold, could add their own features and resell the enhanced service to their customers. Since the basic service rates would be identical for common carriers and firms outside the scope of FCC regulation, there could be no discrimination in favor of a common carrier affiliate. Because of the resale conception, the FCC stated that there was less need for strict separation than in its prior computer proceedings formulations. It emphasized that it was seeking a compromise between the abilities of common carriers to act in a predatory manner toward noncarriers and the diseconomies of structural separation. The former was an argument in favor of structural separation, the latter opposed it. The FCC's so-called compromise was to require only AT&T and GTE to form separate subsidiaries (on reconsideration the requirement did not apply to GTE). The key notion used to require AT&T to form a separate subsidiary was market dominance. Without explaining how a closely regulated firm can abuse its monopoly power, the FCC concluded that structural separation imposed on dominant carriers "will aid to diminish the likelihood of abuses of monopoly power through either (1) denial of access to the 'bottleneck' i.e. local exchange and toll transmission facilities or (2) cross-subsidization from the monopoly service to competitive enhanced and CPE markets."[95] The decision did not discuss why regulators would be unable to guard against such abuses; rather, it was assumed that they could not. Indeed, notwithstanding the size of the record compiled in the *Computer II* proceeding, there is virtually no discussion of the FCC's or PUC's actual experiences in such matters.

While there is clearly a place for economic theory in decisions, the final decision employed little else in its discussions of the separate subsidiary issue. Theoretical studies on the benefits of competition overrode any empirical studies of AT&T's innovation that stemmed from vertical integration and communication among the components of the Bell system.[96]

Having decided that AT&T should form separate subsidiaries, the FCC's next step was to elaborate a complicated scheme of the activities that could be conducted jointly on behalf of parent and subsidiary and those that had to be separated. The subsidiary would have its own operating, marketing, installation, and repair personnel. Certain kinds of information could be shared, other kinds could not. To assure arm's-length dealings, the parent and subsidiary could not share space, and the implication was clear that any fraternization would be risky. The rules were so detailed and complex that they were tantamount to a deeper regulator presence in the day-to-day operation of both businesses than had ever occurred. The strict delineation between business operation and regulatory supervision that Theodore Vail had spelled out and that was cardinal to the regulated network manager system had been devastated by the separation rules.[97] The final blow dealt to AT&T followed from the series of post-*Carterfone* interconnection decisions. Not just computer communications devices but all CPE, including the basic telephone, were to be deregulated pursuant to calendar schedules:

> We [the FCC] conclude that in light of the increasing sophistication of all types of customer-premises equipment and the varied uses to which such equipment can be put while under the user's control, it is likely that any given classification scheme would serve to impose an artificial, uneconomic constraint on either the design of CPE or the use to which it is put.[98]

The FCC's primary concerns were with sophisticated business users rather than ordinary residential subscribers, most of whom would want nothing more complicated than "POTS"—plain old telephone service. Once consumer sovereignty was established in CPE, the concept of end-to-end responsibility was completely undermined. Subscribers would now be able to own or lease any CPE—and pay for the cost of repairs. CPE would be removed from tariff regulation (detariffed) and would have to be offered through the separate subsidiary. In this way, CPE provision and transmission service would be "unbundled." Unbundling, as the FCC indicated in the dense paragraphs on the subject, might cause CPE costs for residential subscribers to be greater than the transmission savings from "unbundling," but the FCC would deal with that problem later on.[99]

Computer II left AT&T with a promise that it would be allowed to engage in enhanced services over the opposition of the Justice Department. CPE was, with few exceptions (such as coin-operated telephones and certain multiplexing equipment), deregulated with little thought given to its effect on AT&T's various public service obligations. In its dissatisfaction with the final decision, AT&T was joined by many of the industries and trade associations that had participated in the inquiry (although often for different reasons) as well as Commissioner Joseph Fogarty. Attacking the decision's partiality, Fogarty concluded that the assumptions pertaining to the alleged benefits of separation were treated as truths, whereas countervailing hypotheses were treated as unproven assumptions subject to considerable doubt. In so doing, Fogarty charged, the FCC was not protecting the interests of the general public but rather the private interests of individual competitors.[100] Forgotten in the decision was the upward pressures on local rates. Of course, the attitudes that Fogarty criticized in the *Computer II* final decision were only the most recent manifestation of the attitude found in most FCC post-*Carterfone* decisions.

THE AFTERMATH OF *COMPUTER II*

Almost every major participant in *Computer II* filed notices of appeal with the U.S. Court of Appeals for the District of Columbia and requested the FCC to reconsider the matter. In its 98-page Petition for Reconsideration, AT&T raised issues concerning service restrictions, intercorporate transactions between AT&T and its subsidiary, the financial consequences of the *Computer II* rules, and the transition to the new structural and behavioral changes.[101] Other participants criticized nearly every aspect of the decision, including AT&T's right to participate at all in enhanced services.[102]

The order on reconsideration, adopted on 28 October 1980, affirmed the basic definitions that were made, released GTE from the separate subsidiary requirement, changed some of the dates concerning CPE deregulation, and altered some accounting practices. Existing CPE and that installed until March 1982 (embedded CPE) would remain part of the rate base and continue under state regulation. But a separate proceeding would be initiated to consider the detariffing of embedded CPE and such technical matters as CPE maintenance. Some relaxation on what subsidiaries may do was permitted.[103] The opinion on reconsideration indicated that applying the new fundamental distinctions would not be easy. Two novel AT&T services were held to be enhanced services because they stored information and retrieved it by computer: Dial-It involved the storage of information, such as a story, which AT&T customers could retrieve by dialing a number; and Custom Calling II allowed a caller to leave a message when the line was busy. Again, although storage was involved, the information was not transformed. The FCC made it clear that it would interpret the concept of a basic service narrowly; that is, only a channel of communication would be considered a basic service.

The controversies continued before the courts and the FCC following the *Computer II* reconsideration. AT&T and the FCC were on one side of the controversy and the Justice Department and most other *Computer II* participants were on the other. Each sought to convince the Federal District Court with jurisdiction over the 1956 consent decree to uphold their respective views on the proper interpretation of the decree.[104] When Judge Vincent Biunno decided in September 1981 in favor of the AT&T-FCC position on the 1956 consent decree, the path was cleared for AT&T to form and operate its separate subsidiary.[105] But controversies over a host of implementation and accounting issues remained,[106] which were still not resolved when in November 1982 the Court of Appeals upheld the *Computer II* rules against numerous challenges.[107] Yet when the Court of Appeals upheld the FCC's *Computer II* decision, the emphasis shifted to another momentous event in the interface between government and AT&T. The Justice Department and AT&T had entered into a consent settlement of the 1974 antitrust case calling for dramatic structural changes in the industry. AT&T had created its new unregulated progeny—ironically named American Bell, the antecedent of AT&T—in June 1982. Of course, this structure would have to be revamped in the light of the 1982 antitrust settlement (the Modified Final Judgment, or MFJ). The FCC would have to consider *Computer II* in view of the new corporate entities created by the MFJ and, at the same time, it would have to continue solving the problems arising under *Computer II*.

The events became even more complicated. On 5 July 1985, the Commission launched its third computer inquiry. In *Computer III*, the FCC asked whether it should eliminate the separate subsidiary require- ments of AT&T and whether it should revise the tests to determine which enhanced services should be regulated. The FCC even admitted that it might have to re-regulate some unregulated services.[108] The agency lifted AT&T's separate subsidiary burden as the *Computer III* inquiry continued into 1987.[109] As this indicates, the FCC's idea of competition was something quite different than market competition, in which the economic arena, not the tribunals of government, deter- mines outcomes. The public interest standard that prevailed in tele- communications at this time was not protecting competition but the competitors.

CHAPTER 9

"NO" FOR AN ANSWER:
UNITED STATES V. AT&T

AN OVERVIEW

Even AT&T's sternest critics conceded that the company's handling of the divestiture of its local operating companies and of setting up the new Bell-operating companies was done in exemplary fashion. Breaking up was indeed easy to do—although extremely expensive. And in our roles as taxpayers and ratepayers, we helped to pay for it. Even the Justice Department, in February 1987, proposed that the regional Bell-operating companies (BOCs) created as a result of the AT&T divestiture should be allowed to enter certain long-distance, manufacturing, and information services from which they were barred in the settlement at the insistence of the Department.[1] Judge Harold F. Greene, who presided over most of the *United States* v. *AT&T* case, was irked during a June 1987 hearing by the Justice Department's shift in position on the need to divorce local operation from other facets of telecommunications. AT&T's attorney Howard Trienens told the court that the proposed decree changes "will cause to reemerge the very controversies we thought we were getting rid of when we signed the decree."[2] The Justice Department's theoretical concerns on alleged regulatory irresponsibility, cross-subsidization, and vertical integration, which were the critical underpinnings of *U.S.* v. *AT&T*, seem to have been reversed. Judge Greene, still a true believer in the virtues of the consent settlement (MFJ), claimed at one point that the Justice Department appeared "as if it had taken some valium and is very relaxed" about such concerns.[3] Was it all worth it? In this chapter, we attempt to answer this question by examining the *United States* v. *AT&T* case and the events that led to the MFJ.

Emboldened by the success of MCI and others and prodded by them, the Antitrust Division brought suit in February 1974, reinforcing the position of AT&T's rivals that policies profiting them were in the public interest. While the Justice Department always claimed to represent the consumers when it enforced the antitrust laws, we should bear in mind R. H. Coase's perceptive question: "Which consumers' viewpoint will be heard?" All public policies and conceptions of the public interest involve wealth redistribution issues.[4] The AT&T divestiture may have benefited MCI and large business subscribers but not necessarily the middle- or lower-class residential subscriber. What is clear, however, is that the Justice Department's action further threatened the regulated network manager system and further undermined the older conception of the public interest. Some persons even claimed that the Justice Department's action threatened the universal service goal, as economist E. E. Zajac noted in 1981:

> In my view, a disinterested, objective observer of the American scene would conclude that a basic level of telephone service is regarded as an economic right. The evidence is all around us; starting with the universal service mandate in the Communications Act of 1934. . . .
> In order to achieve that mandate, the price of basic telephone service has been kept low compared to costs principally through separations and settlements payments.[5]

Behind the continuing attacks on AT&T was the sense that no matter what the company had to face, it would still find a way to discharge its obligations. In other words, the very success of the older conception of the public interest was a factor in its undoing. Henry E. Boettinger, an AT&T executive who headed the *TELPAK* tariff development task force, pointedly testified:

> It reminded me actually of a meeting with Mr. Strassburg [Common Carrier Bureau Chief] that occurred in 1960, and I said, it was on the teletype thing, I said Bernie, why do you hit us so hard. He says, no matter what we do to you guys, you always find a way to cope. It may very well be that that philosophy was the motivation behind the great gamble that they took.[6]

Now it was time for the Justice Department to take the biggest gamble of all with American telephone service.

Behind most of the charges leveled against AT&T was an attack on the company's vertical integration. Critics claimed that vertical integration within a large firm enables that firm to utilize market power against smaller, nonvertically integrated competitors. For example, AT&T was allegedly able to thwart MCI's long-distance service by refusing interconnection; and the Bell local operating companies purchased a disproportionate amount of CPE from Western Electric, allegedly thwarting the competitive opportunities of rival CPE manufacturers.

Since the telephone industry was closely regulated, it was necessary for the Justice Department to couple the vertical integration argument with one that claimed the regulatory agencies were unable to supervise adequately the behavior of the regulated firms. In earlier chapters, we found these claims unconvincing, but it was crucial to the Justice Department's case to show that regulation had and would continue to fail. For this reason, the Justice Department argued that the only appropriate relief would be to dissolve the ties between and within the various levels within AT&T's structure. Before we examine the 1974 *AT&T* case in detail, we must first look at integration in the telephone industry. Most importantly, we must understand why the Antitrust Division's claim that integration is used to attain market power is false. Integration takes place for sound business reasons, as a brief history of GTE illustrates.

GTE AND INTEGRATION

In the post–World War II era, virtually every major actor in telecommunications has horizontally and vertically integrated. The Bell system continued to expand horizontally by absorbing more and more local companies, acquiring these both during good and bad times. Thus, AT&T's Virginia subsidiary, the Chesapeake & Potomac Telephone Company of Virginia, absorbed seven independent companies from 1912 to 1935. A typical transaction involved the acquisition of a relatively small operation. For example, on 1 January 1945, the New England Telephone & Telegraph Company acquired the properties of the Northern Telephone Company, operating three northern Vermont exchanges.[7] Most of AT&T's acquisitions occurred because the acquired firm was in financial distress. The FCC concluded, in one of the few contested hearings, that AT&T did not have a policy of outbidding independents and that both AT&T and GTE, the largest independent, had programs that substantially improved the acquired companies, installing more modern, efficient equipment and transmission lines.[8] Therefore, AT&T acquisitions were generally approved because rates would be reduced and service improved—the public service criteria.

General Telephone and Electronics (GTE), the second largest telephone company before the AT&T breakup, underwent similar development, although its history began much later. GTE began as the General Telephone Corporation in 1935, an investment and holding company, when it acquired the assets of the bankrupt Associated Telephone Utilities. In the early 1930s, Associated served about 300,000 telephones in parts of twenty-five states, the most important of which was California. Beginning with operating revenues of $11 million in 1935, the company increased these to $85 million in 1951. In that significant year in GTE's history, the person who was to leave as lasting an imprint on the company as Theodore J. Vail left on AT&T assumed the company's presidency. When Donald C. Power became president, the company had acquired many local operating companies but only one small switching equipment manufacturer—the Leich Electric Company.[9] When Power took over GTE, it had approximately 1.4 million telephones, constituting about 20 percent of the non-Bell market. By 1969, as a result of Power's policies, GTE served approximately 9 million telephones, constituting about 46 percent of the non-Bell market. In addition, it had become vertically integrated and a major participant in equipment manufacture. From 1946 to 1955, GTE quadrupled its operating revenues and boosted net income even more rapidly,[10] and by 1984, its revenues and sales were in excess of $14.5 billion and its operating income was about $2.9 billion.[11] Hence, Power's policies of vertical and horizontal integration had significantly contributed to the company's spectacular financial success.

Many of GTE's acquisitions were quite small. For example, in 1954, GTE acquired the Marshfield Telephone Company in Wisconsin, which served almost 5,000 telephone stations. But two acquisitions during Power's years with GTE were crucial to the company's overall performance and illustrate what horizontal and vertical integration can achieve. In 1955, General Telephone, the then largest independent local operating system, merged with Theodore Gary and Company, which was not only the second largest system but also controlled the Automatic Electric Company, the second largest manufacturer of telephone equipment in the country. As early as 1930, approximately three-fourths of the world's telephones used Automatic Electric (AE) equipment. AE continued its technological progressiveness thereafter so that at the time of the Theodore Gary merger it was the largest domestic manufacturer of switchboards and telephones for independent telephone companies.[12] Integration of General Telephone and Theodore Gary was expected to allow AE to achieve even greater scale economies and sharply reduce fixed costs per unit of output. In addition, the acquisition would strengthen General Telephone's research efforts.[13] But since General Telephone could not monopolize the telephone industry or even come close to AT&T's size, what net benefits did it see in integration? According to a *Business Week* analysis, the increased size resulting from the merger was expected to increase the rate of growth. Power used AT&T as a model in his attempt to achieve a greater growth rate and to make the company more efficient. He expected the vertical integration of a controlled supplier to result in lower equipment costs than if purchases were made in the open market. With control of a captive equipment manufacturing firm, the supply of CPE and other telephone equipment would henceforth be prompt and adequate. The problem of prompt and adequate supply had become especially critical as the company expanded its local telephone operations.[14] The assurance of prompt and adequate supply would, of course, make the company more efficient.

But how would the acquisition of more local operating companies make GTE more efficient? Power's first step after acquiring Theodore Gary was to reorganize management, using AT&T's federal plan as a model. He added centralized specialist functions at headquarters that would assist each of the local operating companies by providing information on how better to perform certain functions. These included financial, engineering, marketing, public relations, and other functions. Increasingly, local managers consulted the headquarters experts for the solutions to problems, and feedback from one local operating company to the headquarters was shared with others. Accounting systems were made uniform and many economies of scale in purchasing large quantities were achieved.[15] In these ways, the whole GTE system was more efficient than each component operating separately. And, as the company grew, the need for captive suppliers grew commensurately.

General Telephone's next major consolidation was in 1959, when it merged with Sylvania Electric Products (a leading firm in electronics, lighting, television, radio, metallurgy, and chemistry) and became General Telephone and Electronics (GTE). *Business Week* stated that, "At first blush, the combination seemed as odd as a wedding of a great dane and a bobcat."[16] But, on closer examination, Power's plan made a great deal of sense in light of anticipated technological development in telecommunications. Although Power had established General Telephone Laboratories in 1957, it was still very small, especially in comparison to Bell Labs. Sylvania, in contrast, had long experience in electronics research, much of which was related to data processing. At the time, Sylvania sought to move more heavily into the data field, and the potential applications in telecommunications were substantial. Thus, in a period of rapid technological change, the Sylvania acquisition was to play a major role in making GTE more efficient through technological progressiveness. Automatic Electric would produce many of the new products for the GTE system.[17] Then, in 1983, GTE completed its imitation of AT&T's structure when it acquired Southern Pacific Company's telecommunications services, the most important component of which was SPRINT, a long-distance carrier. This acquisition was approved by Judge Harold F. Greene in December 1984, subject to certain conditions agreed to by GTE and the Justice Department.[18] Central to Judge Greene's approval was the fact that GTE lacked "monopoly power," thus distinguishing that situation from AT&T's. But, as this brief history of GTE shows, monopoly is not the point of the integrated structure that both companies attained.

The SPRINT acquisition was not as successful as most of GTE's other ones. Consequently, to stem large losses, GTE shed SPRINT into a new company that combined SPRINT and United Telecommunications' long-distance unit.[19] Nevertheless, the details of GTE's history illuminate the overall lesson: telephone companies perceived clear benefits in adopting integrated structures patterned on AT&T's. The point of adopting such an integrated structure, in GTE's case as in AT&T's, was not to attain monopoly power—GTE had no hope of doing so—but to achieve certain efficiencies and economies that benefit each component of the integrated operation. Indeed, IBM acquired substantial shares in MCI in 1985, purchased Rolm (a leading PBX manufacturer), and forged close links with other firms in diverse areas of telecommunications.[20]

THE MEANING OF INTEGRATION IN TELECOMMUNICATIONS

The behavior of the telecommunications industry strongly points to the conclusion that comparative costs at the margin are lower when firms choose internal organization rather than market mechanisms for many telecommunications activities. That is, it is cheaper for each firm to do some things internally than to acquire those things on the open market.[21] Obviously, each firm has different decisions to make in that respect, and each arrives at different structures. Further, such decisions are not permanent; companies frequently shed divisions. As we explore the *United States* v. *AT&T* case, it is important to appreciate that large companies attain the shapes that they do not in response to the idea that they are monopolists but in response to rational economic criteria. The long history of AT&T and the short one of GTE show this.

The costs of a more fragmented structure may be particularly high in the deployment of new technologies. For example, one study of the development of TD microwave systems conducted on behalf of AT&T analyzed the key events

> to determine when and if they would have occurred if the participating parties were not commonly owned and were relying upon contracts. Our analysis showed that contracting would have added from 2 to 5 months to the development of each TD microwave system, or a total of 28 months for the entire family of systems. In the integrated Bell System contracting would not have been necessary.[22]

According to the study, additional capital costs conservatively estimated at $675 million would have been incurred. It is in industries that are both technologically progressive and highly interactive that integration is most beneficial. The constant mutual adjustment of the component parts of the network led to integrated research planning, design, and manufacturing within one firm. Again, the interactivity of the network virtually called for a command structure—the network manager—that would make the cost-quality and other trade-off decisions improve the network and institute better coordinated and more efficient product designs. As the case of the TD microwave system indicates, the net transaction costs involved in planning, negotiating, contracting, and supervising can often be lower within a single firm than within several when a product or service is (1) integrated into a highly interactive network, (2) highly complex, and (3) technologically dynamic. A company may, of course, take the wrong path. But it is still more likely that experienced management will understand a business better than inexperienced Justice Department attorneys.

The Bell system was able to achieve technological coordination in development and a high degree of compatibility between each service and product in the network. It had the ability to raise capital for expansion and improvements that smaller communications firms could not undertake singly. It had resources large enough to absorb the costs involved in universal service through rate averaging and so on. Its great resources allowed Bell Labs the luxury of incurring great risks in long-range scientific and technological work. Further, the Bell system clearly achieved many economies of scale. Finally, as the GTE example shows, the Bell system's vertical structure could rationalize flows by assuring that the needed CPE, wire, switching and transmission equipment, and so forth were efficiently supplied without shortfall, quality impairment, delay in supplying products, or other difficulties. As economic historians Harold Livesay and Patrick Porter have shown in the case of manufacturing, these and not monopolistic aspirations have been the fundamental reasons for vertical integration.[23]

THE BEGINNINGS OF THE *AT&T* CASE

In the spring of 1968, Antitrust Division Chief Donald Turner expressed his dissatisfaction with the settlement terms of the 1956 *Western Electric* suit. His comments caused such great activity in AT&T stock that trading had to be stopped temporarily.[24] Not only were many Antitrust Division staff and others (notably some legislators) dissatisfied with what they conceived to be a "sellout" in 1956, but the Antitrust Division had become active in intervening in FCC proceedings, including *Carterfone* and *Computer I*. Not surprisingly, the Antitrust Division's intervention was always on the side of more competition, for its task was to protect competition through the antitrust laws.

To understand *United States* v. *AT&T*, it is important to be aware of the prevailing attitude within the Antitrust Division. Suzanne Weaver's important survey of prevailing attitudes in the Antitrust Division during the period under consideration sheds much light on what we might term the Division's ideology:

> The lawyers strongly oppose any attempts to balance the value of competition against that of other economic or social goals. They do not accept . . . that some desired social goal will not be well served by maximum competition. . . . [While there is a] massive presumption within the division in favor of competition, it is not clear that its idea of competition is an economically coherent one.[25]

One facet of incoherence about competition is that the word meant both the number of competitors and a standard of conduct—two very different concepts. For example, an analysis of the relationship between criminal price-fixing cases and industry concentration has shown that 94 percent of the cases brought in 1955–1965 involved industries in which the four largest firms accounted for less than 60 percent of the industry's sales.[26] In other words, these cases involved many competitors but not one of the presumed major behavioral benefits of competition—price rivalry. The Antitrust Division chose whichever concept it considered most appropriate at the time, while at the same time ignoring that regulated monopoly may achieve positive performance results in some industries that competition may attain in others. Thus, under the Antitrust Division's ideology, if one of AT&T's rivals is protected by placing a floor under AT&T's rates, benefits are assumed to occur because there are several firms providing the service. Under this ideology, the actual performance of the industry under regulated monopoly is ignored. This ideology is critically important in understanding the Antitrust Division's approach to its case against AT&T.

Antitrust Division attorneys, as we have seen, have prosecuted many cases against small firms that have engaged in clearly illegal practices such as collusive price fixing. Nevertheless, Suzanne Weaver reports that the Antitrust Division favors bringing action against large firms. Although small and large firms both engage in illegal conduct, Weaver concludes that

> the presence of a large firm in an investigation will prompt not simply a search for the anti-competitive effects but a search that tends to construe even probably harmless things in an anti-competitive light. . . . [T]he presence of bigness in a case at hand will convince many lawyers that they will find "something bad" about the situation if only they look long and hard enough.[27]

However, many factors determine whether the Justice Department will bring a novel and difficult case such as *AT&T*. Complex cases consume substantial resources and, of course, a Department loss in a big case can be embarrassing. For this reason, it is more likely that an Attorney General will consent to bringing a big case when additional factors are present. In *United States* v. *AT&T*, although there was dissatisfaction with the 1956 *Western Electric* consent judgment and the Antitrust Division had consistently taken positions in conflict with AT&T's before the FCC, these factors were probably not enough to push the case. Certainly, Senator Phillip A. Hart's Industrial Reorganization Act proposals and his specific attacks on AT&T provided valuable support.[28] Almost every potential and actual SCC and CPE firm appeared before Hart's Subcommittee complaining about AT&T in 1973 and 1974. But while administrators do not ignore legislative pressures, they will not move simply because a certain legislator may want them to do so. Often there are legislators who are as vehemently opposed to an action as those who are in favor of it.

Two major factors greatly influenced the Justice Department's decision to bring the *AT&T* case. First, the case was endorsed by President Gerald Ford because it supported the administration's economic program and its broad concept of the public interest. Second, intense disturbances and pressures present in the judicial area forced the Justice Department to pursue action. That is, the numerous private antitrust suits brought against AT&T and the pressures exerted by AT&T's rivals, most importantly by MCI, would have made it appear as if inaction on the Justice Department's part would seem like avoidance of its duty. For example, in ITT's antitrust suit against GTE's acquisition of the Hawaiian Telephone Company, other operating companies, and equipment manufacturers, the Federal District Court criticized the Justice

Department for the 1956 *Western Electric* settlement and subsequent Antitrust Division inaction in the telecommunications field.[29] That this 1972 decision was largely reversed in 1975 did not diminish its ability to prod the Justice Department in 1973 and 1974.[30]

President Ford was touring Japan when the 1974 *AT&T* suit was filed. Although he was not directly consulted, he was apprised of the suit while he served as vice-president.[31] He was also aware of an AT&T investigation concerning the possibility of a lawsuit, a fact widely publicized months before the filing. For example, in a December 1973 *Business Week* report, it was noted that AT&T had been served with subpoenas for documents and that "[m]any in the communications industry are certain that it is a precursor to further action—either an antitrust suit or reopening a 1956 consent decree."[32] There were actually two AT&T investigations being conducted at this time. However, President Ford had ample opportunity to make his views known; that he did not reject the suit implies his approval. Moreover, Antitrust Division staffers asserted that the president was kept informed of the investigation.[33] Thus, the AT&T antitrust suit was in accord with the administration's program and, according to *Telecommunications Reports*, received Ford's "full approval."[34] Only a few months before the suit was brought, Clay T. Whitehead, Director of the Office of Telecommunications Policy, appeared before the Hart Subcommittee and told Congress that "[t]he antitrust laws should be enforced to ensure that regulatory mechanisms cannot become a haven for escape from competition. . . . Finally, a restructuring of the communications industry may be necessary if competition and monopoly are to coexist constructively."[35] Whitehead claimed that the only appropriate monopoly area was local-loop transmission and that all other services, including long distance, and equipment should be open to competition.

Yet another critical event that influenced the Justice Department's decision to bring the *AT&T* suit involved President Ford's economic advisers. Drawing a close connection between inflation—then considered the nation's most pressing economic problem—and economic regulation, the economists

> agreed that government regulation was a major cause of the high and rising cost of living, and that reforming it was one of the few useful things that could be done to control inflation. The consensus on this point was striking, being shared by economists of every political stripe—a fact not lost on President Ford.[36]

Further, only three days before the *AT&T* suit was announced, Hart committee staffmember Bernard Nash, referring to President Ford's October address calling for tougher antitrust enforcement, concluded: "I view speeches like Ford's as creating a tone from the top down." Ford's focusing on antitrust action as a principal way to combat inflation "probably unwraps a lot of things enforcement people have hesitated to do because they didn't have any administration support" during the Nixon presidency.[37] The prospective *AT&T* divestiture case was thus viewed as the single most important test of invigorated antitrust enforcement.

Although the Antitrust Division was backed by the Ford administration, it also needed support for its view that the FCC and state regulators were incapable of resolving telecommunications issues adequately. To the Antitrust Division, the burgeoning number of private antitrust suits brought against AT&T was evidence of the FCC's inadequacy, in that AT&T's rivals were unable to obtain relief through the agency or the PUCs and had to resort instead to private antitrust action. The Division argued further that both small and large firms had brought such cases, and that many private controversies had become public ones. The Antitrust Division used these facts together with its view of AT&T's use of the regulatory process to contest such cases as SCC or *Carterfone* and to justify its conclusion, as stated in *Business Week*, that "the regulatory process was no longer able to contain AT&T's power."[38] Also, the lengthy records of the earlier regulatory proceedings and private antitrust cases were expected to save the Justice Department considerable time, effort, and money in preparing its case. The advice and materials provided by AT&T's competitors led Antitrust Division counsel Philip Verveer to proclaim, "We have not wanted for competitors who felt aggrieved and who have educated us in the business."[39]

The firm that provided the most important lessons for the Antitrust Division was MCI, which had brought its carefully prepared antitrust suit against AT&T in March 1974. MCI began its meetings with Antitrust Division officials as early as 1973. While its influence was certainly important in the Justice Department action, much more was involved. The information that MCI would provide and its collaboration in other ways would be of great value to and would save the Justice Department considerable resources in compiling data purporting to show that AT&T had violated the Sherman Act. Further, MCI's collaboration demonstrated that the Justice Department would have major support in the case—a clear incentive to take action. And, as Judge Greene reiterated during the examination of MCI officials, the MCI-related episodes were among the most important in the *AT&T* case.[40] William McGowan was not exaggerating when he commented, after his 1980 Chicago Federal District Court verdict against AT&T, that "[f]ully half of the Justice case against AT&T is our case."[41]

THE COMPLAINT

The complaint in *United States* v. *AT&T* was filed on 20 November 1974, in the District of Columbia Federal District Court, and the trial began on 15 January 1981. After several postponements, the Justice Department concluded the presentation of its case on 2 July 1981; the defendants began their case on 3 August 1981 and terminated it on 18 December 1981. The settlement agreement into which the Antitrust Division and AT&T entered in January 1982 terminated the trial portion of the case. However, AT&T was scheduled to resume its case after the New Year's Day holiday and to complete its presentation on or about 20 January 1982. The Justice Department was then scheduled to present its rebuttal case, and the trial was scheduled to end by 10 February 1982.

Given the size of the record, it is likely that if the settlement had not intervened, Judge Greene would have not prepared a decision until late in 1982 or early 1983. An appeal to the Court of Appeals by one or both sides would have been inevitable as would an attempt to have the Supreme Court consider some of the questions the case raised. Thus, the settlement, modified and approved by Judge Greene on 11 August 1982, occurred almost 8 years after the complaint was filed. Without a settlement, the case could have taken as many as eleven or twelve to resolve. We should also consider that in 1987, Judge Greene was still being asked to consider problems under his 11 August 1982 order (MFJ).

The complaint was only 14 pages long—much shorter than the 1949 *United States* v. *Western Electric* complaint. Yet it spawned a volume of paper of legendary proportions.[42] The pretrial phase had included 296 days of depositions and 45,000 pages of material. The trial testimony was recorded on 25,047 transcript pages. The plaintiff called 94 witnesses; the defendants listed 244 witnesses and 55 written testimonies. The Antitrust Division marked 8,103 exhibits totaling about 183,000 pages, but only 2,071 exhibits (totaling about 46,000 pages) were put in evidence. However, AT&T marked 15,477 exhibits of approximately 618,000 pages, of which only 2,521 totaling approximately 98,000 pages were received as evidence when the trial was suspended. In addition, of course, there were numerous motions and other procedural matters as well as court decisions based on the disputes between the parties. Finally, there were 73 stipulation packages, which constituted the basic organizing principle of the case (these are discussed later in more detail).

How did such a relatively small complaint generate such a torrent of paperwork? In general, monopolization cases under Section 2 of the Sherman Act are usually big cases because the stakes are high (a company may, after all, be restructured if it loses such a case). For example, in the classic 1911 Section 2 cases, Standard Oil and American Tobacco were broken up.[43] Also, the high stakes tend to make monopoly cases bitterly contested. In addition, they entail the presentation of numerous facts showing that the defendant(s) has monopoly power and intends to acquire and/or maintain it. In contrast, a price-fixing case under Section 1 of the Sherman Act is proved when evidence of collusion is shown. That is, if A and B agree to fix prices, the courts will not inquire about their size, market power, or anything else. But if a company is charged with monopolizing, the courts will conduct an inquiry into the peculiarities and nature of the industry, the defendants' market positions within it, and the specific acts undertaken to acquire or maintain monopoly power. This can involve a written history of the industry and of the defendants' place within it.

The Antitrust Division named AT&T, Western Electric, and Bell Labs as defendants, charging them with three offenses: monopolization, attempt to monopolize, and conspiracy to monopolize. The other conspirators not made defendants included the local operating companies in which AT&T held shares, such as New Jersey Bell and Pacific Telephone & Telegraph. While there are different elements required than in the monopolizing charge, the attempt and conspiracy charges essentially fell within the claim that AT&T engaged in monopolization under Section 2. Further, the government's complaint was framed in terms of two elements required to prove monopolization. First, the defendants had to possess monopoly power in the relevant market. *Monopoly power* was defined as the power to control prices or to exclude competition. While this test has no readily apparent meaning and has been treated in a number of ways, the fundamental question is whether "a firm has a substantial degree of power to exclude competitors by reducing price and still be profitable."[44] The relevant product or service market is based on the notion of reasonable interchangeability. Do products serve the same use so that small reductions in price in one product result in large numbers of buyers turning to it from other products? If this occurs, both products are part of the same product market—they exhibit high cross elasticity of demand. Thus, in one leading case, cellophane and other flexible wrappings were part of the same product market.[45]

Thus far we have looked at the element of monopoly power, but the possession of such power alone is not sufficient to constitute a Sherman Act monopolization offense. One may, for example, attain monopoly power as a result of producing a product that is better than one's competitor's. Or one's service, distribution, design, and so on may be so superior that all customers turn to it. Attaining a monopoly position in such ways is lawful; indeed, that is what competition is about. And if one attains market dominance as a result of such superior performance, the process of competition has worked well. In the words of Joseph Schumpeter:

> The fundamental impulse that sets and keeps the capitalist engine in motion comes from the new consumer goods, the new methods of production or transportation, the new markets, the new forms of industrial organization that capitalist enterprise creates.[46]

Consequently, the second element in the offense of monopolization is that the charged firm's conduct goes beyond normal and honest business conduct. In the *AT&T* case, the Justice Department considered its burden of proof in the following terms:

> Willful acquisition or maintenance of monopoly power does not require a showing of specific intent. . . . Where the offense alleged is monopolization, the requisite showing is one of a general or deliberate purpose or intent to exercise monopoly power. . . . It is sufficient to show that a monopoly results as the necessary consequence of a defendant's conduct or business arrangements.[47]

In other words, the Justice Department sought to ease its burden considerably by abnegating the second element of a monopolization charge. However, the Justice Department still had to show as many situations of purportedly predatory conduct as it could locate.

Only two pages in the complaint actually sketched the actions about which the Antitrust Division complained, yet they did not tell what the government intended to prove. The charges included that (1) Western Electric supplied the telecommunications equipment needs of the Bell system, thereby eliminating competition from other manufacturers and suppliers; (2) AT&T obstructed the interconnection of SCCs and other carriers; and (3) AT&T obstructed the interconnection of customer-provided CPE into the Bell system.[48] Thus, the Justice Department's case was based on only three factors: (1) the Bell system's vertical integration and procurement practices; (2) MCI's rate and interconnection complaints against AT&T; and (3) CPE interconnection cases. Clearly, the second and third factors were viewed as examples of predatory conduct. Based solely on these alleged actions—and without mention of the FCC's or PUCs' involvement in the events described in the complaint—the Justice Department called for AT&T's dismemberment. It hoped the court would require AT&T to divest all Western Electric stock and that Western, in turn, would be required to divest "assets sufficient to insure competition in the manufacture and sale of telecommunications equipment."[49] Additionally, the Justice Department called for AT&T to divest some or all of the Bell-operating companies, and requested the court to impose unspecified, nonstructural relief. In short, the Justice Department wanted AT&T to serve as nothing more than a long-distance company with some connection to Bell Labs.

Any complaint of this sort will adversely affect the price of securities of the company being charged. However, since an accusation is not proof of guilt, it is felt that the government should attempt to minimize the harm done to an accused company. In this instance, the time chosen to announce the antitrust suit could not have been worse from AT&T's perspective. Whether spite, indifference, or misunderstanding was the cause we will never know, but the fact remains that every responsible Justice Department official knew or should have known that AT&T was at the time in the process of making the largest offering of fixed-income securities ever made by an American corporation. The investigation had been going on for many months and the securities sale would have been completed in a few days. The $600 million offering was withdrawn the day after the complaint was filed.[50]

THE ANSWER

That AT&T would vehemently denounce the antitrust suit, and that MCI and the other firms that had brought private actions against AT&T would be delighted with it, are not surprising. The recorded responses of the investment community were largely negative. A First Boston Corporation securities analyst noted that Western Electric was one of the best manufacturing companies in the country and that a spin-off company would raise prices.[51] According to an AT&T survey, newspaper editorials ran three to one against the suit.[52] A *Wall Street Journal* editorial summarized this generally negative stream of sentiment against the suit:

> While the Justice Department can't promise any consumer benefits that might result from its suit to break up AT&T, it is sure of one thing. This is the largest antitrust action ever filed.
> So much for the mentality of modern day trustbusters. As long as they can tackle the biggest of all "big businesses" what is the difference whether the massive expenditure of federal money and effort is likely to cut anyone's phone bills? What the Justice Department suit attacks is not monopoly but vertical integration.
> A study [by] Touche, Ross & Co., the accounting firm, completed for the Federal Communications Commission earlier this year . . . was something of a disappointment to federal regulators and trustbusters.
> Its conclusion was that "the general effects of the interrelationship of Bell Systems companies are a reduction of cost and investment." . . . Out of all this we arrive at one question: Where is the problem that justifies risking possible damage to the efficiency of a vital part of the U.S. infrastructure. . . . If there is a problem that justifies all this we can't find it.[53]

AT&T sought, of course, to capitalize on the sentiment in its favor. After the suit was filed, de Butts announced that AT&T was not in violation of the law and that the action was undertaken in complete disregard of the interests of the general public. Fragmentation of responsibility, the principal goal of the suit, would lead to deterioration of telephone service. The regulated network manager system, de Butts pointed out, had withstood constant examination by state and federal regulatory agencies, courts, and legislative bodies almost from its inception. Notwithstanding criticism of certain specific activities, the system, on balance, had worked remarkably well. Virtually every household had telephone service, the level of telecommunications technology was the highest in the world, and costs had been kept down by productivity gains at twice the pace of the general economy. Finally, de Butts stated on several occasions that AT&T would not settle the suit.[54]

In contrast to the complaint, AT&T's formal answer was 23 pages long and replete with details. But, more importantly, instead of starting with recent times, as the complaint did, the AT&T answer briefly traced the history of the industry from the telephone's invention to the suit. The purpose of the history was to show why and how the regulated network manager system had evolved. In contrast to the Justice Department's portrayal of AT&T, the company showed that other models of government-business relationships in the telephone industry were tried in the past but found wanting. Accordingly, the regulated network manager system evolved, not all at once but gradually, in response to public service goals. It noted that with the enactment of the Communications Act of 1934,

> Congress has determined that telecommunications carriers should be regulated, and the telecommunications industry should be structured, under the standard of the public interest in good, universally available, service at reasonable rates rather than under the policy of favoring competition applicable to enterprises generally under the Sherman Act.[55]

AT&T then showed how it had been under constant scrutiny (much of this hostile) since well before the enactment of the 1934 Act. The FCC was invited by Congress to request new powers and enforcement tools if existing ones were found to be inadequate. Yet with minor exceptions, the agency concluded that it already had sufficient power to regulate AT&T and the other public service companies. But, AT&T questioned, was this because the FCC was under AT&T's influence or because it had given up in response to the futility of adequately regulating the public service firms? The question was, of course, a vital one, in that a major underpinning of the Justice Department case was the inadequacy of regulation and, therefore, the need to dissolve AT&T. Not only had AT&T's component telephone companies been adequately regulated, but Western Electric and Bell Labs as well. In view of the numerous contests that AT&T and its constituent companies lost by 1974 at the federal and state levels, there was almost a mythical quality to the notion of inadequate regulation. The proof of adequate regulation could be found in the high quality of telephone service, in AT&T's modest profit rates, and in the fact that the "interstate rates of the Bell System are substantially at the level of 20 years ago, and rates for local service have increased at only about one-third of the rate of increases of prices in the economy generally."[56] In short, then, AT&T claimed it had not behaved like a monopolist; that is, its monopoly position in long distance and many local markets came about not from predatory practices, but for the same reason that the tiny Tatum Telephone Company was the local monopolist in Tatum, Texas. The gradual evolution of the telephone industry was in the direction of single market providers. It noted, too, that the FCC had demonstrated in many decisions that it, and not AT&T, had the power to exclude or license new competitors. The FCC and the PUCs had the power to control rates through a variety of regulatory techniques. For these reasons, AT&T lacked monopoly power in the antitrust sense regardless of its size. Further, AT&T asserted that the court lacked jurisdiction over the matter because a comprehensive regulatory scheme inconsistent with antitrust primacy governed telecommunications. (While the FCC had modified the old regulated network manager system in favor of what is termed here *contrived competition*, it was still a comprehensive system. No matter how *ad hoc* FCC regulation had become, the numerous SCC, satellite, interconnection, long-distance, rate, technical, and other decisions showed that FCC regulation was so comprehensive that there was no room for antitrust enforcement.) Finally, AT&T's answer argued that the matter had already been tried and settled by the parties. Since AT&T had fully complied with the terms of the 1956 consent decree, the Justice Department could not bring another suit on the same cause of action: "The 1956 judgment is *res judicata* and constitutes a bar with respect to the cause of action asserted herein."[57]

OPENING SKIRMISHES

The case was first assigned to Judge Joseph C. Waddy, who became a federal judge in 1967 after serving in the District of Columbia Municipal Court. Waddy had not previously presided over an antitrust suit but, noted *Telecommunications Reports*, his background in domestic relations with the Municipal Court might help him face "the largest divorce suit in history."[58]

At the outset of the case, AT&T could pursue several alternatives simultaneously. First, it could seek to override both the Justice Department's and the FCC's actions by requesting legislation that would restore, to a large extent, the regulated network manager system with AT&T as network manager. Second, it could fight the antitrust suit on its own merits, including pressing the affirmative defenses of *res judicata* and FCC exclusive jurisdiction. Third, it could engage in trial tactics that could delay the proceedings interminably and lead to controversies on procedural and due-process grounds. Under this last possibility, the case would become so bogged down in procedural and due-process controversies that it would eventually be dismissed. In any event, it was far too early to consider settlement.

The opening phases of the case showed that it would be a substantial one. In December 1974, the Justice Department requested that AT&T collect and submit a large number of documents. The following example of the Justice Department's request demonstrates the burden it sought to impose:

> All documents prepared, sent, or received since January 1, 1930, which relate or refer in whole or in part to, or which constitute instructions, directives, or suggestions regarding the purchase by AT&T or any Bell company of telecommunications equipment from Western Electric.[59]

In turn, AT&T asked the court to require the federal government "to turn over all documents relating to the telecommunications industry, including those having to do with Bell's performance in providing the government's own telecommunications system." An AT&T spokesperson explained that the request was relevant because the government's documents would show that "the Bell System's organization and performance have resulted in the world's best and most reasonably priced telecommunications service."[60] Needless to say, this was viewed as irrelevant under the Justice Department's theory of the case, yet it never once challenged AT&T's overall performance. Rather, the Justice Department's antitrust theory focused more on the alleged harm to MCI and other competitors than on the well-being of the general public. In its view, the benefits of competition outweighed the benefits of AT&T's overall performance.

AT&T asserted that the Justice Department's document demand was unreasonable in that it would require 20,000 hours of effort and cost more than $300 million to comply. Even a scaled-down request would entail a search costing $125 million. Moreover, AT&T's general counsel Mark Garlinghouse stated that AT&T particularly objected to transporting the massive amount of material to the Justice Department and marking each document by the paragraph number in the complaint to which it pertained. Taking the offensive, AT&T demanded that the court order federal government agencies to preserve all documents pertaining to telecommunications, a request with which Judge Waddy complied. With this step, AT&T stated another important theme in its defense: its structure and conduct were largely attributable to the government's mandates and not to its own independent "intention."[61] Thus, according to AT&T, intent, one of the critical components in the charge of monopolizing, was missing.

While the document battle progressed, in a 20 February 1975 court hearing, Judge Waddy expressed concern that his court lacked jurisdiction over the matter on the basis of the *res judicata* and FCC exclusive jurisdiction defenses. Because he felt that these were threshold matters, he suspended discovery, except for his order requiring government agencies to maintain their telecommunications documents.[62] AT&T argued that under the 1956 consent decree, it had divested itself of all unregulated activities. In the process, AT&T was constrained to forego commercial opportunities based on Bell system technological advances. Since the 1956 decree made all AT&T practices (including the setting of Western Electric prices) subject to comprehensive FCC and PUC regulation, AT&T argued that all parts of the enterprise were fully regulated. Thus, together the 1956 decree and the regulatory scheme under the Communications Act preempted the jurisdiction of the Federal District Court for the District of Columbia. If any court had jurisdiction, AT&T argued, it was the Federal District Court for the Northern District of New Jersey, which supervised the enforcement of the 1956 decree.[63]

The Justice Department's position held that there was an overriding public policy in favor of enforcing the antitrust laws. Accordingly, courts were ousted of jurisdiction only "where specific discrete conduct is expressly or implicitly immunized by particular provisions of an act of Congress." The Justice Department made the same argument that MCI had in its first antitrust suit against AT&T: that the Communications Act did not explicitly immunize from the suit the firms regulated by the FCC. On the *res judicata* charge, the Justice Department argued that the 1956 decree "does not provide these defendants perpetual immunity from the antitrust laws."[64] It declared that even though the New Jersey District Court retained jurisdiction over the 1956 decree, the Justice Department could elect to initiate new action so to remedy a continuing violation if the earlier remedy had been ineffective. In response, AT&T claimed that

> The Antitrust Division is engaged in a deliberate and concerted effort to undercut the public interest standard upon which the regulatory process is based and to substitute for that standard—even in pervasively regulated industries—the standard of competition embodied in the Sherman Act. . . . [It is engaged in] a war on the regulatory process itself.[65]

Obviously, AT&T had in mind the antiregulatory and pro-Sherman Act approach that the Justice Department had used before the FCC and other economic regulatory agencies.

Of course, we can never know how Judge Waddy would have decided the case if his death in 1978 had not prevented him from presiding over the trial or reviewing the settlement. AT&T's lead counsel, George Saunders, felt that Waddy would have given the Antitrust Division "the back of his hand."[66] It was clear that Judge Waddy was skeptical of the Antitrust Division's claims, for during the July 1975 hearing on whether the court's jurisdiction should be ousted, Waddy told Department attorneys that he was "having trouble finding out exactly what you're complaining about."[67] When the Department's chief counsel, Philip Verveer, read a series of allegations of improper Bell system conduct, Judge Waddy asked whether the FCC asserted jurisdiction over each one. Verveer answered affirmatively in each case. Yet, in response to remarks by Saunders, Waddy understood the Justice Department to contend that the antitrust laws applied because agency regulation was inadequate. He asserted that the Department was "attacking a course of conduct which the FCC cannot stop."[68] In short, as Judge Waddy conceived it, the Justice Department would have to show that FCC regulation had failed.

It was not until 1 October 1976, that Judge Waddy made his first jurisdictional ruling. In the decision, he "initially concluded that the present suit is not barred by the doctrine of *res judicata* because of the 1956 settlement in New Jersey."[69] The operative word is *initially*, for Waddy supplied no reasons to support his conclusion. At this point, he was willing to give the Justice Department the benefit of the doubt so as not to delay further the proceeding. On the issue of FCC jurisdiction, Waddy asked the agency to supply a brief outlining its views on whether antitrust jurisdiction was preempted. It was apparent from the tenor of his decision that the FCC's views would weigh heavily in his next decision. The FCC, generally sympathetic to competition and AT&T structural reform, concluded that the court should "resolve the remaining jurisdictional question by asserting its jurisdiction over the subject matter and the defendants."[70] It was clear from these remarks that it feared Judge Waddy might otherwise turn the matter over to the FCC. In addition, a strong FCC position in favor of agency preemption undermined the many antitrust suits brought by the SCCs and interconnect companies. Thus, while claiming that there were areas that antitrust may not touch, the agency concluded that its orders did not immunize carriers and their conduct from the antitrust laws.

On 24 November 1976, Judge Waddy issued his ruling, concluding that AT&T was not immune from Sherman Act prosecution. Obviously relying on the FCC's views, the court did not closely examine the regulatory scheme or history of telecommunications to determine whether an inherent inconsistency existed between the antitrust laws and FCC regulation. Rather, relying on several maxims and the Supreme Court's 1973 *Otter Tail Power* decision, it reasoned that

> Merely because Congress has authorized the Commission to regulate the telecommunications industry (even assuming that regulation is viewed as pervasive) does not automatically necessitate the conclusion that the antitrust laws are to be displaced. . . . The Court is satisfied that it has jurisdiction of at least *some of the aspects* of the case [emphasis added].[71]

Imposing a nearly impossible burden, the court virtually required AT&T to show that under every conceivable circumstance telecommunications was exempt from antitrust coverage. Relying largely on the FCC's conclusion that the antitrust laws could apply to some telecommunications matters, Judge Waddy was unwilling to delay the beginning of pretrial proceedings for a long time. As long as the antitrust laws were not clearly inapplicable to every transaction covered in the Antitrust Division's vague complaint, the pretrial events would begin. As the evidence developed, Judge Waddy contemplated referring particular issues to the FCC: "At this stage in the proceedings, however, the issues must be more sharply defined through discovery and other proceedings."[72]

The court was clearly influenced by the Supreme Court's 1973 *Otter Tail Power* decision in which the defendant power company refused to sell power at wholesale to municipal power systems and to transfer power from other companies over its lines (a practice called "wheeling"). It claimed these activities were exempt from the antitrust laws because they were subject to Federal Power Commission (FPC) regulation. But in that case, the FPC had no authority over wheeling and, therefore, could not supervise refusals to wheel[73]—a critical difference between *Otter Tail* and the *AT&T* case. The FCC, as the Justice Department conceded, could assert jurisdiction over all practices complained of. The court, in brief, refused to examine the 1934 Act in detail, relying instead on an easy comparison.

CONGRESSIONAL INTERLUDE

Notwithstanding the adverse ruling, it was clear that Judge Waddy was skeptical about the merits of the Justice Department's case against AT&T. At the very least, he indicated that the complaint was extremely vague. Pointedly, he asked the Division's lead counsel in a November 1976 hearing, "Specifically what is your cause of action? What are you really claiming?"[74] Thus, AT&T could reasonably feel that it might prevail in a trial on the merits. In any event, the agreements concerning discovery into which AT&T and the Justice Department entered were expected to clarify the issues sufficiently and to move the case forward.[75]

Nevertheless, AT&T was not exclusively pursuing its judicial option, as there was a small possibility that it could reverse the direction taken by the FCC and the Justice Department through congressional action. The likelihood of doing so was small for several reasons. First, only 5 to 10 percent of the bills introduced into Congress in any session are actually enacted into law. Telecommunications bills, including major rewrites of the 1934 Communications Act, have been introduced in almost every session from 1976 to 1987. To date, notwithstanding the increasing public interest in the subject, the major changes have been made by the FCC and the courts. Despite innumerable speeches and legislative hearings, no major legislation has been enacted. Legislative participants like Representatives Lionel Van Deerlin and Timothy Wirth have drawn considerable media attention through their criticism of action or inaction within nonlegislative arenas, but they have been unsuccessful in changing policy. Even with the attention and considerable energy that Congress has devoted to the subject, it has not been an important actor in telecommunications policy since 1934. The policy divisions within Congress and among the numerous interest groups affected by telecommunications policy have been too great to negotiate a legislative consensus. Further, the FCC and the courts have acted in response to policy issues, thereby reducing the pressures on Congress to do more than talk and hold hearings. Most legislators are, therefore, able to play their favorite role as critics or proponents of some set of ideal policies without considering costs. Often they capitalize on a prejudice such as hatred of large corporations or the predisposition in favor of small competitors. Therefore, AT&T had only a slim chance to move Congress in the directions it desired.

Many legislators, MCI, other SCCs, and the interconnect industry would oppose AT&T. The FCC, the Office of Telecommunications Policy in the Executive Office of the President, and the Justice Department would also vigorously fight legislation that was perceived as anticompetitive. Moreover, we must remember that the Ford and Carter administrations favored deregulation and increased competition. In addition, there was the enmity of many legislators who routinely opposed any economic proposal supported by a giant business firm as well as that of other legislators who firmly believed that the new policies would improve telecommunications service. The latter group included some members of the important House Communications Subcommittee.

However, AT&T hoped that through a coalition that would mobilize public opinion, the influence of its interest group opponents could be countered. Congress would then be compelled to enact legislation that would restore the regulated network manager system. AT&T's allies included the independent telephone companies, banded together in the United States Independent Telephone Association (USITA), and the Communications Workers of America (CWA). Although the CWA and other unions had often taken positions strongly at odds with AT&T, they generally supported the Bell system on this issue because of their fears of imported rather than domestically made equipment and of the new entrants' largely nonunion labor.[76] With CWA's support, AT&T hoped that the entire AFL-CIO would follow. The idea of new legislation was introduced by John de Butts in February 1976:

> We in our business have decided that the time has come to call the public's attention to its stake in this matter. . . . It is for this reason that the telephone industry has decided to seek a resolution of the issues confronting it in the only forum I have long felt had the necessary perspective to resolve them—the Congress of the United States.[77]

The bill endorsed the vertically integrated, regulated network manager system, declaring that the system was essential to maintaining reasonable charges and universal service. The bill declared that no compensatory charge would be declared unlawful because it was too low—a clear slap at the FCC's protection of MCI—and no SCC could be authorized to provide service unless it showed that its operation would not result in increased charges for local telephone service. Finally, the bill affirmed the right of the PUCs to regulate CPE interconnection even though the equipment was used, in part, for interstate transmission.

Given the array of opposition to the bill that would develop, including governmental institutions, legislators, and communications interests such as MCI that had already shown considerable skill in the political arena, the only hope that the supporters of the bill—styled the Consumer Communications Reform Act—had was to rouse a groundswell of public opinion in its favor. Senator Vance Hartke, a liberal Democrat, set the proponents' tone when he introduced the bill, stating that "Congress must and should act now to see that the interest of all the American public, rather than a few large businesses, is served."[78] Meanwhile, AT&T wrote to its three million shareowners recommending that they actively support the bill.[79] Opponents of the bill portrayed it as nothing more than an AT&T power grab, labeling it the "Bell Bill." However, it drew surprisingly large congressional support from both sides of the aisle (including 171 House members), and liberals and conservatives in both political parties supported it.

However, in the subcommittee the bill was attacked as crass special interest legislation. USITA countered by claiming that opponents of the bill were pro-IBM, ITT, and other giant business interests.[80] The proponents' task of creating a public groundswell required that the public be educated in the complexities and history of telecommunications policy—a nearly impossible task.[81] The communications bill died. There was much congressional activity after this—speeches were made, bills were drafted, hearings were held, and legislators sought to capitalize on the public interest in telecommunications policy. But, for AT&T, the legislative option was exhausted.

In 1977, because its options were more limited as a result of Judge Waddy's jurisdictional decisions and congressional inaction, AT&T focused its attention on fighting the case. Appeals of Judge Waddy's jurisdictional rulings to the Court of Appeals and the Supreme Court failed, as the FCC joined the Antitrust Division in supporting the decision.[82] When the Supreme Court declined to review the judge's jurisdictional decision in November 1977, AT&T shifted its attention to procedural issues, the most important of which involved an attempt to compel the Justice Department to narrow the charges.[83] It must be appreciated that the Justice Department did not prepare such an ambiguous complaint unintentionally; rather, ambiguity was intended to prolong the time before it would be required to specify the charges against AT&T. In so doing, the Justice Department hoped to obtain as much information as it could from the private antitrust suits against AT&T then in progress. Accordingly, it resisted AT&T's narrowing efforts, and 1977 ended with pending battles on the language and scope of the pretrial orders.

JUDGE GREENE TAKES CHARGE

As the discovery disputes progressed in 1978, Judge Waddy became terminally ill with cancer. The case was reassigned to Judge Harold F. Greene, who had been sworn in as a Federal District Court Judge on June 22. Greene was uniformly regarded as a resolutely fair trial judge and an excellent judicial administrator. A central fact of Greene's life was that he and his family had escaped Nazi oppression, which gave him firsthand experience of a government's potential for abuse. His principal professional experience before becoming Chief Judge of the D.C. Court of General Sessions was with the Justice Department in the area of civil rights.[84] Although Judge Greene had been with the Justice Department, it should not be assumed that he was biased in favor of the prosecution in the *AT&T* case. Good lawyers are role players; they can operate effectively as prosecutor, defense counsel, and judge. And Judge Greene was an excellent attorney. Moreover, as we saw in the case of legislation affecting AT&T, attitudes toward telecommunications policy cut across traditional liberal-conservative lines. Although Judge Greene's associations were with liberal Democrats, we should not assume that this necessarily biased him in favor of the government's side. Time would reveal his predilections.

Judge Greene had the immediate task of getting the proceedings moving. Almost 4 years had elapsed since the complaint was filed, yet little progress had been made. Greene wanted to avoid another *United States* v. *IBM* scenario, which began in January 1969 and was still far from completion. As a group studying big antitrust cases for the National Commission for the Review of Antitrust Laws and Procedures reported in January 1979 on the *IBM* case: "The number of non-substantive issues generated during discovery and trial is also prodigious. As of November 27, 1978, Judge Edelstein had issued 59 opinions, 127 memorandum endorsements, 21 pretrial orders, 13 amended pretrial orders, and 63 stipulations and orders."[85] The Advisory Panel also discussed Judge Waddy's handling of the *United States* v. *AT&T* case, pointing out that virtually no discovery had taken place since the complaint was filed. While the report was filed after Judge Greene took charge, he undoubtedly knew of the existence of President Carter's National Commission for the Review of Antitrust Laws and Procedures, of which delay was a major topic of investigation. However, we cannot assume that delay is simply a defense tactic. The issues raised in procedural matters are often important ones, especially if they concern the government's potential for abuse—a subject about which Greene would be sensitive. Once a case is brought, the government lawyers involved are much like those in the private sector—they do not necessarily seek justice but rather they seek to win and score heavily over their opponents. Judge Greene would have the difficult task of balancing fairness to the defendants with moving the case at a quicker pace.

One of Greene's first acts was to issue an order on 6 July 1978, directing the parties to file status memoranda on all issues preliminary to the trial. Then, on 11 September 1978, after reviewing prior proceedings, Judge Greene issued his first important decision in the case.[86] The decision was organized into four subjects. First there was the question of jurisdiction. Second was one of AT&T's principal defenses: that the United States government to a large extent compelled the conduct of which it now complained. But the Justice Department, in addition to disputing this contention, also argued that the government was not a monolith and that the Justice Department could not be prevented from complaining about conduct in which the FCC and other agencies implicitly or explicitly concurred. Third was that the plaintiff sought access to documents produced in private antitrust suits brought against AT&T. And fourth, Judge Greene would use the decision to plot the future course of action in the case. Once again the court rejected the argument that regulation was sufficiently pervasive to preempt completely the antitrust laws. In any event, there was no reason for this question to prevent discovery proceedings. If after discovery the court was wrong about jurisdiction with respect to some of the defendants' conduct, those issues would be referred to the FCC under the doctrine of primary jurisdiction. The practical consequences of the second issue were that it is considerably easier to obtain documents in discovery from the other party to the suit than from a third party. Therefore, if the court upheld the Justice Department's position that only it was the plaintiff, it would be more difficult for AT&T to obtain documents from the approximately forty government agencies (including the FCC). Conversely, if AT&T prevailed on this point, it would be easier for it to obtain a veritable mountain of documents for inspection, copying, and so forth. Generally, the government agencies (other than the Department of Justice) objected to various parts of AT&T's discovery demands and would not voluntarily produce some documents or parts of others. They agreed to show documents to the magistrate appointed by Judge Waddy without the need for a subpoena. Judge Greene, in deciding the issue, first observed that one of AT&T's most important arguments was that its conduct largely resulted from government directives and policies. Moreover, AT&T claimed that its structure and practices benefited the United States government. Noting that AT&T's argument was plausible, that the United States as a plaintiff was the entire executive branch (except the independent regulatory agencies of which the FCC was the most important), and that any relief would be national in impact and scope, Greene rejected the plaintiff's argument. On a more practical level, a voluntary system would not work in that it would lack incentive for a government agency to produce numerous documents voluntarily. While he could not order the production of documents from the FCC because of its nominal independence from the executive branch, Greene promised to assist AT&T in securing documents from it—if the defendant would pare down its request.

The third major issue concerned documents produced by AT&T in private antitrust suits. At stake were approximately 2.5 million pages of AT&T documents that were in the records of the *Litton* and *MCI* cases. Judge Greene, noting that it would be too time-consuming for the Department of Justice to duplicate the document-selection process when it was already available, held for the government on the issue.

THE ORGANIZATION OF THE *AT&T* CASE

Judge Greene's basic strategy in administering the *AT&T* case involved several considerations, the most important of which was a trial without a jury. By allowing nearly all evidence and testimony within a broad range of tolerance into the record, Greene avoided the pitfalls involved in deciding issues of inclusion and exclusion, many of which lead to appeals. Greene would, after all, be able to evaluate the quality of evidence based on his legal skills and experience. At the same time, he assured AT&T that it would be able to obtain the evidence it needed for its defense. Although a record replete with the testimony and exhibits of both sides would help to guarantee fairness, it would also cause interminable delay. *Business Week* commented on the enormous potential for chaos:

> AT&T claims that its "thorough study" of Justice's original demands for pretrial discovery of documents would require the Bell System to sort through 7.2 billion pages of material and submit 1.2 billion pages to the government for copying. By its own estimate, the Antitrust Div. will have to examine several million documents and hundreds of depositions from witnesses.[87]

Judge Greene's next task, then, was to outline procedures that would bring order and speed to this morass of documents without injuring his commitment to fairness. He began with the Justice Department's complaint, characterizing it as "sweeping, broad, and vague. This has not only had the effect of making it difficult for defendants to formulate their defenses, but it has also been an obstacle to discovery."[88] In an attempt to narrow the issues, Judge Greene devised a unique system that would both structure the case and reduce the volume of material needed as evidence. Although modified somewhat, the basic contours of Greene's original plan governed the administration of the case.

Thus, Pretrial Order No. 12 asked the parties to file four successive Statements of Contention and Proof (SCP) over an 18-month period. The plaintiff's first SCP was to show (1) the government's legal and factual contentions, (2) a list of witnesses and the documentary evidence that would support each contention; and (3) the extent to which the evidence was in plaintiff's hands or where it could be found. The defendants' first SCP was to be organized in a manner similar to plaintiff's. After the filing of the first SCPs, the magistrate was to conduct a conference designed to simplify the issues, arrive at stipulations of uncontroverted facts, and reduce further unnecessary discovery. At the conclusion of the first pretrial conference, then, the parties would have a list of stipulations to which they both agreed and another of contentions about which they differed. It was hoped that the second SCPs would further narrow and simplify the issues and that the second pretrial conference would increase the number of stipulations and reduce the contentions. In this way, considerably less need for testimony and exhibits would exist when the trial began. However, Judge Greene allowed sufficient flexibility in the procedure to enlarge existing contentions or to add new ones in the second SCP. Thereafter, the magistrate was instructed to be more stringent in applications for new contentions. The discovery process was scheduled to terminate on 1 April 1980.[89]

THE JUDICIAL PROCESS

Although Greene's pretrial process did not work exactly as planned, it marked a good beginning to what would lead to an orderly trial. The plaintiff's 530-page first SCP was filed on 1 November 1978, and outlined the nature of the telecommunications industry and its technology and participants. The document also described the structure of the Bell system and AT&T's role in it, and it stated the major themes of the Justice Department's case as well as the purported factual support. The themes included were (1) the alleged exclusionary acts that result from vertical integration, (2) the abuse of monopoly power to thwart competition—so-called predatory acts; and (3) the inability of state and federal regulation to control the acts of the defendants. The markets examined were broadly telecommunications transmission and equipment, and a discussion of the applicable law was followed by another of the relief necessary to remedy the violations of the law.[90]

The defendants' first SCP, a 490-page document, was structured somewhat differently in keeping with its theory of the case. It began with a more detailed discussion of the technology of telecommunications, showing that the vertical and horizontal structures of the Bell system were due more to the technology of telecommunications than to any intent to monopolize the industry. The defendants also described the development of telephone regulation and the reasons for its increasing pervasiveness, including the widespread adoption of the monopoly idea and the growth of federal regulation. Seeking to show that the regulated network manager system worked well, the historical exposition included as well material on the remarkable performance of the Bell system, such as the accomplishments of Bell Labs—topics that the Justice Department largely viewed as irrelevant. The lengthiest portion of the document consisted of rebuttals of the government's charges. Finally, AT&T argued its affirmative defenses and the proposed remedy, and an appendix described how it intended to prove its case.[91]

The second SCPs were expected to be more brief than the first, merely detailing additions and deletions to the original statements. Although they were brief in comparison to the first and third statements, the second statements did provide some important information about the parties' respective strategies. The plaintiff's second statement indicated that the AT&T acts to which it would devote most attention were those concerning the SCC's, principally MCI, and AT&T's responsive tariffs. The Justice Department clearly intended to rely on material presented by the plaintiffs in private antitrust suits. A second line of attack would be the introduction of evidence on a vast number of matters concerning CPE, AT&T procurement practices, private-line interconnection, and so on. While the evidence in each such matter would be brief, if not sketchy, the cumulative impression that the Department hoped to create was that AT&T was a persistent predator.[92] The defendants briefly responded to these new charges in their 21 May 1979 second statement. They also complained that the government was abusing the process that the judge had devised.[93] Clearly, AT&T was saving its detailed responses for the third statement.

At the same time it filed the second statements, the Antitrust Division asked the court to abandon the stipulation/contention process in favor of the standard one, in which each side would request specific admissions of the other. The latter process, while more traditional than Greene's novel procedure, would have delayed the meticulous organization of the case that was at the heart of the stipulation/contention process. It must be recalled that the *MCI* v. *AT&T* case was still pending in the District Court for the Northern District of Illinois, and the trial would not begin until February 1980. Although the Antitrust Division had received more than 1.5 million pages of documents and attorneys' work from MCI, it still had an incentive to delay the organization of its case until it saw the case presented by its ally and AT&T's defense. AT&T vigorously objected to the abandonment of the stipulation/contention process, a position that was upheld by Judge Greene. However, for the same strategic reason the Antitrust Division sought to divide the case into two parts that would be separated by a substantial period of time—a trial of the "background" portions and another of the "more substantive" issues. Because the distinction was an artificial one and sharply protested by AT&T, the judge turned down the Antitrust Division's request.[94]

Nevertheless, in late October 1979, the Justice Department filed an appeal from an order issued by the court-appointed Special Masters, which required each side to submit detailed statements of facts on certain matters and to recast certain contentions in more neutral and precise terms. The government was "not able to comply with the Special Masters' plan because it has not had an opportunity to review its evidence on a subject matter basis and is unable to provide anything more than a summary narrative."[95] Judge Greene sharply criticized the Justice Department for not revealing its case and for delaying the proceedings:

> The government's several submissions to the Court exhibit an excessive rigidity possibly borne of inadequate preparation. . . . Defen-

dants are quite correct in their assertion that "the stipulation negotiations must . . . identify the true nature of the dispute between the
parties with respect to each episode." Any effort to devote the negotiation conferences merely to the goal of arriving at the stipulation
of a list of isolated, fragmentary facts would hardly advance the progress of this case or the cause of justice.[96]

Most importantly, the process of organizing the case had taken a
major leap forward because of the insistence of the Special Masters,
AT&T, and the judge that the case be organized in the Third Statement
of Contentions and Proof by substantive topics or episodes. By September 1980, when Judge Greene rendered his next important decision in
the matter, the organization of stipulations and contentions into
eighty-two separate episodes, many with subparts, had moved the case
to a new level. Once again, the Judge criticized the Justice Department
for using dilatory tactics: "It appears that in this respect [discovery] the
government wishes to do now that which it should have done years ago.
. . . It now seeks to make up for lost time."[97] (By this time MCI had
won its extraordinary antitrust victory over AT&T at the Federal District Court level.) Greene, however, would not allow the Justice Department to delay the case by engaging in additional discovery to build
its case. Both sides would have to engage in the trial and the remaining
pretrial simultaneously.

THE EPISODES AND THE EVIDENCE

As the trial in United States v. AT&T drew near, Judge Greene continued
to facilitate the admission of vast amounts of testimony and exhibits
into evidence in a way that he hoped would speed up the proceedings.
Thus, in March 1980, Greene established rules that allowed each side
to produce written testimony but that gave the opposing sides the right
to object—a process that was far less time-consuming than strict oral
testimony.[98] Equally importantly, since much of the evidence was comprised of the reports and decisions of state and federal agencies (most
importantly, the FCC's), the court established ground rules for treating
these documents as well. While holding that most such documents

were reliable, Judge Greene cautioned that "[i]t is important to emphasize the limited purpose for which these materials are being admitted."[99] That is, the court would not admit these materials alone as
conclusive evidence of any practice; rather, it would consider them in
conjunction with other evidence intended to rebut agency findings.
Thus, as a result of these rules established by Judge Greene, the eighty-
two episodes and the Stipulation/Contention Packages developed. The
latter material constituted the most important documents in the *AT&T*
case; they made the case as administratively manageable as possible.
Essentially, the parties' third SCPs were based on the episodes and followed the formats of the Stipulation/Contention Packages; that is, they
summarized many of the stipulations and contentions in each episode.
This eliminated the need for a fourth SCP.

The third SCPs were considerably longer than the first ones. The
plaintiff's was organized in two volumes and consisted of 1,872 pages;
AT&T's 2,154-page, three-volume SCP also included a 6-page list of
episodes. For each episode, the stipulation/contention process was divided into three stages. An initial set of negotiations determined the
basic areas of agreement and disagreement and outlined the stipulations
and contentions. After further negotiations and review, the stipulation
was printed in final form and signed by the parties. The stipulations
appeared in numbered paragraphs that corresponded to the plaintiff's
and defendants' contentions and summaries of how each party intended
to prove the contentions at the trial, including the names of witnesses,
descriptions of exhibits, and citations of documents. The stipulations
were in the form of factual summaries to which both parties agreed,
extensive quotations from private documents, or official reports such
as FCC decisions. At first, the stipulations and contentions paralleled
each other, but time pressures made this impossible in later episodes
(we must remember that the trial and other matters occurred simultaneously). When the settlement procedures were taking place, time
pressures also necessitated that some episodes be merged and others
divided, such that there were seventy-three final packages instead of
eighty-two.[100]

Both episode lists had much in common; for example, episodes one
through seven and nine dealt with the technology of telecommunications as well as the history of government-industry relations through
the *Carterfone* decision. Most of that material, which has been discussed
in this book, was a part of AT&T's defense that its structure and perfor-

mance were to a large extent attributable to a combination of the nature of telecommunications technology and government regulation. The heart of the government's case was embodied in the episodes concerning specialized common carriers, most critically MCI, and the AT&T tariff offerings (Series 11,000 and HI/LO).

These were the most important and detailed episodes in the government's case. The government's most important witnesses included MCI's William McGowan, whose testimony covered approximately 600 transcript pages, and other MCI officials who testified on FX, CCSA, EXECUNET, and other matters of controversy between MCI and AT&T. Its principal expert witness was Professor William H. Melody, whose 500-page testimony argued that the various AT&T tariffs were not compensatory. Through these testimonies and exhibits, the Justice Department hoped to show that the FCC, although well intentioned, was unable to control the monopolist AT&T.

It is important to appreciate the importance of these episodes to the government's case, for not only did MCI furnish the Justice Department with 1.5 million pages of materials from its first antitrust suit against AT&T, but it provided the work of its attorneys as well. In the words of the Court of Appeals, District of Columbia Circuit:

> MCI furnished the Government the documents, depositions, and exhibits that MCI had discovered from AT&T. MCI also furnished certain documents pertaining to a "database" consisting of computerized abstracts of documents, deposition transcripts and exhibits received from AT&T during discovery. MCI's counsel had prepared the database.[101]

Considering the importance of the MCI episodes to the Justice Department, it is instructive to note the disposition of MCI's principal private antitrust suit against AT&T. In January 1983—approximately 1 year after the Justice Department and AT&T reached a settlement and four months after Judge Greene's basic decision on that settlement—the Seventh Circuit Court of Appeals reversed most of the trial court's findings in *MCI* v. *AT&T* and explicitly rejected Dr. Melody's testimony and the cost concepts he advanced. The Seventh Circuit found that each of AT&T's private-line tariffs was compensatory.[102] The Seventh Circuit upheld the jury's findings on the FX and CCSA issues only by permitting the jury to interpret the FCC's complex SCC decision.

However, even though the SCC portion of the government's case was the most elaborate, the other parts of the case were important as well. The cumulative effect of the many episodes used to show AT&T's alleged abuse of its monopoly position was intended to prove regulators' failure in controlling AT&T's destructive conduct. Usually these episodes involved a representative of a company supposedly abused by AT&T, who purported to show that the company's product or service was remarkable and innovative and that AT&T's conduct harmed the company. Further, AT&T had to justify its conduct in the more complex world of telecommunications; for example, it had to show technical reasons for not purchasing certain equipment from independent manufacturers or for not interconnecting with particular CPE. From Greene's decision on the motion to dismiss, it is clear that these episodes made a major impression on the court and that AT&T would endure a difficult burden in its defense. Nonetheless, the defendants' third statement and the Stipulation/Contention Package indicated that AT&T had a plausible and convincing justification for each such incident. For example, consider episode 44, "Intercom Devices: Pritec." Pritec Corporation was a manufacturer of intercom equipment that, in 1971 and 1972, was installed into Illinois Bell's system through an interface device known as the STC coupler that was manufactured by two independent suppliers to Western Electric.

During late 1971 the boom in hand-held calculators and CB radios, which used some of the same components as the STC, led to temporary shortages that delayed Pritec interconnection. Pritec complained to the FCC and Illinois Bell about the adverse impact on its business. In any event, the shortage was eliminated in 1972 due to sharp increases in production.[103] When the STC was unavailable, one of the Western Electric suppliers did manufacture a different connecting arrangement that Pritec sought to substitute for the STC. Illinois Bell's refusal on the grounds that the substitute device was defective and not in compliance with the Bell system technical standards presented factual issues. Such disputes can readily be resolved through private litigation or by regulatory agencies. To seek divestiture on the basis of such incidents as Pritec, which involve disputable facts, is like killing a gnat with a howitzer.

Later episodes dealt with Bell system procurement practices. In these, the Justice Department essentially reiterated its vertical integration theory of the *Western Electric* case, but with one difference: it used as examples up-to-date devices like repertory dialers, line cards, and transfer keys. Although, as we know from our evaluation in earlier chapters, the vertical integration argument was theoretically wanting, the FCC—through the interconnection and *Computer I* and *Computer II* decisions—sought to eliminate any CPE-type problems of which the Department complained. In the area of central office equipment, the Justice Department was in the peculiar position of deploring AT&T for favoring its own equipment over that offered by Japanese firms.[104] Since procurement decisions of central office equipment involve a multitude of complex engineering decisions for each such piece of equipment, there were no egregious examples of AT&T willfulness here. Consequently, it was doubtful that Justice Department attorneys and their allies would be able to argue vertical integration successfully in view of AT&T's reasonable cost and engineering reasons for the decisions taken by Western Electric and the other Bell system companies. The last episode—the remedy—was based on the cumulative impact of all other allegations, including the failure of regulation or any relief short of dismemberment to control AT&T.

THE MOTION TO DISMISS

The government's presentation of evidence began on 15 January 1981, following an unsuccessful attempt to settle. At the conclusion of the plaintiff's case, in which about one hundred witnesses were called and thousands of documents introduced, AT&T filed a 553-page memorandum in support of its motion to dismiss the complaint on the ground that the Antitrust Division had failed to state a cause of action. Because the defendant takes no risk in making such a motion at the close of the plaintiff's case, it is not an uncommon action. Also, the defendant may obtain a better sense of the points the court considers most important as well as its general views on the case, and thus adjust the examination of witnesses accordingly. Consequently, the general rule is that such motions are rarely granted before the close of the entire case, as stated by the Fifth Circuit Court of Appeals:

> Except in unusually clear cases the district judge can and should carry
> defendants' Rule 41(b) motion with the case—or simply deny it,

since the effect will be the same—let the defendant put on his evidence, and then enter a final judgment at the close of the evidence.[105]

This rule is applied because "an appellate reversal for error in granting the motion may require an entire new trial."[106] Thus, in consideration of the effort required in a case as important as *United States* v. *AT&T*, we can appreciate Judge Greene's caution in deciding to follow this general principle.

However, Judge Greene's 40-page decision strongly rejected many of the arguments raised in AT&T's motion to dismiss, indicating that the court would support major portions of the government's case. Greene's general attitude may be surmised in this 1983 statement: "It is antithetical to our political and economic system for this key industry to be within the control of one company."[107] Thus, Judge Greene again decided that the court's jurisdiction was not hindered because of implied antitrust immunity. Instead of delineating at this stage those activities that the FCC and PUCs could not effectively regulate, Greene stated: "This claim has previously been addressed and rejected by the Court. . . . The intent of Congress to repeal the antitrust laws through a regulatory scheme must be clear if a court is to find an immunity from these laws. . . ."[108] Prior decisions had been based on the notion that because records on specific practices had not been established, the court could not conclude that the antitrust laws did not apply to at least some of the events encompassed by the government's vague complaint. But with the Antitrust Division's presentation of its case, it was now time to conduct a detailed examination of the FCC's and PUC's ability to regulate. Thus, to defer to the "intent" of the late nineteenth-century Congresses that debated the Sherman Act rather than to explore in detail the legislative intent behind the Communications Act of 1934 was a clear defeat for AT&T.

After supporting the plaintiff's implied antitrust immunity argument, the court then failed to follow the mandate of *RCA Communications*, an important Supreme Court case that dealt with the FCC and competition: "That there is a national policy favoring competition cannot be maintained today without careful qualification. It is only in a blunt, undiscriminating sense that we speak of competition as an ultimate good."[109] Instead, the court assumed in nearly all instances that the antitrust laws applied. Not only was regulation given little consideration but, under the standards of the Sherman Act, other important considerations were cast aside. For example, the court did not consider that Japanese competitors would benefit from the procurement portions of plaintiff's case and adversely affect the nation's balance of trade. Also considered irrelevant was the fact that AT&T continued to be

> an organization that has made fundamental contributions to human knowledge recognized by eight Nobel prizes, that has provided the fundamental technological underpinnings not only for the telecommunications industry but for other industries as well, and that has provided the people of this country with the best telecommunications service at the lowest prices.[110]

The court's application of the antitrust laws led to its finding that AT&T gained monopoly power through various barriers to entry, such as bottlenecks, entrenched customer preferences, the regulatory process, large capital requirements, access to technical information, and disparities in risk.[111] In contrast, our examination of AT&T's performance has shown that all indicia of monopolistic behavior were absent; the company neither charged monopoly prices nor made monopoly profits. For example, if we invested $1,000 in Dow Jones Industrial stocks in 1917, our average return in 1987 would be $33,809. Fourteen unregulated company's returns would be in excess of $100,000, but AT&T's return would be $7,106, ranking sixty-seven among one hundred of the largest companies.[112] Hence, neither profit nor prices reflected monopoly power in the Sherman Act sense, largely because of state and federal regulation.

Further, in its evaluation of AT&T's alleged monopoly power, the court also disregarded the power of state and federal regulators to permit entry and exit as well as to control rates, routes, competition, and so forth. Only by ignoring the control that regulators have over virtually every aspect of a telephone company's behavior, was it possible for the court to conceive that AT&T had the power to exclude competitors or to control prices. And the only way the court could demonstrate that AT&T had monopoly powers was to assume that the FCC had been "captured" by AT&T, which, of course, cannot be assumed without also ignoring the history of telephone regulation and AT&T's many defeats before the regulatory agencies. As we have seen, the FCC rendered decisions during the post–World War II period that were usually at odds with the positions sought by AT&T. The agency had conducted a general investigation into AT&T's rates and had permitted new firms to enter many phases of the telecommunications business while at the same time temporarily precluding AT&T's entry into domestic satellites and otherwise handicapping it against other competitors. The court viewed AT&T's resistance to many of these changes as a violation of the antitrust law, without considering the fact that the FCC compelled changes in AT&T's conduct.[113] In much the same way the court found that AT&T had the power to exclude competitors notwithstanding the entry of numerous competitors. For example, the plaintiff's witnesses, Richard M. Moley, Rolm vice-president, and Richard Masi, manager of marketing operations of the Siemens Corporation, spoke of the increasingly competitive nature of the growing PBX market.[114] However, the court did not emphasize the many successful competitive firms but instead those that had failed to succeed in the market, and it blamed AT&T for their failure.[115] Similarly, the court supported the government in ignoring AT&T's total procurement practices, including numerous purchases from outside suppliers, as well as the high quality of Western Electric equipment. Instead, the Justice Department focused on a small number of questionable purchases, substituting its business and engineering judgment for that of the experienced engineers and management persons who made such decisions on a daily basis.[116]

AT&T, then, had lost on nearly every point decided by Judge Greene in the motion to dismiss. Although AT&T sought to down-play the decision, commenting that "[i]t is important to remember that Judge Greene has not found us guilty of antitrust violations,"[117] the company knew that the decision indicated a high probability of losing the case. Indeed, AT&T responded by enlarging its witness list in an attempt to counterargue parts of the decision.[118] But, at the same time, other important events occurred. Most notable was Judge Buinno's 3 September 1981 *Western Electric* decision, construing the 1956 judgment in AT&T's favor so that it could offer enhanced services through a separate subsidiary in keeping with the FCC's *Computer II* proposals. This placed the prospect of a negotiated settlement in a new light, for AT&T's leadership realized that Theodore Vail's conception of the public interest was shattered and that the company would soon have to adjust to a new one.

CHAPTER 10

WHAT'S MY LINE?

WHY SETTLE?

When the old AT&T broke up on 1 January 1984, and was replaced by a new AT&T and seven regional Bell-operating companies (BOCs), an era had come to an end. The new AT&T was no longer in the local-loop business and its two principal fields—equipment manufacture and long-distance transmission—were subject to varying mixes of regulation and limited competition. The end of the old AT&T marked the atrophy of the public service principles that had matured with the company. While it was questionable whether the new conception of the public interest would serve the general public as well as the old one had, there was no question that the new policy regime would lead to a proliferation of new players in the telecommunications arena.

In this final chapter, we examine the attempts to settle the *United States* v. *AT&T* case and the settlement into which the parties entered, as well as the events that occurred from the time of the agreement to the actual breakup. An understanding of the agreements as well as the attempts that failed does not imply that the case should have been brought in the first place, but rather that we need to consider the positions in which the Justice Department and AT&T found themselves. Of course, AT&T did not wish for a major antitrust complaint to be filed against it, nor did the company want to defend against the mountain of evidence that the Justice Department placed in the record. AT&T did not seek the strong denial of its motion to dismiss, and it did not choose to be in the position it was in. But once on the defensive, AT&T had to operate within the real world. Thus, settlement implied neither AT&T's guilt nor approval of the terms compared to other *ideal* arrangements. Of course, the peculiarities and personalities of the actors involved played roles in the settlement process and its terms. Moreover, there are a variety of terms that can occur in a settlement; the more complex the matter, the greater the flexibility. Nevertheless, as we follow the settlement, we will see a logic to it that overrides the personalities who participated. It was a settlement compatible with the politics of the times and the numerous events that led to it. *EXECUNET* had changed the shape of the long-distance market, while the private antitrust suits against AT&T (primarily MCI's) contributed to the viability of many new firms. The FCC did its part by permitting considerable rivalry in equipment markets. Local loops were the only segment of the traditional telephone system whose monopoly status was largely unchallenged. The logic of these events was to separate sharply activities governed by monopoly from those in which a kind of competition—no matter how constrained—prevailed.

From the Justice Department's perspective, many factors favored settlement.[1] First, much of what it sought in the 1974 complaint had been accomplished or was in the process of being achieved in other proceedings. *EXECUNET* and its aftereffects had opened up the long-distance market to at least a form of competition. The FCC's computer and interconnection proceedings were opening up the CPE market to easy entry. A divorce of AT&T from the operating companies would do the same for the switching and transmission equipment markets. Because so much had already been settled, the Justice Department had greater room for flexibility in arranging a settlement without invoking the ire of AT&T's rivals. The *AT&T* case was so unique that it would have little precedent value. In contrast, the Justice Department had sought decisions in antitrust cases with little economic impact in order to establish an important precedent. For example, it pursued a merger case in which the acquiring and acquired firms constituted only 7.5 percent of the Los Angeles grocery market.[2] In that case, the Justice Department welcomed a court test that would eventually lead to a Supreme Court decision. Notwithstanding the Justice Department's victory in Judge Greene's denial of AT&T's motion to dismiss, there was much to lose from a lengthy prolongation of the case. At the conclusion of the trial, the record would have been so immense that much time necessarily would elapse before a final decision would be announced by Judge Greene. The inevitable appeal to the Court of Appeals would add years to the case as well, and it was far from certain that the Justice Department would win at the Court of Appeals level. An appeal to the Supreme Court would extend the time still further. The uncertain status of the telecommunications industry during these critical years could not help AT&T or its opponents plan effectively for the future. Nor could it help the Justice Department politically. Congress and members of the Executive Branch were already preparing a variety of remedies, and as different as these were, all could be implemented considerably more quickly than antitrust relief. Finally, even if the Justice Department won the case on its merits, it is far from certain that drastic relief involving divestiture would have been upheld. In summary, then, the Justice Department had many reasons to attempt to settle the matter.

AT&T, too, had to consider the various trade-offs of litigation and settlement. In addition to the enormous resources consumed in litigation, prolonging the matter through the Supreme Court stage would limit the company's ability to engage in long-range planning. The company certainly did not want to put resources in a division that it may have had to divest. Again, such uncertainty enhanced risk and, therefore, probably made it more difficult and costly for the company to borrow funds, especially in the form of long-term bonds. Moreover, the ultimate outcome of AT&T's attempt to modify the 1956 consent decree was equally uncertain, in that the Justice Department challenged AT&T on this interrelated matter as well. From AT&T's perspective, settlement considerations required the company to come to grips with the kind of structure that would be the least worse alternative. AT&T also appreciated that Judge Greene would have to approve the terms of a settlement and that its many enemies in Congress and the private sector would closely scrutinize and exert influence on its terms.

AT&T'S SETTLEMENT CONSIDERATIONS

On 31 January 1979, John de Butts retired after 42 years with the Bell system, the last seven of which were as chairman of the board. Although de Butts regretted the erosion of the regulated network manager system, he planned for future contingencies during his last years with the company. Asher Ende, a former FCC staffer, captured the essence of de Butts's accomplishments: "de Butts is the Moses who took the people to the edge of the promised land, and [incoming chairman Charles L.] Brown is the Joshua who must fight the Canaanites."[3] De Butts instituted a massive reorganization of the company that emphasized marketing in a way AT&T had never before done. Three new vice-presidencies were created along the lines of broad business sectors: business services, residential services, and network services. The company's new marketing department recruited Archibald J. McGill, a former IBM marketing vice-president, to become a marketing manager. Under de Butts's leadership, AT&T would place increased importance on its competitive offerings and less importance on its noncompetitive sectors, principally local telephone service. De Butts sought to "make the Bell System as strong in marketing as it is strong in technology,"[4] which would characterize AT&T's negotiating strategy in the years to follow. Although the company expected its efforts in the competitive sectors to be increasingly important, it knew that sophisticated buyers of the products and services would be particularly sensitive to the technological progressiveness of their purchases. In this way, marketing and technology were intimately linked. This, in turn, was closely tied to AT&T's retaining control of most of Western Electric, which would design and manufacture the new products and services, and of Bell Labs, which would undertake the research.

Based on its past record, AT&T could be reasonably confident of its ability to do well in the new competitive environment.

> A key reason for this confidence lies in the unique resource of Bell Laboratories. For a high technology business such as ours to continue to innovate, it must be fueled by constant research that extends the boundaries of scientific knowledge and translates it into useful technology. . . . In short, Bell Laboratories assures the Bell System of being on the leading edge of new technology.[5]

Thus, AT&T was far more reluctant to give up the research, development, and implementation of new technology—Bell Labs and Western Electric—than it was to give up long-distance or local-operating transmission. Justifying in 1983 what took place, AT&T chairman Charles L. Brown noted: "We faced the prospect of an even more disastrous divestiture—being gutted—by having Western Electric and Bell Labs

cut out of the system. We would have lost control of our own technology."[6] However, it was more difficult for AT&T to determine if long
distance or local loop was more important. It was clear that retaining
long distance would be preferred to keeping local service, as long distance had been far more susceptible to technological progressiveness
and declining costs than had local service. But an even more subtle
chain of reasoning led to the preference for long distance: local-loop
service might even become a burden in AT&T's overall strategy. In
AT&T's 1979 *Annual Report*, published shortly before the May 1980
Computer II final decision, Chairman Brown emphasized: "Our third
concern is the need—in an era of rapidly developing competition—to
free the Bell System from the constraints of the 1956 Consent Decree.
No longer does it make sense to deny the Bell System the opportunity
to compete in unregulated markets."[7] At the same time, more than 90
percent of AT&T's construction budget had been going to the local
operating companies. Yet some of the states, particularly California
and Louisiana, were adamantly resisting local rate increases. The 1979
Annual Report spoke of a cash squeeze in California, which was "seriously
jeopardizing the Pacific Company's ability to finance construction and
good service."[8] Although AT&T's Killoch study on costs, expenses, and
flows was, like all studies involving cost-accounting assumptions, subject to criticism, there was no reason to believe that AT&T did not
accept its results and conclusions. The Killoch study was submitted
as evidence in legislative and administrative proceedings. One of its
conclusions was that direct revenue in local service covered less than
60 percent of costs, even using the allocation methods advocated
by William Melody. Later, AT&T studies continued to show similar
shortfalls.[9]

These perceptions placed AT&T in a difficult dilemma—if it continued to place resources in local operating companies to the same extent
it had in the past, its return on investment likely would be considerably
lower than if it placed those same resources in competitive activities
that could open up as the result of the *Computer II* liberalization. But,
on the other hand, as *Fortune* reporter Bro Uttal observed,

> If AT&T does start putting its money where the best returns are, its
> relations with state regulators will worsen. . . . If state commissioners
> suspect their current woes are being increased because Bell is "di-
> verting" investment to Baby Bell or using monopoly revenues to sub-
> sidize its competitive activities, rate setting could become confisca-

tory even outside such notoriously pinch-penny states as California and Louisiana.[10]

One way to avoid the dilemma would be to divest the operating companies, such that state regulators could not complain about funds diverted from their "proper" place in local-loop construction. Even the alternative of local rate increases was considered risky, for AT&T planners must have been aware of the future bypass threat. Because costs per channel of satellite and microwave systems had been falling, local rate increases would make it increasingly attractive for more business customers to circumvent the local exchanges of the public-switched network by constructing their own local private networks.[11] Although the threat was not an immediate one and the FCC did not raise it as an issue until 1980, it was probably considered by AT&T planners long before its public airing.[12] Further, it suggested not that the local operating companies should be let go, but rather that if any part of the Bell system should not be retained, it should be all or part of the local operating companies.

As the United States v. AT&T case progressed, it became apparent that the judicial management would probably preclude the kind of legal entanglements that would create lengthy delays or major procedural errors. Therefore, settlement prospects became increasingly more important. Corporate Planning, an AT&T department designed to consider the company's future, grew from less than fifty people in 1972 to about two hundred 10 years later. It developed the Case B and other studies intended to compare alternative futures for the company under various structural arrangements. In June 1978, Corporate Planning established a new task force devoted to strategic planning. The task force concluded that resolution of the 1974 case and modification of the 1956 consent decree were highly desirable goals. However, it noted that some form of structural modification was needed. When the task force presented its views to Chairman Brown in 1979, it did not specify the particulars of structural modification, as these would depend on hard bargaining. Nevertheless, it concluded: "If required, reduce horizontal integration—to retain vertical integration."[13] This meant that some or all of the operating companies would be the victims of the Justice Department's case—if it came to that.

320 CLOSING THE RING

ATTEMPTS AT SETTLEMENT

Prior to the enactment of the Antitrust Procedures and Penalties Act—
the so-called *Tunney Act*—in 1974, only the parties to the suit had to
agree for a consent decree to be entered. The Tunney Act arose in large
part because of congressional suspicion about the 1956 *Western Electric*
consent decree and the settlement terms of an antitrust suit against ITT
during the Nixon administration.[14] Under the procedures set up by the
Act, the Justice Department is required to submit for industry and public comment a copy of the proposed decree and a public impact statement that analyzes the decree and its probable impact. After public
comments, the court is required to hold a hearing on the decree, making findings about whether the decree is in the public interest and what
its probable effects will be. Since the court has the power to "take such
other action in the public interest as the court may deem appropriate,"
the parties must consider what the court will do in reaching its final
terms of agreement.[15] In turn, since the court considers the public's
comments, the parties must take these into account as well. While
legalistic arguments were made to circumvent the Tunney Act procedures in the *AT&T* case, both sides knew that Judge Greene would reject
the idea. Only a voluntary dismissal could circumvent the Act, and
Greene's independence made it clear that he would resist settlement.

Although settlement was discussed almost from the outset of the
case, the first serious attempt to settle occurred at the end of 1980 and
the beginning of 1981. During the waning days of the Carter administration, both sides requested that the trial, then scheduled to begin on
15 January 1981, be postponed pending settlement negotiations. The
parties stated that they had a framework for negotiations but that many
complex and controversial features still needed to be resolved. Judge
Greene, claiming not to understand why the parties waited so long to
begin serious negotiations, turned down their request. Greene noted
that the unresolved issues, which might derail the settlement, and the
time required contributed most to his decision. In addition, incumbent
Assistant Attorney General Sanford Litvack had not consulted with incoming Reagan administration officials about the settlement plans.[16]
However, only one week later the parties reported that they had
worked intensively on settlement and that a complete, detailed agree-

ment had been prepared, in which there remained no complex or controversial issues to be resolved. Judge Greene described the agreement as "essentially complete,"[17] but noted that the new administration still had not been consulted about the terms. After both sides planned to remedy this problem quickly, Judge Greene agreed to interrupt the trial proceedings until 2 February 1981, at which time the attorneys for both sides were to report back to the court. If at this time they were agreeable to the filing of a formal consent decree within 30 days, the court would delay the case further. However, if they could not agree to this by February 2, the trial would proceed.

Attempts to settle United States v. IBM had failed, in part, because of widespread leaks on the proposed terms. Accordingly, few people on both sides in the AT&T case knew the details of the proposals. Nevertheless, in an early statement, Assistant Attorney General Litvack indicated that (1) the 1956 consent decree would be vacated or modified so as to allow AT&T to enter into enhanced services and (2) the structure and operations of AT&T would be altered.[18] Even without knowing the details of the proposed settlement—and the differences that remained—opposition was beginning to mount. MCI, equipment manufacturers, and the American Newspaper Publishers' Association were mounting efforts to convince the new administration to reject the proposed settlement—whatever it might be. The newspaper publishers were fearful of AT&T's ability to enter the electronic classified advertising business, which could divert advertising revenues from newspapers to telecommunications.[19]

When the settlement's terms were revealed, they surprised many observers. First, AT&T would have been required to divest Pacific Telephone & Telegraph and its minority interests in Cincinnati Bell and Southern New England Telephone.[20] AT&T would have given up problems in the case of PT&T and its minority shareholdings in two companies, which, though parts of the Bell system, it did not control. By the divestiture of these local operating companies, the Justice Department would have arranged the creation of independent firms whose behavior on interconnection and other issues could readily be compared to the Bell local operating companies. If the Bell companies were found wanting in some respect, the FCC could use the three former Bell system companies operating independently as models of appropriate behavior.[21] Further, the 1956 consent decree would have been vacated, allowing AT&T to enter noncommunications businesses. However, consistent with the *Computer II* rules, a fully separated subsidiary would provide CPE and enhanced services. The Long Lines Department and the interstate long-distance network would have been placed under the control of a different, fully separate subsidiary. Essentially agreeing with the *Computer II* final decision conception of separate subsidiaries, the separated components of AT&T would deal in a nondiscriminatory way with other components of the company. For example, under the post-*EXECUNET* FCC decisions, local operating companies would treat AT&T long-lines, MCI, Southern Pacific, and other long-distance carriers in a nondiscriminatory manner. Finally, AT&T would have been required to spin off parts of Western Electric, which would have created a rival in the equipment business with the technological and business acumen to compete with Western Electric. While the new company would have been considerably smaller than Western Electric, it would have been a viable competitor. Although not pleased with this aspect of the proposed settlement, top AT&T officials felt that it was more important to end the case and end the Antitrust Division's opposition to the company's entrance into unregulated businesses. Based on the performance of Western Electric and Bell Labs, AT&T's management felt that the company could become a powerful force not only in the older regulated fields but also in the development and manufacture of unregulated products and enhanced services, such as call-forwarding and tapping into remote data banks.[22]

In addition to the time pressures that Judge Greene imposed on the parties, there were several other reasons contributing to the agreement's failure. First, renowned antitrust scholar William F. Baxter, appointed to head the Antitrust Division, had ideas very different from those who guided Antitrust Division personnel in the proposed settlement. Second, Judge Greene had been eminently fair in his treatment of the parties, and before the motion to dismiss was denied, AT&T could reasonably feel that it had a good chance to win the case if it went to trial. Shortly before the trial resumed, AT&T stated: "We feel obligated to make it plain that the beginning of trial will present us with an altogether new set of circumstances, and therefore a changed basis for appraising what might constitute a reasonable disposition of our contentions with the Justice Department."[23] Third, the Justice Department was dissatisfied with all versions that had been prepared of the proposal guaranteeing all long-distance carriers equal access to local telephone systems.[24] Yet among these reasons for the proposed agreement's failure, the most important was Baxter's vigorous opposition. On 9 April 1981, Baxter rejected the Carter administration's antitrust team's settlement proposals because they would have left unregulated services under AT&T's control. On the same day, the Antitrust Division filed a memorandum in the U.S. District Court for the Northern District of New Jersey, opposing modification of the 1956 decree on the ground that AT&T was barred from offering services that were not rate regulated. And, in the same period, Baxter rejected a Defense Department request to dismiss the suit against AT&T because of the adverse impact it would have on defense arrangements. Instead, Baxter intended to litigate the case, and would discuss settlement with AT&T only if it agreed to complete separation of all AT&T-regulated activities from unregulated ones.[25] As we will see, Baxter maintained a consistent and rigorous stance from the time he assumed office through to the 8 January 1982 agreement.

TOWARD A SETTLEMENT

Baxter's strong criticism of the proposed 1981 settlement would form the basis of the Justice Department's future negotiating position. Baxter held that AT&T should be divided into two piles of assets: the regulated side would be comprised of those involved in local loops, and the competitive side would include equipment, enhanced services, data processing, and long distance. "We are well into the morn of the day when long lines should not be regulated at all. . . . [Long distance should be] put over on the competitive pile. The local loops would be on the other."[26]

However, placing assets into two piles and strictly separating them tells us nothing about how the separation should be effected. There are three possible ways in which such a separation can take place. First, there can be accounting regulations that separate regulated from unregulated activities. The 1956 consent decree adopted this solution with respect to separating Western Electric's activities from those of both local and long-distance transmission. Second, in the *Computer II* solution, a strictly separated subsidiary operates within competitive markets, and criteria, such as nondiscrimination between customers, attempt to assure that the regulated and unregulated components of the company do not favor each other. Third, there is dissolution and divestiture along certain lines, such as those proposed by Baxter and his predecessors. Obviously, within each category there can be many different solutions and the categories are not necessarily mutually exclusive, as parts of each framework could have been used in a comprehensive solution to the AT&T "problem."

The Reagan administration was split on how to proceed. Those who opposed any structural tampering with the Bell system wanted to drop the *AT&T* suit in fear that it might lead to divestiture. Notwithstanding the divisions, the administration could not publicly appear to vacillate—it had to take a unified stand on this issue like any other one. Secretary of Commerce Malcolm Baldridge, appearing in June 1981 before the Senate Commerce Committee, noted that the administration looked to Congress to solve the problem, complaining that the FCC was slow and indecisive. The dominant view within the administration favored the solution of fully separated affiliates and rejected divestiture. In Baldridge's words, the separate affiliate solution represented "a compromise by which the public can benefit from AT&T participation within the areas of its expertise, while still continuing to be protected from AT&T control of the bottleneck facilities and potential anti-competitive conduct."[27] Thus, the administration favored legislation that would be clear and comprehensive, embody the separate subsidiary requirement, and uphold AT&T's right to enter unregulated markets. We should note that the FCC and the Justice Department were at this time battling the same issue before the Federal District Court for Northern New Jersey. Congress then had the opportunity to quickly resolve the issue. But even though it favored a legislative solution, the administration was unwilling to state that it would drop the *AT&T* suit.[28] In keeping with the administration's strategy, however, the Justice Department in August requested Judge Greene to suspend the suit until 30 June 1982, to give Congress time to enact comprehensive legislation with which a decision in the case might conflict. Nevertheless, Judge Greene denied the request.[29]

The legislative option was still alive in October 1981, when the Senate passed a consensual bill by an overwhelming 90–4 margin. However, certain events of early November eliminated the option, demonstrating the difficulty in enacting legislation on a complex issue with diverse viewpoints. The Senate legislation was pending in the House, but Representative Timothy Wirth sought to have his own different views enacted into law. A November 3 staff report, prepared under Wirth's guidance, endorsed the system of contrived competition: "In many markets, the full force of competition, and the protective surveillance and allocative guidance that it provides, has yet to develop to the point where complete deregulation will further the public interest."[30] Wirth also introduced a bill that was substantially different from the Senate's; it would have required the FCC to classify carriers as dominant and regulated or unregulated, and to treat the dominant carriers in an unfavored fashion. Only one carrier would be classified as dominant.[31]

Although events were stagnated on the legislative front, they advanced rapidly on the judicial one during this period, further moving the parties toward a settlement. On 3 September 1981, Judge Vincent Biunno of the Northern District of New Jersey, which had continuing jurisdiction over the 1956 final judgment, held that AT&T could offer detariffed CPE and enhanced services through a fully separated subsidiary in accordance with the *Computer II* rules.[32] Before AT&T could savor that victory, however, Judge Greene denied AT&T's motion to dismiss on September 11. A major consequence of Greene's decision and its widespread publicity was that the forces within the administration seeking dismissal of the suit were seriously undermined. The pressure to drop the case came principally from (1) Commerce Secretary Baldridge, who claimed the suit was putting American leadership in telecommunications in jeopardy; (2) Defense Secretary Caspar Weinberger, who held that a fragmented Bell system would endanger the national defense effort; and (3) a cabinet task force on telecommunications, which recommended that the case be voluntarily dismissed. However, Judge Greene's denial of the motion to dismiss supported the views of Baxter and others who sought a strong pro-competition stance within the administration.[33] Thus, dismissal of the case would have left the administration vulnerable to charges of selling out to AT&T and of tampering with the judicial process. As a result, when Baxter was called before a House Government Operations Subcommittee on 4 November 1981 to explain apparent inconsistencies in his stands on settling the case, he was in an influential position and used the opportunity to amplify his views on a settlement. Although Baxter was willing to continue litigating the case, he knew that as many as 5 years might pass before a final disposition was announced. He therefore reiterated the same type of settlement that he had sought when first assuming office:

> At the present time we are asking that local basic telephone service, which is usually referred to as exchange service, be separated from the rest of the enterprises. . . . The reason we focus on those local exchange services is because these are the activities that represent natural monopolies. . . . The number of such companies is less important than that they be separated from the rest of the enterprise.[34]

Baxter held that regulation should be lifted from AT&T's activities because it was unnecessary, except for a short transition period.

Hence, paving the way toward a settlement in the case were AT&T's victory on the *Computer II* rules and its defeat on the motion to dismiss, together with the Justice Department's defeat on *Computer II* and its victory on the motion to dismiss.

THE AGREEMENT

When AT&T's Board of Directors met promptly at 10:30 A.M. on 16 December 1981, Charles Brown scrapped his prepared statement and instead described the Baxter divestiture plan that had been under discussion between Baxter and AT&T general counsel Howard Trienens. After Brown had been thoroughly questioned by the others present, the Board authorized him to enter divestiture talks with the Justice Department. Baxter and his staff began preparing an agreement based on regulated and unregulated divisions of the company. Baxter did not care whether AT&T kept the local operating companies or the competitive parts of the business, as long as it did not keep both. AT&T received a first draft of the proposed consent decree on December 21. After Brown reviewed the original proposal, a modified proposed decree, little different from the first one, was prepared. At most, half a dozen Justice Department employees, AT&T's directors, and, perhaps, ten of its employees knew of the momentous events that were taking place.[35]

As the agreement took shape, the lawyers turned their attention to the legal vehicle that was to embrace what they did. As we have seen,

AT&T wanted to eliminate the restrictions in the 1956 consent decree. Both sides wanted to consolidate the New Jersey and District of Columbia cases before one judge—Judge Greene. Therefore, they concluded that the agreement was a modification of the 1956 consent decree. Judge Biunno was asked to transfer the matter to Judge Greene's court but not to examine the substance of the agreement. Little known is that Judge Biunno did, in fact, approve the decree before transferring it to Judge Greene, who conducted his own review. Further, both sides argued that the Tunney Act did not apply to modifications of decrees but, expecting to lose on that issue, they followed the Tunney Act procedures. Brown then presided over a meeting with operating company presidents on 5 January 1982, who were told the details and sworn to secrecy. On January 6, Brown, in accordance with his understanding with Baxter, assured Defense Secretary Weinberger that the agreement would not adversely affect American defense posture. The following day, the White House was informed of the agreement. On January 8, Baxter, AT&T general counsel Howard Trienens, and aides signed the agreement in Baxter's office. Explaining the company's incentives to sign, AT&T vice-president Alfred C. Partoll explained that the antitrust suit had been a "brooding presence" that had now disappeared; the settlement "would lift a giant cloud" because it rescinded the 1956 decree restricting AT&T from entering noncommunications businesses. But others in the company viewed the pending divorce with considerable regret.[36]

At the heart of the settlement was the requirement that AT&T would spin off the Bell-operating companies and submit a plan that would restructure the BOCs into viable entities. AT&T would no longer be in the local exchange business (except for its minority ownership in Cincinnati Bell and Southern New England Telephone, which the settlement did not affect). Also, AT&T would retain control of Bell Labs and Western Electric and continue to operate its intercity long-distance network. The company would furnish all CPE, including that furnished by the local Bell companies, but license and supply contracts then in effect between Western Electric and the local operating companies would be cancelled. The new operating companies would, thus, be free to choose their own suppliers. Because the local operating companies would be suddenly divorced from Bell Labs—their principal resource for scientific and technological information and research—AT&T agreed to provide the new operating companies, on a priority basis, with research, development, and support services until September 1987. Finally, AT&T promised that it would not acquire the stock of any spun-off Bell-operating company.[37]

The settlement also specified the obligations of the new Bell-operating companies. Foremost among these was to provide each long-distance carrier and information service provider (that is, a company that transforms and communicates information) access into local loops equal in type, quality, and price to that provided to AT&T and its affiliates. For example, if a person dialed "1" to access AT&T's long-distance service, each new operating company would have to make arrangements to treat the other long-distance carriers equally. The new operating companies would offer their customers a choice of which long-distance carrier they wanted that would be accessed by dialing "1." Similarly, each BOC was forbidden to discriminate in treatment between AT&T and other suppliers of various services, CPE, and switching and transmission equipment.

However, the most controversial aspects of the MFJ followed from Baxter's rigorous distinction between regulated and unregulated businesses. The new operating companies (with a few exceptions relating to emergencies) were forbidden to manufacture or distribute CPE or other telecommunications products. For the same reason, they were excluded from the interexchange long-distance and information service businesses. More generally, the BOCs agreed not to provide any other product or service, except local telephone service and local access, "that is not a natural monopoly service actually regulated by tariff."[38] Among the most important nonregulated services were the Yellow Pages. In 1982, industry directory revenues were $40 billion, of which AT&T's share was $3.5 billion. Advertising income from this source had grown 8 to 10 percent a year from 1978 through 1983.[39] Notwithstanding the threat of financial trouble among the BOCs, they were not given any service that was clearly not a natural monopoly. The Justice Department would have solved the problem by allowing the BOCs to grant "use-specific licenses" for the information contained in its file of telephone subscribers and the machine-readable listings compiled from the file. In this way, each BOC would be able to derive considerable revenue by licensing such information to as many users as they wished.[40] Baxter's rigor was not to prevail on these issues—Greene modified the MFJ after considering the numerous statements filed under the Tunney Act procedures.

THE TUNNEY ACT DECISION

Although the parties to the settlement formed a united front once they entered into the agreement, virtually every other interest criticized some aspect of it. Frequently, these criticisms were quite varied; for example, some deplored the breakup while others felt that the breakup did not go far enough. The criticism continued in the formal comments authorized under the Tunney Act. More than 600 individuals and organizations filed comments comprising approximately 8,750 pages. The Antitrust Division reported that "[t]he comments could have filled about 1,500 pages of the *Federal Register* at a cost to the Antitrust Division of more than $600,000."[41] Senator Robert Packwood, who chaired the Commerce Committee that prepared the Senate bill, feared that local rates would rise markedly as a result of the agreement; whereas Representative Wirth, clearly undercut by the settlement, announced that he would hold hearings on his bill and the settlement.[42] As former Antitrust Division Chief Litvack stated, the settlement "represents a striking victory for the government in that it achieved all the essential goals of the lawsuit."[43]

Both the Justice Department and AT&T sought to complete the arrangements called for in the settlement as quickly as possible and to do so without undue shock to the component parts of the new system or subscribers. In February 1982, AT&T took the first step in reconstructing the twenty-two operating companies into more economically viable entities by reorganizing them into seven larger regional operation firms. In this way, smaller BOCs like Diamond State Telephone, which covered Delaware, would be better able to withstand the shock of divestiture. Each regional company, which in fact constituted the firms eventually spun off, had local operations that were greater than GTE's. While most observers accepted the soundness of the spin-off plan, GTE complained that its manufacturing divisions had a much better opportunity to sell to the former Bell-operating companies—the twenty-two autonomous decision-making bodies—than to the seven new BOCs.[44]

Much depended on Judge Greene's Tunney Act approval. In May 1982, Greene indicated that he would consider the comments as carefully as he had other aspects of the case, ordering AT&T and the Justice

Department to write briefs on the questions raised.[45] Finally, on 11 August 1982, Judge Greene rendered his opinion and order agreeing to accept the MFJ subject to certain modifications that applied to both the new operating companies and AT&T.[46] First, the new operating companies would continue to provide the printed Yellow Pages. Second, they could lease or sell CPE to their customers but they could not manufacture them. In this way, Greene argued, they would not favor their manufacturing subsidiaries—thus solving the vertical integration problem. Third, the new BOCs could enter other business markets if they were able to show that monopoly power would not be used to impede competition in the markets. Under this provision Judge Greene has been deluged by the operating companies with requests to enter new lines of business. Fourth, while the new BOCs were prohibited from offering information and enhanced services, AT&T was precluded from engaging in electronic publishing over its own transmission facilities for 7 years. Many of these changes were deviations from the rigorous division into competitive and regulated activities that Baxter had devised. Further, they reveal Greene's concern that without such opportunities and benefits, the new operating companies might not become viable entities. Apparently concerned also about the possible adverse impact of the decree on the universal service goal, Greene did not object to a subsidy flow from the long-distance user to the local subscriber.[47]

However, Greene would soon realize that he had not replaced the FCC as a decision-making body and that the MFJ would not resolve many of the controversies and problems within the industry. In December 1982, the FCC adopted its long-debated access charge rule (not to be confused with equal access), under which each local subscriber would be charged a flat fee to link into the toll network.[48] The flat fee was intended to help local telephone companies avoid having to raise business subscriber rates. Traditionally, business rates had subsidized residential rates, but now the reduced costs of bypass technologies afforded more firms the opportunity to bypass local loops if they considered local rates unacceptable. The access charge solution was expected to eliminate the incentive to bypass by shifting charges to residential subscribers. The resulting controversy, into which Congress, the FCC, PUCs, the Executive Branch, and others were drawn, would continue for some time. More importantly, it would show, even as early as 1982 and 1983, that the AT&T breakup had exacerbated rather than solved many of the industry's problems. Yet access charges would be only one of numerous controversies into which Judge Greene would be drawn as a result of his obligation to supervise the enforcement of the decree. Nevertheless, on 24 August 1982, when the Justice Department and AT&T signed a revised agreement incorporating the changes that Greene required, they undoubtedly believed that the agreement would solve more problems than it would create.[49]

AT&T's plan for reorganization would become effective within the 18 months following the entry of the approved MFJ. The new operating companies were to have sufficient facilities, personnel, systems, and rights to technical information so to allow them to provide good performance—an obligation that AT&T fulfilled in exemplary fashion. In December 1982, AT&T filed its 471-page Plan of Reorganization.[50] Under the plan, the former twenty-two BOCs were reorganized into seven newly formed regional holding companies (RHCs)—later named Pacific Telesis, U.S. West, Southwestern Bell, Ameritech, Bell South, Bell Atlantic, and NYNEX. Approximately 75 percent of AT&T's assets were assigned to the RHCs. Further, all Bell-system territory in the continental United States was divided into 161 geographical areas called Local Access and Transport Areas, or LATAs. The LATAs were generally centered on a city or other identifiable community of interest, and each one marked the boundaries within which RHC-operating company subsidiaries could provide telephone service. Thus, an operating company could provide local service and intra-LATA long distance, but inter-LATA long distance would be provided by AT&T and the other interexchange carriers, such as MCI (which argued that the LATAs were too large). For example, because one LATA in Ohio included Cleveland, Akron, and Lorain, a long-distance call from Cleveland to Akron would be handled by the Ohio Bell subsidiary of Ameritech but a call from Cleveland to Columbus, Ohio, would be served by an interexchange carrier.[51] Certain exceptions permitting RHCs to cross LATA lines (such as the New York City–suburban New Jersey corridor) were permitted. The plan also required each new BOC to provide all interexchange carriers equal access by 1 September 1986, as well as information access. Finally, for the seven RHCs AT&T set up a central services organization called Bellcore, which the RHCs jointly owned. Bellcore's function was to provide the RHCs and their subsidiaries technical assistance, such as network planning, engineering, and software development. Patterned after Bell Labs, the new company would also provide consulting services and serve as a central contact point for coordinating the efforts of the RHCs in meeting national security requirements.[52]

On 8 July 1983, Judge Greene issued a decision largely accepting the plan of reorganization but requiring certain changes. First, he expanded the patent licensing powers of the RHCs. Second, AT&T would no longer be permitted to use the logo or name "Bell" (except in the case of Bell Telephone Laboratories). According to Greene, the continued use of "Bell" by AT&T would have caused such confusion that an Illinois Bell subscriber, for example, would have assumed that AT&T "is the natural or 'official' long distance company to be used in conjunction with the local services provided by the several Bell Operating Companies."[53] Symbolically, though, Greene's decision on this point was appropriate—it marked the end of a long period in telecommunications history (even if it didn't mark the end of controversy within the industry). In early August, AT&T, with some reluctance, and the Justice Department agreed to Greene's modifications of the reorganization plan.[54] In November, AT&T sent to its shareholders a prospectus detailing the stock distribution plan (seven RHC shares for every ten AT&T shares held). And at midnight on the last day of 1983, the Bell system that had been gradually constructed for more than a century broke up.

BELL'S STAR

One lesson from AT&T's history stands out above all others: major changes in public policy can occur even though an existing public policy regime leads to highly effective performance. Although those seeking changes often employ economic and technological arguments and use legal discourse, it is in the realm of politics that we can best understand the radical restructuring that occurred in the telecommunications industry and in the policies governing it. In this sense, overall performance is not the central criterion in these types of decisions. Major economic and technological opportunities attract those like William McGowan and Thomas Carter to telecommunications, just as they provided major incentives for Alexander Graham Bell and Elisha Gray in the 1870s. But unlike other industries, would-be entrepreneurs in the telecommunications industry have had to operate within the context of extensive economic regulation that favored an entrenched rival. They had to persuade the decision makers in a variety of different institutions—most importantly, the Justice Department, FCC, and the courts—of their policy preferences being in the public interest. Although their burden has been substantial in view of AT&T's overall excellent performance, the new entrepreneurs have succeeded in their endeavors. Further, their activities represent skillful political maneuvering, in that their success was not achieved through exerting greater "pressure" than AT&T but because they were able to persuade most of the autonomous policymakers that their preferences were in the public interest.

MCI and other AT&T opponents realized that administrators are usually not apt to change reasonably satisfactory policies drastically. Therefore, AT&T's rivals could not have directly challenged the overall performance of the Bell system without losing. Instead, they first used apparently reasonable arguments and modest requests. They then sought to show the FCC that it could better discharge its statutory responsibilities under the Communications Act by allowing new firms to enter designated segments of the market not served adequately or at all by AT&T. Their demands were tied to more general sentiments in the American public philosophy: give a new firm that wants to take a risk the chance to show what it can do; favor the small firm when it takes on the giant; capitalize on anti-big business, antimonopoly, and, specifically, anti-AT&T sentiment. The concomitant of these activities is to gather allies willing to join the effort. Certainly, the ability of the newcomers to attract major industries and firms—such as the petroleum industry, IBM, the securities industry, the computer industry, and Westinghouse—willing to participate actively in proceedings increasingly isolated AT&T and its allies. At the same time, AT&T's opponents skillfully brought into the fray important governmental actors who had nothing pecuniary to gain from the victories of AT&T's rivals but much to gain ideologically. The Antitrust Division, for example, which seeks to enforce the antitrust laws, has consistently sought to restrict the application of the economic regulatory statutes. MCI and other AT&T opponents had to attract such allies and congressional sympathizers by showing them that their private interest represented the public interest.

AT&T, of course, had to defend itself. It sought to persuade the FCC that the regulated network manager system and the excellent performance of the entire industry would be endangered if the FCC yielded to the requests of new entrants and their allies. The new entrants, however, simultaneously claimed to represent only modest change and the wave of the future. AT&T's opponents were abetted by the Bell system's very success. The FCC was persuaded that it could afford to accept these minor risks because the new entrants would not greatly affect AT&T. Claiming that they would advance technology, the new entrants placed the FCC in a defensive position, for if the agency appeared to be technologically backward it would have been in violation of its fundamental mandate under the Communications Act. Indeed, technological progressiveness was linked to an even higher public interest standard—national economic well-being. The new entrants, their business clients, and their supporters within the FCC and the Antitrust Division had the advantage of matching their vague promises against the existing carriers' performance. They could always *claim* they could perform better. Using an argument based on microeconomic theory—that new entrants spur technological progress—they successfully portrayed AT&T, one of the world's most technologically advanced institutions, as backward, and themselves, with virtually no scientific or engineering record, as the wave of the future.

Although the FCC opened the door to the new entrants, their initial promises were not fulfilled. Gradually, the FCC's overriding commitment became one to particular competitors rather than to free competition. Under the principles of free competition, AT&T would have bested its smaller rivals with ease. Seizing the FCC's commitment to competitors, the newcomers' strategy was to demand more and to claim that AT&T's resistance indicated its desire to monopolize. In the Ford administration, AT&T's rivals benefited from a powerful new movement that demanded sweeping deregulation of all industries subject to economic regulation. Deregulation—the new conception of the public interest—was supported by the Ford, Carter, and Reagan administrations, which claimed it could solve such larger concerns as combatting inflation and modernizing America's infrastructure. Free-market conservatives, single-mindedly pursuing the virtue of economic efficiency to the exclusion of all other values, joined hands with Naderites in advocating deregulation, suspicious that the activities of economic regulatory agencies were dominated by those they regulated. Lost in this movement for deregulation was the fact that the performance of the American telephone industry was quite different from that of the railroad, trucking, airline, banking, and other industries subject to intensive economic regulation. AT&T was caught in a sweeping generalization that was backed by a widely accepted view that all heavily regulated industries were economically backward. The Antitrust Division, with the support of the Ford administration, acted in 1974. And the collective assaults on AT&T by private interests, activists courts, the FCC, and the Antitrust Division led to the extraordinary transformation of the telecommunications industry.

The end result was not free competition in the traditional sense; rather, AT&T still could not practice free competition in many ways and Judge Greene became a second regulatory agency beside the FCC. Supervision of the industry and protracted proceedings illustrate that AT&T and its offspring were still being intensively regulated, their conduct sharply restrained. Thus, in 1987, Congressman Edward Markey urged that AT&T be denied the opportunity to compete on equal terms because the "marketplace isn't optimally competitive yet."[55] One wonders when it will be "optimally competitive."

OUT OF TOUCH

Activist judges are a part of our time. Private companies naturally pursue their private interests. The Antitrust Division and its sympathizers pursue the enforcement of the antitrust laws to the exclusion of other considerations; indeed, if the professional antitrusters had their way many other large corporations would have suffered AT&T's fate. But it is the conduct of the FCC that is the most interesting and difficult to explain. Much of what followed the agreement in the *AT&T* case depended on the agency's inability to resolve the issues quickly.

The history of telephone regulation shows that the FCC and the state PUCs are autonomous agents whose commissioners and staffs are mostly honest and diligent. If regulatory agencies are "captured" by the large firms or industries they regulate, AT&T was not among them, as it lost numerous contests before the FCC. In fact, there has never been sufficient evidence to support the view that regulatory agencies consistently obey those interests they regulate. Rather, as this book attempts to show, the FCC and PUCs (like other regulatory agencies) are bound to a public interest standard. But the application of the standard to concrete situations is not mechanical or immediately obvious. The old public interest theory of regulatory behavior claimed that agencies sought to protect the consumer against exploitation by certain large industries—railroads, gas works, telephone companies, and so on. The "capture" theory and its offshoots were an overreaction to the older and simpler conception. The new public interest theory embraces the variety of responses that regulatory agencies make, takes seriously the reasons advanced for actions, and reconciles the specific decisions. The FCC (and, by extension, the PUCs) has often been subject to a variety of different impulses pulling in contrary directions. Under the new public interest theory, there is a hierarchy to these impulses. At the apex are the overriding obligations of the agency, often spelled out in the preamble to the statute that created the agency. To a considerable extent, the particular rules were developed in contested cases. Gradually, principles were created and a general framework developed in the same manner that the Anglo-American Common Law evolved over the centuries. For example, the law of contract was elaborated and integrated over a long period of time. Similarly, in the public utility field, numerous decisions held that telephone companies should have end-to-end responsibility under the public service principle. However, the new public interest theory takes into account not only the obligations of an agency but the activities of private interests as well. Indeed, without understanding their role, we cannot understand how the old public service conception became unraveled. The regulatory agencies and the regulated firms were jointly responsible for the performance of the telephone industry. In this sense, the regulators had to be concerned with the viability and health of AT&T and the independent telephone industry. But this does not mean that AT&T could influence the regulators' behavior for its own benefit. First, regulators can and have prodded regulated companies to perform better or more efficiently—they have the right to obtain information and to punish transgressions. Second, the very success of a regulated firm can ironically contribute to agency experimentation at its own expense, for if the agency makes a mistake in permitting an experiment, the costs imposed on the industry will not be very large. Third—and a central theme of this book—

new entrants and others can attempt to persuade regulatory agencies that their goals will be better accomplished through policies that favor new entrants. The main point here is that it is *persuasion* and not pressure or influence that usually moves an agency to adopt new policies that modify or reverse older ones. As we know, MCI and others effectively persuaded the FCC that their private interests constituted the public interest. The apex of the hierarchy was thus tied to private interests.

But when a regulatory agency establishes a policy that it believes is in the public interest, it does not necessarily follow that the policy is the best one for the public. Indeed, much of this book argues that the FCC gradually supplanted a carefully developed structure of telephone regulation with many exceptions that became quite ambiguous under the term deregulation. Of course, there were some FCC commissioners, such as Benjamin Hooks, who rejected the agency's new path and consistently followed the views summarized by Theodore Vail:

> Experience also has demonstrated that [regulatory] "supervision" should stop at "control" and "regulation" and not "manage," "operate" nor dictate what the management or operation should be beyond the requirements of greatest efficiency and economy. . . . State . . . regulation should be of such character as to encourage the highest possible standard in plant, utmost extension of facilities, highest efficiency in service . . . rigid economy in operation.[56]

These views had been elaborated into clear standards.

Although not every clear standard of conduct embodied in law deserves to be obeyed, clear standards generally allow us to pose clear questions: Is there a better set of standards? What are the costs and benefits of each set of standards? When standards are ignored and when precedents that led to the efficient achievement of goals are cast aside, costs and benefits are also ignored. The erosion of principle and rational precedent in the administrative area, in turn, encourages social experiments in the judicial and legislative areas. Certainly, the FCC should have periodically reexamined the underlying public service principles in light of technological advances and economic change. One can dissent from the breakup rules allowing long-distance rivalry and those that deregulated ordinary CPE and inside wiring—and gave consumers the right to pay for repair. But even in the case of complex CPE where changes were needed, the FCC did not carefully scrutinize or modify the older rules to meet contemporary circumstances. First, it made

numerous *ad hoc* decisions that gradually modified the older public interest standard. Then, under the banner of deregulation, it drastically
changed existing rules without comparing the costs and benefits of
various public interest conceptions. The FCC's continued lack of clarity
exacerbated conflicts that continued well beyond the AT&T breakup.

As a result of the AT&T breakup and the changes that have taken
place, the American people have been subjected to long-term risks for
reasons that had little if anything to do with AT&T's overall performance. The breakup of AT&T and the diversion of resources from science and engineering to advertising on prime-time television may constitute a long-term silent crisis. But as the course of events charted
here shows, these risks and costs ultimately stem from political causes,
not economic or technological necessity.

NOTES

Chapter 1
Hello, Central: The Telephone in Perspective

1. Editorial, "The Largest Antitrust Suit," *Wall Street Journal*, 22 November 1974, 18.

2. Stuart Jackson, "Business Week/Harris Poll: The Public Sees the Little Guy As the Loser," *Business Week*, 3 December 1984, 89.

3. New York Central Securities v. United States, 287 U.S. 12, 24 (1932).

4. FCC v. RCA Communications, Inc., 346 U.S. 86, 97 (1952).

5. Quoted in W. Brooke Tunstall, *Disconnecting Parties* (New York: McGraw-Hill, 1985), 3.

6. Richard B. DuBoff, "The Telegraph and the Structure of Markets in the United States, 1845–1890," in *Research in Economic History*, vol. 8, ed. Paul Uselding (Greenwich, Conn.: JAI Press, 1982), 256, 257.

7. Wolff Packing Co. v. Court of Industrial Relations, 262 U.S. 522, 534 (1923).

8. Breck P. McAllister, "Lord Hale and Business Affected with a Public Interest," *Harvard Law Review* 43 (1930): 769. For a contrary but less persuasive view, see IBM, "Reply Comments," in *In the Matter of Policy and Rules Concerning Rates for Competitive Common Carrier Services and Facilities Authorizations Therefor*, CC Docket No. 72–252 (April 4, 1980). Essentially, IBM employs an argument to counteract the possibility of FCC regulation of computer-related services.

9. Brass v. Stoesser, 153 U.S. 391 (1894).

10. Henry C. Adams, "Introduction," in Frank H. Dixon, *State Railroad Control* (New York: Thomas Y. Crowell, 1896), 9.

11. *Congressional Record*, 1910, 45: 5534.

12. Nash v. Page, 80 Ky. 539 (1884).

13. Salt River Valley Canal Co. v. Nelssen, 10 Ariz. 9 (1906); Wheeler v. Northern Colorado Irrigating Co., 17 P. 487 (S. Ct. Colo., 1888).

14. McCarter v. Firemen's Insurance Co., 73A.80, 84 (N.J.E., 1909).

15. Alexander Graham Bell's 25 March 1878 speech, reprinted in John E. Kingsbury, *The Telephone and Telephone Exchanges* (1915; reprint, New York: Arno Press, 1972), 89–92.

16. James D. Reid, *The Telegraph in America* (New York: Derby Brothers, 1879), 594–666.

17. State v. Nebraska Telephone Co., 22 N.W. 237, 238, 239 (Neb., 1885).

18. Hockett v. State, 5 N.E. 178, 182 (1886).

19. Budd v. New York, 143 U.S. 517 (1892).

Chapter 2
The Bells Are Ringing

1. There is an enormous literature on the disputes concerning the invention of the telephone. The most important sources on which the text relies are David A. Hounshell, "Elisha Gray and the Telephone: On the Disadvantages of Being an Expert," *Technology and Culture* 16 (April 1975): 133–61; Lloyd W. Taylor, "The Untold Story of the Telephone," *American Physics Teacher* 5 (1937): 250; Fred De Land, *The Invention of the Electric Speaking Telephone*, AT&T Archives, Box 1098; William Aitken, *Who Invented the Telephone?* (London: Blackie and Son, 1939), chs. I–XIV; George B. Prescott, *Bell's Electric Speaking Telephone* (New York: D. Appleton & Co., 1884); Robert V. Bruce, *Bell: Alexander Graham Bell and the Conquest of Solitude* (Boston: Little, Brown, 1973); and W. James King, "The Telegraph and the Telephone," in *The Development of Electrical Technology in the Nineteenth Century*, Paper 29, Bulletin 228 (Washington, D.C.: United States National Museum, 1962), 312–18.

2. The most important legal materials are Telephone Cases, 126 U.S. 863 (1887); *The Deposition of Alexander Graham Bell in the Suit Brought by the United States to Annul the Bell Patents* (Boston: American Bell Telephone Co., 1908); John E. Kingsbury, *The Telephone and Telephone Exchanges: Their Invention and Development* (New York: Longman, 1915), ch. V; Charles H. Swan, *Narrative History of the Litigation on the Bell Patents, 1878–1896* (1903), AT&T Archives, Box 1098. Other case material includes American Bell Tel. Co. v. American Cushman Tel. Co., 35 F. 734 (N.D. Ill., 1888); American Bell Telephone Co. v. People's Telephone Co., 22 F. 309 (S.D., N.Y., 1884).

3. Details on the *Western Union* battle are based on Rosario Joseph Tosiello, *The Birth and Early Years of the Bell Telephone System, 1876–1880* (New York: Arno Press, 1979), 81–3, 484–91; Alvin F. Harlow, *Old Wires and New Waves* (1936; reprint, New York: Arno Press, 1971), 409–11; Robert W. Garnet, *The Telephone Enterprise* (Baltimore: Johns Hopkins University Press, 1985), ch. 4; and Federal Communications Commission, Special Investigation, Dkt. 1, Exhibit 2096F, *Financial Control of the Telephone Industry* (Washington, D.C.: Government Printing Office, 1937), 13–29. Gifford's views are recorded in Affidavit of George Gifford, 19 September 1882, AT&T Archives, Box 1006. Details on Gould's involvement are found in Maury Klein, *The Life and Legend of Jay Gould* (Baltimore: Johns Hopkins University Press, 1986), 276–82.

4. R. H. Coase, "The Nature of the Firm," *Economica* IV (New Series) (November 1937): 404. For a similar showing of organizing within single firms in the petroleum industry, see John G. McLain and Robert W. Hough, *The Growth of Integrated Oil Companies* (Boston: Graduate School of Business, Harvard University, 1954), especially p. 513.

5. See Leonard S. Reich, *The Making of American Industrial Research* (Cambridge: Cambridge University Press, 1985), 144.

6. Biographical material on Vail is based primarily on Albert Bigelow Paine, *In One Man's Life* (New York: Harper & Row, 1921). Although an example of the "hero worship" genre, Paine contains much factual information. The best general source of information on the early phase of telephone history is Garnet, *The Telephone Enterprise*.

7. See Garnet, *The Telephone Enterprise*, 76–80. The certificate of incorporation is reprinted in Arthur W. Page, *The Bell System* (New York: Harper & Brothers, 1941), 214–16.

8. Harold C. Livesay and Patrick G. Porter, "Vertical Integration in American Manufacturing, 1899–1948," *Journal of Economic History* XXIX (September 1969): 495–96.

9. See Garnet, *The Telephone Enterprise*, 14–17, 138; FCC, Special Investigation, Dkt.

1, Exhibit 130, *Origin and Development of the License Contract* (Washington, D.C.: Government Printing Office, 1936); FCC, *Investigation of the Telephone Industry in the United States* (Washington, D.C.: Government Printing Office, 1936), 18–26.

10. Johnson County Home Telephone Co., 8 Mo. P.S.C.R. 637 (1919).

11. On patent policies, see FCC, Special Investigation, Dkt. 1, Exhibit 1989, *Patent Structure of the Bell System, Its History and Policies and Practices Relative Thereto* (Washington, D.C.: Government Printing Office, 1936). The conclusion on franchise battles is based on an examination of every pre-1920 issue of *Telephony*, then the leading independents' trade journal.

12. AT&T, *1907 Annual Report*, 18.

13. AT&T, *1910 Annual Report*, 32, 33.

14. As examples of the view of merchants on the undesirability of telephone competition, see the reports of the Merchants Association of New York opposing the grant of a competing franchise: *Telephone Competition from the Standpoint of the Public* (New York: New York Telephone Co., 1906), AT&T Archives, Box 1082; and Special Telephone Committee, Merchants Association of New York, *Supplemental Telephone Report, Further Inquiry into the Effect of Competition* (1905).

15. Stuart Daggert, "Telephone Consolidation Under the Act of 1921," *Journal of Land & Public Utility Economics* VII (1931): 27.

16. United States v. AT&T, Civil Action No. 74–1698 D.D.C. (1974) Stipulation/Contention Package, Episode 5, para. 580–82, 615–73.

17. Ibid., par. 579.

18. R. H. Coase, "Discussion," in *A Critique of Administrative Regulation of Public Utilities*, ed. Warren J. Samuels and Harry Trebing (East Lansing, Mich.: Institute of Public Utilities, Michigan State University, 1972), 311–16.

19. James Q. Wilson, "The Politics of Regulation," in *The Politics of Regulation*, ed. James Q. Wilson (New York: Basic Books, 1980), 370.

20. Pacific Telephone & Telegraph Co., 15 Cal.R.C.R. 993, 994 (1918).

21. See, for example, a leading 1920s scholarly work: Ellsworth Nichols, *Public Utility Service and Discrimination* (Rochester, N.Y.: Public Utilities Reports, 1928), 479.

22. See United States v. AT&T, Stipulation/Contention Package, Episode 4, para. 31, 32, 39, and 412, and Episode 5, para. 505–10, 534–36.

23. See A. H. Griswold, "The Radio Telephone Situation," *Bell Telephone Quarterly* 1 (April 1922): 6–8; and AT&T, *1918 Annual Report*, 28.

24. The principal sources used for the discussion of the early history of radio are Hugh G. J. Aitken, *Syntony and Spark—The Origins of Radio* (New York: John Wiley, 1976); Hugh G. J. Aitken, *The Continuous Wave: Technology and American Radio* (Princeton, N.J.: Princeton University Press, 1985); W. Rupert MacLaurin, *Invention to Innovation in the Radio Industry* (New York: Macmillan, 1949); Gleason Archer, *History of Radio to 1926* (New York: American Historical Society, 1938); Hiram L. Jome, *Economics of the Radio Industry* (Chicago: A. W. Shaw, 1925); Federal Trade Commission, *Report on the Radio Industry* (Washington, D.C.: Government Printing Office, 1924); and Erik Barnouw, *A Tower in Babel* (New York: Oxford University Press, 1966).

25. Quoted in William Peck Banning, *Commercial Broadcasting Pioneer* (Cambridge, Mass.: Harvard University Press, 1946), 68.

26. The principal sources on the creation of the FCC and the background on which the text relies are United States Senate, *A Study of Communications by an Interdepartmental Committee* (Washington, D.C.: Government Printing Office, 1934) [known as the *Roper Report*]; House of Representatives, *Preliminary Report on Communications Companies* (Wash-

ington, D.C.: Government Printing Office, 1934) [known as the *Splawn Report*]; House Committee on Interstate and Foreign Commerce, *Federal Communications Commission, Hearings* (Washington, D.C.: Government Printing Office, 1934); Senate Committee on Interstate Commerce, *Commission on Communications, Hearings* (Washington, D.C.: Government Printing Office, 1929); Philip T. Rosen, *The Modern Stentors* (Westport, Conn.: Greenwood Press, 1980); and G. Hamilton Loeb, *The Communications Act Policy Toward Competition: A Failure to Communicate* (Cambridge, Mass.: Harvard University Center for Information Policy Research, 1977).

Chapter 3
Silence That Dreadful Bell: The New Deal
and the *Western Electric* Case

1. On the New Deal and its business attitudes, see especially Ellis W. Hawley, *The New Deal and the Problem of Monopoly* (Princeton, N.J.: Princeton University Press, 1966), pt. 4; and David Lynch, *The Concentration of Economic Power* (New York: Columbia University Press, 1946), chs. 1, 2, 7, and 9.

2. Temporary National Economic Committee, *Investigation of Concentration of Economic Power: Final Report and Recommendations* (Washington, D.C.: Government Printing Office, 1941), 691.

3. *Events in Telecommunications History* (New York: AT&T, 1979), 29–31.

4. Quoted in "American Telephone and Telegraph Company," *Fortune's Favorites* (New York: Alfred A. Knopf, 1931), 4.

5. Federal Communications Commission, *Investigation of the Telephone Industry in the United States* (Washington, D.C.: Government Printing Office, 1939), 543; and FCC, *Third Annual Report* (Washington, D.C.: Government Printing Office, 1937), 88–90.

6. FCC, *First Annual Report* (Washington, D.C.: Government Printing Office, 1936), 14, 15, 54–6; and FCC, *Second Annual Report* (Washington, D.C.: Government Printing Office, 1936), 53.

7. See Arthur W. Page, *The Bell Telephone System* (New York: Harper & Row, 1941), 188.

8. See the information given in the following AT&T sources: Page, *Telephone System*, 143–48; and AT&T, *Brief of Bell System Companies on Commissioner Walker's Report on the Telephone Investigation* (1938), 248–56 [hereafter cited as *Bell System Brief*].

9. FCC, *Fourth Annual Report* (Washington, D.C.: Government Printing Office, 1939), 24.

10. See, generally, FCC, *Proposed Report, Telephone Investigation* (Washington, D.C.: Government Printing Office, 1938) [also called the *Walker Report*]. For a good summary, see "FCC's Trial Balloon on AT&T," *Business Week*, 9 April 1938, 17, 18.

11. "Wrong Number," *Business Week*, 28 March 1936, 11.

12. FCC, Special Investigation, Dkt. 1, Exhibit 2096E, *Politics of Control* (Washington, D.C.: Government Printing Office, 1937).

13. N. R. Danielian, *AT&T: The Story of Industrial Conquest* (New York: Vanguard Press, 1939), 411.

14. Page, *Telephone System*, 169, 170; and FCC, *Politics of Control*, chs. V–VII.

15. FCC, *Proposed Report*, 574, 575.

16. AT&T, *Bell System Brief*, 230, 231.

17. FCC, *Fifth Annual Report* (Washington, D.C.: Government Printing Office, 1940), 19.

18. FCC, *Investigation of the Telephone Industry*, 597.

19. See Smith v. Illinois Bell Tel Co., 282 U.S. 133 (1930); and Lindheimer v. Illinois Bell Tel Co., 292 U.S. 151 (1930). See also "Direct Regulation of the American Telephone and Telegraph Company," *Yale Law Journal* 48 (1939): 1018; and the cases collected in Carl I. Wheat, ed., "The Regulation of Interstate Telephone Rates," *Harvard Law Review* 51 (1938): 878, fn. 63.

20. FCC, *Investigation of the Telephone Industry*, 588.

21. Material on AT&T's role in talking motion pictures is taken from Tino Balio, *The American Film Industry*, rev. ed. (Madison: University of Wisconsin Press, 1985); Frank H. Lovette and Stanley Watkins, "Twenty Years of 'Talking Movies': An Anniversary," *Bell Telephone Quarterly* XXV (Summer 1946): 82–92; S. Millman, ed., *A History of Engineering and Science in the Bell System: Communications Sciences, 1925–1980* (New York: AT&T Bell Laboratories, 1984); FCC, Special Investigation, Dkt. 1, Exhibit 1946A, *Electrical Research Products Inc.* (Washington, D.C.: Government Printing Office, 1937); and AT&T, *Supplement to the Brief Filed December 5, 1938 by Bell System Companies on Commissioner Walker's Proposed Report on the Telephone Investigation* (1939).

22. See Hawley, *The New Deal*, 387–88; and George W. Stocking and Myron W. Watkins, *Cartels in Action* (New York: Twentieth Century Fund, 1947), passim.

23. United States v. Paramount Pictures, 334 U.S. 131 (1948).

24. "Washington Outlook," *Business Week*, 18 December 1946, 16; and United States v. Pullman Co., 50F. Supp. 123 (E.D. Pa., 1943) affd. 330 U.S. 806 (1947).

25. Harold G. Livesay and Patrick G. Porter, "Vertical Integration in American Manufacturing, 1899–1948," *Journal of Economic History* XXIX (September 1969): 495–96.

26. Details of AT&T's postwar plans are contained in "Item: 12 Million New Telephones," *Fortune*, June 1950, 81–6, 139–46; and *Telecommunications Reports*, 27 September 1945, 19–21.

27. *Telecommunications Reports*, 1 February 1946, 22.

28. "What Is AT&T's Future?" *Business Week*, 31 May 1947, 64.

29. House Committee on the Judiciary, Antitrust Subcommittee, *Consent Decree Program of the Department of Justice*, Hearings, pt. II, vol. 3 (Washington, D.C.: Government Printing Office, 1958), 3564–568.

30. "Washington Outlook," *Business Week* 18 December 1940, 16.

31. *Telecommunications Reports* 17 December 1948, 17.

32. Quoted in Charles Zerner, "U.S. Sues to Force AT&T to Drop Western Electric Co.," *New York Times*, 14 January 1949, 1, 3.

33. House Committee, *Consent Decree Program*, part 2, vol. 3, 3603–605, 3606–611.

34. Ibid., 3616.

35. Quoted in *Telecommunications Reports*, 19 January 1949, 10.

36. Complaint, United States of America v. Western Electric Co., Civil Action No. 17–49 (January 14, 1949), 68–72.

37. Answer, United States of America v. Western Electric Co., Civil Action No. 17–49 (April 24, 1949), para 3.

38. Ibid., para. 16, 17.

39. See, for example, Complaint, para. 125.

40. "Consent Decree: Both Sides Win," *Business Week*, 3 March 1956, 80, 85; and "The Impact of Two Historic Antitrust Decrees," *Business Week*, 4 February 1956, 26–28.

41. *Telecommunications Reports*, 7 February 1950, 11, 12.

42. "Final Judgment," para. IX in House Committee, *Consent Decree Program*, part II, vol. I, 1851.

43. House Committee, *Consent Decree Program*, part II, vol. I, 2198–201, 2313–342; vol. III, 3451–453, 3817–822, 4458, 4461.

44. Ibid., vol. III, 3963–965.

45. See "Consent Decree," 80, 85; *Telecommunications Reports*, 16 May 1955, 1, 2; House Committee, *Consent Decree Program*, part II, vol. I, 2112–129, 2139, 2159, 2198, 2200, 2201.

46. House Committee on the Judiciary, Antitrust Subcommittee, *Consent Decree Program of the Department of Justice Report* (Washington, D.C.: Government Printing Office, 1959).

Chapter 4
The Voice of Change

1. Quoted in Hush-A-Phone Corp., 20 FCC 391, 413–14 (1955).

2. House Committee on Energy and Commerce *Telecommunications in Transition: The Status of Competition in the Telecommunications Industry* [majority staff report] (Washington, D.C.: Government Printing Office, 1981), 181.

3. See, for example, Joe S. Bain, *Industrial Organization* (New York: John Wiley, 1959), ch. 7.

4. Leonard Waverman, "The Regulation of Intercity Telecommunications," in *Promoting Competition in Regulated Markets*, ed. Almarin Phillips (Washington, D.C.: Brookings Institution, 1975), 209–33.

5. Walter Adams and James W. Brock, "Integrated Monopoly and Market Power: System Selling Compatibility Standards and Market Control," *Quarterly Review of Economics and Business* 22 (Winter 1982): 32.

6. R. H. Coase, "The Nature of the Firm," *Economica* IV (New Series), (November 1937): 404, 405.

7. Correspondence, Theodore N. Vail to Great Southern Telephone and Telegraph Co., 13 October 1884, in AT&T Archives, Box 1212.

8. See, for example, correspondence, C. N. Fay to Theodore N. Vail, 17 October 1884, in AT&T Archives, Box 1212; and M. F. Tyler to Theodore N. Vail, 20 October 1884, in AT&T Archives, Box 1212.

9. Some advertisements for such devices are found in "Foreign Attachments—1892–1894," in AT&T Archives, Box 1212.

10. American Bell Telephone Co. to G. F. Hudson, 19 June 1894, memorandum no. 249047, in AT&T Archives, Box 1212.

11. "Something Up to Date for All Telephone Receivers" (n.d.), in AT&T Archives, Box 1353.

12. "Danger Lurks in the Telephone," in AT&T Archives, Box 1353.

13. See, for example, correspondence, H. K. McCann to J. D. Ellsworth, 7 January 1909, in AT&T Archives, Box 1353; and H. K. McCann to J. D. Ellsworth, 27 February 1909, in AT&T Archives, Box 1353.

14. See correspondence, L. G. Richardson to George V. Leverett, 24 June 1911, in AT&T Archives, Box 1353.

15. Correspondence, Bancroft Gherardi to R. W. Devonshire, 5 May 1922, p. 1, in AT&T Archives, Box 1353.

16. See Oliver E. Williamson, *The Economic Institutions of Capitalism* (New York: Free Press, 1985), 18–22.

17. See United States v. AT&T, Stipulation/Contention Package, Episode 4, para. 52, 62; *Allocation of Microwave Frequencies Above 890 Mc*, 27 FCC 359, 397 (1959); F. L. Howe, *This Great Contrivance* (Rochester: Rochester Telephone Corp., 1979), 102.

18. Hush-A-Phone Corp., 20 FCC 391, 413 (1955); Gardner v. Providence Telephone Co., 49 A. 1004 (1901); Cammen v. American Tel & Tel Co., 2 FCC 351 (1936); and United States v. AT&T, Civil Action no. 74–1698, D.D.C. (1974), Stipulation/Contention Package, Episode 4, para. 44.

19. Pennsylvania PUC v. Bell Telephone Co. of Pa., 20 Pa. PUC 702, 706–707 (1940).

20. National Labor Relations Board v. Jones & Laughlin Steel Corp., 301 U.S. 1 (1937).

21. Littlepage v. Mosier Valley Tel Co., PUR 1918E 425, 432. See also Bluffs v. Winchester Tel Co., PUR 1915A 928, 929; Badger Mutual Tel Co., PUR 1926A 361, 364.

22. In Re Green, 17 Cal RCR 744 (1920); Riverview Tel Co., PUR 1916B 442.

23. Hotel Sherman Co. v. Chicago Tel Co., PUR 1915F. 776.

24. Quick Action Collection Co. v. N.Y. Tel Co., PUR 1920D 137, 144.

25. City of Los Angeles v. Southern California Tel Co., 2 PUR (NS) 247, 251 (1933).

26. As in Doehart v. Pacific Tel & Tel Co., 90 PUR (NS) 185 (1951).

27. See Customers of the Concordia Teleph Co., 3 PUR 522 (1934).

28. J. S. Bradley, "A New Bell System Service in Classified Telephone Directories," *Bell Telephone Magazine*, October 1928, 266–73.

29. Pacific Teleph & Teleg Co., 40 PUR 441 (1961); and New England Teleph & Teleg Co., 36 PUR 3d 319 (1960).

30. See, for example, Murphy-Reier Inc. v. Illinois Bell Teleph Co., 26 PUR 3d 540 (1958).

31. Cazenovia Teleph Corp., 17 PUR 3d 394, 398 (1957). The use of auxiliary covers was considered in some cases to be misleading and therefore unfair competition. See Michigan Bell Teleph Co. v. Wharram, 82 PUR (NS) 94 (1949).

32. New York Telephone Co., PUR 1932A 262, and PUR 1932A 433.

33. Bureau of the Census, *Historical Statistics of the United States*, part 2 (Washington, D.C.: Government Printing Office, 1975), 783.

34. United States v. ATT, Stipulation/Contention Package, Episode 6, para. 6.

35. United States v. AT&T, Defendants' Third Statement of Contentions and Proof, vol. I, 339–43.

36. *Telecommunications Reports*, 11 July 1935, 2.

37. United States v. AT&T, Stipulation/Contention Package, Episode 1, para 34.

38. Ibid., para 35 and materials cited therein.

39. *Telecommunications Reports*, 31 January 1972, 25.

40. *Telecommunications Reports*, 15 February 1945, 17.

41. "What Is AT&T's Future?" *Business Week*, 31 May 1947, 59.

42. *Telecommunications Reports*, 1 June 1954, 3–6, 15–17; and 21 March 1955, 9–12.

43. "For the Bell System, All Phones Are Ringing," *Business Week*, 9 January 1965, 65–70.

44. Ibid., 69.

45. United States v. AT&T, Defendants' Third Statement, vol. II, 1117–124.

46. These and the following AT&T arguments are synthesized from the materials in a company folder entitled *Interconnection—Foreign Attachments 1965-66-68*, AT&T Archives, Box 2077. The material includes speeches and memoranda designed to persuade the public and opinion-makers in favor of AT&T's interconnection views. Some of the material is undated and otherwise unidentified.

47. See especially, AT&T, "The Nationwide Communications Network," Information Department memorandum, 18 September 1968, in AT&T Archives, Box 2077.

48. E. Goldstein, "Switching, Signaling and Charging," speech, 10 April 1968, AT&T Archives, Box 2077, 6, 7.

49. "A Summary of the Bell System's Petition for Reconsideration" (n.d.), in folder entitled *Interconnection—Foreign Attachments 1965-66-68*, AT&T Archives, Box 2077.

50. *Telecommunications Reports*, 29 November 1946, 15.

51. Use of Recording Devices, 11 FCC 1033 (1947).

52. *Telecommunications Reports*, 24 January 1946, 18.

53. *Telecommunications Reports*, 18 October 1946, 4, 5; 27 September 1946, 7, 8; 27 August 1947, 4; and 9 January 1948, 9.

54. *Telecommunications Reports*, 28 November 1947, 5; and Use of Recording Devices, 1037–40.

55. Jordaphone Corporation of America, 18 FCC 644 (1954).

56. *Telecommunications Reports*, 15 July 1949, 31.

57. *Telecommunications Reports*, 12 June 1950, 7; 16 April 1951, 27.

58. *Telecommunications Reports*, 5 February 1951, 27, 28.

59. *Telecommunications Reports*, 12 February 1951, 6.

60. *Telecommunications Reports*, 2 July 1951, 16–18.

61. *Telecommunications Reports*, 19 November 1951, 1–3.

62. Doehart Corp. v. Pacific Tel & Tel Co., 90 PUR (NS) 185 (1951).

63. Gulf Tele-Magnet Corp. v. Southern Bell T & T Co., 87 PUR (NS) 33 (1951).

64. Jordaphone, 18 FCC 644 (1954); *Telecommunications Reports*, 10 May 1954, 1, 2, 16–18; 12 February 1951, 4–6.

65. See S. Millman, ed., *A History of Engineering and Science in the Bell System: Communications Sciences (1925–1980)* (New York: AT&T Bell Laboratories, 1984), 206, 207; and R. Brown, "The Outlook for Radio Relaying," *Bell Laboratories Record* (October 1945): 365–67.

66. *Telecommunications Reports*, 11 July 1935, 2.

67. M. C. Biskeborn, W. G. Nutt, and B. Wargotz, "CLOAX—The Next Generation Coaxial Cable," *Bell Laboratories Record* (July 1969): 195–98; Joseph Udelson, *The Great Television Race* (University, Ala.: University of Alabama Press, 1982), 92–93; Millman, *Communications Sciences*, 33, 34; and *Telecommunications Reports*, 17 July 1935, 4–8.

68. *Telecommunications Reports*, 26 October 1944, 14.

69. Correspondence, Keith S. McHugh to Dear Mr. ———, 17 March 1944, in AT&T Archives, Box 67.

70. *Telecommunications Reports*, 10 May 1945, 25. For the same considerations applied to FM broadcasting, see "FM Program Transmission: A Bell System Service," *Bell Telephone Magazine* (Winter 1944–1945): 261, 262. See also Keith S. McHugh and George L. Best, "The Bell System's Interest in Program Television," *Bell Telephone Magazine* (Spring 1944): 11, 12; and Laurance G. Woodford, "The Bell System's Progress in Television Networks," *Bell Telephone Quarterly* (Autumn 1946): 150–51.

71. C. C. Taylor, "Radio Telephone Service in Chesapeake Bay," *Bell Laboratories Record* (August 1941): 358–62.

72. For details on the engineering problems of early postwar microwave, see H. T. Friis, "Microwave Repeater Research," *Bell Systems Technical Journal* (April 1948): 183–246.

73. *Telecommunications Reports*, 16 March 1944, 5, 6; and United States v. AT&T, Stipulation/Contention Package, Episode 10, para 16.

74. United States v. AT&T, Stipulation/Contention Package, Episode 10, para. 131.

75. Donald C. Beelar, "Cables in the Sky and the Struggle for Their Control," *Federal Communications Bar Journal* 26 (1967): 26–32.

76. Mackay Radio and Telegraph Co. Inc. et al., 39 FCC 1 (1939).

77. United States v. AT&T, Stipulation/Contention Package, Episode 10, para. 38, 39.

78. Federal Communications Commission, *Eleventh Annual Report: Fiscal Year Ended June 30, 1945* (Washington, D.C.: Government Printing Office, 1946), 7, 8; and Frequency Allocation, Non-Government, 39 FCC 68, 69–73 (1945).

79. United States v. AT&T, Stipulation/Contention Package, Episode 10, para. 17–19; and M. D. Fagen, ed., *A History of Engineering and Science in the Bell System: National Service in War and Peace (1925–1975)* (New York: Bell Telephone Laboratories, 1978), 335–38.

80. Frequency Allocation, Non-Government, 39 FCC 68, 159 (1945).

81. United States v. AT&T, Stipulation/Contention Package, Episode 10, para. 25–30.

82. *Telecommunications Reports*, 19 December 1946, 29, 30; 3 January 1947, 16.

83. Bus Transportation Frequencies, 39 FCC 257 (1946).

84. United States v. AT&T, Stipulation/Contention Package, Episode 10, para. 23; and *Telecommunications Reports*, 4 June 1947, 12.

85. *Telecommunications Reports*, 12 June 1947, 18–22.

86. Frequency Band 1,000–13,200Mc, 39 FCC 298, 299 (1948).

87. United States v. AT&T, Stipulation/Contention Package, Episode 10, para. 47; and *Telecommunications Reports*, 30 April 1948, 5, 6.

88. *Telecommunications Reports*, 18 June 1948, 6, 7.

89. United States v. AT&T, Stipulation/Contention Package, Episode 10, para. 48–52.

90. State Agricultural and Industrial School, 4 N.Y. PSCR 219, 221–222 (1914). See also *Telecommunications Reports*, 18 June 1948, 7, 8.

91. Philco Corporation v. American Telephone & Tel Co., 80F. Supp 397 (E.D. Pa., 1948).

92. *Telecommunications Reports*, 9 October 1948, 12, 13.

93. *Broadcasting*, 14 February 1949, 67; and *Telecommunications Reports*, 4 February 1949, 33.

94. *Broadcasting*, 17 March 1949, 38; 28 March 1949, 54–L; and 15 August 1949, 41.

95. *Broadcasting*, 12 September 1949, 60, 85; and 5 December 1949, 3; *Telecommunications Reports*, 24 October 1949, 31, 32; and 5 December 1949, 13–16.

96. Television Charges and Regulations, 42 FCC 1 (1949).

97. Ibid., 23.

98. Ibid., 31.

99. *Broadcasting*, 27 March 1950, 5, 17.

100. *Telecommunications Reports*, 13 March 1950, 12, 13, 29–31.

101. *Telecommunications Reports*, 10 May 1950, 10; 3 July 1950, 28.

102. *Telecommunications Reports*, 26 June 1950, 23; 10 July 1950, 16.

103. *Telecommunications Reports*, 6 November 1950, 8, 9; 15 January 1951, 12, 13.

104. Western Union Telegraph Co. et al., 17 FCC 152 (1952).

105. Ibid., 173.

106. J. E. Belknap and Associates, 18 FCC 642 (1954).

Chapter 5
The Warning Bell

1. Communications Act of 1934, Title I, Section 1.

2. New York Central Securities v. United States, 287 U.S. 12, 24 (1932).

3. FCC v. RCA Communications Inc., 346 U.S. 86, 97 (1952).

4. Hush-A-Phone Corp., 20 FCC 391, 398 (1955).

5. Ibid., 399.

6. *Telecommunications Reports*, 4 February 1949, 30.

7. *Telecommunications Reports*, 20 May 1949, 11, 12.

8. *Telecommunications Reports*, 23 January 1950, 40; Hush-A-Phone Corp., FCC Dkt. 9189 (1950).

9. *Telecommunications Reports*, 30 January 1950, 6, 41.

10. *Telecommunications Reports*, 3 April 1950, 28, 29.

11. Hush-A-Phone Corp., 20 FCC 418–21 (1950).

12. *Telecommunications Reports*, 23 January 1950, 7.

13. *Telecommunications Reports*, 19 February 1950, 9, 10.

14. Hush-A-Phone Corp., 20 FCC 391, 424 (1955).

15. The legal literature is enormous on these points. See, generally, the cases and discussions in Walter Gellhorn, Clark Byse, and Peter L. Strauss, *Administrative Law: Cases and Comments*, 7th ed. (Mineola, N.Y.: Foundation Press, 1979), 249–343.

16. See, especially, Bernard H. Siegan, *Economic Liberties and the Constitution* (Chicago: University of Chicago Press, 1980), chs. 1, 2.

17. Greater Boston Television Corp. v. FCC, 444 F.2d 841, 850 (D.C. Cir., 1970).

18. Hush-A-Phone Corp. v. United States, 238 F.2d 266 (D.C. Cir., 1956).

19. Ibid., 269.

20. Hush-A-Phone Corp. v. AT&T, 22 FCC 112 (1957).

21. *Telecommunications Reports*, 22 April 1957, 4.

22. *Telecommunications Reports*, 20 May 1957, 18; 23 September 1957, 16.

23. Typical post-*Hush-A-Phone* state PUC decisions are Netsky v. Bell Telephone Co. of Penn., 65 PUR 3d 145 (1966); Peters Sunset Beach v. Northwestern Bell Telephone Co., 60 PUR 3d 363 (1965); and Harmony of Ft. Lauderdale v. Southern Bell Telephone & Telegraph Co., 69 PUR 3d 261 (1967). For an overview of the FCC's attitude, see *Telecommunications Reports*, 1 May 1961, 6.

24. *Telecommunications Reports*, 28 May 1956, 12, 13.

25. *Telecommunications Reports*, 1 June 1954, 4.

26. "For the Bell System All Phones Are Ringing," *Business Week*, 9 January 1965, 66.

27. Quoted in G. E. Schindler, Jr., ed., *A History of Engineering and Science in the Bell*

System: Switching Technology (1925–1975) (New York: Bell Telephone Laboratories, 1982), 226.

28. Ibid., 335–68.

29. *Telecommunications Reports*, 19 December 1946, 29; 3 January 1947, 16.

30. *Telecommunications Reports*, 7 February 1947, 11.

31. Ibid., 12, 13.

32. *Telecommunications Reports*, 24 October 1947, 30.

33. *Telecommunications Reports*, 5 December 1947, 21, 22.

34. Ibid.

35. *Telecommunications Reports*, 18 February 1952, 31.

36. *Telecommunications Reports*, 3 August 1953, 24, 25.

37. *Telecommunications Reports*, 1 March 1954, 1–4.

38. *Telecommunications Reports*, 21 January 1957, 1.

39. *Telecommunications Reports*, 22 April 1957, 1.

40. FCC v. RCA, 346 U.S. 86, 97 (1952).

41. *Telecommunications Reports*, 10 June 1957, 9.

42. *Telecommunications Reports*, 17 June 1957, 7.

43. *Telecommunications Reports*, 24 June 1957, 3, 4.

44. National Association of Manufacturers Committee on Manufacturers' Radio Use, *Notice of Appearance*, in FCC Dkt. 11866, Box 2227, 1; Above 890Mc and Statement of Committee on Manufacturers' Radio, NAM, by Victor G. Reis, in Box 2228, 1586.

45. National Retail Dry Goods Association, *Notice of Appearance*, Box 2227, 382–91; and *Telecommunications Reports*, 15 July 1957, 1.

46. Automobile Manufacturers Association, Statement of Evidence, in FCC Dkt. 11866, Above 890Mc, Box 2227, 850.

47. Testimony of William H. Morris, in Above 890Mc, Box 2228, 1121, 1122.

48. "Proposed Testimony, W. M. Rust, Jr.," in Above 890Mc, Box 2228, 1648, 1649.

49. Testimony of E. J. Strawn, in Above 890Mc, Box 2228, 1659, 1660.

50. See United States v. AT&T, Civil Action no. 74–1698 D.D.C. (1974), Stipulation/Contention Package, Episode 11, Defendants' Contentions 9 and 10.

51. Statements of J. C. Carrington and H. Ray Weaver, in Above 890Mc, Box 2226, 2522, 2719–2729.

52. Allocation of Microwave Frequencies Above 890Mc, 27 FCC 359, 412 (1959).

53. Ibid., 404, 405, 414.

54. Ibid., 408.

55. Ibid., 411.

56. *Telecommunications Reports*, 7 March 1960, 13, 14.

57. Allocation of Frequencies in Bands Above 890Mc, 29 FCC 825 (1960).

58. United States v. AT&T, Defendants' Third Statement of Contentions and Proof, vol. 2, 845.

59. United States v. AT&T, Stipulation/Contention Package, Episode 14, para. 10, 13.

60. Ibid., para. 15, 16, 19, 20.

61. Quoted in ibid., para. 22. See also para. 21, 23, 24.

62. Ibid., para. 31A, 31B, 32, 33.

63. *Telecommunications Reports*, 23 January 1961, 1–4; 30 January 1961, 7; 13 February 1961, 1–5; and 1 May 1961, 6.

64. *Telecommunications Reports*, 13 March 1961, 1–2. See also United States v. AT&T, Stipulation/Contention Package, Episode 14, para. 59.

65. *Telecommunications Reports*, 20 March 1961, 5.

66. *Telecommunications Reports*, 27 March 1961, 1–4; 17 April 1961, 1–3; 15 May 1961, 10, 11; and 22 May 1961, 1–4; United States v. AT&T, Stipulation/Contention Package, Episode 14, para. 63, 64, 66.

67. *Telecommunications Reports*, 7 August 1961, 3. See also United States v. AT&T, Stipulation/Contention Package, Episode 14, para. 68.

68. *Telecommunications Reports*, 11 September 1961, 1, 2; United States v. AT&T, Stipulation/Contention Package, Episode 14, para. 70.

69. *Telecommunications Reports*, 13 November 1961, 13; 11 September 1961, 9.

70. See, for example, *Telecommunications Reports*, 5 December 1960, 22–27; and 20 August 1962, 1–5, 25–33.

71. *Telecommunications Reports*, 16 July 1962, 9; and United States v. AT&T, Stipulation/Contention Package, Episode 14, para. 91, 93.

72. TELPAK, 38 FCC 370, 378 (1964).

73. Ibid., 395.

74. *Telecommunications Reports*, 20 August 1962, 12–19, 42–46.

75. TELPAK, 37 FCC 1111, 1112 (1964).

76. Bureau of the Census, *Historical Statistics of the United States: Colonial Times to 1970*, part 2 (Washington, D.C.: Government Printing Office, 1975), 783.

77. "Behind the Communications Mess," *Business Week*, 18 November 1967, 66–74.

78. For a good summary of the early events in satellite communications, see Jonathan F. Galloway, *The Politics and Technology of Satellite Communications* (Lexington, Mass.: D.C. Heath, 1972), ch. 2–4.

79. Quoted in Galloway, *Satellite Communications*, 23.

80. *Telecommunications Reports*, 7 August 1961, 10.

81. For details see Domestic Communications—Satellite Facilities, 22 FCC 2d 86 (1970).

82. "Domestic Communications Satellite Fight Opens. Ford Fund Offers Plan," *Wall Street Journal*, 2 August 1966, 9; and United States v. AT&T, Defendants' Third Statement of Contentions and Proof, vol. II, 766–69.

83. "AT&T Drops Opposition to TV Networks Operating Own Communications Satellites," *Wall Street Journal*, 16 October 1969, 9.

84. Joseph Schumpeter, *Capitalism, Socialism and Democracy*, 3d ed. (New York: Harper & Row, 1950), 83.

85. American Telephone & Telegraph Company, *1970 Annual Report*, 8.

86. Bell Telephone Laboratories, *Engineering and Operations in the Bell System* (New York: Bell Telephone Laboratories, 1977), 377, 378; and Schindler, *A History of Engineering*, 385–88.

87. See, for example, New York Telephone Co., 82 PUR 3d 417 (1970); and New England Telephone & Telegraph Co., 81 PUR 3d 171 (1969).

88. Schindler, *A History of Engineering*, 398.

89. *Telecommunications Reports*, 31 January 1972, 25.

90. "AT&T Should Run Mails," *Wall Street Journal*, 10 April 1967, 4.

91. On the steps that telephone companies took to accommodate antique and decorator phones, see Hawaiian Telephone Co., 61 PUR 3d 552 (1965); and *Telecommunications Reports*, 31 May 1966, 39.

92. *Telecommunications Reports*, 26 September 1966, 22, 23.

93. Allocation of Microwave Frequencies Above 890Mc, 27 FCC 359, 414 (1959).

94. Netsky v. Bell Telephone Co. of Penn., 65 PUR 3d (1966); Racine Flash Cab Co. v. Wisconsin Telephone Co., 65 PUR 3d 321 (1966); and Electronic Detectors Inc. v. New Jersey Telephone Co., 62 PUR 3d 186 (1965).

95. See *Telecommunications Reports*, 26 September 1966, 22, 23.

96. Peters Sunset Beach, Inc. v. Northwestern Bell Telephone Co., 60 PUR 3d 363, 368 (1965). On AT&T's understanding of its obligations, see the following materials in *Interconnection—Foreign Attachments, 1965–66*, AT&T Archives, Box 2077: statement of William M. Ellinghaus, August–September 1966; memorandum, "Antique Telephones and Unauthorized Extensions" (n.d.); correspondence, Lee C. Tait and R. W. Kleinert to Mrs. Gering, 25 October 1965, with attachments; and Donald F. MacEachern, "Unauthorized Equipment—A Foreign Attachment Problem," speech before United States Independent Telephone Association, 19 October 1965.

97. Patti Hartigan, "At Home with Tom Carter," *On Communications* (February 1985), 24. See also *Telecommunications Reports*, 7 November 1960, 20.

98. United States v. AT&T, Stipulation/Contention Package, Episode 42A, para. 177.

99. See, especially, M. A. Adelman, *The World Petroleum Market* (Baltimore: Resources for the Future, 1972), 30, 31, 201.

100. This summary is drawn from the Record, Vol. 2, *Use of the Carterfone Device in Message Toll Telephone Service*, FCC Dkt. 16942 and 17073.

101. Carter v. American Telephone & Telegraph Co., 250 F.Supp. 188 (N.D. Tex., 1966).

102. Carterfone Record, vols. 2 and 8 (1968).

103. Carterfone, 13 FCC 2d 430, 434 (1968). Carter admitted, however, that the device did not function properly with some kinds of telephones. See also *Telecommunications Reports*, 17 April 1967, 35.

104. Carterfone, 434.

105. Ibid., 420, 423–24.

106. Ibid.

107. Ibid., 425.

108. Ibid., 424.

109. "New Jolt for Ma Bell and Friends," *Business Week*, 19 August 1967, 9.

110. "FCC Staff Eyes Competition for Mother Bell," *Business Week*, 18 May 1968, 52.

111. Carterfone, 14 FCC 2d 571 (1968).

112. See *For Release: 11 A.M. Thursday, August 29, 1968*, "Remarks of H. I. Romnes" and "Remarks of Ben S. Gilmer" (29 August 1968); correspondence, D. E. Emerson to Ben F. Waple, 29 August 1968, and other AT&T Information Department releases in *Interconnection—Foreign Attachments*, AT&T Archives, Box 2077.

113. H. I. Romnes, "Dynamic Communications for Modern Industry," speech before the Annual Meeting of the American Petroleum Institute (13 November 1967), AT&T Archives, Box 2077, 4, 5, 7. See also United States v. AT&T, Stipulation/Contention Package, Episode 42B, para. 309.

114. AT&T "Foreign Attachment" Revisions, 15 FCC 2d 605, 609–610 (1968). See also the reconsideration in 18 FCC 2d 871 (1969).

Chapter 6
Ringing in the New: The Rise of MCI

1. Bureau of the Census, *Statistical Abstract of the United States: 1986* (Washington, D.C.: Government Printing Office, 1985), 547, 548.

2. United States v. AT&T, Civil Action no. 74–1698, D.D.C. (1974), Stipulation/Contention Package, Episode 5, para. 507, 509, 535, 536.

3. Senate Subcommittee on Antitrust and Monopoly, Committee on the Judiciary, *The Industrial Reorganization Act*, part 6 (Washington, D.C.: Government Printing Office, 1974), 4423.

4. Roland Mueser, ed., *Bell Laboratories Innovation in Telecommunications, 1925–1977* (Murray Hill, N.J.: Bell Telephone Laboratories, 1979), 39–41, 95–104, 125–29, and 162–66.

5. Bell Telephone Laboratories, *1971 Annual Report*, 14.

6. For details of the advances that Bell Labs made in the physical sciences, see S. Millman, ed., *A History of Engineering and Science in the Bell System: Physical Sciences (1925–1980)* (New York: Bell Telephone Laboratories, 1983).

7. United States v. AT&T, Stipulation/Contention Package, Episode 4, para. 26–31.

8. Dan Cordtz, "The Coming Shake-Up in Telecommunications," *Fortune*, April 1970, 158.

9. William J. Baumol, Otto Eckstein, and Alfred E. Kahn, "Competition and Monopoly in Telecommunications Services," in *The Industrial Reorganization Act*, part 2, 1342.

10. See Bernard Schwartz, ed., *The Economic Regulation of Business and Industry*, vol. IV (New York: Chelsea House, 1973), 2500.

11. Illinois State Telephone Co. v. Illinois Commerce Commission, 73 PUR 3d 525, 527, 528 (1968).

12. Quoted in United States v. AT&T, Stipulation/Contention Package, Episode 21, para 2.

13. Ibid., para. 2–5.

14. Ibid., para. 6, 7.

15. Ibid., para. 8.

16. Ibid., Defendants' Contention 4.

17. Ibid., para. 10–14.

18. Ibid., para. 15–17.

19. *Telecommunications Reports*, 11 October 1965, 1–4; 31 January 1966, 20, 21.

20. United States v. AT&T, Stipulation/Contention Package, Episode 21, para. 18–23.

21. *Telecommunications Reports*, 21 March 1966, 23, 24.

22. *Telecommunications Reports*, 20 February 1967, 34.

23. *Telecommunications Reports*, 31 July 1967, 9.

24. Quoted in ibid., 10.

25. *Telecommunications Reports*, 2 October 1967, 9.

26. Microwave Communications Inc., 18 FCC 2d 979 (1967).

27. Ibid., 986.

28. Ibid., 994. See also 991.

29. Ibid., 1004.

30. See, for example, United States v. AT&T, Trial Record, 3578, 3579.

31. Joseph A. Schumpeter, *Capitalism, Socialism and Democracy*, 3d ed. (New York: Harper & Row, 1950), 84, 85.

32. *Events in Telecommunications History* (New York: AT&T, 1979), 59, 60.

33. *Telecommunications Reports*, 6 May 1968, 6–13.

34. *Telecommunications Reports*, 18 November 1968, 5–7.

35. Larry Kahaner, *On the Line* (New York: Warner Books, 1986), chs. 3–4. This undocumented book is an unabashed laud of MCI, although Kahaner conducted interviews with MCI officials and obviously had their confidence. However, the book does contain useful information on MCI's background.

36. *Telecommunications Reports*, 23 December 1968, 14, 15.

37. United States v. AT&T, Stipulation/Contention Package, Episode 15, para. 11.

38. Quoted in ibid., para. 16.

39. MCI's statement on Series 11000 is reported in *Telecommunications Reports*, 23 June 1969, 14, 15. Cost data on the offering is summarized in United States v. AT&T, Stipulation/Contention Package, Episode 15, para. 24–27, 35, 36.

40. Kahaner, *On the Line*, 60.

41. Quoted in *Telecommunications Reports*, 14 July 1969, 24.

42. Microwave Communications Inc., 18 FCC 2d 953, 954 (1969).

43. Ibid., 959.

44. Ibid., 960.

45. Ibid., 966.

46. Ibid., 978.

47. *Telecommunications Reports*, 18 August 1969, 10; and "The Round AT&T Lost," *Business Week*, 6 September 1969, 68, 70.

48. FCC v. RCA Communications Inc., 346 U.S. 86 (1952).

49. Microwave Communications Inc., 18 FCC 2d 953, 972 (1969).

50. Ibid., 973–76.

51. *Telecommunications Reports*, 13 October 1969, 26.

52. Microwave Communications Inc., 21 FCC 2d 190 (1970).

53. *Telecommunications Reports*, 22 December 1969, 25.

54. United States v. AT&T, Stipulation/Contention Package, Episode 22, para. 1–3.

55. *Telecommunications Reports*, 22 December 1969, 27, 28.

56. "AT&T's Bell Labs Claims New Device for Computers," *Wall Street Journal*, 6 April 1970, 8; "Bell Labs Develops Laser," *Wall Street Journal*, 1 September 1970, 10; Mueser, *Bell Laboratories Innovation*, 98; and David Fishlock, "Mission Control for the New Wave," *Financial Times*, 9 February 1987, 10.

57. *Telecommunications Reports*, 22 June 1970, 44–46.

58. Specialized Common Carrier Services, 24 FCC 2d 318 (1970).

59. United States v. AT&T, Stipulation/Contention Package, Episode 22, para. 7; *Telecommunications Reports*, 20 July 1970, 1–7, 17–23; and Specialized Common Carrier Services, 24 FCC 2d 328–38 (1970).

60. Specialized Common Carrier Services, 24 FCC 2d 324 (1970).

61. See, for example, Allocation of Frequencies Above 890Mc, 27 FCC 359, 370 (1959).

62. See AT&T (Railroad Interconnection), 32 FCC 337 (1962).

63. *Telecommunications Reports*, 28 September 1970, 10.

64. See the excellent summary in *Telecommunications Reports*, 5 October 1970, 1–8, 41–49.

65. *Telecommunications Reports*, 1 June 1971, 1, 2.

66. Specialized Common Carrier Services, 29 FCC 2d 870 (1971).

67. Ibid., 904.

68. Ibid., 906.

69. Ibid., 951.

70. MCI, *Proposed Findings of Facts and Conclusions of Law*, FCC Dkt. nos. 16509–19, 8. For a compilation of similar MCI statements, see United States v. AT&T, Defendants' Third Statement of Contentions and Proof, vol. 1, 676.

71. AT&T Revisions to the Wide Area Telecommunications Service (WATS), Tariff FCC No. 259, 59 FCC 2d 671, 674 (1976); and G. E. Schindler, Jr., ed., *A History of Engineering and Science in the Bell System: Switching Technology (1925–1975)* (New York: Bell Telephone Laboratories, 1982), 342.

72. United States v. AT&T, Stipulation/Contention Package, Episode 1, para. 72; and Bell Telephone Laboratories, *Engineering and Operations in the Bell System* (New York: Bell Telephone Laboratories, 1977), 63, 64.

73. United States v. AT&T, Stipulation/Contention Package, Episode 1, para. 73, 74; Episode 17, Appendix; and Episode 24, para. 222, 223; Schindler, *A History of Engineering*, 358, 359.

74. Quoted in United States v. AT&T, Stipulation/Contention Package, Episode 23, para. 15.

75. Ibid., para. 15, 25, 26, 32–37.

76. *Specialized Common Carrier Services*, 29 FCC 2d 870, 940 (1971); and 24 FCC 2d 318, 347, 348 (1970).

77. United States v. AT&T, Trial Record, 3713; and Kahaner, *On the Line*, 67, 68.

78. United States v. AT&T, Stipulation/Contention Package, Episode 23, para. 52.

79. Ibid., para. 69.

80. Ibid., para. 55, 59; and Plaintiffs' Contentions and Defendants' Contentions, para. 32, 33, 36–38; *Telecommunications Reports*, 5 September 1972, 6; and United States v. AT&T, Trial Record, 3935.

81. United States v. AT&T, Stipulation/Contention Package, Episode 23, para. 62. See also Episode 23, para. 61, 63, 64, 69–72, and Plaintiffs' Contentions and Defendants' Contentions 57 and 61.

82. Ibid., Episode 26, para. 1–7.

83. Ibid., para. 38, 50–52; Plaintiffs' Contentions and Defendants' Contentions, para. 48–54.

84. Ibid., Episode 26, para. 67.

85. Ibid., para. 74.

86. Ibid., Episode 26, Plaintiffs' Contentions and Defendants' Contentions, para. 88, 117; and Episode 26, para. 109, 113, 114, 115, 117.

87. International Tel & Tel Co. v. General Tel & Electronics Corp., 351 F. Supp. 1153, 1180–82 (D. Hawaii, 1972), rev'd. 518 F 2d 913 (9th Cir., 1975).

88. United States v. AT&T, Stipulation/Contention Package, Episode 26, para. 103.

89. Ibid., para. 112.

90. United States v. AT&T, Defendants' Third Statement of Contentions and Proof, vol. I, 648.

91. United States v. AT&T, Trial Record, 4306, 4307.

92. United States v. AT&T, Stipulation/Contention Package, Episode 23, para. 74 and Defendants' Contention 81.

93. Ibid., Episode 24, para. 22.

94. Ibid., para. 28.

95. See, generally, Ibid., Episode 24, para. 22 and Defendants' Contentions, para. 13–15, 17.

96. Ibid., Episode 24, Defendants' Contentions, para. 6.

97. AT&T—"Foreign Attachments" Tariff Revisions, 15 FCC 2d 605, 609–10 (1968).

98. Ibid., 608.

99. United States v. AT&T, Stipulation/Contention Package, Episode 24, para. 46; and ATT—"Foreign Attachments" Tariff Revisions, 18 FCC 2d 871 (1969).

100. See William McGowan's testimony in United States v. AT&T, Trial Record, 3818, 3819, and Stipulation/Contention Package, Episode 24, para. 51, 52.

101. Ibid., Episode 24, Defendants' Contentions, para. 57. See also Defendants' Contentions, para. 58–60.

102. Quoted in ibid., para. 63.

103. Ibid.

104. Ibid., para. 86.

105. Ibid., para. 222–36, and Defendants' Contentions, para. 80, 81.

106. Quoted in ibid., Episode 24, para. 102, and Defendants' Contention 85.

107. Quoted in ibid., Episode 24, para. 154 (see, generally, Section 7).

108. Ibid., para. 176, 179, 180, 181.

109. Ibid., Plaintiffs' Contention 182; and United States v. AT&T, Trial Record, 3878, 3943, 3993, 4023–27, and 4047.

110. United States v. AT&T, Stipulation/Contention Package, Episode 24, para. 198 and Plaintiffs' and Defendants' Contentions, para. 198.

111. See ibid., Episode 24, Defendants' Contention 190, for an example of an ex parte contact.

112. Ibid., Episode 24, Section 10; and United States v. AT&T, Trial Record, 3967–973.

113. "Trustbuster Hart Tilts with AT&T," *Business Week*, 4 August 1973, 15, 16.

114. See, generally, United States v. AT&T, Episode 29.

115. On the collaboration between MCI and the FCC's Common Carrier Bureau, see United States v. AT&T, Trial Record, 3787.

116. Specialized Common Carriers, 44 FCC 2d 467, 470 (1973).

117. MCI Communications Corp. v. American Telephone & Telegraph Co., 369 F. Supp. 1004, 1029 (E.D. Pa., 1973).

118. MCI Communications Corp. v. American Telephone & Telegraph Co., 496 F. 2d 214, 221 (3d Cir., 1974).

119. Bell System Tariff Offerings, 46 FCC 2d 413, 441 (1974).

120. Ibid., 427.

121. Ibid., 426.

122. AT&T Charges, Regulations, Classifications and Practices for Voice Grade/ Private Line Services (High Density–Low Density), 58 FCC 2d 362, 366–67 (1976); AT&T Charges for Interstate Telephone Services (Phase II), 64 FCC 2d 1, 81 (1977); and United States v. AT&T, Stipulation/Contention Package, Episode 29, para. 468.

Chapter 7
The Broken Connection: Computers and Interconnection

1. Leslie Wayne, "AT&T's New Challenge," *New York Times*, 4 February 1982, D1, D8.

2. See Roland Mueser, ed., *Bell Laboratories Innovation in Telecommunications, 1925–1977* (Murray Hill, N.J.: Bell Telephone Laboratories, 1979), 42, 101, 102, 166, 185, 186.

3. United States v. AT&T, Civil Action no. 74–1698 D.D.C. (1974), Trial Record, 13993.

4. Smith v. Illinois Bell Telephone Co., 282 U.S. 133 (1930).

5. Peter Temin and Geoffrey Peters, "Is History Stranger than Theory? The Origin of Telephone Separations," *American Economic Review: Papers and Proceedings* 75 (May 1985): 326.

6. See Peter Temin and Geoffrey Peters, "Cross-Subsidization in the Telephone Network," *Willamette Law Review* 21 (Spring 1985): 199–223.

7. John D. de Butts, "The Time Is Now for the Communications Industry," in *Proceedings, Eighty-fifth Annual Convention, National Association of Regulatory Utility Commissioners* (Washington, D.C.: National Association of Regulatory Utility Commissioners, 1974), 287.

8. Ibid., 288.

9. Ibid., 291.

10. Early developments are recounted in Herman H. Goldstine, *The Computer from Pascal to Von Neumann* (Princeton, N.J.: Princeton University Press, 1972).

11. Senate Committee on the Judiciary, Subcommittee on Antitrust and Monopoly, *Industrial Reorganization Act, Hearings*, part 7 (Washington, D.C.: Government Printing Office, 1974), 5040, 5041; Alvin J. Harman, *The International Computer Industry* (Cambridge, Mass.: Harvard University Press, 1971), 9–13; and Saul Rosen, "Electronic Computers: A Historical Survey," *Computer Surveys* (March 1969): 7–36.

12. United States v. International Bus Machs. Corp., Trade Cases, para. 68, 245 (S.D. N.Y. Jan. 25, 1956); and Manley B. Irwin, "The Computer Utility: Competition or Regulation," *Yale Law Journal* 76 (1967): 1302, 1303.

13. S. Millman, ed., *A History of Engineering and Science in the Bell System: Communication Sciences (1925–1980)* (New York: AT&T Bell Laboratories, 1984), 359; and Goldstine, *The Computer*, ch. 12.

14. Millman, *A History of Engineering*, 366–79.

15. Gerald W. Brock, *The Telecommunications Industry* (Cambridge, Mass.: Harvard University Press, 1981), 269.

16. David Farber and Paul Baran, "The Convergence of Computing and Telecommunications Systems," *Science*, 18 March 1977, 1169.

17. United States v. AT&T, Defendants' Third Statement of Contentions and Proof, vol. II, 1276–89; and Plantiffs' Third Statement of Contentions and Proof, vol. II, 1500–05.

18. An excellent summary of the *Telequote* episode, on which the text primarily relies, appears in "Computer Services and the Federal Regulation of Communications," *University of Pennsylvania Law Review* 116 (December 1967): 328–46.

19. Ibid., 329.

20. New York Telephone Co., 44 PUR (N.S.) 265, 269–70 (1942).

21. R. M. Fano and F. J. Corbato, "Time-Sharing on Computers," *Scientific American*, September 1966, 129–40.

22. Rosen, "Electronic Computers," 31–34.

23. "The FCC Computer Inquiry: Interfaces of Competitive and Regulated Markets," *Michigan Law Review* 71 (1973): 173–76.

24. Reported in *Telecommunications Reports*, 25 October 1965, 1–3, 36.

25. W. J. Golden, Jr., 61 MCC 57, 58 (1952).

26. See Delbert E. Smith, "The Interdependence of Computer and Communications Services and Facilities: A Question of Federal Regulation," *University of Pennsylvania Law Review* 117 (April 1969): 847–53.

27. Aeronautical Radio, Inc. v. AT&T, 4 FCC 155, 162–63 (1937).

28. See *Telecommunications Reports*, 21 February 1966, 7.

29. Smith, "The Interdependence," 849, 850.

30. *Telecommunications Reports*, 21 March 1966, 5.

31. Interdependence of Computer and Communication Services, 7 FCC 2d 11, 15 (1966).

32. Ibid., Supplemental Notice of Inquiry, 7 FCC 2d 19 (1967).

33. *Telecommunications Reports*, 9 January 1967, 19–21.

34. Smith, "The Interdependence," 850.

35. Western Union Telegraph Co., 11 FCC 2d 1, 9 (1967). See also *Telecommunications Reports*, 26 December 1967, 1–5, 28.

36. *NARUC Bulletin*, 15 January 1968, 6.

37. *Telecommunications Reports*, 4 March 1968, 15–18.

38. See the summary in *Telecommunications Reports*, 11 March 1968, 4–16, 29–47.

39. AT&T—"Foreign Attachments" Tariff Revisions, 15 FCC 2d 605 (1968).

40. The *SRI Report* is summarized in *Telecommunications Reports*, 12 May 1969, 1–8.

41. *Telecommunications Reports*, 28 July 1969, 16–20.

42. Computer Use of Communications Facilities, Report and Further Notice of Inquiry, 17 FCC 2d 587, 589–90 (1969).

43. Ibid., Tentative Decision, 28 FCC 2d 291 (1970).

44. Ibid., 297.

45. Domestic Communication-Satellite Facilities, Notice of Proposed Rulemaking, 22 FCC 2d 810, 811 (1970).

46. Ibid., Second Report and Order, 35 FCC 2d 844, 847–48 (1972).

47. Computer Use of Communications Facilities, Tentative Decision, 28 FCC 2d 291, 305 (1970).

48. Donald A. Dunn, "Policy Issues Presented by the Interdependence of Computer and Communications Sciences," *Law and Contemporary Problems* 34 (Spring 1969): 374.

49. *Telecommunications Reports*, 25 May 1970, 9–11.

50. *Telecommunications Reports*, 8 June 1970, 1–3; 15 June 1970, 24; 22 June 1970, 7–9, 30–38; 8 September 1970, 4–10.

51. Computer Use of Communications Facilities, Final Decision and Order, 28 FCC 2d 267 (1971).

52. Ibid., 289.

53. Ibid., Memorandum Opinion and Order, 34 FCC 2d 557 (1972); *Telecommunications Reports* 26 April 1971, 1–3; and 24 May 1971, 22, 23.

54. *Telecommunications Reports*, 19 April 1971, 8–10.

55. *Telecommunications Reports*, 9 February 1970, 1–3.

56. "Interdependence of Communications and Data Processing: An Alternate Pro-

posal for the Second Computer Inquiry," *Northwestern University Law Review* 73 (1978): 312.

57. GTE Service Corporation v. FCC, 474 F. 2d 724 (7th Cir. 1973).

58. Ibid., 732.

59. Computer Use of Communications Facilities (Order), 40 FCC 2d 293 (1973).

60. AT&T "Foreign Attachment" Provisions, 15 FCC 2d 605 (1968); and 18 FCC 2d 871 (1969).

61. Electronic Detectors, Inc. v. New Jersey Bell Tel Co., 62 PUR 3d 186, 190 (1965).

62. United States v. AT&T, Stipulation/Contention Package, Episode 42B, para. 319–25.

63. Ibid., para. 327, 330, 332.

64. Ibid.

65. *Telecommunications Reports*, 22 June 1970, 4, 5.

66. United States v. AT&T, Stipulation/Contention Package, Episode 42B, Defendants' Contentions, paras. 315, 316.

67. Ibid., Defendants' Contention, para. 336.

68. Ibid.

69. A summary of the Dittberner Associates report appears in *Telecommunications Reports*, 31 August 1970, 1–4, 22–25. Extensive portions of the report are reprinted in United States v. AT&T, Stipulation/Contention Package, Episode 42B.

70. United States v. AT&T, Defendants' Third Statement of Contentions and Proof, vol. 2, 1167.

71. NARUC Committee on Communications, *An Investigation into the Economic and Quality of Service Impact on Telephone Service Subscribers* (Washington, D.C.: NARUC, 1974), 11. See also 78–91.

72. Ibid., 13, 50–60.

73. *Telecommunications Reports*, 8 September 1970, 21.

74. *Telecommunications Reports*, 1 February 1971, 12, 13; and 15 February 1971, 6.

75. United States v. AT&T, Stipulation/Contention Package, Episode 72A, para. 414–19; *Telecommunications Reports*, 8 March 1971, 1–5; and 14 June 1971, 1–3, 31, 32.

76. United States v. AT&T, Stipulation/Contention Package, Episode 42B, para. 440.

77. Ibid., para. 445.

78. *Telecommunications Reports*, 10 October 1972, 1–6.

79. *Telecommunications Reports*, 2 October 1972, 1, 2.

80. NARUC, *An Investigation*, 40–42; and *Telecommunications Reports*, 17 January 1972, 9, 10.

81. See, for example, *Telecommunications Reports*, 7 September 1971, 5–12; and 10 January 1972, 12, 13, 25.

82. *Telecommunications Reports*, 23 April 1973, 3–5.

83. Interstate and Foreign MTS and WATS, Notice of Inquiry, 35 FCC 2d 539 (1972); and *Telecommunications Reports*, 25 October 1971, 1–3.

84. *Telecommunications Reports*, 15 May 1972, 5, 6. On the continuing Common Carrier Bureau hostility toward AT&T in the certification proceedings, see, for example, *Telecommunications Reports*, 20 December 1971, 1–4.

85. Interstate and Foreign MTS and WATS, Notice of Inquiry, 35 FCC 2d 539, 542 (1972).

86. United States v. AT&T, Defendants' Third Statement of Contentions and Proof,

vol. II, 1149. According to AT&T seventeen state commissions were undertaking interconnection impact investigations during this period.

87. United States v. AT&T, Stipulation/Contention Package, Episode 42B, para. 642–47, and Defendants' Contentions, para. 634.

88. Rochester Telephone Corp., 91 PUR 3d 370 (1972).

89. Ibid., 378, 379.

90. *Telecommunications Reports*, 19 July 1971, 26–28.

91. *Telecommunications Reports*, 28 February 1972, 11, 12.

92. *Telecommunications Reports*, 30 May 1972, 6–8.

93. New York Telephone Corp., 79 PUR 3d 410 (1969).

94. Rochester Telephone Corp., 91 PUR 3d 370, 377 (1972).

95. Ibid., 394.

96. See, for example, the Missouri case of Slavin v. Southwestern Bell Telephone Co., 8 PUR 4th 624 (1975); and Phonetele, Inc. v. California Public Utilities Commission, 11 Cal. 3d 125 (1974).

97. See *Telecommunications Reports*, 22 February 1972, 1–6, 20, 21; and 10 April 1972, 11.

98. *Telecommunications Reports*, 2 October 1972, 2, 3.

99. *Telecommunications Reports*, 16 October 1972, 20, 21.

100. Quoted in *Telecommunications Reports*, 30 April 1973, 1.

101. Alvin von Auw, *Heritage and Destiny* (New York: Praeger, 1983), 141.

102. United States v. AT&T, Trial Record, 14060. See also 14055–59, 14061–67.

103. de Butts, "The Time Is Now," 289.

104. Telerent Leasing Corp. et al., 45 FCC 2d 204, 220 (1974).

105. North Carolina Utilities Comm. v. FCC, 537 F. 2d 787 (4th Cir., 1976).

106. *Telecommunications Reports*, 21 January 1974, 14, 15; see also 23 October 1973, 1–7, 24–31.

107. *Telecommunications Reports*, 28 May 1974, 10.

108. Customer Interconnection, 46 FCC 2d 214 (1974).

109. Interstate and Foreign Message Toll Telephone Service et al., Recommended First Report and Order, 53 FCC 2d 221, 224–25 (1975).

110. Ibid., Memorandum Opinion and Order, 53 FCC 2d 219 (1975).

111. *Telecommunications Reports*, 22 July 1974, 19, 20; and 25 November 1974, 10–12; United States v. AT&T, Stipulation/Contention Package, Episode 42B, para. 720.

112. Bureau of the Census, *Abstract of the United States: 1986* (Washington, D.C.: Government Printing Office, 1985), 545; and AT&T, *1974 Annual Report*, 6, 11–13.

113. AT&T, 53 FCC 2d 473 (1975).

114. Interstate and Foreign Message Toll Telephone, etc., First Report and Order, 56 FCC 2d 593 (1975).

115. Ibid., 600.

116. Ibid., 597.

117. United States v. AT&T, Stipulation/Contention Package, Episode 42B, para. 737–40.

118. Interstate and Foreign Message Toll Telephone Service, Memorandum Opinion and Order, 57 FCC 2d 1216 (1976).

119. Ibid., 58 FCC 2d 716 (1976).

120. Interstate and Foreign Message Toll Service, Second Report and Order, 58 FCC 2d 736, 737 (1976).

121. Ibid., 740.

122. See, for example, Interstate and Foreign Message Toll Telephone, etc., Memorandum Opinion and Order, 59 FCC 2d 83 (1976); Interstate and Foreign Message Toll Telephone Service, Supplemental Notice of Proposed Rulemaking, 64 FCC 2d 1039 (1977); Interstate and Foreign Message Toll Telephone Service, Memorandum Opinion and Order, 64 FCC 2d 1058 (1977); Interstate and Foreign Message Toll Telephone Service, Third Report and Order, 67 FCC 2d 1255 (1978).

123. Interstate and Foreign Message Toll Telephone Service, Memorandum Opinion and Order, 70 FCC 2d 1800, 1811 (1979).

124. Telephone Industry's Primary Instrument Concept, 67 FCC 2d 606 (1978).

125. Primary Instrument Concept, 68 FCC 2d 1157, 1158 (1978).

126. Customer Interconnection, First Report, 61 FCC 2d 766, 769 (1976).

127. Ibid., 772.

128. Arthur D. Little, Inc., "The Relationship Between Market Structure and the Innovation Process," AT&T Exhibit No. 52, FCC Docket 20003.

129. Systems Applications, Inc., Regulatory Policy Changes and the Future of the Independent Telephone Industry (January 1976), III–19.

130. Customer Interconnection (First Report), 61 FCC 2d 766, 902–4 (1976).

Chapter 8
Busy Signals: MCI's Renewed Attack
and *Computer II*

1. Franklin M. Fisher, John J. McGowan, and Joen E. Greenwood, Folded, Spindled and Mutilated (Cambridge, Mass.: MIT Press, 1983), 1.

2. See the summary in Congressional Quarterly, Inc., Congress and the Nation, vol. IV (Washington, D.C.: Congressional Quarterly, 1977), 572.

3. See Complaint, Kellogg Co. et al., FTC Dkt. 8883 (1972); and Complaint, EXXON Corporation et al., FTC Dkt. 8934 (1973).

4. Jimmy Carter, "Remarks on Signing S. 1946 (Staggers Rail Act of 1980) into Law," Weekly Presidential Documents, 14 October 1980, 2226.

5. "AT&T/DOJ Antitrust Proceedings," Memorandum from Commissioner Fogarty, 21 January 1982, 1.

6. Bell System Tariff Offerings, 48 FCC 2d 413 (1974).

7. United States v. AT&T, Civil Action no. 74–1698, D.D.C. (1974), Stipulation/Contention Package, Episode 24B, AT&T Stipulation 75A.

8. United States v. AT&T, Transcript of Testimony, 3875, 3878, 3882, 3889, 3891.

9. Ibid., 4023–26.

10. Ibid., 4006, 4007.

11. Ibid., 4008, 4009.

12. Ibid., 4046.

13. Ibid., 3836, 4047–49, 4089.

14. Telecommunications Reports, 3 December 1973, 6.

15. Telecommunications Reports, 12 November 1973, 12, 13.

16. Telecommunications Reports, 11 March 1974, 1.

17. Ibid.

18. Bell System Tariff Offerings, 46 FCC 2d 413, 427 (1974).

19. Eastern Railroads Presidents Conference v. Noerr Motor Freight Inc., 365 U.S. 127 (1961); and United Mine Workers v. Pennington, 381 U.S. 657 (1965).

20. *Telecommunications Reports*, 8 April 1974, 1, 2.

21. MCI Communications Corp. v. American Telephone & Telegraph Co., 462 F. Supp. 1072, 1078–79 (N.D. Ill., 1978).

22. Gordon v. New York Stock Exchange, 422 U.S. 659, 682 (1975).

23. Good examples include Essential Communications v. American Telephone & Telegraph, 610 F. 2d 1114 (3d Cir. 1979); and SOUND Inc. v. AT&T Co., 1980–82 Trade Cases, para. 53, 514 (8th Cir. 1980).

24. Reprinted in Bernard Schwartz, ed., *The Economic Regulation of Business and Industry*, vol. IV (New York: Chelsea House, 1973), 2426.

25. "AT&T and the Antitrust Laws: A Strict Test for Implied Immunity," *Yale Law Journal* 85 (1975): 254–79.

26. The author whose focus was entirely on suits brought by the government also includes a fifth factor: whether the agency has the power to grant the relief requested. In the case of the FCC, he concludes that it had the same powers as the court had in *United States* v. *AT&T*. He noted, however, that "more recent cases have not subscribed to this requirement." Ibid., 262. In any event, because no agency has the power to grant treble damages, the logic of including this criterion would be to exclude *all* private antitrust suits. Since this could readily defeat the considerations in the first four criteria because courts in private suits announce principles of law just as they do in suits brought by the government, this fifth factor should clearly be excluded.

27. Hawaiian Telephone Co. v. FCC, 498 F. 2d 774 (D.C. Cir. 1974).

28. FCC v. RCA Communications Inc., 346 U.S. 86, 97 (1952).

29. "AT&T and the Antitrust Laws," 276.

30. MCI Communications Corp. v. American Telephone & Telegraph Co., Brief of Appellant, p. 177, 708 F. 2d 1081 (7th Cir. 1983).

31. See, for example, *Telecommunications Reports*, 4 February 1980, 11; 3 March 1980, 19; 2 June 1980, 11; and 9 June 1980, 24.

32. *Telecommunications Reports*, 24 March 1980, 23.

33. Quoted in "The Potential Fallout from AT&T's Defeat," *Business Week*, 30 June 1980, 45.

34. Robert Metz, "MCI's Future vs. AT&T," *New York Times*, 23 October 1981, 34.

35. *Telecommunications Reports*, 23 June 1980, 14.

36. *Telecommunications Reports*, 7 May 1979, 17, 18; and 16 November 1981, 3–5.

37. *Telecommunications Reports*, 26 April 1982, 9–13.

38. An excellent analysis appears in Spencer Weber Waller, "The New Law of Monopolization," *DePaul Law Review* 32 (1983): 595–623.

39. See MCI Communications Corp. v. American Telephone & Telegraph Co., 708 F. 2d 1081, 1111–23 (7th Cir. 1983).

40. Leslie Wayne, "MCI Loses Some Sparkle," *New York Times*, 12 February 1984, F1, 8.

41. Steven Erenhouse, "$37.8 Million to MCI in AT&T Suit," *New York Times*, 29 May 1985, 29, 38; and *Telecommunications Reports*, 27 May 1985, 1–3, 30, 31.

42. *Telecommunications Reports*, 25 November 1985, 5, 6.

43. MCI Telecommunications Corporation, 60 FCC 2d 25, 26 (1976).

44. United States v. AT&T, Transcript of Testimony, 5613–19; *Telecommunications Reports*, 21 April 1980, 9; and United States v. AT&T, Stipulation/Contention Package, Episode 24B, Plaintiffs' and Defendants' Contentions, para. 76A.

45. United States v. AT&T, Episode 24B, AT&T Stipulation, para. 76.

46. Ibid., para. 77, 77A.

47. United States v. AT&T, Defendants' Third Statement of Contentions and Proof, vol. 1, 694.

48. Steve Coll, *The Deal of the Century* (New York: Atheneum, 1986), 88, 89.

49. MCI Telecommunications Corporation, 60 FCC 2d 25, 36 (1976).

50. Rochester Telephone Corp. v. United States, 307 U.S. 125, 146 (1939); see also SEC v. Chenery Corp., 332 U.S. 194 (1947).

51. See the concurring opinion in Ethyl Corp. v. Environmental Protection Agency, 541 F. 2d 1 (D.C. Cir. 1976).

52. See the comments of William H. Allen, quoted in Walter Gellhorn, Clark Byse, and Peter L. Strauss, eds., *Administrative Law: Cases and Comments*, 7th ed. (Mineola, N.Y.: Foundation Press, 1979), 343, 344. An example of Judge Wright's negative attitude toward regulatory agencies is his attack on the Civil Aeronautics Board in Moss v. Civil Aeronautics Board, 430 F. 2d 891, 893 (D.C. Cir. 1970).

53. Chevron U.S.A. Inc. v. National Resources Defense Council Inc., 104 S. Ct. 2778 (1984).

54. MCI Telecommunications Corp. v. FCC, 561 F. 2d 365 (D.C. Cir. 1977).

55. Ibid., 375.

56. Ibid., 378.

57. AT&T Company et al., 67 FCC 2d 1455 (1978).

58. MCI Telecommunications Corp. v. FCC, 580 F. 2d 590 (D.C. Cir. 1978).

59. See, for example, Competitive Carrier Rulemaking, 85 FCC 2d 1, 22–24 (1980).

60. United States v. AT&T, Stipulation/Contention Package, Episode 42B, AT&T Stipulations, para. 93A, 93A.1, 93A.2, 93A.3; and Exchange Network Facilities (ENFIA), 71 FCC 2d 440 (1979).

61. *Telecommunications Reports*, 4 February 1980, 8, 9.

62. *Telecommunications Reports*, 31 March 1980, 9, 10; 19 May 1980, 29; and 30 June 1980, 13; Exchange Network Facilities (ENFIA), 90 FCC 2d 123 (1980).

63. *Telecommunications Reports*, 9 March 1981, 13, 14; and 27 April 1981, 4.

64. *Telecommunications Reports*, 18 May 1981, 15, 16; and 8 June 1981, 20, 21.

65. *Telecommunications Reports*, 29 June 1981, 15.

66. MTS/WATS Market Structure, 97 FCC 2d 682, 710 (1983).

67. Brian O'Reilly, "More than Cheap Talk Propels MCI," *Fortune*, 24 January 1983, 68.

68. Almarin Phillips, "Theory and Practice in Public Utility Regulation: The Case of Telecommunications," in *Economic Regulation: Essays in Honor of James R. Nelson*, Kenneth Boyer and William G. Shepherd, eds. (East Lansing, Mich.: Institute of Public Utilities, 1981), 194.

69. "Interdependence of Communications and Data Processing," *Northwestern University Law Review* 73 (1978): 313, 314.

70. N. R. Bradley Lambert, "The Effect of the Second Computer Inquiry on Telecommunications and Data Processing," *Wayne Law Review* 27 (1981): 1543.

71. For a modest 1976 forecast of growth in computer communications, see Vinton G. Cerf, "The Future of Computer Communications," in *Planning Conference on Computer Communications, November 8–9, 1976* (Washington, D.C.: FCC, 1976).

72. "Who Will Supply the Office of the Future?" *Business Week*, 27 July 1974, 42.

73. Victor Block, "AT&T Plans Fight over Rejection by CCB of Dataspeed 40 Tariff," *Telephony*, 15 March 1976, 19.

74. AT&T, Revisions to Tariffs 260 and 267 Relating to Dataspeed 40, 62 FCC 2d 21 (1977).

75. Computer Inquiry, Notice of Inquiry and Proposed Rulemaking, 61 FCC 2d 103 (1976).

76. Computer Inquiry, Supplemental Notice of Inquiry, 64 FCC 2d 771 (1977).

77. Quoted in *Telecommunications Reports*, 6 June 1977, 3; see also 23 May 1977, 4, 5.

78. *Telecommunications Reports*, 13 June 1977, 12.

79. Ibid.

80. Second Computer Inquiry, FCC Docket no. 20828, Reply Comments of AT&T (17 October 1977), 8.

81. Ibid., 41.

82. Computer Inquiry, Tentative Decision, 72 FCC 2d 358, 393 (1979).

83. Ibid., 394.

84. Resale and Shared Use of Common Services, 60 FCC 2d 261 (1976), and 62 FCC 2d 588 (1977); American Telephone & Telegraph Co. v. FCC, 572 F. 2d 17 (2d Cir. 1978).

85. Computer Inquiry, Tentative Decision, 72 FCC 2d 358, 430 (1979).

86. "The FCC Backs Bell on Data Processing," *Business Week*, 4 June 1979, 65.

87. *Telecommunications Reports*, 8 October 1979, 2.

88. Ibid., 4. See also Second Computer Inquiry, Reply Comments of IBM (7 December 1979), FCC Docket no. 20828.

89. Second Computer Inquiry, Comments of the United States Department of Justice (12 October 1979), FCC Docket no. 20828, 16, 17.

90. *Telecommunications Reports*, 21 April 1980, 10.

91. Second Computer Inquiry, Final Decision, 77 FCC 2d 384 (1980).

92. Ibid., 419, 420.

93. See Robert M. Frieden, "The Computer Inquiries: Mapping the Communications/Information Processing Terrain," *Federal Communications Law Journal* 33 (Winter 1981): 79–82.

94. Second Computer Inquiry, Final Decision, para. 271–79.

95. Ibid., para. 216.

96. Ibid., para. 212.

97. Ibid., para. 233–64.

98. Ibid., para. 139.

99. Ibid., para. 163–66.

100. Second Computer Inquiry, (Final Decision), Statement of Commissioner Joseph R. Fogarty, slipsheets 1–22.

101. Second Computer Inquiry, Petition for Reconsideration of AT&T (12 June 1980), FCC Docket no. 20828.

102. *Telecommunications Reports*, 23 June 1980, 15–18; 16 June 1980, 5–9, 30–33; 11 August 1980, 2–6, 30–32; and 8 September 1980, 5, 16–18.

103. Second Computer Inquiry, Memorandum Opinion and Order, 84 FCC 2d 50 (1980).

104. *Telecommunications Reports*, 30 March 1981, 1–4, 28, 29; and 6 April 1981, 1, 2.

105. *Telecommunications Reports*, 7 September 1981, 1–3.

106. See, for example, Second Computer Inquiry, Memorandum Opinion and Order on Further Reconsideration, 88 FCC 2d 512 (1981).

107. Computer and Communications, etc. v. FCC, 693 F. 2d 198 (1982).

108. *Telecommunications Reports*, 29 July 1985, 1–4, 28, 29; Amendment of Section 64.702 of the Commission's Rules, cc Docket no. 85–229. See the excellent analysis in Richard E. Wiley and Howard D. Polsky, "Understanding the *Computer III* Inquiry," *Telematics* (November 1985): 3–8.

109. *Telecommunications Reports*, 23 September 1985, 1–3; 19 May 1986, 5–7, 36; and 30 March 1987, 1–4, 31.

Chapter 9
"No" for an Answer: *United States* v. *AT&T*

1. United States v. Western Electric Co., "Report and Recommendations of the United States Concerning the Line of Business Restrictions Imposed on the Bell Operating Companies by the Modification of Final Judgment."

2. "Judge Greene Shows Irritation at Shift over Bell Breakup," *Wall Street Journal*, 30 June 1987, 36.

3. *Telecommunications Reports*, 6 July 1987, 1.

4. Ronald H. Coase, "Discussion," in *A Critique of Administrative Regulation of Public Utilities*, Warren J. Samuels and Harry M. Trebing, eds. (East Lansing, Mich.: Institute of Public Utilities, 1972), 313.

5. E. E. Zajac, "Is Telephone Service a Right?" in *Proceedings of the Institute of Public Utilities, Eleventh Annual Conference: Energy and Communications in Transition* (East Lansing, Mich.: Institute of Public Utilities, 1981), 102.

6. United States v. AT&T, Civil Action no. 74–1698, D.D.C. (1974), Transcript of Testimony, 17435.

7. *Moody's Public Utility Manual*, vol. 1 (New York: Moody's Investor Service, 1982), 95, 128.

8. See Wisconsin Telephone Co., 27 FCC 1 (1959).

9. Details on GTE's development are taken from *Moody's Public Utility Manual*, 1936–2011; International T&T Corp. v. General Telephone & Telegraph Corp., 351 F. Supp. 1153 (D.C. Hawaii, 1972); AT&T Archives, Box 74; and a sketchy GTE pamphlet, *A History of GTE* (n.d.).

10. "Ladies Day in Wall Street," *Business Week*, 5 February 1955, 46, 48.

11. GTE, *1984 Annual Report*, 33.

12. "Battle for World's Telephones Becomes Three Cornered Affair," *Business Week*, 22 October 1930, 12; and AT&T Co., Treasury Department, *Financial and Other Statistics of the General Telephone System: 1955*, 4, in AT&T Archives, Box 74.

13. "From a Telephone Merger: A Giant Among Independents," *Business Week*, 10 September 1955, 158.

14. "Why General Aims to be a 'Baby Bell,' " *Business Week*, 24 March 1956, 153.

15. Ibid., 154, 155.

16. "When Phones Wed Electronics," *Business Week*, 15 November 1958, 79.

17. Ibid., 79–81; and *A History of GTE*, 7.

18. U.S. v. GTE Corp., 1985–1 Trade Cases, para. 66, 354 (D.D.C., 1985).

19. "GTE Will Shed Sprint and Take Big Write Off," *Wall Street Journal*, 17 January 1986, 3.

20. Andrew Pollock, "The Battle of the Titans: Part II," *New York Times*, 30 June

1985, F1, F26; John Marcom, Jr., and Eileen White, "IBM-MCI Pact Portends Big Changes," *Wall Street Journal*, 27 June 1985, 2, 22.

21. R. H. Coase, "The Nature of the Firm," *Economica* IV (New Series), November 1937, 404.

22. United States v. AT&T, Defendants' Exhibit D–T–125, "Testimony of Malcolm Schwartz," 125.

23. Harold C. Livesay and Patrick G. Porter, "Vertical Integration in American Manufacturing, 1899–1948," *Journal of Economic History* XXIX (September 1969): 495–96.

24. "Media Gets a Message from Justice," *Business Week*, 8 June 1968, 110, 112.

25. Suzanne Weaver, *Decision to Prosecute* (Cambridge, Mass.: MIT Press, 1977), 169, 170. See also *Telecommunications Reports*, 22 February 1971, 26, 27.

26. James M. Clabault and John F. Burton, *Sherman Act Indictments* (New York: Federal Legal Publications, 1966), 130.

27. Weaver, *Decision*, 170.

28. "Trustbuster Hart Tilts with AT&T," *Business Week*, 4 August 1973, 15, 16.

29. International T&T Corp. v. General Tel & Elec Corp., 351 F. Supp. 1153, 1185–86 (D. Hawaii, 1972).

30. International T&T Corp. v. General T&E Corp., 518 F. 2d 913 (9th Cir. 1975).

31. Steve Coll, *The Deal of the Century* (New York: Atheneum, 1986), 71.

32. "The Justice Dept. Aims at AT&T Again," *Business Week*, 8 December 1973, 41.

33. Mitchell C. Lynch et al., "Fighting Bell," *Wall Street Journal*, 21 November 1974, 1.

34. *Telecommunications Reports*, 9 December 1974, 8.

35. Senate Subcommittee on Antitrust and Monopoly, Committee on the Judiciary, *The Industrial Reorganization Act*, part 6 (Washington, D.C.: Government Printing Office, 1974), 3844, 3845.

36. Paul Weaver, "Unlocking the Gilded Cage of Regulatory Reform," *Fortune*, February 1977, 180.

37. Kenneth Bacon and Mitchell Lynch, "On the Offensive?" *Wall Street Journal*, 18 November 1974, 1.

38. "Why the Justice Department Took AT&T to Court," *Business Week*, 30 November 1974, 70.

39. "The Antitrust Lawyers Roll Up Their Sleeves," *Business Week*, 30 November 1974, 69.

40. United States v. AT&T, Transcript of Testimony, 3836, 3837; "AT&T's Western Electric and Long Lines Are Prime Focus of Justice Agency Suit," *Wall Street Journal*, 21 November 1974, 6; and Coll, *The Deal*, 55, 56.

41. "The Potential Fallout from AT&T's Defeat," *Business Week*, 30 June 1980, 45.

42. Details are contained in a 17 September 1982 Department of Justice release, *Facts and Figures From the U.S. v. AT&T Case*, 1, 2.

43. United States v. American Tobacco Co., 221 U.S. 185 (1911); and Standard Oil Co. of New Jersey v. United States, 221 U.S. 1 (1911).

44. Lawrence A. Sullivan, *Handbook of the Law of Antitrust* (St. Paul, Minn.: West Publishing Co., 1977), 77.

45. United States v. E. I. DuPont de Nemours & Co., 351 U.S. 377 (1956).

46. Joseph Schumpeter, *Capitalism, Socialism and Democracy*, 3d ed. (New York: Harper & Row, 1950), 83.

47. United States v. AT&T, Plaintiffs' First Statement of Contentions and Proof, 515, 516.

48. United States v. AT&T, Complaint, 12, 13.

49. Ibid., 14, 15.

50. *Telecommunications Reports*, 25 November 1974, 1; Coll, *The Deal*, 67, 70; and Mitchell C. Lynch et al., "Bond Befuddlement," *Wall Street Journal*, 25 November 1974, 1, 21.

51. Peter T. Kilborn, "Efficiency Is Mark of Western Electric," *New York Times*, 21 November 1974, 68.

52. *Telecommunications Reports*, 2 December 1974, 8.

53. Editorial, "The Largest Antitrust Suit," *Wall Street Journal*, 22 November 1974, 18.

54. "Statement by AT&T Chairman on Suit," *New York Times*, 21 November 1968, 68.

55. United States v. AT&T, Answer, 10.

56. Ibid., 12.

57. Ibid., 23.

58. *Telecommunications Reports*, 16 December 1974, 18.

59. *Telecommunications Reports*, 20 January 1975, 10.

60. *Telecommunications Reports*, 20 January 1975, 10.

61. *Telecommunications Reports*, 24 February 1975, 1–6.

62. United States v. American Telephone & Telegraph Co., 1976–2 Trade Cases, para. 61,097 (D. D.C., 1976).

63. *Telecommunications Reports*, 10 February 1975, 1–4; and 7 April 1975, 7–10.

64. *Telecommunications Reports*, 31 March 1975, 1, 2.

65. Ibid., 3.

66. Coll, *The Deal*, 123.

67. *Telecommunications Reports*, 28 July 1975, 1.

68. Ibid., 3.

69. United States v. American Telephone & Telegraph Co., 1976–2 Trade Cases, para. 61,097, p. 69,966 (D. D.C., 1976).

70. *Telecommunications Reports*, 8 November 1976, 7; see also 5 January 1976, 1–4.

71. U.S. v. AT&T, 1976-2 Trade Cases, para. 61,163, p. 70,248 (D. D.C., 1976).

72. Ibid., 70,249.

73. Otter Tail Power Co. v. United States, 410 U.S. 366 (1973); and *Telecommunications Reports*, 29 November 1976, 9, 10.

74. *Telecommunications Reports*, 22 November 1976, 3.

75. *Telecommunications Reports*, 20 December 1976, 1, 2, 27, 28.

76. See House Committee on Interstate and Foreign Commerce, Subcommittee on Communications, *Competition in the Telecommunications Industry* (Washington, D.C.: Government Printing Office, 1977), 1167–84.

77. *Telecommunications Reports*, 9 February 1976, 1.

78. *Telecommunications Reports*, 29 March 1976, 2.

79. *Telecommunications Reports*, 5 April 1976, 2.

80. *Telecommunications Reports*, 27 December 1976, 1.

81. For details, see Richard Harris, *The Real Voice* (New York: Macmillan, 1964).

82. *Telecommunications Reports*, 10 January 1977, 1–4; 31 January 1977, 3, 4; 7 February 1977, 6; 21 March 1977, 6, 7; 4 April 1977, 10, 11; 25 April 1977, 28; 6 June 1977, 7; 18 July 1977, 2, 3; and 12 September 1977, 4, 5.

83. *Telecommunications Reports*, 5 December 1977, 6–8; 12 December 1977, 10; and 19 December 1977, 5–7.

84. Biographical details from Coll, *The Deal*, 123–31; and Robert E. Taylor, "Activist Judge," *Wall Street Journal*, 30 December 1983, 1, 12.

85. Peter M. Gerhart, "Report on the Empirical Case Studies Project," in *Report to the President and the Attorney General*, vol. II, National Commission for the Review of Antitrust Laws and Procedures (Washington, D.C.: Government Printing Office, 1979), 22.

86. United States v. American Telephone & Telegraph Co., 416 F. Supp. 1314 (D. D.C., 1978).

87. "The AT&T Case Comes Alive," *Business Week*, 11 September 1978, 105.

88. United States v. American Telephone & Telegraph Co., 416 F. Supp. 1314, 1344 (D. D.C., 1978).

89. Ibid., 1345–47.

90. United States v. AT&T, Plaintiffs' First Statement of Contentions and Proof, passim.

91. United States v. AT&T, Defendants' First Statement of Contentions and Proof, passim.

92. United States v. AT&T, Plaintiffs' Second Statement of Contentions and Proof, passim.

93. United States v. AT&T, Defendants' Statement in Lieu of a Second Statement of Contentions and Proof, passim.

94. United States v. American Telephone & Telegraph Co., 83 FRD 323 (D. D.C., 1979).

95. Ibid., 84 FRD 350, 352–53 (D. D.C., 1979).

96. Ibid.

97. Ibid., 88 FRD 47, 50 (D. D.C., 1980).

98. U.S. v. AT&T Co., 1980–1 Trade Cases, para. 63,244 (D. D.C., 1980).

99. United States v. American Telephone & Telegraph Co., 498 F. Supp. 353 (D. D.C., 1980).

100. Antitrust Division, Justice Department, *Facts and Figures from the U.S. v. AT&T Case*, 17 September 1982, 1.

101. U.S. v. AT&T Co., 1980–2 Trade Cases, para. 63,533, p. 76,859 (D.C. Cir. 1980).

102. MCI Communications Corp. v. American Telephone & Telegraph Co., 708 F. 2d 1081 (7th Cir. 1983).

103. See United States v. AT&T, Plaintiffs' Third Statement of Contentions and Proof, vol. II, 1150–57; and Defendants' Third Statement of Contentions and Proof, vol. II, 1194–1200.

104. United States v. AT&T, Plaintiffs' Third Statement, vol. II, 1581–1606; and Defendants' Third Statement, 1770–1814.

105. Riegel Fiber Corp. v. Anderson Gin Co., 512 F. 2d 784, 793 N.19 (5th Cir. 1975).

106. SEC v. Murphy, 626 F. 2d 633, 659 (9th Cir. 1980).

107. Quoted in Taylor, "Activist Judge," 12.

108. United States v. American Telephone & Telegraph Co., 524 F. Supp. 1336, 1345 (D. D.C., 1981).

109. Federal Communications Commission v. RCA Communications Inc., 346 U.S. 86, 91–92 (1953).

110. United States v. AT&T, Memorandum in Support of Defendants' Motion for Involuntary Dismissal Under Rule 41B, 21.

111. United States v. American Telephone & Telegraph Co., 524 F. Supp. 1336, 1348 (D. D.C., 1981).

112. Peter Newcomb, "No One Is Safe," *Forbes*, 13 July 1987, 142, 144.

113. United States v. American Telephone & Telegraph Co., 524 F. Supp. 1336, 1352–53 (D. D.C., 1981).

114. United States v. AT&T, Transcript of Testimony, 7619–22 and 10422–23.

115. United States v. American Telephone & Telegraph Co., 524 F. Supp. 1336, 1351 (D. D.C., 1981).

116. See United States v. AT&T, Memorandum in Support of Defendants' Motion, Section IV.

117. *Telecommunications Reports*, 14 September 1981, 3.

118. *Telecommunications Reports*, 28 September 1981, 8, 9.

Chapter 10
What's My Line?

1. The framework is based on Richard Posner, "The Behavior of Administrative Agencies," *Journal of Legal Studies* 1 (June 1972): 305–47.

2. United States v. Von's Grocery Co., 86 S. Ct. 1478 (1966).

3. "Behind AT&T's Change at the Top," *Business Week*, 8 November 1978, 115. A major source of information on AT&T's strategy in settlement is Peter Temin with Louis Galambos, *The Fall of the Bell System* (Cambridge: Cambridge University Press, 1987), chs. 6–7.

4. AT&T, *1978 Annual Report*, 3.

5. Ibid., 24.

6. Quoted in W. Brooke Tunstall, *Disconnecting Parties* (New York: McGraw-Hill, 1985), 16.

7. AT&T, *1979 Annual Report*, 3.

8. Ibid., 15.

9. Senate Subcommittee on Antitrust and Monopoly, Committee on the Judiciary, *The Industrial Reorganization Act*, part 6 (Washington, D.C.: Government Printing Office, 1974), 4428–34; and J. H. Alleman, *The Pricing of Local Telephone Service* (Washington, D.C.: U.S. Department of Commerce, 1977), 111, 112.

10. Bro Uttal, "How to Deregulate AT&T," *Fortune*, 30 November 1981, 75.

11. See Jane L. Racster et al., *The Bypass Issue: An Emerging Form of Competition in the Telephone Industry* (Columbus, Ohio: National Regulatory Research Institute, 1984), chs. 1–4.

12. MTS/WATS Market Structure, Second Supplemental Notice of Inquiry, 77 FCC 2d 224, 235 (1980).

13. Quoted in Alvin von Auw, *Heritage and Destiny* (New York: Praeger, 1983), 327.

14. Lawrence A. Sullivan, *Handbook of the Law of Antitrust* (St. Paul, Minn.: West Publishing Co., 1977), 758, 759.

15. 15 United States Code Annotated 16(f).

16. U.S. v. American Telephone & Telegraph Co., 1980–81 Trade Cases, para. 63,705 (D. D.C., 1981).

17. Ibid., para. 63,711, p. 77,795 (D. D.C., 1981).

18. Telecommunications Reports, 12 January 1982, 3.

19. *Telecommunications Reports*, 26 January 1981, 18.

20. *Telecommunications Reports*, 2 March 1981, 3.

21. Steven Coll, *The Deal of the Century* (New York: Atheneum, 1986), 143.

22. Ibid., 144; *Telecommunications Reports*, 2 March 1981, 3; and AT&T, *1980 Annual Report*, 2, 3, 11, 19, 21.

23. *Telecommunications Reports*, 2 March 1981, 1.

24. Coll, *The Deal*, 175, 176.

25. *Telecommunications Reports*, 13 April 1981, 3.

26. Ibid., 4.

27. Senate Committee on Commerce, Science and Transportation, *Telecommunications Competition and Deregulation Act of 1981* (Washington, D.C.: Government Printing Office, 1981), 126; see also 121–25, 131–33.

28. Ibid., 131.

29. *Telecommunications Reports*, 3 August 1981, 1, 2.

30. *Telecommunications Reports*, 12 October 1981, 4–7; and House Subcommittee on Telecommunications, Consumer Protection and Finance, Committee on Energy and Commerce, *Telecommunications in Transition: The Status of Competition in the Telecommunications Industry* (Washington, D.C.: Government Printing Office, 1981), XIII.

31. *Telecommunications Reports*, 14 December 1981, 1–4, 17, 18; and Coll, *The Deal*, 294, 295.

32. United States v. Western Electric Co., 531 F. Supp. 894 (N.D. N.J. 1981).

33. Robert E. Taylor and James A. White, "AT&T's Accord," *Wall Street Journal*, 19 January 1982, 1, 14.

34. House Subcommittee of the Committee on Government Operations, *Departments of Justice and Defense and Antitrust Litigation* (Washington, D.C.: Government Printing Office, 1982), 4.

35. Details are based on Taylor and White, "AT&T's Accord," 1, 14.

36. "The Historic AT&T Settlement As Seen by Those Who Took Part," *New York Times*, 11 January 1982, 1, 28.

37. United States v. Western Electric, Modification of Final Judgment, Section I.

38. Ibid., II, 3.

39. "How the Bell Breakup Is Rewriting the Yellow Pages," *Business Week*, 23 January 1984, 132.

40. United States v. AT&T, Civil Action no. 74–1698, D. D.C. (1974), Competitive Impact Statement, 29, 30.

41. *Federal Register*, 17 May 1982, 21214.

42. Ernest Holsendolph, "AT&T to Split Up, Transforming Industry," *New York Times*, 9 January 1982, 24.

43. *Telecommunications Reports*, 8 February 1982, 5.

44. Ernest Holsendolph, "AT&T Would Set Up Seven Regional Units," *New York Times*, 20 February 1982, 21, 23; and James A. White, "AT&T to Spinoff Its 22 Operating Subsidiaries into 7 Regional Firms in First Step to Reorganize," *Wall Street Journal*, 22 February 1982, 4.

45. *Telecommunications Reports*, 31 May 1982, 6–9.

46. United States v. American Telephone & Telegraph Co., 552 F. Supp. 131 (D. D.C., 1982).

47. Ibid., 169.

48. Market Structure (Phase I), 93 FCC 2d 241 (1982).

49. U.S. v. Western Electric Co., 1982–2 Trade Cases, para. 64,900 (D. D.C., 1982).

An excellent examination of Judge Greene's modifications appears in Geoffrey M. Peters, "Is the Third Time the Charm?" *Seton Hall Law Review* 15 (1985): 269–71.

50. United States v. Western Electric, AT&T's Plan of Reorganization.

51. See Appendix to Application of BOCs for Approval of LATAs, HI-H19 and United States v. Western Electric, 569 F. Supp. 1067 (D.D.C., 1983).

52. See "A Research Arm for the Bell Holding Companies," *Business Week*, 5 March 1984, 72.

53. U.S. v. Western Electric Co. Inc., 1983–2 Trade Cases, para. 65,756, p. 69,855 (D. D. C., 1983).

54. Andrew Pollack, "AT&T, U.S. Agree on Final Aspects of Bell Breakup," *New York Times*, 4 August 1983, 1, 30.

55. Bob Davis, "Commerce Agency Urges Deregulation of AT&T, Says Business Is Competitive," *Wall Street Journal*, 23 January 1987, 15.

56. AT&T, *1910 Annual Report*, 32, 33.

INDEX

Above 890Mc case, 126–34, 135, 139, 147
Adams, Henry C., 27
Adams, Walter, 87
AE (Automatic Electric Company), 277, 278
AFL-CIO, 298
AIS (Automatic Intercept System), 155
Allen, William, 256
Altec Service Corporation, 67
American Bell, 271
American Bell Telephone Company, 40, 41–43
American Can Company, 69
American Newspaper Publishers' Association, 321
American Speaking Telephone Company, 36, 41
American Tobacco, 286
Antitrust cases. *See* specific cases
Antitrust immunity issue, 245–48
Antitrust laws, 68, 293, 295–96
Antitrust principles, 16, 50, 55
API (American Petroleum Institute), 10, 20, 127–28, 131, 151, 161
Arcata Communications, 221
Area-code system, 71
Army, U.S., 178
Arthur D. Little Company, 191
Ashley, George, 164
Associated Telephone Company, 121–22
Associated Telephone Utilities, 276
Automobile Manufacturers Association, 131

Bader, Michael, 164, 170, 183
Baker, Donald, 49–50, 243
Baldridge, Holmes, 73–74

Baldridge, Malcolm, 324
Banking industry, 58
Basic transmission service, 267
Baumol, William, 157
Bausch & Lomb Optical Company, 69
Baxter, William F., 322, 323, 326–27, 328
Beelar, Donald C., 108
Bell, Alexander Graham, 29, 37, 40, 332; patent of, 31, 33, 34–36
"Bell Bill," 298
Bell Labs, 4, 15, 22, 40, 75; and coaxial systems, development of, 95; and computer development, 201; and the consent decree of January 1956, 77; creation of, 37; funding for, 280; R&D record of, 49, 304; and *United States* v. *AT&T*, 286, 288, 317, 327; and the UNIX system, 155
Bell of Pennsylvania, 190–94
Bell Patent Association, 36
Bell patents, 4, 7, 78–79; Alexander Bell's original, 31, 33, 34–36; expiration of, 14, 36, 88; postwar policy regarding, 78
Bell System Tariff Offerings (1974), 193
Bell Telephone Company (a corporation), 41
Bell Telephone Company (a Massachusetts trust), 40–41
Billingsley, James R., 263, 266
BOCs (Bell-operating companies), 273, 314, 327, 328, 330
Boettinger, Henry E., 274
Boundary problem, the, 54–57, 206
Brass v. *Stoesser* (1894), 27
Broadband Rate Planning Group, 135
"Broadband Report," 135–36
Broadcasting: boom, 56; toll, 56–57
Brock, Gerald, 201

Brock, James W., 87

Brown, Charles L., 23, 317, 318, 319, 326

Bunker-Ramo Corporation, 202–5, 208

Bruch, Dean, 183

Business-government collaborations, 26, 48–54, 290

Business Week, 63, 72, 73, 141–42, 150; analysis, of GTE's acquisitions, 277, 278; on the 1974 AT&T suit, 283, 284, 302

Bus Transportation Frequencies case, 111

Butts, John de, 23, 24, 196–99, 243; and the regulated network manager system, 289–90, 316–17

California Farm Bureau Federation, 171

California Forestry Service, 127

California Railroad Commission, 91–92

Candygram, 207

Capital contribution concept, 181–84

Capitalism, 54, 60

Capitalization, 42–43

Capital movements, 25

Cartels, international, 68

Carter, Jimmy (Carter administration), 240, 297, 300, 320, 323, 334

Carter, Thomas F., 147–48, 332

Carter Electronics, 20, 148, 151

Carterfone, 147–48, 220–21

Carterfone decisions (1968), 6, 120, 127, 144, 146–52; and equipment connection requests, 191; and interconnection policy, 224, 230, 233, 269; prelude to, 140–42; and tariff revisions, 184, 185; and *United States* v. *AT&T,* 307

CAs (connecting arrangements), 223, 224

CBEMA, 261

CB radios, 88–89

CCSA (common control switching arrangement), 177–78, 184–90, 191, 192–94; controversy, 242, 253, 254, 259

Celler, Emanuel, 79–80, 83

Central Freight Lines, 129

Centrex, 127

Certification issue, 216–20, 228, 229

Channel sharing, 159

Channel splitting, 159

Chesapeake & Potomac Telephone Company of Virginia, 275

Chrysler, 145

CIA (Computer Industries Association), 261

Cincinnati Bell, 40, 321

Clark, Tom, 72, 74

Clayton Act, 244

Coase, R. H., 38, 39, 50, 274

Coaxial cables, 19, 60, 62, 95; and the television industry, 105–6, 107, 112

COMAS, 145–46

Commerce, Department of, 49

Commerce, interstate, 15, 90

Commodity exchanges, 25

Common Carrier Bureau, 102–3, 116, 117, 122; and the *Carterfone* case, 148, 151; and Dataspeed, 261–62; and the interconnection question, 209; and MCI, 162; and the *Rochester Telephone* decision, 226; and the SCC Investigation, 170–75. *See also* FCC (Federal Communications Commission)

Common Law: Anglo-American, 336; English, 25–26

Communications Act of 1934, 8, 15, 17, 21, 58, 60; and the *Above 890Mc* case, 129; and the antitrust immunity issue, 246, 247; and computer communications, 208, 223; and *Computer II,* 264; and the FCC, 96, 333; and the *Hush-A-Phone* case, 124; and the *MCI* v. *AT&T* case, 256–57, 294; public interest requirements of, 115; and the regulated network manager system, 290; rewrites of, 297; Section 214, 171; Section 202, 139; and the Telequote controversy, 204; and the television industry, 113, 115, 117; and *United States* v. *AT&T,* 294, 311; violations of, 62, 100

Communications Satellite Act (1962), 143

Competition, 22, 23, 26, 54, 164; and the Communications Act of 1934, 129; contrived, 8, 10, 199, 291; free, 7, 8,

208; vs. natural monopoly, 214; and public service, 29, 44–47, 50; regulatory function of, 50, 198, 199

Computer and Business Equipment Manufacturers Association, 233

Computer industry, 10, 16, 154; and interconnection issues, 195–235; postwar growth of, 94, 95

Computer I decisions, 202–16, 260, 281, 310

Computer II decisions, 239–72; and *United States* v. *AT&T*, 310, 318, 322, 324, 325–26

Computer III decisions, 272

COMSAT (Communications Satellite Corporation), 143–44

Cone Mills Corporation, 189

Congress, 9, 11–12, 41, 58, 228; House Small Business Subcommittee on Regulatory Agencies, 146; House Subcommittee on Communications, 232; and the 1949 *Western Electric* suit, 59, 75; and *United States* v. *AT&T*, 296–99, 316, 330–31

Consumer Communications Reform Act, 298

Continental Telephone, 214

Cooper, Basil B., 103

Cox, Kenneth, 179, 183, 191

CPE (customer premises equipment), 3, 5, 63, 84–85; as computer input devices, 207–8; and *Computer II*, 271; full-scale competition in, 230–33; and interconnection policy, 100; liberalization of, 197; maintenance of, 90–93; marketing and design of, in the postwar period, 95–96; protection from, technical standards for, 221; rival manufacturers, AT&T's, 196, 275

CPI (consumer price index), 53, 94, 141, 155, 229

Creamskimming, 20, 21, 113, 115; and the common-carrier argument, 129–30; and MCI's Chicago–St. Louis line, 157, 159–60, 164–65, 167–68, 169, 199; and private-microwave system operation, 133

Creative destruction, 145

Credit card explosion, 98

Cross-subsidy arrangements, 9, 10, 14, 273

Cudahy, Richard D., 251

CWA (Communications Workers of America), 298

Danielian, N. R., 64

DATAPHONE, 202

Dataspeed, 261–62, 264

DATRAN (Data Transmission Company), 170, 174–75, 176, 182–83

Deerlin, Lionel van, 297

Defense, Department of, 51, 75, 77, 78, 79–80; and *United States* v. *AT&T*, 325

Department store chains, 20

Deregulation, 59, 334, 337; and economic problems, 26; and the Ford administration, 7, 334; public response to, 9

Dial access issue, 180

Dingman, James, 143

Direct-distance dialing, 127

Dittberner Associates, 218–19

Dow Jones Industrial: Average, 72; stocks, 312

Dumont, 110, 111–12

DuPont, 69

Eastern Oregon Telephone Company, 167

Eastman, Joseph B., 58

Eastman Kodak, 69

Eckstein, Otto, 157

Economic theory: and justice, 26; use of, to justify business goals, 7–8. *See also* Monopoly argument, natural

Economies, controlled, 7

Edison, Thomas A., 31, 36

Eisenhower administration, 59, 77, 80, 142

Electronic Industries Association, 213

Electronic Secretary, 103

Ende, Asher, 317

End-to-end responsibility, 18, 19
ENFIA tariff, 258–60
England, 45
Enhanced services, 267
ERPI (Electrical Research Products Inc.), 66–67
EXECUNET, 241–42, 253–56, 257, 258, 259, 260; and the long-distance market, impact on, 315; tariff, 23
Executive branch, the, 50, 68
Experimental license, 108

Favoritism, 12–13
FBI (Federal Bureau of Investigation), 73
FCC (Federal Communications Commission), 3, 20–23; and anticompetitive legislation, 297; and AT&T, investigation of (1934), 60, 61–66, 155; and AT&T acquisitions, 276; and AT&T service quality, reports on, 156; Common Carrier Bureau—see Common Carrier Bureau; and the Communications Act, 96, 333; computer inquiries, 13, 202–35, 315; and contrived competition, 291; and CPE, 92; creation of, 6, 57–58; decision-making patterns of, 11; decisions, post-EXECUNET, 322; and the equipment market, 315; and the Hush-A-Phone case, 121–25; and the ICC, 14; and interconnection policy, 107–18, 196; and judicial activism, 240–41; jurisdiction of, 293, 295, 301; liberalization actions of, 6, 16–17; and MCI, 154–70, 298, 337; and the MCI v. AT&T case, 241, 252, 254–72; and the New Deal, 8, 14, 15; and new entrants into the telephone industry, in the late 1960s, 20–22; and new standards of competition, 23; and the 1974 MCI moves, 23; during the 1960s, 15–19, 20–22; and public interest, conception of, 118; and the regulated network manager system, 119–52, 292; responsibilities of, 119; and spectrum allocation, 107–13; STI

investigation, 62–66; and United States v. AT&T, 293, 299, 307, 311, 330–38; after World War II, 19, 85, 95–96, 101–4
Federal rate jurisdiction, 48
Federal Register, 329
Federal Trade Commission, 68, 69, 240
Fiber optics, 156
Fire insurance, 28–29
First Amendment, 244
First Boston Corporation, 289
Flexibility, 159
Floating rate issue, 181
FM (frequency modulation), 97
Fogarty, Joseph R., 241, 270
Ford, Gerald, 282, 283, 284
Ford administration, 7, 297, 334
Ford Foundation, 144
Fortune, 157, 318
Freeport Sulphur, 132
FTS (Federal Telephone System), 178
FX (foreign exchange), 177, 184–90, 191, 192–94; and the CCSA controversy, 242, 253, 254, 259

Garlinghouse, Mark, 293
General Accounting Office, 51
General Electric, 16, 54, 69–70; and the patent pool agreements, 55–56; and the television industry, 112, 116
General Motors, 69, 182, 190
General Telephone of the Southwest, 148, 149
Gifford, George, 37
Gifford, Walter, 61
GNP (gross national product), 49, 94
Goeken, John D., 162, 165, 181, 188–89
Gould, Jay, 36–37
Grady, John, 245, 246, 249, 251
Grain elevators, 27
Gray, Elisha, 33, 34–35, 36, 332
"Gray Book," 136
Great Atlantic and Pacific Tea Company, 69
Great Depression, 49, 60–61, 71, 79

Great Northern Railroad, 27
Greene, Harold F., 24, 189–90, 242, 246; and GTE's acquisitions, 278; and MFJs, 273, 285; and *United States* v. *AT&T*, 299–311 *passim,* 315–16, 320–32 *passim*
GSA (General Services Administration), 138
GTE, 151, 159, 183; and *Computer I*, 214, 215; and *Computer II*, 268, 271; and integration, 275–79; local operations of, 329; and the MCI Chicago–St. Louis route, 169, 170

Hanson, O. B., 106
Harris, Laurence E., 183, 184
Hart, Philip A., 191, 240, 282, 283
Hartke, Vance, 298
Hawaiian Telephone Company, 282
Henry, William, 148
HI/LO tariffs, 191, 193–94, 199; and the *MCI* v. *AT&T* case, 249, 252; and *United States* v. *AT&T*, 308
Honeywell, 200
Hooks, Benjamin, 234, 337
House Communications Subcommittee, 297, 232
House Small Business Subcommittee on Regulatory Agencies, 146
Hubbard, Gardiner, 36, 40, 41
Hughes Aircraft, 144
Humble Oil, 131
Hush-A-Phone, 149
Hush-A-Phone case, 89, 120, 121–25, 133, 135; and liberal interconnection policy, 136, 147, 232, 233
Hyde, Rosel H., 168–69

IBM, 10, 13, 16, 20, 239; and AT&T, conflict with, 196, 200–201; and the boundary question, 206–7; and *Computer II*, 263–64, 266, 267; dominance of, in the computer industry, 200; and the *Mackay* decision (1939), 108, 109; and MCI, 279; System 360, 200. *See also United States* v. *IBM* (1956)
ICC (Interstate Commerce Commission), 14, 17, 28, 57, 58; and the Willis-Graham Act, 48
I. G. Farben, 68
Illinois Bell, 160, 180, 189
Illinois Commerce Commission, 160, 180
Illinois Public Utilities Commission, 91
Industrial Communications Association, 126
Inflation rates, 4
Information revolution, 24
Integration, 34, 38–39, 275–80. *See also* Vertical integration
Interdata Communications, 165
Interstate Commerce Act, 247
IPVC wire, 196
ITT (International Telephone & Telegraph), 183, 214, 299, 320

Japanese firms, 310, 312
Javits, Benjamin A., 146
Jewett, Frank, 95, 106
Johnson, Nicholas, 97, 146, 152, 164, 168
Johnson, Lyndon, 146
Johnson administration, 239
Jordaphone case (1954), 102–4
Jourolomon, Leon, Jr., 71–72
Judicial activism, 124, 240–41
Justice, Department of, Antitrust Division, ideology of, 281–82. *See also specific cases*

Kahn, Alfred, 157
Karnopp, Walter, 167
Keating, Kenneth, 74
Kennedy administration, 143
Keystone Telephone Company, 44
Keystone Tubular, 190, 191

Kingsbury Commitment, 48
KTSs (key telephone systems), 220, 229

Labor, Department of, 53, 155
Labor costs, 53
Laissez-faire doctrine, 13, 25, 27
Large-volume users, 10
Larkin, Edward, 226
LATAs, 331
Lee, Robert E., 169
Leich Electric Company, 276
Leming, T. L., 188–89
Little, Arthur D., 234
Litvack, Sanford, 320, 321, 329
Livesay, Harold, 43, 280
Lobbying, 51, 166
Long-distance service, 3, 5, 10, 53; costs, reduction of, 19, 60, 61; and MCI, 153–54; during the 1930s, 60, 61, 62; revenues, and local service, 197; and technological advances, 19; and Vail, 41–42, 269
Louisiana PSC, 103
LRIC (long-run incremental cost), 251
LSV system, 196

McAllister, Breck, 26–27
McGill, Archibald J., 317
McGowan, William, 165–66, 180, 190, 285, 332; and MCI's 1974 offensive, 241, 242, 243, 244
McHugh, Keith, 106
Mackay decision (1939), 108–9
Mackay Radio & Telegraph, 108
Manitoba, 45
Mann-Elkins Law (1910), 48, 96
Markey, Edward, 335
Marshfield Telephone Company, 276
Martin, W. H., 122
Masi, Richard, 313
MCCs (miscellaneous common carriers), 170
MCI (Microwave Communications), 5, 142, 153–94, 274–75; and computer communications, 208; and the EX-ECUNET tariff, 23; and the FCC, 154–70, 298, 337; and IBM, 279; initial entry of, into the telephone industry, 21–22; and large business subscribers, 10, 20; political power of, 4, 167; and public interest arguments, 7–8; and United States v. AT&T, 153, 242–43, 284–85, 288, 322, 333
MCI v. AT&T cases, 23, 223, 239–72, 305, 306; impact of, 315
Media, 13, 52, 72–73
Melody, William H., 308, 318
Mergers, backward vertical, 43
MFJs (modified final judgments), 273–74, 328, 330
Micom, 165
Microwave relay, 19, 87, 95, 136; long-distance transmission characteristics of, 111; pollution, 127; private-line, 132–34, 135; and spectrum allocation issues, 105, 106–7, 108, 109, 110. See also Spectrum allocation
Microwave Users Council, 128
Military communications, 71
Miller, Richard W., 126
Minority share ownership, 43, 44
Minute Maid Corporation, 129, 132
Missouri Public Service Commission, 44–45
MIT, 202, 204–5
Moley, Richard M., 313
Monopoly argument, natural, 13, 26, 44–47, 64; and interconnection tariffs, 85–87; and the Nixon administration, 214
Morgantown Post, 75
Morris, William H., 131
Morse Code, 30
Motion picture industry, 66, 67, 69
Motorola, 133, 136, 138
MTS, 224, 242, 253–54, 257

Nadar, Ralph, 52, 334
NAM (National Association of Manufacturers), 130, 136, 209, 213
NARUC, 51, 78, 80, 216, 228; and the

Carterfone case, 149, 151; and the certi-
fication issue, 216, 219–20; and CPE,
technical standards for protection
from, 221, 222; de Butts speech before
the, 197, 199
NAS (National Academy of Sciences),
217–18
Nash, Bernard, 284
National Aeronautics and Space Agency,
148
National Bell Telephone Company, 36,
41
National Commission for the Review of
Antitrust Laws and Procedures, 300
National Industrial Recovery Act, 8
Nationalization, 45, 47, 58
National Recovery Administration, 58
National Retail Merchants Association,
147, 148, 151, 209
Nazism, 69, 299
NBC (National Broadcasting Company),
106, 114
NCSUs, 223, 224
New Deal, the, 8, 14, 34, 58, 59–80; and
federal jurisdiction, concept of, 15
New England Telephone and Telegraph,
92, 100, 275–76
New England Telephone Company, 40–
41
New Jersey Bell, 286
New Jersey Board of Public Utility Com-
missioners, 91
New Jersey Court of Errors and Appeals,
28
New York Central Securities (1932) decision,
17
New York Herald Tribune, 74–75
New York–Penn Microwave Corporation,
170
New York Public Service Commission
(PSC), 92–93, 114, 145, 204; and *Roch-
ester Telephone Company* decision, 224
New York Stock Exchange, 10
New York Telephone Company, 93, 145
New York Times, 252
Nixon, Richard M., 153
Nixon administration, 173, 214, 320
Noerr-Pennington Doctrine, 244–45
Northern Telephone Company, 276

NRDGA (National Retail Dry Goods Association), 130
Number 5 Crossbar, 178

Office of Management and Budget, 51
Office of Telecommunications Policy,
297
Oligopoly, 191
Osborne, H. S., 97
Otter Tail Power decision (1973), 295, 296
Ownership, direct, 38–39

Pacific Telephone & Telegraph, 40, 72,
92, 286; and *United States* v. *AT&T*, 321
Packwood, Robert, 329
Paramount decision (1948), 69
Partoll, Alfred C., 327
Patent pool agreements, 56, 57
Patents, 7, 37; Bell—*see* Bell patents; li-
censing of, compulsory, 78–79, 83
PBXs, 155, 178, 220, 229, 279
Peters, Geoffrey, 197, 198
Petroleum industry, 127–28, 131
Philco, 110, 112, 113, 114, 127
Phillips, Almarin, 196, 259–60
Piece-out, 186
Pluralism, 18
Podell, Bertram, 228
Politics of Control, 64
Porter, Patrick, 43, 280
Postal Service, U.S., 146
Power, Donald C., 129–30, 276–78
Price-fixing, 281
Pricing: flexibility, 176; independent,
noncollusive, 16
Primary business test, 206
Pritec, 309
Profits, 49, 98
Public interest, 13, 51, 52, 118; argu-
ments, 7, 10, 154; conceptions of, 7,
16–17, 77–78, 83–84; and the Ford
administration, 282; and the public
service principle, 24, 25; service of,
and competition, 50

Public service standard, 7, 9, 12–14, 24–33, 119–21; and antitrust principles, 16; application of, 12–14, 22; in broadcasting, 57; and capitalist competitive principles, 54; erosion of, 84; Gifford on, 61; and interconnection rights, 93; and MCI, 156–57; after World War II, 84

PUCs (Public Utility Commissions), 14, 15, 50–53, 335–36; constraints on, 50–52; critics of, 50, 52; and equipment prices, investigation of, 78; and the *Hush-A-Phone* case, 125; and interconnection policy, 90–93, 122, 124; and rate increases, 97; after World War II, 19–20, 65–66, 72, 97

Pullman Company, 69–70

Radio industry, 16, 54, 55, 77, 114

Radio spectrum, allocation of, 84, 107, 108. *See also* Spectrum allocation

Radiotelegraph service, international, 17

Railroad industry, 13, 25, 27–28

RAMAN laser, 155

Rate averaging, 10, 14, 18, 20, 22; AT&T's departure from, 194; and HI/LO tariff offerings, 191; and pricing flexibility, 176; and unrestricted choice of interconnection arrangements, 185

Rate proceedings, 65–66, 80

Raytheon Manufacturing Company, 110, 112

RCA, 55, 57, 105, 311; and IBM, competition between, 200; and the *Mackay* decision (1939), 108, 109

RCA case (1952), 120

Reagan administration, 239, 334

Recession of 1937, 68

Reed-Bulwinkle Act, 68

Regulated network manager system, 6, 8–9, 20, 33, 289–90; achievements of, 49; and the boundary problem, 54–57; and competition, 198–99; and Con-

gress, 297; development of, 8, 14; erosion of, 15, 48–49, 54–57, 119–52, 317; evaluation of, 53; and the FCC, 119–52, 292; virtues and drawbacks of, 22; after World War II, 19

Reid, Charlotte T., 193

Republican Party, 77, 80

Resale and Shared Use decisions, 265

RETMA (Radio-Electronics Television Manufacturers Association), 128, 129

RHCs, 331–32

Roberts, Bert C., Jr., 241, 242, 254

Rochester Telephone Company, 170, 199, 224–27, 228, 229, 231

Rochester Telephone Company decision, 224, 226

Rolm, 279, 313

Romnes, H. I., 151

Roosevelt, Franklin Delano, 8, 59, 60

RTC program, 224–27, 228, 229, 231

Rural Electrification Administration, 4

Rust, W. M., Jr., 131

SAI (Systems Applications, Inc.), 234

Sanders, Thomas, 36, 40, 41

Satellites, 19, 95, 142–44, 191

SCAN (Switched Circuit Automatic Network), 178

SCC Investigation, 170–94, 208

SCCs (Specialized Common Carriers), 241; and *United States* v. *AT&T*, 288, 295, 308–9

Scheinman, Stanley, 242

Schumpeter, Joseph, 145, 164, 287

SCPs (Statements of Contention and Proof), 303–4, 306, 307

Second Atlantic Cable, 24–25

Securities issues, 58

Self-righteousness, judicial, 124

Senate Commerce Committee, 324

Senate Interstate Commerce Committee, 247

Separations (revenue allocation issues), 197

Series 11000 tariff offering, 165–66, 308
Settlements (revenue allocation issues), 197
Sharfman, Herbert, 163
Sharwell, William G., 265
Shell Oil, 131
Sherman Act, 244; and *United States* v. *AT&T*, 284, 286, 294, 295, 311
Sherman Antitrust Law, 16, 17, 68, 70, 75; and the *Carterfone* case, 148
SICOM (Securities Industries Communications Service), 208–9
Signal-to-noise ratios, 4
Sinclair Refining Co., 131
Smith, Adam, 26
Socialism, 7
Southern Bell, 132, 221
Southern New England Telephone, 40, 321
Southern Pacific Communications Corporation, 170
Southern Pacific Company, 170, 278
Southwestern Bell, 148, 149
Soviet Union, 142
Spectrum allocation, 107–10, 115, 125–34
Spectrum economy, concept of, 115–16
Sperry-Rand, 200
SPRINT service, 258, 278
Sputnik I, 142
SRI (Stanford Research Institute), 210
Staggers Rail Act, 240
Standard Oil, 286
State Department, 51
STC, 309
Steel industry, 69
STI (Special Telephone Investigation), 62–66, 73, 74, 247
Stipulation/Contention Packages, 307, 309
STL, 112
Stock prices, 72, 74–75
Strassburg, Bernard, 192, 193, 205, 206; and the *Computer I* inquiry, 209
Strawn, E. J., 131
Supreme Court. *See specific cases*
Sylvania, 278

Taft, William Howard, 25
Tariffs: *Bell System Tariff Offerings* (1974), 193; and the "Broadband Report," 135; EXECUNET, 23; HI/LO—*see* HI/LO tariffs; and the *Hush-A-Phone* case, 125; post-*Carterfone*, 184, 185, 186–87, 216–20, 225; Series 11000 offering, 165–66, 308
Tatum Telephone Company, 291
Tax rates, 9
TBA (Television Broadcasters Association), 112–13
TD microwave systems, 279–80
Telecommunications Reports, 73, 126, 129, 244, 283
Telegraph: importance of, 24, 25, 28; and interconnection restrictions, 113–15; public policy toward, 30, 32; and the telephone, comparison of, 30–31
Telemagnet, 102, 103
Telephone, invention of, 6–7, 29; as a public service, 29–33; and the telegraph, comparison of, 30–31
Telephone directories, 92–93, 330
Telephone handsets, 100–101
Telequote controversy, 202–5, 206
Television Broadcasters Association, 127
Television industry, 13, 57, 77, 84; postwar growth of, 94, 97; and transmission technology, politics of, 105–7, 110–13; *Western Union* case, 115–18
TELPAK, 134–40, 146, 242
Temin, Peter, 197, 198
Terminal equipment manufacturers, 13
Theodore Gary and Company, 277
Time sharing, 204–5
Timken Roller Bearing Company, 69
TNEC (Temporary National Economic Committee), 60
Trade press, 13
Transmission technology, 9, 105–7, 110–13
Transportation industry, 7, 58
TRC (Tariff Review Committee), 185
Trienens, Howard, 273, 327
Truman, Harry, 68
Truman administration, 59; Antitrust Division, 68–69, 73–74, 76, 105

Tunney Act (1974), 320, 327–32
Turner, Donald, 280

U-Dryvit Auto Rental Company, 100
United Fruit, 55
United Shareowners of America, 146
United Shoe Machinery Corporation, 69
United States Air Force, 148
United States v. *AT&T*, 5–6, 34, 142, 199,
    259, 273–338; and *Computer II*, 262;
    and MCI, 153, 242–43, 284–85, 288,
    322, 333; and monopoly of the video
    market, charges of, 105, 108; motiva-
    tions for, 50; and the 1949 *Western Elec-
    tric* case, parallels between, 77; and
    PUCs, effectiveness of, 48; and the
    SCC Investigation, 175–76
United States v. *IBM*, 77, 300, 321
United States v. *Pullman Company*, 69–70,
    71, 73–74
United States v. *Western Electric* (1949), 59–
    80, 115–18, 280; investor response to,
    74–75; and the STI investigation, 62–
    63; and television transmission, con-
    trol of, 114–15. *See also Western Electric
    consent decree of 1956*
United Telecommunications, 232, 278
United Telephone, 214
Univac, 200
Universal service, 10, 14, 18, 46–47
UNIX system, 155, 201, 212
U. S. Alkali Export Association, 69
USITA, 136, 151, 233, 234, 298, 299
U.S. Rubber, 69
Uttal, Bro, 318–19

Vail, Theodore J., 8, 33, 41, 44, 48; and
    interconnection policy, 88; and the
    public interest standard, 45–46, 52,
    313; on regulation, 337; strategy of, in
    dealing with independents, 47

Vertical integration, 69, 70, 71, 273;
    AT&T's defense of, 76; critics of, 275;
    and *United States* v. *AT&T*, 288, 309,
    310. *See also* Integration
Verveer, Philip, 294
Video programming transmission, 5
Vietnam War, 146
Voice service, 264

Waddy, Joseph C., 291–96, 299, 300
Walker, Paul A., 62, 63–64, 73, 247; and
    ERPI, 67; and the *Mackay* decision
    (1939), 108–9
Walker Report, 63–65, 71, 73, 74, 78
Wall Street Journal, 9, 289
WATS (Wide Area Telephone Service),
    177, 224, 242, 254, 257
Weaver, Suzanne, 281–82
Weinberger, Caspar, 325, 327
Western Electric, 16, 40, 43, 60; control
    of, AT&T's, 317, 322; and CPE, 222,
    275; Research Laboratories, 40; and
    United States v. *AT&T*, 286, 288, 310,
    327. *See also United States* v. *Western Elec-
    tric* (1949)
Western Electric consent decree of 1956,
    76–80, 83, 201, 261, 267–68; and the
    Tunny Act (1974), 320, 327; and *United
    States* v. *AT&T*, 283, 313, 318, 323, 327
Western Union, 8, 13, 31, 36; and com-
    puter communications, 207, 213, 214;
    contest with Bell interests, 36–37, 41;
    and interconnection rates, 180, 181–
    84; and MCI's Chicago–St. Louis route,
    169, 170, 248–49; and *MCI* v. *AT&T*,
    248–49; and the Telequote contro-
    versy, 203–5; television relay rates of,
    113; and the TELPAK case, 137
Westinghouse, 10, 20, 55, 56
Whitehead, Clay T., 283
Willis-Graham Act, 48
Wilson, James Q., 52
Wired Music, 93

Wire service, 25
Wirth, Timothy, 297, 325, 329
Wright, Skelly, 23, 256, 257, 258

Yale Law Journal, 247
Yellow Cab Company, 69
Yellow Pages, 330

Xerox Corporation, 223, 225, 267

Zajac, E. E., 274